About the Author

He was introduced to birds at the tender age of five, when taken to his local park in Birmingham to feed the ducks. His first real involvement was egg collecting, but he quickly became more interested in watching and studying birds. Over the next eighty years, he has studied birds in most European countries, plus Egypt. He has written many features for various publications; jointly presented a countryside radio programme for BBC Radio Birmingham; was a tutor for both Birmingham and Keele universities teaching bird study, and has taken parties of birders on study tours in the UK and Europe.

Searching:
An Autobiography of a Birder

Brian C. George

Searching
An Autobiography of a Birder

Olympia Publishers
London

www.olympiapublishers.com
OLYMPIA PAPERBACK EDITION

A CIP catalogue record for this title is
available from the British Library.

ISBN: 978-1-78830-591-4

This is a work of creative nonfiction. The events are portrayed to the best of the
author's memory. While all the stories in this book are true, some names and
identifying details have been changed to protect the privacy of the people
involved.

First Published in 2020

Olympia Publishers
Tallis House
2 Tallis Street
London
EC4Y 0AB

Printed in Great Britain

VOLUME I

A CELEBRATION OF AN EIGHTY YEAR LOVE
AFFAIR WITH BIRDS

INTRODUCTION

I first became aware of birds at the tender age of five, almost eighty years ago. When the weather permitted, my parents would take me to the local park on a Sunday afternoon to feed the ducks. I quickly learned what mallards, swans, coots and moorhens looked like, and back home, I had occasional house sparrows and starlings for company. Birds were beginning to become an accepted part of my life; unwittingly, at that stage.

I was fortunate in the fact my father was in a reserved occupation, so when the War commenced, his technical skills were more important to the war effort than he be in a uniform. Although, he did have a uniform of sorts, he was a member of the Home Guard or 'Dad's Army' as it is better known these days.

My father was a keen angler and, on the odd occasions I saw him, he would take me fishing down the local canal: the 'cut', as us Brummies knew it. One day, a miracle occurred; well, a miracle as far as I was concerned – a bit of pure magic. My father had his rod in a rest whilst he was puffing on his pipe, and a kingfisher landed on the tip of his rod not ten feet away. For a few seconds only, I gazed at the most beautiful thing I had ever seen; I did not realise we had birds of such exquisite beauty.

My father told me what the bird was, a kingfisher, and from that moment on, if you will excuse the pun, I was hooked. Birds became the driving passion for me, I wanted to see as many as I could, get to know all their names and learn all about them. Wonderful dreams for a lad of six, who did not even have a book to help him. This was corrected at my next birthday, I was given a copy of the *Observer's Book of British Birds*, which I cherished for many a year.

As with many young boys of that period, egg collecting was carried out without realising the damage we were doing, although my group of three did have a certain honour among thieves: we only ever took one egg from a nest, and only if one of us needed it for our collection;

otherwise, the nest was undisturbed. This went on for most of the war years, but as we quickly obtained an egg of each of the local species, this interest started to wane, but not entirely for me.

There were few books on the market in those days – certainly few within the budget of my family's income – but on my 12th birthday I became the proud possessor of a second-hand set of *The Handbook of British Birds*; five volumes published by Witherby, a classic in its day, and they still sit proudly on my book case. Out of date they may now be, but they are still a lovely set of books to handle. I have jumped a few years here so let us get back on track.

I also obtained a pair of opera glasses from my grandmother; to me, these were a powerful new instrument through which to study birds. Compared with today's binoculars, they were probably only 2 or 3x's magnification, but for me they opened up a new world. I never went anywhere without those round my neck.

Just prior to the advent of war in 1939, my family had moved from Saltley to the suburbs of Birmingham, Great Barr, my first taste of countryside. Here, we had fields and country lanes; I could chase after butterflies, get involved with birds, walk miles without any fear, go fishing with my father – a completely new world was opening up. Then war came.

As mentioned earlier, I was fortunate in one respect, my father was in a reserve occupation, he was a skilled wire-drawer and his skills were necessary for the war effort, so the nearest he got to fighting was in the Home Guard; although, he was bombed out on more than one occasion as the Luftwaffe attacked the factory where he both worked and carried out his Home Guard duties. I did at least have the advantage of growing up with him, and thanks to his love of fishing; I got out to also see my birds.

In 1945, the war ended, and I had the surprise of my life at Christmas that year: I became the proud owner of a bicycle. My parents had been saving up at the local shop by making weekly club card payments for this machine, there was no H.P. in those days, and a completely new world was about to open up for me. I now had my cycle, my opera glasses and my Observer's book in my pocket, and I always had my set of books back home for reference – I could not go wrong!

THE FORMATIVE YEARS

There were three of us who were the keen egg collectors, Roland 'Polly' Watson, who is no longer with us, and Brian 'Nipper' Wood, who now lives in Eire.

Nipper and I still keep in touch and he still has his love of birds. All three of us by 1945 had cycles so we could spread our net far and wide in pursuit of our hobby.

As mentioned earlier, there is a certain honour among thieves, there certainly was among us three egg collectors.

We never took more than one egg from a nest; we never returned to it to take more; we only had one egg per species in our collections so many a nest found was left safe and secure, and we never shared our information with other collectors.

'Polly' was a very good tree climber, not that 'Nipper' and I were bad, thus he was a very useful guy to be part of the team. We learned where certain birds made their nests, and knowing exactly where to look, we grew quite experienced in identifying the various eggs so we always knew what nest we had found should no adult bird be in attendance. Without realising it, we were developing a very sound field craft; the birth of three naturalists was nigh.

I was the oldest of the three, although we are only talking months. All of us were interested in sport, especially cricket and football, at which we did quite well. We even ran our own football team and played against other local sides down at the neighbourhood park where we could hire a pitch. We never had enough money to hire a dressing room, so we cycled or walked down to the park in our soccer gear; I cannot see Wayne Rooney doing that somehow! We were very fortunate: we had two leather footballs, real balls, which my father had salvaged from his works after an evening of bombing. We treasured these two balls as though they were solid gold, taking turns to take them home to apply dubbin. No two balls were ever treated with such reverence, and it also had a fringe benefit for me: as both balls were mine, I always played as I was captain!

Back to birds. We got into several scrapes whilst out egg collecting; we were chased out of more than one private wood or garden. The local constable took us to task on more than one occasion, with the odd clip behind the ear to emphasise a point. He would not be allowed to do that now, but we respected him and, if we needed assistance, we would seek him out.

I always remember one occasion. We had located a sand martin colony at a local quarry, this was an egg we all needed; the question was, how to get down to them. The quarry cliff was a good 20 feet deep and sheer, with deep water at the base. We decided the only way to get an egg was to be dangled on a rope and lowered down, but we needed a few willing hands to do that; we were not going to risk one on the rope being lowered by two holding the rope. We managed to get one or two friends who were not egg collectors to join us – off we went.

I had drawn the short straw, the rope was attached to me and down the cliff I was lowered. I had a tin in my pocket stuffed with cotton wool and quickly had helped myself to three eggs, all from different nests needless to add. I had put the eggs safely in the tin and was just about to call up to be lifted, when I found myself being hauled up very quickly. On arriving at the top, whom did I see: our local bobby. You knew you were in trouble when he addressed you as, 'Master George'; you were always, 'son', when he was in a good mood. 'What were you doing, 'Master George?'

'Nothing officer' I replied.

'Nothing, when hanging on the end of a rope?' was the retort.

For a few minutes the conversation went along similar lines, until sensing he was beginning to lose patience, I told him.

Out of my pocket came the tin, in which three delicate and small eggs lay. 'You had better take them back 'Master George.' I was about to tell him I did not know which nesting holes I had taken the eggs from, there were about 100 pairs in this colony, when I thought better of it. Our constable was a good policeman, but he obviously knew little about sand martins. I was lowered down once again, put the three eggs in three different holes, three young sand martins were going to grow up with foster parents although they would never know it. I was hauled back up, given one final lecture, and we were sent on our way.

It was several years later when I bumped into our by now retired bobby. He remembered me and I had quite a surprise because he still remembered our little sand martin incident. We were joking about this when he suddenly said to me, 'I don't suppose you put the eggs in the right nests did you?' I just looked at him and we both burst into laughter; even though he was retired, he was still a damn good bobby!

Two incidents of birds who knew how to deal with egg molesters are worth recounting; firstly, a mute swan. Swans are not to be tampered with, but in the innocence of youth all things are possible. I had a mute swan's egg, my colleagues had not, so we sussed out a mute swan's nest which was get-at-able. The bird had nested on the shores of a small island in a local pool, and we had watched her for several days until she had laid six eggs, time for one to go walk-about.

A punt lay handily nearby, so off we went; believe me 'Just William' has nothing on us. We pulled up near the nest expecting the female to come off the nest to investigate us, when one of us would have darted to the nest and taken an egg. The swan had not read the script, she just sat tight. We started to flick as few small stones in her direction when one of them hit her. Enough was enough. Off she came, grunting and snorting; the lady was not amused. I ran and picked up an egg, sat down in the punt, and off we poled back to shore.

We had completely forgotten about the male. He was swimming further up the pool, had seen what was going on and was rapidly flying down the lake to investigate. He only had one object in mind, to repel all boarders. The swish, swish of his wings came louder and louder; I was crouched low down in the punt with the egg in my lap. When the swan arrived, he banked just above us and with his wing flicked one of my friends straight into the pool; in doing so, he completely lost the pole.

Fortunately, he could swim so we pulled him in and paddled frantically back to shore. Needless to say, when we returned home, we had some explaining to do to his mother. We thought it only right he should have the egg.

The second incident concerns a tawny owl. You never tangle with a tawny owl if you can help it. We had found this tawny owl nesting in an old tree stump, ten feet or so above the ground, in a very climbable tree.

We visited the tree regularly to see how she was progressing with her egg laying. Normally, we just had to kick the stump for her to flee the nest, a quick climb up, count the eggs and be on our way.

The last time we checked, she had laid her fourth egg a few days later and we decided the time was ripe to take one, as her clutch should be complete by now.

We arrived, kicked the tree, repeated the process to make sure, and up the tree scrambled 'Nipper'; well, I think it was 'Nipper'. It certainly was not me. He shoved his hand in the hole, let out a shriek, and out flew madam tawny owl leaving 'Nipper' having lived up to his name and truly 'Nipped'! The net result of all this was he had a badly scratched and bleeding arm. She had obviously got fed up of people kicking her tree and, from now on, would ignore it all. There was not a lot we could do for a badly bleeding arm, apart from wrap our handkerchiefs round it, so we cycled off to Coleshill, the nearest town, to find a chemist. Here, after telling a few 'lies' to explain the injury, the chemist did at least clean and wrap up the wound, and off home we cycled with more explaining to do.

Could it be that these two events made me consider the merits of egg collecting, and turn me into a bird watcher instead?

I did have one final fling in the collecting game. I obtained a pet jackdaw; although, to be fair, it did not start off as a pet. I found the fledgling bird on the ground. It had obviously fallen from a nest and could not yet fly, so I took it home with every intention of only keeping the bird until it could fly away. Jacky, as it obviously came to known, had other ideas.

Within a matter of ten days, Jacky could fly so taking it down to the field at the bottom of the grove in which we lived, the great release was to take place. I lobbed Jacky up in the air, he, I had by now realised it to be a male, flew round in a few circles and promptly landed back on my shoulder. He had learned this trick as I had tried to teach him to fly. After repeating the manoeuvre several times, with the same result each time, I had no option but to give up, and walk Jacky home sitting quite happily on my shoulder.

Jacky's home had been an old parrot cage. We had once had a parrot and, while I had been taking Jacky out, my mother had cleaned the cage and put it away.

She was not amused when I walked back with the bird on my shoulder. Anyone would have thought I was Captain Hook; he always had a parrot on his shoulder, I believe. This was the start of a six-year relationship between man and bird.

During the day, Jacky spent most of his time flying free round the neighbourhood. All the neighbours grew to know him and, to a certain degree, tolerated him. He came back home for food when required and, at night, went to sleep in his parrot cage with a dark sheet covering it so he did not wake us up at dawn.

Jackdaw are members of the crow family, which is classed as one of the most intelligent group of birds, and Jacky's behaviour certainly seemed to confirm this.

They are, without a doubt, the most curious of birds and the antics and situations mine got into were widespread, but two in particular are worthy of mention; one even made the local press.

Those of us old enough to remember the last war will also remember rationing and the short supply of various products, especially the exotic type of fruits such as oranges. It is amazing to see how common they are today, but not back in '46.

My mother came dashing out, put some money in my hand, and sent me off down to the local Co-op as they had received a supply of oranges. I jumped on my bike and shot off. Jacky, who had been moping around, had obviously seen me go and chased after me to investigate; at the time, I was unaware of this. The Co-op was only a couple of minutes away by bike, and I obviously had other things on my mind.

Jacky had become very adept at roding on my handlebars; I had these taped – us 'racing cyclists' always did this – and Jacky had found he could grip his claws round the taped area and ride along with me. I think it is safe to presume he was after a free lift!

The Co-op was traditional pre-war design: one end a butchers; the centre, and largest area, groceries; and the other end being the green grocery department which was shuttered not having doors. From my approach, the green grocery area was first.

I placed my bike against the shop wall and nipped into the green grocers. The continuing first part of this narrative is pure presumption on my part. Jacky, no doubt, came round the corner just as I vanished. A shopper was probably going into the grocery department and Jacky followed them in through the now open door. I came out of the shop clutching a brown paper bag in which lay four precious oranges, which was all we were allowed to buy. This narrative now returns to being factual.

As I came out, I heard screams and shrieks coming from the grocery department, shouts of 'Watch my baby's eyes', 'Where has this horrible, large black bird come from?' and so forth. Above this could be heard the call 'chak, chak' being repeated continuously; straight away, I knew Jacky was in the shop. I was the only one with a pet jackdaw locally.

I rushed in, pandemonium was rife, and flying about in sheer panic was Jacky.

Do you remember how some of the Co-ops of that period had a system of money being transported in small cups from sale point to the cashiers who were in an office?

These were whirring across the store adding to Jacky's fright; fortunately, he heard my call and swiftly flew down onto my shoulder. To say I exited the store at speed is putting it mildly; I grabbed my bike and swiftly cycled off home.

I said nothing to my mother, but when my father came home from work, he showed me the evening paper and pointed to a piece about a vicious bird terrorising shoppers, and asked me the obvious question. I could hardly lie, but my father had a sense of humour, and Jacky was quarantined for a week or so until the story had died down. I must admit for several days, anytime I saw a policeman, I thought he was after me. Our local bobby must not have been informed about it as he would have known who the villain of the piece was. I learned two things that day: firstly, how the press could exaggerate as my jackdaw had now become at least a raven judging by the size of the bird being reported, and also the comments of the passer-by; what they claim to have witnessed, I do not know.

Now for event number two, this one nearly broke up a long friendship between my parents and one of our neighbours. Shortly after the war finished, a 'craze' developed for adding leaded lights to existing windows; this involved strips of lead which were stuck to the outside of the windowpanes forming various patterns, and our neighbour had invested in this. They had a very simple pattern, just strips running diagonally across the window with the final strip crossing over all the others. After a while, this strip started to peel off just an inch or so, and this was where Jacky came in – unfortunately.

He was a regular visitor to their garden; they kept poultry just as my father did so there was always grain about, and Jacky would not miss out on this. You would have thought we never fed him! On one of these visits, he must have noticed this piece of dangling lead, which to a member of the crow family presented a challenge indeed.

The first I learned about this was when I heard the lady of the house shouting something not very complimentary about Brian George's bloody bird. I went to see what it was all about, and I could understand her feelings. Jacky was flying backwards with the lead in his bill, slowly stripping the lead off the window; he was having a whale of a time. I ran into their garden quickly to stop Jacky doing further damage and retreated just as quickly to avoid further abuse. My father was at home on this occasion so I went in and told him about it all. He was not amused, as neither was I, judging by how my ear was ringing!

Round to our neighbour he went, apologising for the behaviour of my bird and offering to repair the damage. Fortunately, the lead strip had not been broken, it was just dangling loose, so all that was needed was a tube of the right glue. This, needless to say, was not cheap so my pocket money was much reduced over the next few weeks. Once the repair had been carried out, it presented no further challenge to Jacky, and convinced us leaded lights were not for the George's. I did not tell my father Jacky had saved him spending some money by his actions. That would not have been tactful somehow.

Enough of Jacky, apart from to say we had him until I was nearly nineteen. He actually died whilst I was in Egypt in the forces, but what a pet and what a companion at times. I smile about him now just narrating these two stories. One extra thing before I forget: crows are good mimics, and jackdaws especially so. Although we never set out to try to teach him to talk, he did pick up one or two things. He could say a very clear 'Hello', he knew his own name of 'Jacky' which was distinct from his call of 'chak, chak', and finally, which always caused some amusement, he would shout out 'Brian' in almost the same tones as my mother. The times I went in to ask what she wanted, when it was not her, it was Jacky. At times like this, I am sure I could see a smile on his face. Thanks for the memories, Jacky!

By now the three egg collectors were splitting up; we had all moved onto different schools so we did not see each other so frequently. I went to a Commercial School where I stayed until I was over sixteen, and homework became very much the order of the day. I stopped running my own football team as I had reached the dizzy heights of playing both football and cricket for my school, which just goes on to show how poor they must have been.

We managed the odd cycling trip, although 'Polly' had learned about girls; to 'Nipper' and I, they were still pastures yet to be explored.

My school, Aston Commercial School, ran a summer camp for senior students where we stayed for a month, having normal lessons in the morning and in the afternoons worked on local farms. We slept under canvas in large bell tents and the girls slept in old military style billets. The camp was at Broom on the River Arrow, between Alcester and Bidford-on-Avon, a beautiful spot in rural Warwickshire. The work on the farms was not heavy: potato picking, pea picking and, if you were lucky, hay making where we were able to use pitchforks under close supervision, needless to say. Fortunately, the summer of '48 was very pleasant. Well, it was for our four weeks.

Along with a couple of friends, we used to go out in the evening for a walk along the Arrow. Here we saw a kingfisher, a little grebe, found a heron's nest in the reeds and I heard and saw my first ever turtle dove. We all thought the latter was a cat in a tree as its call is a soft cat-like purr; it was only when the bird flew out we realised what we had experienced. The heron was also interesting, and it taught me a lesson. Even at such an early age, I realised you do not believe all you read. My book at the time stated herons were colonial birds who nested in trees. No mention was given to the fact that solitary birds may ground nest in dense vegetation, as this one had. It was a good job I had finished with my egg collecting. I never did possess a heron's egg. Up to now, all my herons had been at the top of very tall trees, all beyond my tree climbing skills, and 'Polly's' for that matter. We also thought we had heard nightingales, but our knowledge and experience of that bird was nil. It was only many years later, when I had become accustomed to hearing nightingales, I realised we had.

Come Christmas of '49, my school days were over, I needed to find a job, which in those days you could do without great difficulty. I joined the clerical (not religious) profession as a clerk and started to earn the princely sum of £1 10s old money! (£1.50 today, although this would not be the comparable value to now; probably nearer to £40.00 per week.) This was considerably more than my previous level of pocket money; although, I did now have to make a payment for my keep.

The next year or so passed very quickly and National Service loomed on the horizon. I did not wish to join the Army so I signed on as a short-term regular in the RAF with a four year full-time service, and eighteen months reserve service; the latter was just money for doing nothing, although should any situation arise, you could be promptly called back.

EGYPT AND ALL THAT

After 'square-bashing' I was posted overseas to Egypt. I had originally been drafted for the Far East and had all my injections for that part of the world, some of which were not very pleasant, when Farouk got kicked out of Egypt. To meet this threat, we bolstered up all our military stations in the Canal Zone so, instead of a peaceful posting to the Far East, I was on active service in Egypt, whatever that may mean. This also meant additional injections for me, and I am sure every one I had was with a blunt needle. We did not have disposable needles in those days, you just stood in a line and took your punishment like a man.

Prior to going abroad, the RAF gave us a few 'special holiday' days so I returned home for a short time. My mother was very concerned with my going overseas, but my father took a more philosophical view. I think he envied me the opportunity of travel abroad, especially at the government's expense.

We flew from Blackbush Airport in a York military aircraft, no swank here; you sat in a bucket type seat and off you flew. The flight across the Mediterranean did not go all according to plan. We were due to land in Malta for refuelling, but part of the way across, we ran into a very heavy electrical storm; a very spectacular event, even if frightening at times. We could not land in Malta, so we droned on to north Africa, flying now on two engines to conserve fuel. We eventually landed in Libya, refuelled and breakfasted, for the final leg to Egypt. These flights were not supersonic. I doubt if we exceeded 200 mph, and by the time we reached our destination, we were worn out. These planes were not designed for sleep and comfort; you were in the RAF now young man.

After three days at Fayid I was posted to Deversoir, an RAF station on the side of the Suez Canal where the canal entered the Great Bitter Lake. My active service now began and, to prove the point, I was issued with a .303 rifle and 25 rounds of real ammunition plus a bayonet. The bayonet I think was only for ceremonial purposes, not for use!

I was very fortunate with my posting. I joined a special unit, JAPIC, which stood for 'Joint Air Photographic Intelligence Centre' for which we were all security cleared: Top Secret and all that jazz. Mind you, I may joke now but we took it all very seriously and, even today, I would not talk about some of the things the unit did and accomplished.

One very good side effect of being in this unit was the fact that access was very limited, very few had the necessary passes, so we had to carry out our own guarding and security duties which meant we were not involved in station duties, and I know who was the better off. We missed out on many a parade and inspection.

We may have had more guard duties to perform, but they more than compensated for other things. We were not inspected prior to going on duty and that was some benefit, believe me. When it comes to inspections the military mind goes into orbit, they can see a speck of dust yards away – sometimes, I think they put it there!

One story I must recount happened to me prior to my permanent posting and I caught for three nights station guard duty. On one of these nights, my patrol was to guard one of the aircraft hangers and during my two hours on, four hours off, I must have walked miles round this hanger. Towards the end of one such patrol, I came round the corner and received the shock of my life. Across the hanger doors a large shadow was swaying backwards and forwards, it had two large arms or so it appeared, which were gently moving and I just stood there in almost shock. Fortunately, my naturalist instincts took over, I turned and looked at one of the spot lights which illuminated the hanger. There in front of it was a preying mantis, a stick-like insect which was catching flying insects attracted by the light. The mantis itself was probably only six inches in length, but due to the spotlight its shadow was about fifteen feet long. I could now wipe the sweat off my face and go and study the insect.

How about a dictionary explanation (should it be required): mantis – a genus of orthopterous insects carrying their large spinous forelegs in the attitude of prayer.

There it is, education is a wonderful thing. This was my first encounter with Egyptian wildlife, but with two and a half years ahead of me, it was obviously not going to be my last.

One of the last things I did before leaving good old 'Blighty' was to obtain a second-hand copy of the condensed version of '*The Handbook of British Birds*', I could not bring my five volume set with me for obvious reasons, plus the fact I did not wish to lose it. Having the condensed version in one book was ideal, and I was going to need it as I had already experienced fleeting glimpses of birds I could not identify. Once a member of JAPIC, I was able to settle down and concentrate my efforts.

A short while after my arrival a new face arrived on the scene, Alan Parker. He was also a keen birdwatcher and photographer. He was a cub photographer with one of the London dailies of that time, and we quickly got to know each other. He was older than I as he had served an apprenticeship which delayed his entrance into National Service; he was only doing his two years, as National Service was at that time. Most of our leisure time was spent bird watching and photographing them whenever possible. Mind you, he did most of that, I was just his side kick when it came to photography.

Natural history study was in its infancy in those days. If you expressed an interest as a male, you were thought to be a bit queer; those sort of things were best left up to the fair sex. The other wise-crack of the day was, 'You're interested in birds eh, was she any good?' We, needless to say, just got on with it, and if the chance came in a football match, we left our mark! One or two wise-crackers left the field limping, we knew how to look after ourselves.

My arrival in Egypt coincided with the autumn migration of birds from Europe and home; I had never witnessed anything like this. Thousands of martins and swallows were flying down the Suez Canal on their way south, the areas of vegetation were temporary home to warblers I had been listening to and seeing only months previously. Exotic birds were also flying through; storks, pelicans and many of the larger birds of prey; I quickly began to realise my time in Egypt was not going to be wasted. My only concern was being able to identify all of what I saw.

One bird in particular excited me the first time I saw it, a glossy ibis. What a bird. I know it was not a sacred ibis which graced the tombs of the Egyptian kings, but to me it was the next best thing. This bird is on the British List, although very rare then, it became my number one bird to see in the UK. The question was: 'will I ever do so?'

I was fortunate in being a good marksman and I competed in the odd competition, as well as getting a few shillings a month more in my pay packet for the crossed rifles I wore on my arm. This gave me access to the station armoury and here I managed to borrow a pair of military binoculars. They had several pairs which were rarely used so, when I went off birding, I was able to borrow a pair.

I also managed to obtain a copy of a paperback publication by the MOD of birds of the Nile Delta. This had been written by R.H. Greaves and illustrated by Margaret Greaves; how the MOD came to be involved in the publication of such a book I have no idea, but I was mightily glad they had. The book covered the sixty common birds of the Nile Delta, birds which were highly unlikely to ever reach our shores, so consequently were not in the book I had brought with me. Armed with both binoculars and two bird books, my voyage of discovery was about to commence.

The only question was: would the RAF allow me the time? As mentioned previously, I was on Active Service and had the rifle to prove it.

After taking a few days to settle in and find my way around, I quickly realised that the camp had a goodly collection of birds. Although it was no longer the breeding season, there was still plenty to see, as well as the species mentioned a few lines back.

The first new bird I was able to identify was the crested lark, this bird was quite common and relatively tame. I could regularly see the bird running on the sandy ground where it appeared to be feeding on ants. Could easily be confused with our skylark by the novice, but the crest and bill were much larger. Its bill quite powerful really for a small bird, probably due to the food it commonly ate.

The most exciting and spectacular bird of my early days, and still one of my favourite birds was the hoopoe. The first time I flushed one of these birds I could not believe what I was looking at. For one of the most strikingly plumed birds, they are almost invisible when on the sandy ground of Egypt. My first flew off like a gigantic butterfly as it flapped and bounced a short distance away from me, to promptly vanish as soon as it landed. What a bird, previously just a picture in a book, now I had my own; a bird I was to share the next two and a half years with – service in the RAF was looking better by the day.

The Suez Canal was almost the perimeter of the camp, it was that close, just a couple of minutes' walk, and a few minutes more and I was on the shores of the Great Bitter Lake; these were to become regular haunts of mine. Spur-winged plover was another new species to be found here among the dry sandy shores of the lake. A lapwing-like bird in many respects, unmistakeable in flight as it flew with fairly slow clipped wing beats and its jet black flight feathers. Another feature for me was its longish legs, although being slightly smaller than our familiar lapwing, it always seemed to be taller – not that I ever saw them side by side – lapwings were not birds to be seen in Egypt.

Two early attractions of the Canal, where I could just sit for hours at times, were dolphins and pelicans. We were told, although never substantiated, the dolphins were kept in the Canal as they were the arch enemy of the local Mediterranean shark population, and any shark venturing into the canal would be promptly driven off by a pod of dolphins. It is true I never saw a shark, and most of us regularly swam in the lake and Canal with no warning of shark danger. The only problem I had with this claim was just how did they keep the dolphins in the Canal and stop them swimming out to sea. Not to worry, it was just a joy to see them so often. Months later, I was to swim with a few, but that is another story.

Now the pelicans. We all know 'their beak can hold more than their belly can', but when seen for the first time, what a beak. The white or great pelican is almost swan size, and I learnt they regularly migrated through Egypt in spring and autumn and my arrival in Egypt just caught the end of their autumn passage. Small groups were still flying down the canal, usually low over the water with an almost lazy flap, flap, glide flight. For such a large bird this looked almost effortless, as these large black and white birds glided through, some being accompanied by their browner youngsters. I never did find out where they were flying to for the winter, I just enjoyed their passing by. I could hardly wait for spring to see them on their return journey.

My introduction to Egypt was far exceeding my first thoughts, and the fact I should really have now been in the Far East no longer concerned me. I had much to look forward to, of that I felt sure, and I still had my love of football and cricket to consider.

The football season was just about to start and, after a few trials, I made my unit side and reached reserve status for the station team. Although normally having played in goal, I was selected as a left back for my unit team. As we had a junior first division team goalkeeper available, there was no way I could compete with this guy, who actually played for Luton Town in his latter days. As far as the station team was concerned, I played wherever was needed, which was not very often.

At this stage in the proceedings, Alan arrived on the scene, he was not a bad footballer either, so we had both birds and football to share; we quickly struck up a friendship as mentioned earlier.

One of our first joint ventures introduced us to another rather special bird. Alongside one of the perimeter fences ran the 'Sweet Water Canal', this was not its real name, it was just the name we gave it due to the smell which came from it – especially in the summer months – and it was not sweet. I am sure had you fallen in it, you would have died from almost every disease known to man. The canal was the life blood of the local community whose living conditions were frightful. They seemed to use the water for everything, especially irrigation, and it was amazing just what actually lived in this water.

Back to our special bird. We were studying the canal when a black and white bird flashed by, to suddenly stop and commence to hover almost directly in front of us, before plunging into the water and emerging with some small lizard-like creature in its bill. We could not believe our luck, a pied kingfisher, another picture from a book, and this time I had to thank Margaret Greaves for the illustration.

Compared with our kingfisher, the pied is a big and striking bird, not quite twice the size of ours, but getting on that way. This was not to be our last sighting of this bird, it obviously lived along this stretch of the canal, and we began to look forward to seeing it.

I quickly became aware of a large bird-of-prey which frequented the area where waste food was collected before being taken off to wherever it was disposed of. Several people had a not very polite name for this bird, which I will not use here (these words may now offend British ladies of the 21st century), but I soon became aware of the correct name of the bird: it was a black kite, an exceptionally rare bird back home, only one or two having been reported ever. They were an incredible flying machine, quite unlike any bird-of-prey I had experienced previously, not that I had seen all that many. My previous experience only covered three; kestrel, sparrowhawk and the odd buzzard, so the black kite became my fourth ever.

Another feature which I soon became aware of was the fact that the local kestrels formed small flocks, something I had never seen back home, and it was some little time before I realised I was not looking at our kestrel. These were an entirely different species – the lesser kestrel. What they were doing here in Egypt I did not know, as according to my book, they were a Mediterranean species, but we certainly had this small colony at Deversoir – not that I saw many elsewhere – if at all.

This bird taught me a lesson: look very closely at every bird you see, they may look familiar, but you never know. I quickly began to realise I knew very little and, at this point, I really started to study birds; previous to this, I had only ever played the part.

In Fayid, the Army had an area which can be best termed as a flower garden. Here flowers were grown for the various events where floral decoration was required, and the area was very well maintained. As well as the many flowers a trap had been built, a large Heligoland trap in fact, and here birds were caught and ringed for Cairo Museum.

The Royal Engineers had done a good job on this, it is incredible what they can turn their hands to! Even though we were on active service, it is amazing just what goes on behind the scenes. Alan and I managed to get permission to visit this site, and here we saw many an interesting bird, ringing several; we can only hope our records did in fact reach the museum.

The whole area was well-watered and some very exotic looking flowers were to be seen. The area was also good for flying insects, especially butterflies, some of which looked almost tropical. In addition, the odd snake and lizard were to be seen. One large irrigation ditch ran through the trap which was about eight feet high at the entrance, and whenever we arrived, we always made a drive on the trap. On one occasion, we heard a lot of flapping going on and as we progressed down the hide we saw the reason for it. A largish white looking egret was caught up in the corner of the hide, a buff-backed heron as it was then known, (in all new books it is now called the cattle egret) and this bird possesses a beak like a dagger and it knew how to use it. Discretion was the order of the day, so we just drove the bird back out of the trap and let it go on its way. Come the spring, it would be interesting to see just what we managed to ring; we were hoping for a good selection of warblers and the like who could quite easily be making their way to the UK.

Members of the forces were invariably young men in the 18 to 21 year category and, as I got to know my companions better, I began to hear about 'Dear John Letters'; something completely new to me who had led a sheltered life of birds, football and cricket, never having had a girlfriend. Many of my new acquaintances had girlfriends and moving far away from them was not easy. Overseas camps in those days were principally male, remember we are talking 1951 in my case, and female members of the armed forces were usually only based in the UK. Their only connection with the fair sex was through correspondence – mobiles had not been invented – so many spent most of their time feeling quite depressed and their only respite was receiving mail from their girlfriends. For the girls back home they were mixing with the opposite sex daily at work etc., and in consequence many found new boyfriends. After all absence makes the fond heart wander, or so they do say.

This is where 'Dear John' came in, although it was not necessarily John, it could be Bill, Frank, Tony, anybody. It was just the fact a 'Dear John Letter' was a letter from the girlfriend breaking off the relationship as she had found someone else. Eighteen months or so is a long time to be apart, especially at that age, and the receiver of the letter was just a bit too far away to do anything about it. Many a heart was broken, I was not sorry this was not going to happen to me; my birds did not write letters, although they infuriated me in many other ways. Was I ever going to get to grips with the birds of Egypt, of which there were well over 450?

The worst letter I received late that year was from my mother telling me Jacky had died. She had got up and taken the sheet off his cage to find poor Jacky lying on the cage floor dead. I consoled myself with the thought he had had a good life, wanted for nothing, been a devil on his day, but shared in a home which loved him dearly. Goodbye old friend.

During this, my first winter in Egypt, I had really struggled with the local resident birds but was slowly getting to grips with them. The birds, which come summer would have flown off back to the UK, were not the problem, it was the local birds which are resident in Egypt which were the awkward ones. I did not know just how many 'Little Brown Jobs', LBJs as we call them, existed, and one in particular was driving both Alan and me crackers.

The bird in question was obviously a warbler, and the bird was proving to be a most annoying species. We had not managed a clear view of the bird for all our efforts; it spent its time skulking away in thick vegetation. It was very small, almost wren-like, which was about as close a description as possible, and not until early spring did we positively identify the bird. It commenced to take to circling flights in the sky in which the tail markings showed well, and the way it fanned out its tail was quite distinctive. The outer edges of the tail had largish white areas, and the tip of the tail was all white, in the bright sunlight of Egypt, these white areas almost twinkled in the sun. Thanks to Mr R.H. Greaves, we had a fan-tailed warbler, a bird neither of us had heard of before. If you look for this bird in present day field guides you may find it referred to as the zitting cisticola, but fan-tailed warbler it will always be to me. Sorting out this one gave us both confidence for the future.

It was round this time it became necessary to go out on armed escort duties. Our C.O. was liaising with other officers at distant camps, and I was one of the regular airmen called upon to travel as escort, a duty which was not unpleasant. Our C.O. was a charming man, a D.F.C. decorated pilot in fact, a Squadron Leader, who still flew on occasion. It was on one such escort mission I added another special bird to my Egyptian list.

We were travelling through desert countryside, just a vista of sand and rugged areas of sandstone, this was as I had always imagined the desert to appear. A large greyish looking bird flew across in front of us to land on one of the rugged outcrops – I could hardly believe my eyes. I was looking at my very first vulture not in a cage, an Egyptian vulture in fact. Squadron Leader Bailey (Bill to us, although never called that in front of him needless to say), knew of my interest in birds and asked me what it was. When I told him he stopped the car, had the driver reverse so we could obtain good views of the bird for a minute or so, before the bird flew off. It was also Bill's first ever vulture! It turned out to be the only one I saw during my 30 months in Egypt, I began to wonder why it was called the Egyptian vulture!

This bird was at least recognisable, unlike the fan-tailed warbler, and when I returned and told Alan about it all he was a most disappointed man. We were quickly learning in this birding game you win a few and lose a lot! I was happy, though, another new bird to my list.

A week or so later escort duties called once again, and this time two vehicles were required and Alan managed to win himself the job of being escort in number two. I was again responsible for guarding the C.O., so we were the lead vehicle. It was once again a desert journey and, as we crossed the desolate terrain, we flushed two large black birds, raven of some kind, and as they flew past us I could see they were more brown than black; they were in fact a pair of brown-backed raven, but Bill was not interested in these so we drove on. When talking to Alan at our destination, he too had seen them and agreed with my diagnosis, his conclusion had been identical. I really do believe we were beginning to get quite good at this game! The desert was proving trumps for exciting birds.

During my first winter in Egypt, it was not necessary to always travel to see new and interesting birds. JAPIC HQ had a garden of sorts round it, mainly trees (bamboo types and date palms), and resident in these were palm doves a completely new species to me. They resembled turtle doves slightly, but quickly realised they were not. Here, once again, Margaret Greaves came to my rescue, and another new bird was added to my list.

Another species which was driving both Alan and me mad was the white-vented bulbul, although we did not know it at the time. It was a blackbird type bird with a squarish back to the head, fairly musical in a not unpleasant way, but it was a bird which rarely stood still. After much time and effort, we finally identified it, and another new species was added to our lists. Eventually winter turned into spring, not quite as we knew it at home, as winters here were not as unpleasant as in the UK – snow is a very rare event in Egypt.

With spring came the passage of birds en route to Europe. Hirundines came through in large numbers, swallow probably being the most numerous. Various warblers began to make an appearance, not in large flocks as the hirundines, but 20 or 30 in a small area were common place. Chiffchaff were calling, much as they do at home, and willow warblers could be heard singing away quite merrily, almost making us believe we were at home. Amongst the birds of prey marsh harrier and osprey were to be experienced. These were new birds to me as I had never seen them back home as both were very rare birds in the UK at that time.

My first osprey will remain with me forever as I actually saw it catch a fish in the lake. To see a large bird plunge dive, feet first into the water, vanish in a plume of spray and then appear with a large fish struggling away in its claws, was really memorable, and so it has remained. As the bird flew off, with the fish still struggling, I was able to watch the osprey turn the fish round in its claws and fly off with the fish head on, which no doubt cut down air resistance for the bird. This may have been nature in the raw, but it is what osprey are put on this planet to do, and long may it continue that way.

As the season continued, I began to pick up the more unusual species amongst the general movements. A few white storks started to appear, stonechat and the odd robin, where on earth had he been? Even a few chaffinch passed through, surely none of these commoner species were from the UK, the Mediterranean was probably their destination. Two birds in particular, I remember: two of the most spectacular birds to be found in Europe in my opinion. Firstly, a roller, and what a bird we had there. A true vagrant as far as the UK is concerned, and is still so to this day. They are largish birds being 30 to 32 cm in length, in flight they could be mistaken for stock dove. They love to perch on roadside telephone and power lines where they can survey the ground beneath before dropping down to take insects off the ground. On watching the bird do this, I began to understand why the bird is called a roller: it just rolls off the wires prior to its drop. That may not be the true scientific reason, but it still does for me. What a mega bird.

Could this bird be out shone? Yes it could, and by what – the bee-eater, or European bee-eater as it is now called. If you have a good imagination and can visualise a multi-coloured swallow, then you have your bee-eater.

The first bee-eater I ever saw was perched on the electricity cable which fed our billet, and when I walked outside and saw it sitting there, just a few feet above my head, I could not believe it. They are an incredibly hued bird, a blaze of magical colours, they are almost impossible to describe – if you have a field guide have a look. To avoid confusion, I will give you their scientific name 'merops apiaster'. When seen in flight they are very graceful and elastic in soaring flights, interspersed with a series of rapid wing beats, frequently passing through at altitude.

For the following few days they passed through in small parties, the highest number I saw together being 17, and these were all perched on the cable to our billet. They feed on large flying insects, such as bees, hence their name, but not solely so, and watching a bird feed on a bee made me really appreciate how things have evolved – Darwin had it right I believe.

In Egypt we had a very large dark bee, it was a solitary insect which nested in the holes and cracks of wooden buildings, and we were led to believe it had one hell of a sting, so keep away, which we duly did. Whether this news had been passed on to the bee-eater we never knew, but the way the bird handled the bee was fascinating.

You could watch the bird holding the bee in its stout bill gently stroking the bee on the wire. It always seemed to stroke the bee in the same direction, wiping the tail end of the bee on the wire before swallowing the insect. After watching this on several occasions, I came to the conclusion the bird was stroking the bee to extract the sting and wiping it to make sure the sting was no longer attached to the insect. If this was the case, just how had the bird developed this technique? Evolution is a marvellous thing, and they do say birds have little brains. The people who claim this have never studied birds, obviously.

Unfortunately, the bee-eaters moved through quite quickly; no doubt, this was fully appreciated by the bee population. We now awaited their return in the autumn, the bee-eaters that is, the bees were resident.

During early summer, Alan became involved with his photography with me tagging along as his unpaid assistant. We had constructed a hide from a mixture of canvas and parachute silk, and daubed this with dark paint as camouflage. Ringed plover, and the spur-winged plover mentioned previously, bred on the shores of the Great Bitter Lake, and Alan wished to photograph these.

During the warmer months, we commenced work early in the morning and finished at lunch time which gave us the afternoons free.

We would take the hide down to the lake, walk out near to the nest, erect the hide quickly; Alan would go inside with all his equipment and I would retreat until out of sight. Birds cannot count, so seeing me walk off they would presume things were safe and return to their nest. With the heat in Egypt, birds could stay off their eggs far longer than would be considered safe in the UK. Alan then had a couple of hours to do his photography before I returned and we left the site. I know one thing: I was more than happy with my side of the proceedings. At times, Alan came out of the hide looking as though he had been in a sauna. To have temperatures over 40°C were not unusual.

All photography in those days was in black and white, but that did at least mean we could develop and print all the shots very quickly; the camp had a very good photographic club. It also meant that if the shots were satisfactory, we did not have to trouble the bird further – that always being the most important consideration. The safety of the bird must always be paramount; I wish some of today's digi camera men remembered that, but I am digressing. Just as a point of interest, I still have many of Alan's photographs from those days which bring back happy memories.

It was shortly after this Alan got posted to another camp on Cyprus, so that was the parting of our ways, and we never did meet up again. Being in the forces was very much like ships that pass in the night! I was now the lone 'Birder of Deversoir' so I had to get on with things myself, but this was to hold me in good stead for my 'Birding Life' ahead.

Life was not all birds, the cricket season was now upon us, and although JAPIC was a small unit we had a very useful cricket team, one of our members a Flight Lieutenant was actually a county player for Hampshire and another was a Yorkshire colt in the times when you could only play for Yorkshire if you were born, or your parents were, in the county; how things have now changed. The rest of us were keen, if bumbling, 'amateurs'.

I played wicket keeper, not because I was any good, no one else wanted the job. We played on coconut matting laid out on rolled sandy surfaces, or even just a sandy surface, and the way a ball came off those surfaces was formidable indeed. What a really fast bowler could do was legend, hence wicket keepers were eagerly sort after. Whether you were any good was not the real criteria, the only requirement was you were mad enough to stand up behind the stumps. No matter how many catches were dropped, stumpings missed or extras given away, a wicket keeper's job was secure!

I did have one memorable match when I helped our Flight Lieutenant to collect a hat-trick with two catches and a stumping, he was highly delighted; it was his first hat-trick whilst in the forces. He actually gave us the money for a round of drinks in the NAAFI that evening. Were we now professionals? I had found fame for five minutes, it was never repeated.

It was during this first summer that I learned to swim. The water in the lake was highly salted, and in consequence it made swimming very easy. It was so dense I believe, that to drown, you would really have to work at it. I had never been confident in water and whilst at school had always sorted out a good reason not to do it. Here, I learned to swim in a matter of hours; you could just lie on your back in the water and float. I understand it is the third most salty lake in the world, and the name 'Bitter' was completely understandable, one mouthful was enough. The worst part about swimming in it was the fact that as soon as you came out of the water, due to the heat, you dried off almost instantly, and found yourself covered in salt, which you could brush off it was that thick. At least you did not have to worry about taking a towel with you, all you needed was a quick shower once you returned to base. Ah, idyllic days, and we were being paid for it.

It was one of these excursions where I almost came into conflict with a snake, and it was a big fellow. The shore of the lake was very sandy and some areas were covered with dunes. I was walking through these when the meeting occurred.

Skirting round a particularly soft dune I suddenly came face to face with the snake. It reared up in front of me, as I froze to the spot, I doubt if ten feet separated us. As it started to sway backwards and forwards, I felt myself coming out in a cold sweat. Then, with a sudden movement, the snake turned tail and raced off into the distance. I nearly collapsed with shock. The speed the snake moved at I would have had no chance had it attacked, it would have caught me up in seconds. Do not ask me what snake it was, it may even have been harmless to man, all I know is

33

the fact it was no grass snake, and in the circumstances, I feel I am allowed to exaggerate its size! I can only presume the snake was as frightened of me as I was of it, for which I remain eternally grateful. I smile as I recall the event, but believe me, I was not smiling some sixty years ago, when I thought my demise was due.

I never saw another snake of such size again, but I must confess when out in quiet places on my own, I did make a certain amount of noise so that if one again heard my coming, it may move off. Not a very scientific appraisal of things, but it suited me. I had no wish to surprise a snake again; next time, it may not race off. I do understand they tend to strike first and ask questions afterwards!

Come late autumn, the football season commenced once again and among the influx of new men to the camp came a few more-than-useful footballers and I found my spell as a reserve to the station team was no longer required. I maintained my place in the JAPIC XI, but even that was not for much longer.

We were playing a squadron team in the station league, and it had proved to be a very hard match, with a few nasty tackles taking place which the referee had not really kept under control and tempers were getting a bit frayed. You would never have believed we were drinking with some of these players in the NAAFI the previous night. I went in very hard at one of their players who had given me a rough time, and as I slid in he caught me on the knee – not intentionally I do believe – and click, my knee was out, and I have never felt pain like it. Fortunately for me, the squadron team had arrived in two vehicles, one shot off to the station hospital to warn them of what was coming; I was carried to the other vehicle and driven off down to the hospital. Orderlies with a stretcher were awaiting me and I was rapidly taken into a ward. A young doctor was in attendance and he quickly examined me, not that much of an examination was needed. He warned me that putting the knee back was going to be a painful experience, but in view of the pain I was already in, I doubted it could get much worse.

The doctor may have been a young officer, but he was no mug. He shouted something to a nurse, I turned to look, and crack, my knee was back in place. He was right about the pain but this quickly eased to become just uncomfortable. I was kept in hospital overnight, before returning to my billet. The football match was never completed, let us face it, half of the opposition team had been involved with getting me to hospital.

One advantage of this was being put on 'light duties' for a couple of months and being excused from all parades and guard duties during that period. My football 'career' was also put on hold, with the season being almost completed before I could even be considered.

I was at least able to continue with my bird watching. The return of the bee-eaters was eagerly awaited, and they did not disappoint. Various warblers came through and we had a very heavy movement of wheatear. There had been a bad storm in the Mediterranean, apparently, which had coincided with the wheatears passing through. I also had a very pleasant surprise: I saw my first ever shrike, a red-backed shrike, and what a beauty. On one occasion I saw a passage of white storks, which must have numbered in three figures, these glided over very high in the sky; they had found a thermal or two that was for sure. One thing I noticed with this autumn migration was that it seemed to be over very quickly, species did not hang about for as long as they did in the spring. After a day or two they were gone.

It was now back to winter birding, my second winter in fact. For the first time in Egypt I took particular notice of the crows, which was a good job I did, as they turned out to be hooded crows, not the all black carrion crow back home. A yellow wagtail species also caught my attention, which after careful study, I realised was the blue-headed wagtail; the Egyptian form, Greaves reliably informed me. Another bird which had me going was a very attractive black and white wheatear, but I could find no reference to a wheatear of this type in Greaves, until I realised he referred to the bird as the mourning chat. Waterfowl were always thin on the ground (I should probably have said water here), just the odd teal and shoveler appeared on the lake in winter; the only regular duck being the inevitable mallard, they get everywhere!

After winter comes the spring, and that year I concentrated my efforts on the waders. Could it be I was getting too familiar with bee-eaters? Definitely not, their passage could never be ignored. Waders, even in my early days of bird watching, attracted me, they always were a challenge (and they still are today). Two species I initially took to be ringed plovers, certainly taught me a lesson in bird observation and the fact that small detail can be so important. These birds turned out to be Kentish plover and little-ringed plover, exceptionally rare birds in the UK at that time. (The Kentish still are, but in the last 20 years or so little-ringed plover have commenced to breed.)

That spring also saw an impressive passage of spotted flycatcher with many hundreds moving through in a matter of a few days. One special bird which I managed to find was a bluethroat – although mine had a white throat – there are several races of this particular bird. My list of birds rarely seen in the UK was steadily increasing; I wondered would I ever see some of them when back home? Enjoy them whilst ye may! The summer of '53 was very warm to say the least, so much time was spent swimming in the lake, here I came across snorkelling for the first time. To lie, face downwards in the lovely clear waters of the Great Bitter Lake, was an incredible experience. Sea horses came right up to your goggles and almost seemed to be peering straight into your eyes, up to this time sea horses had appeared as a myth: could there be such a creature? There certainly was.

Was on one such occasion that I came face to face with a dolphin, and for a second or so, I thought I had met up with a shark until it turned and swam directly up to me. What a creature, to see it just two or three feet away is a memory I shall always carry. There were two of them; one kept on returning to gaze at me head on – he probably wondered what I was – the other kept its distance then all too quickly, they were off. Although I saw the dolphins on occasions, afterwards, that wonderful experience was never repeated. Just think, I was being paid by HM Government to experience all of this, and I was still on active service!

Later in the summer, I was walking along the shore of the lake when I noticed a very dark looking bird behaving in a most unusual manner, so I moved behind a dune to study the bird further. I quickly realised I was studying a glossy ibis, mentioned previously, almost as mythological as the sea horses to me. This bird was rushing into a small channel and driving small fish up to the end of it. Here, they leapt out of the water in obvious blind panic, trying to avoid the ibis. For some, it was to no avail; before they could get back into the water, the ibis had swallowed a few before it repeated the process. I have never read of such behaviour: was this a one-off occasion of a bird learning a new technique? I think this observation convinced me more than ever that birds have a well-developed brain and know how to use it. (A view I still hold.)

It was during the back end of that summer that I obtained a 'pet'; I found a chameleon which I kept for a few days. I had now reached the dizzy heights of being a corporal which meant I had my own small room in the corner of the billet. I was i/c (in charge), how's that for promotion! Chameleon are not the most active of creatures, this one spent most of the day curled up asleep in a shoe box. Occasionally, I would take it out and put it on my bed sheets, and no it did not change colour, it just lay there awaiting its dinner. If a fly, of which there were plenty, landed on the sheet out would shoot a long tongue, and with a gulp, the fly was gone. He was more useful than any fly-paper. Time, however, came to put it back into the wild; the chameleon and I, therefore, parted company.

I also met up with my one and only ever scorpion, and what an incredible creature it was, and this one I did not keep as a pet. Whether it was a poisonous one I had no knowledge, but it certainly looked the part so I left it to get on with its own business, just making sure it did not come into the billet. I know one thing, for a few days after this experience, I banged my boots on the floor just in case it was inside! That winter was to be my last in Egypt; my overseas time would finish come March '54 leaving me a little over 12 months service to complete in the UK. The winter of '53 turned out to be one of the coldest experienced in Egypt that century: it actually snowed on occasion and several frosts were experienced. We even felt the cold, and some of the local population died from exposure, they did not have the warm clothing we had nor heating in their homes. I say homes, many looked like just shelters. Being poor in Egypt in those days was not recommended.

During that winter, I came across a few more familiar birds which are residents or winter visitors to Egypt. They have their own house sparrow which only varies with ours slightly. I saw the odd starling, a visitor from southern Europe, the occasional stonechat appeared on the scene and I even chalked up a song thrush; I was in training for when I returned home.

I managed the first two weeks of spring migration before my time was up. I managed to tick off a few interesting warblers during that period. Olivaceous warbler, Sardinian warbler and the graceful warbler being of particular attraction to me.

I waved my farewells to Egypt and its birds, homeward bound I became. My flights in the RAF seemed doomed to have problems.

That time we did manage to land in Malta for refuelling, but the engines would not fire up again, so we spent two days enforced leave in Malta whilst the plane was repaired. We could not do a lot on Malta as we had to stay close to the airfield ready for immediate transportation home, so I had no chance to study Malta birdlife, but at least the beer was drinkable.

We finally landed in dear old 'blighty', where after a couple of weeks holiday, I was posted to RAF Gaydon, a new airfield being built in Warwickshire for the use of Bomber Command.

GAYDON – HOME POSTING

Gaydon was ideally situated for getting home at weekends. We were given several railway warrants a year which gave free travel, but in those days, if you travelled home in your uniform it was not difficult to obtain lifts. I was able to get home for almost free on many an occasion, and found lorry drivers most helpful, they seemed to like company.

As a developing base, workmen were very much in evidence. Parades, inspections etc were limited, the only duty which was still carried out at top level was guard duty; although, we did not carry live ammunition. I was no longer on Active Service, had I ever been was questionable, it was now peace time, but had anyone told the Russians that?

The camp was being developed as a base for the 'V' bombers, and I must say one thing about these enormous aircraft, if you were guarding them in the rain, they certainly provided good shelter; you could have played a football match under their wings. Sorry for that 'slight' exaggeration!

The RAF is a wonderful place to be if you have any ability for sport, or in some cases if you are prepared to give it a try, especially with the more unusual sports. Once again I played football and cricket for my unit team, but never got a look in at camp level, and then I learned about hockey.

At that time I had always thought of hockey as a girls' sport, grown men did not play it, how wrong was I. The camp ran a hockey side which was made up of mainly officers, very few other ranks were ever considered, but with the arrival of the new bombers, flying crews' spare time for hockey was strictly limited. If the camp was going to still run a team, new players were urgently required. I was working for a Pilot Officer who was a keen hockey player. He had both represented the RAF and England, and he started to apply 'pressure' on me to give it a try. One week we had no football matches so I went along for a practice game against a local side from Warwick University. I was put on the wing, whether they thought I would not have much of an influence on the game out wide, I do not know. I managed to actually hit the ball on occasion and stopped it, which is a skill on its own I thought.

Anyway, game over, we retired to the bar after showering, where we had some choice sandwiches and a drink; I was actually bought a whisky by one of the officers. In the RAF other ranks were not allowed spirits or wine, you could only buy beer, cider or soft drinks from the NAAFI. Officers were in a different league. Off camp you drank whatever you liked, it was your money.

The team had another game the following week, and I was again chosen. I did not fool myself this selection was on merit, the team needed 11 players so I was required to make up the numbers. Incidentally, I failed to mention the score of my first game, we lost 6 – 1.

Our next game was against the police training college, if my memory serves me correctly, this was also in Warwick; or, if not, Leamington Spa. The college was the training centre for the Colonial Police Force, we actually had colonies in those days – a lot of the world was still coloured red! Many of the officers being trained were from Malaya, who were probably the top hockey team in the world in those days. It was a safe bet they would be in a different league to us, and as things turned out – they were!

To say we were trounced is an understatement – I doubt if I touched the ball on ten occasions – they rattled up 17 goals, and I think they let us off in the end because we scored two. Not only did they know how to play hockey, they also knew how to entertain. It was not sandwiches here, it was grilled steak and wine; I was beginning to really enjoy my hockey, or at least the fringe benefits.

The benefits from hockey were beginning to dawn upon me. Football teams travelled in a 7-ton truck to their away games, cricket did slightly better, usually travelling by coach; hockey, on the other hand, we went by car. I actually travelled in an open top Jaguar once or twice. Football and cricket players may have been lucky to have a beer and sandwich after the game, you already know what the hockey 'stars' had!

Another thing I tried was cross country running, this too had a regal spark attached to it. Once again being officer dominated, and I made the camp racing team once or twice, just again to make up the numbers. I was never really good at it, but I was stubborn and never failed to finish, albeit well down the field, but this was sufficient for us to win a trophy on one occasion. The only sporting event of any consequence in which I have been a member of a winning team. I had a couple of whiskies for this effort – once again, not paid for by me. I may not have been a top sportsman, but I knew on which side my bread was buttered!

From all this sporting activity, bird watching had taken a back seat and during my last twelve months in the RAF, I did very little; the nearest I got to the countryside was to go fishing with my father. Mind you, I frequently saw kingfisher on these jaunts, and once caught an eel over two feet in length. My father took the eel home and had it jellied; I was not impressed, even though I had caught it.

1954 quickly passed by and I started to prepare for my demob. I had decided not to stay on in the RAF, although I could have done with an almost guaranteed promotion – imagine 'Sergeant George', no I did not think so. Having been born in Saltley, where most of my relatives still lived or worked, I had been lined up for a job as a cost clerk for the Metropolitan, Cammel, Carrriage & Wagon Co, a major supplier to British Rail. Unfortunately, British Rail were involved in a major strike and had no trains running, and the Met. as it was locally known, was almost closed down and was taking on new employees. I stood this for a week or two in the hope the strike would be settled, it was not, so I visited the RAF Employment Agency who looked after ex-RAF members. An interview was quickly arranged with Joseph Lucas, one of the country's top companies at that time. They had a reputation of taking in ex-forces personnel, and I was offered a position in their Buying Office as a Records Clerk. A new career had begun.

THE AFTERLIFE

The work at Lucas's was very interesting and I quickly realised that a career in buying would suit me admirably. The department operated a system of promoting from within, all of us coming in at the lowest level, i.e. Records Clerk, and if we proved our worth promotion followed. You worked in small teams, a Buyer, Progress Clerk and the Records Clerk; our team was responsible for purchasing raw materials, probably the largest group spend of any product, and I enjoyed this.

We worked very closely with the Accounts Department who regularly came into see me regarding invoice clearance and one person in particular, a charming young lady, became almost the regular visitor. We got on very well and after a time I plucked up the courage to ask her out... I say plucked up the courage. As you will no doubt remember, the fair sex and I were not exactly connected. She said yes, and although I was not to know it at the time, this was the start of a 53-year relationship, but more of that later.

Dorothy, which was her name, also had a love of the countryside, so we started off with a common theme, which was to remain with us. It also provided me with the opportunity to pick up on my bird study once again, I now had someone else to share it with.

Dorothy and I hit it off from Day 1, we shared so many interests: theatre (Dorothy was a member of the Lucas Dramatic Society), music, sport, wildlife and walking. After a while, Dorothy obtained a cycle – she had never ridden a bicycle in her life – so I had to ride it home before I could teach her to ride. Needless to say, this was quickly accomplished. I had moved up from my cycle of '45, and was now the proud possessor of a Sun Manxman road racer type. We quickly cut a dash on the roads of Warwickshire!

Cycling in the 50s was a distinct pleasure, not so many cars on the road in those distant days; many of us used our cycles to travel to and from work – it was a different time.

For the next couple of years, we cycled miles round the Midlands before progressing up to a motor scooter, a Lambretta; I do not even know if they still exist. At least with power between our legs, we were able to travel further afield; we frequently smiled about our last holiday prior to marriage.

We were spending a week in Dorset and Devon – Dorothy's parents were in Dorset, mine in Devon. We 'motored' down, and on a very steep hill Dorothy had to get off the scooter and walk up the hill, due to the heavy load the machine was carrying – we had two full suitcases on the back – it could not make the hill. We had not pre-booked any accommodation as the decision to holiday had been a last minute event.

In Bournemouth we attempted to obtain digs, and this became very difficult, most boarding houses had rooms, but they were not prepared to rent them out to un-married couples; even though we wanted separate rooms. Whether they thought we would be visiting each other's room during the night I do not know. Eventually, we found two boarding houses which were next door to each other who let us have a single room in each. So for three days we took it in turns to breakfast together in one, and eat our dinner in the other.

Now for four days in Devon, staying at Torquay. Rooms in the town were like gold dust, so we went inland, and here we came across a farm with vacancies. The farming community were much more accommodating; single rooms were quickly obtained. One memory from this farm was the fact you had to run the gauntlet of their geese. They had a collection of Chinese geese, or swan geese as they are also known, and at times they could be very nasty, especially when attacking your bare legs, and although we were not cycling on this occasion, we wore shorts in the warm weather. Happy days of innocence.

As our marriage grew nearer, we managed to raise the money to place as a deposit for our house and started to make plans accordingly. For the previous two years, both Dorothy and I had Saturday jobs: she worked as a shop assistant in a store in Birmingham, I worked mornings only with my local window cleaner/chimney sweep, but it did what we wanted – helped us raise the cash necessary. Three weeks prior to our wedding calamity struck, the builder went broke, so the house would not be completed on time, if ever.

The Estate Agent responsible for selling the properties, managed, do not ask me how, to retrieve our deposits, which promptly went as deposit for another house; this property, however, was not due for completion for nearly 12 months. Too late to change the wedding, so for a year we lived with my parents, who were very good, before stepping out into the world on our own.

Our new home was in Aldridge, a Staffordshire large village in those days before it became part of Walsall, which became absorbed into the new West Midlands County.

You will have noticed little mention of birds has occurred recently, moving to Aldridge was to change this. Our new home had been built on ground which was once part of a plant nursery, well before the days of Garden Centres, this place just sold plants, equipment and other gardening requirements. As part of the site it also had two tennis courts which were available to hire, these formed our rear garden boundary, and as we both played the game I must confess, Dorothy did so with more skill than I – we frequently booked one of the courts. This was ideal during the summer evenings, if no one else required the court we could play till the light had gone.

Another advantage was the fact that bird life within the nursery was very good, and once I started to put out food for the birds they quickly moved in. One of my first priorities had been to make a few nest boxes and put these up in advantageous positions. You will notice I said make, we are talking here of over fifty years ago when bird supplies and equipment were not readily available. If you wanted peanuts you bought them from the green grocer, in their shells, and threaded these onto cotton so you could hang them in the tree or wherever. The blue tits etc., then had to hack their way through the shell to reach the nut inside; they were not spoiled like they are today! The seed you obtained was seed for cage birds or aviaries, not the mysterious mixtures obtained now-a-days, but the birds survived. Feeding the birds had not quite arrived in those days, and very few people did so. I wonder who we should really credit for starting the feeding the birds craze; should it be the RSPB, or Mary Poppins? After all, she sang the song 'Feed the birds'. Mind you, I never managed to buy it at 'tuppence a bag'!

Our new home was just minutes away from open country, and

interesting places such as Barr Beacon, Chasewater and Walsall Arboretum were but a short distance away by scooter.

It was at the Arboretum I became aware of an unusual duck for the first time: a bird I subsequently identified as a ruddy duck, or North American ruddy duck as it was called in those distant days. A dapper fellow with an incredible blue bill. This bird was not in many of the field guides of the day, certainly not mine, but the one or two which were at the Arboretum certainly brightened up the duck scene. They apparently were offshoots of a few which had escaped from the Slimbridge Wildfowl Trust in Gloucestershire – the Trust being the brainchild of Peter Scott. These 'Yankees' obviously had found England to their liking, but I did not mind, they rapidly became one of my favourite ducks.

One very interesting spot we found, which was within walking distance, was Stubber's Green. Here we had a large lake on which sailing took place and next door, so to speak, was a small settlement pond on which a decent range of duck could be seen. This pond was reed lined providing nesting conditions for reed warbler, sedge warbler and reed bunting, it was also a popular feeding area for martins and swallows; at times, flies were there in vast numbers making hunting easy. It was here I had my first real encounter with water rail, a pair bred there. For Dorothy it was her first experience of the bird, and I had only seen the bird once or twice in my life previously, so we were both more than happy.

A pair of mute swans also nested on the pond, which was a popular area for children to feed the ducks. On one occasion, the swans caused a major traffic jam. It was late in the summer and they had five large cygnets. The family had walked out onto the road after food, and some of the cygnets had decided to sit down on the roadway, making it impossible for motorists to pass. No amount of gentle persuasion was going to move these birds and, when anyone got too close, one of the adults became very aggressive; you do not mess about with a mute swan. The jam increased in size with the usual response from some motorists: if it cannot be fixed, blow your horn!

I must confess we were beginning to enjoy the situation, our sympathy lay fully with the swans, and to see people waving their arms at the birds – and promptly fleeing when the swans retaliated – was almost pure comedy. By now, all the cygnets had sat down completely blocking the road; you could not have got a cycle through.

As much as we were enjoying the situation, something needed to be done, so we moved in. I managed to pick up a cygnet, not that it appreciated the fact, and popped it back into the pond just escaping a savage jab from dad, the cob. At this point a 'miracle' occurred, the cygnets all got up and swaggered back to their pond, followed by their parents, who again had a go for me in their passing.

Traffic could start to flow, one or two of the motorists did at least thank us, the majority did not, and the swans just continued to sail majestically on their pond. Did they fully appreciate the problem they had created, I somehow doubt it!

Just outside Aldridge was a very interesting area of damp woodland, this lay just off the A454 and proved to be a very productive area, especially in the summer months when it was full of bird song. You could hear, if not see, at least eight warblers, woodcock nested and a pair of tawny owls could be seen; they had a favoured ivy covered oak in which they nested and roosted up. Our commoner breeding birds were all accounted for and a sparrowhawk also nested regularly. On a bright summer evening this made a very pleasant walk from home; if you drove there was parking, not that you needed much space for a scooter!

Barr Beacon was close by, one of the highest points in the area, on a clear day you could see miles. We quickly realised this was the point to come for passing migrant birds, especially at night time in spring and autumn. One very late but balmy autumn night, we experienced a passage of fieldfare and redwing; we could not see the birds obviously, but we could sit back and hear their passing. Early one spring we experienced a passage of curlew, now there is a sound for you, nothing is so evocative as the call of the curlew – well, not if you have any soul. Wheatear were to be seen most years on both spring and autumn passage, and the pure music of skylarks filled the air, had Vaughan Williams been here I wondered? Stonechat, not a common bird so far inland in those times, also put in an occasional appearance; they found the isolated gorse patches much to their liking, and I am convinced the odd pair did in fact breed. On one occasion, we actually saw a peregrine pass over the Beacon, now that was a very rare and unusual sight in those days – we are talking of 1959 here – and we also had the thrill of seeing a roding woodcock, a new experience for us. These were wonderful times of discovery, and all occurring on our doorstep.

Chasewater Reservoir was a large canal feeder reservoir and was slowly becoming a favoured roosting spot for winter gulls, and many a frustrating hour was spent here trying to identify the various gulls coming in to roost. This started my love/hate relationship with the species. No real studies had been made on gulls so literature on the subject was somewhat limited. I am sure many of the decisions made in those days would not stand up now. Juvenile gulls, summer plumaged birds, winter plumaged birds and birds in transition, the permutations are limitless and many an experienced birder tries to avoid them wherever possible. It is only in recent years I have tried to get to grips with them, and I am still struggling! In 1960, I moved up in the world. I became an Assistant Buyer at Joseph Lucas – this put a pound or two more in the pocket. We were able to move up into car ownership, a little Austin A35 which cost the princely sum of £110.00, but we did feel posh, no more freezing to death on two wheels, and petrol in those days was about four shillings a gallon (direct comparison being 20p) which compares with about £6.00 today. Halcyon days! We also managed to have our first real holiday since our marriage, we had honeymooned I forgot to mention, so we were not completely deprived!

Our first holiday by car and Cornwall was our destination, which seemed almost like the end of the world in those days. There was no flexibility over holidays. Lucas was in the motor trade and summer holidays were fixed, roughly the last week in July and the first week in August; you either went away or you did not. We had booked up digs in Marazion, which overlooked St. Michael's Mount, at least as a married couple we had no problem with a room! The hostess was charming, rooms lovely and clean, and she was no mean cook. Hotel holidays were rather posh in those days, and well beyond our financial situation.

It was on this holiday that sea birds, for the first time, came into the picture. Puffin, guillemot, razorbill, cormorant, shag and fulmar had been but pictures in a book; you did not see many of these near Birmingham! The puffin is everyone's friend, the one bird instantly recognisable by one and all, you do not have to be a birder to love this little fellow. To split the guillemot and razorbill took a little more work, but the results were worth the effort, and the same thing could be said with the cormorant and shag. We also quickly learned the fulmar was no gull, and that was a relief!

At low tide you could walk across to St. Michael's Mount, a small island covered in thrift, a lovely picture, and here I came across turnstone for the very first time, and what a delightful little bird it really is. It shows no fear of man, just almost runs round your feet as it busily forages for food, doing exactly as it name implies: turning over the stones. I was certainly knocking up new species on this holiday; well, we both were for that matter.

Another flamboyant beauty to our list was the noisy but spectacular oystercatcher, they seemed to be everywhere. These boldly marked black and white birds with their incredible red bill and legs seemed to have one object in life, be as noisy as possible but charm the viewer at the same time – they succeeded on both counts.

A local man in the village where we were staying learned about our interest in birds and he offered to take us to see one of the last choughs to be seen in Cornwall. They had long considered the Cornish Chough to be a species in its own right, and were really concerned about its future; after all, it is part of Cornish history as well as featuring on the Coat of Arms of the county. He would not take us too close and we just had very distant views of the bird. To this day, I do not really know whether we saw one or not. They were right to be concerned about the bird because it did vanish completely from the county, although I am now pleased to report they are again back in Cornwall, so their demise was only temporary. On some of Cornwall's more remote beaches ringed plover were to be found. I never actually located a nest but, by their actions, I suspected the odd pair were breeding. At least I was familiar with this bird, which brought home memories of my period in Egypt.

It was during this holiday we saw one of Britain's rarest birds of that period, a peregrine falcon. It was an extremely rare bird at that point in its history, and to see one hunting feral pigeons along the coast near to Lands End was our scoop of the week. It did not actually catch anything, but what an example of power and grace.

Back home in Aldridge life was going to be rather boring after this, our first real holiday as a married couple had certainly exceeded all our expectations, and it was the birds which had done that for us. Our love of birds, which remained with us for the rest of our lives, and in my case still does, really commenced here in Cornwall.

Only one holiday a year was possible in those early days, both from the point of view of how many days holiday a year you were allowed, and secondly, and probably the most important, the cost.

Work wise, probably the most important promotion of my career was to be made. I became a Buyer and I was transferred to a new factory recently opened in Cannock. Here the main products being produced were headlamps and ignition coils, in which a large amount of raw materials were used, steel, brass, copper and bronze, materials which were to become my forte. With this promotion, I also received a very much appreciated increase in salary, and we quickly decided it was time for a hotel holiday. Where to go?

After much thought we decided to visit the Lake District, and this was the start of a love affair which has lasted right up to today. We found a delightful hotel near to Elterwater, in a small village called Chapel Stile, situated on the banks of the Great Langdale Beck, and this was lovely walking country. As well as our love of birds we had developed a liking for walking, and in the Lakes you can certainly combine the two which we did to good effect.

The beck introduced us to two new birds which have long remained favourites: the dipper and the goosander, which both bred along the beck. You only needed to walk out of the hotel gardens quietly to see the dippers going about their business; they were obviously nesting nearby. Then if you walked down along the beck towards Elterwater you came into the territory of a pair of goosander – two magical birds as far as we were concerned.

Above Chapel Stile was some very rough countryside, not country to meander in. Here you needed additional skills which we did not possess, but we could at least manage some of the lower slopes. Here was home to buzzard, raven and ring ouzel, cracking birds for us from the lowlands of the Midlands, and on one of these forays we picked up some very exciting news: golden eagle had commenced to breed in the Lakes, and we were given clear instructions of where to see them. I was very pleased to have spent time studying maps and being able to work out map references, as I now had the map reference of a golden eagle's eyrie. Could you ask for more? It was a good job I was not an egg collector!

After receiving this news, we had a couple of days with decent weather forecast so off to Haweswater we went. It was a lovely walk down the Riggindale Valley, we heard ring ouzel, saw common sandpiper, wheatear, stonechat, redstart, heard wood warbler and saw a peregrine falcon, what more could you ask for, only the eagle.

The RSPB had set up a security watch group here to protect the eagle from egg collectors and the like, and in the distance, we could see their encampment so we knew exactly where to go. They were a very enthusiastic group of volunteers, you instantly felt the golden eagle was safe in their hands. As we arrived, one of them called us over; in a mounted telescope, he had the male eagle sitting out on a ledge in clear view. This was to be our first ever sighting of a golden eagle in England; well, in Great Britain for that matter, and what a bird.

In the bright sunlight of the day, you quickly realised where the name golden came from; you could not have called this fellow anything else. We spent over an hour enjoying this bird and on one occasion he gave us a fly-past; in the air, you could really appreciate his size. This was the start of a love affair, and for the next few years we never failed to visit the site. Unfortunately, they are no longer there.

Shortly after this holiday, Dorothy found employment locally – no longer trips to Birmingham for her – and this made things far easier at home. She was able to come home at lunch time, prepare our evening meal, should this be necessary, and upon my arrival home the meal may well be ready. This enabled us to put our evenings to good effect, whether that be work or pleasure. We also took on a new member of the family, a dog.

We had always had dogs when at home, so now we could look after one properly, it was a natural progression. Our dog was a basset hound, Kennel Club name Rytow Melody, our name Meg, and she quickly came to rule the roost. To be a basset hound owner you have to be slightly mad: they are untrainable, and have a mind of their own, which once made up, nothing on earth will alter it. They will eat you out of house and home if once given the chance, but they are the most lovable and friendly of animals you could wish for. Dogs are the finest excuse I know for going on walks, and Meg was more than happy to do so.

Fortunately, the hotel we used for our holidays in the Lake District welcomed dogs, they had a spaniel of their own who frequently joined us on our excursions, so the hotel owner was more than happy to see us.

Four or five more years passed by and Aldridge was beginning to grow in size, becoming more of a small town than a village so we looked around for a move into the local countryside, and this is how we came to live in Yoxall – where I have remained ever since. Travelling to Cannock was no problem for me and Dorothy quickly obtained employment at a local agricultural implements manufacturer a couple of hundred yards away from where we lived.

We moved in a couple of days before Easter, which was early that year, and on the day we actually moved in it snowed, not the greeting we had expected! It had all cleared by the Good Friday, and it was on that day we both knew we had made the right move. We were standing on the front lawn, the builder had laid this for us, when we heard the sound of a bird which was to become very much a part of our life for the next few years, a curlew called. There is a no more evocative sound than this, it makes the hair on the back of your neck stand up – well, it does if you have a soul – and we were hearing it from our own home. Needless to say, we now knew the name we were going to call our home, 'Curlew', and the plaque still sits proudly on the wall. We were now deep in the country, I quickly made it my business to get to know the local farmers and obtained permission to walk their land; I think they were quite surprised to be asked. Most of the farms were sheep or cattle, little was grown in those days. The land was all in the flood plain of the River Trent, which made the land suitable for such ventures and provided good cover for birds and other creatures. The village of Yoxall had its own small river, the Swarbourn, and we quickly realised this river was home to kingfisher and grey wagtail, two of our most colourful birds, and along with Meg, we walked many a mile along its banks. We not only enjoyed the birds, the dragonfly and damselfly population along the river was wonderful; something else we now had to get to grips with. A new dawning was upon us, the peace of the countryside was all around us, and it was here for free. A new life had begun.

It was on one such walk that Meg flushed a sitting curlew, there, almost under our feet, lay three of the most beautifully marked eggs you could wish to see. Our first ever curlew's nest, and still my only one. We quickly back-tracked and watched the bird return to her nest, no damage had been done, and we had shared a treasured moment with what was rapidly becoming our favourite bird. You can now probably understand my comments a line or two above, 'a new dawning was upon us'.

The river had a reasonable population of trout, brown trout I was reliably informed by a local angler, and we sat for many a minute just watching these elegant fish swim past; no wonder the grey heron was a constant visitor to these waters.

Walking the river also produced another exciting breeding bird, a common sandpiper was nesting along the bank. To us 'townies', birds such as these were previously either pictures in a book, or birds you may meet up with when on holiday; we now had them on our doorstep, so to speak.

In those distant days of the past, skylark were a common bird and many a May and June day was filled with their pure song. Vaughan Williams, with his 'Lark Ascending' got quite close, but you can never beat the original – the true sound of the English countryside. I trust I have not offended my Welsh and Scottish friends by calling this an English sound, but I do believe it is a commoner bird in England than elsewhere in the UK. I am very pleased to see they are slowly making a comeback, this incidentally is being written in 2017, nearly 50 years on!

YOXALL - WHERE IT ALL STARTED.

Yoxall is not only in the middle of beautiful countryside, it is also very close to the Derbyshire Dales – Dovedale is less than 45 minutes away – so, all very close to home, was this wild and magnificent countryside awaiting our exploration?

Near to hand is a wonderful area of wild countryside – Cannock Chase – which quickly became one of our favourite areas for visiting. Fallow deer roamed free, interesting butterflies were to be seen, and on very warm days common lizards put in an appearance. When we saw the latter, it became necessary to put Meg on a lead; for some reason these little creatures fascinated her, and they needed our protection.

Our birding at this time was all solitary, just the two of us enjoying the countryside, it had not yet become the popular country pursuit it is today. We were out late one warm June evening, it was just getting dark, when we heard a sound the like of which we had never experienced before. From a nearby dead tree, a churring sound could be heard, we froze; what on earth was it? The sound was almost mechanical, and eventually we saw a most unusual looking bird lying longways on a branch in the tree, but what was the bird? We had no idea, and I could not put it into a family group, it was such a strange bird.

Out came my set of bird books, and I must confess I just started at the beginning and looked at the pictures. There were family groups I could obviously ignore so I did not have to look at every illustration, the bird was obviously not a duck or gull etc. Slowly working my way through I found what I was looking for, the bird was a nightjar, I did not even know we had them in our part of the country. They were a very local and almost rare bird even then, as they still are today. A very specialised heathland species, and we had them on our doorstep – Cannock Chase.

In past times the bird was viewed almost mythologically, and many called it a goat sucker as it was firmly believed they sucked the milk from goats at night. They are a true species of the night when they come out to hunt night time flying insects, moths and the like. Needless to say, we had to go back and visit this mystical bird again, and I continue to do so right up to this day. They are a summer migrant, just with us for a few months each year, but what a bird.

Thanks to the Chase, I commenced to get to grips with the various warblers that came back each summer. Birds I had seen on passage when in Egypt were here seen breeding in the UK. Willow warblers and chiffchaffs were common in those days and the Chase used to echo to their song and calls. Blackcaps, garden warblers, common whitethroats and lesser whitethroats added to the bird sound, and even a few wood warblers were regularly seen and heard. When added to by redstarts, pied flycatchers, spotted flycatchers and tree pipits plus our native species, a wide range of birds could be experienced, all less than twenty minutes from home.

Earlier I mentioned the fact Dorothy had obtained employment locally, and one of the products the company manufactured was animal proof fencing for farms and the like. Near to where we lived a large reservoir had been opened a few years previous, Blithfield Reservoir, and the company had supplied many miles of wire fencing which provided security at the reservoir. One of the senior officers of South Staffordshire Water Company, to whom the reservoir belonged, was a regular visitor to the works and Dorothy got to know him well. On one occasion, he asked about me. When Dorothy told him of our interest in birds he kindly obtained permission for us to make visits to the reservoir for the purpose of birding. This was almost like having your own private nature reserve as the only other people using the water were the angling and sailing club members, for which they paid heavily. The variety of birds seen was very good, and we had all this to ourselves, and for free. The Chase and Blithfield Reservoir quickly became the two areas most frequently visited, and as by now we had purchased our first pairs of binoculars, we could see the birds far better than previously. Progress was slowly being made. We also found field guides were becoming more readily available, so an early Collins bird guide was obtained; my Observers book could now retire. So with a field guide and binoculars, a new world most certainly had opened up. As things progressed, I became very interested in writing about wildlife topics. My local church published a monthly magazine, and I started to write a small piece for the magazine, this concerned the wildlife to be seen locally. Not just birds, I was now becoming interested in most aspects of the countryside, and with flowers for instance, they do not move off. It now became necessary to obtain more books on various subjects, and number one priority became a field guide for wild flowers. Once obtained, this book certainly was much used. Instead of binoculars it was now a magnifying glass.

Thanks to writing for the church magazine I started to appreciate habitats, the inter-dependence and relationship of animals, insects and plants, without the latter there would be no life at all. Where would we be without wheat? Our holidays to the Lake District had now become an annual event, the golden eagle had to be visited regularly, and was. On one such holiday, we visited the nature reserve on Walney Island in Lancashire. Here a very large colony of gulls nest, a mixed colony of black-headed. lesser black-backed and herring gulls, hundreds of nests spread over a large area. You are able to walk through the colony, but if you did you were taking your life in your own hands. Gulls are not people friendly and the wear of head gear is necessary. We were walking through, ducking the attacking gulls, when a herring gull came at me, knocked my hat off, and a lesser black-backed gull attacked me from the rear, claws drawing blood on my head. The fact they both attacked me at the same time may have been a coincidence, but it almost looked pre-planned. I learned one thing, when seen so close, both of these gulls are large birds.

Another special bird which bred here is the eider. One bird had chosen to breed on the edge of the car park and I nearly ran her over. As I pulled in to park, I suddenly realised an eider duck was sitting in the grass just in front of my car; fortunately, I was able to stop. The bird just sat there on her nest with not a care in the world about me or my car. I was able to walk right up to her and actually stroke her, and she seemed to enjoy it. When I went back to the information hut and told them about the bird they quickly arranged for a temporary fence to be erected round the nest site, and I moved my car away. To be so close to nature can be both a painful experience as well as a very beautiful experience; I had managed both. Bird behaviour was something I was becoming more interested in. Identification was not enough, I wished to learn all I could.

It is necessary to know what you are actually looking at, but I was after more: the why's and the wherefore's. An incident here at Walney really showed me how birds try to protect their young. The beach at Walney was well populated with oystercatchers and we were watching one pair in particular which had two very small and downy chicks running free, I doubt if they were above two days old. The parent birds were keeping a very close eye on their young when one adult dashed forward, calling loudly, as a lesser black-backed gull dived down towards the two young birds. Before the adult could do anything, the gull plucked up one of the young birds by its stubby wing and flew off. One of the adult oystercatchers promptly flew off after the gull and, to our amazement, it attacked the gull by stabbing at it with its long red bill. This either hurt or surprised the gull which, with a yelp, dropped the young bird which fell to the ground. Due to the low weight of the bird it did no harm, it just jumped up and quickly ran into vegetation nearby where it joined up with the other chick and a parent. Dorothy and I could not believe what we had just witnessed, bravery and skill of the highest order, a moment of bird behaviour never to be forgotten. Real bird watching, I learned a lot on that day. You read a lot regarding brain power of wild creatures, or lack thereof depending upon who is commenting. In my youth if you were called 'bird brain', it meant you were of little brain; after my experiences on that day – birds certainly moved up the ladder in my opinion. What all three examples showed was decisions made, not instinct taking over, and to make decisions you need a well-developed brain.

Visits to the Lakes were showing me a lot, and on a following holiday, we called in at the RSPB Reserve – Leighton Moss – a superb reserve in my opinion. It has a first class restaurant where we had dinner, and then made a quick visit to the reserve, little realising we were in for a treat. As we walked into the first hide a lady in the hide put her finger to her lips, obviously wishing us to be silent. We made our way into the hide and looked where she pointed. Sitting out, in full view, was an otter. Dorothy had never seen one before and she could not possibly have had a finer view. It sat there for about a couple of minutes before it dropped into the water and swiftly swam away; what a start to our holiday. Making our way on we suddenly stopped. A deep booming was coming from a nearby reedbed, a bittern was calling. We could not see the bird, but there is no mistaking that call. Our day was not yet over, from the next hide we went in, bearded tits were very active – well, two of them were. Near the hide they had a nest, which was just about visible in the thick reeds, and judging by their many visits it obviously contained young. At that point a birder rushed into the hide, 'Come quickly,' he said. Just up the pathway from the hide was an amazing sight, a yellow-billed cuckoo was sitting out on the top of a small tree. The yellow-billed cuckoo is a native of North America and a very rare bird for the UK, and up to that day had just been a picture in my field guide. Only five birders were enjoying this bird and we only had the pleasure for a few minutes before the bird flew off and vanished from our sight. We all went back to the Information Centre to report our findings where I think they thought we were imagining things. The bird was not seen again and I do not believe our reports were accepted, but we all knew we had seen one and it is remaining proudly on my Life List.

This was my first encounter with 'authority' where I quickly learned that the reporting of rarities was not readily accepted, and after several battles with rarity committees, I no longer inform them of anything I see.

A magnificent start to our holiday, an otter and three rather special birds, one of which, the cuckoo, was a 'Lifer'; it cannot get much better than that and we still have the Lakes to come.

I think I had better have a few minutes talking to you about lists because they will be mentioned many a time on the following pages. Birders are big list keepers. Most have a garden list; a local list; a UK list; day or holiday lists and, if they go abroad, lists covering the countries visited. These would be maintained on an annual basis but one list, the big one, is their Life List; hence my talk of a 'Lifer' a line or two above. I have a friend who even keeps a list of birds he sees on TV news programmes and the like – they do say you have to be a bit mad to be a birder! After optics, a field guide plus your own knowledge and experience, the two most important items in any birders pockets are a notebook and pencil, no birder goes without these.

The Lakes again proved to be most enjoyable. We walked miles with Meg for company, saw the golden eagle again, and experienced many birds, including among these terns. Living as we do in the middle of the country, terns were not birds regularly seen, they were principally birds of passage each spring and autumn. Two species: were usual, the Arctic and the common tern; the latter has actually now commenced to breed at a few isolated areas in the county. The other white terns, Sandwich, roseate and little terns were very rarely seen being coastal breeding species.

The RSPB have a very interesting reserve at Hodbarrow, just north of Morecambe Bay, on the Duddon Estuary, and here three species of terns breed: common, little and Sandwich; the chance of seeing the last two could not be missed. The RSPB have sited a bird hide very close to the breeding colony of the terns and very good views can be obtained. We had chosen a good day to go, the reserve was very quiet, visitors few, and dogs are allowed here – as long as they are kept under tight control – so Meg came with us. If you are interested in a quiet life, do not go tern colony watching. The noise a few hundred terns can make is staggering – as much as I love the birds, I would not wish to live next door to them. The three terns seen here cover the complete range of sizes in the UK. The Sandwich is our largest and looks almost gull-like; the common is the archetypical tern, white with a black cap, long, narrow pointed wings and with a pale grey upper surface, and long tail streamers – no wonder they were once referred to as sea swallows and the little is our smallest. A very pleasant time was spent here with the terns. Before leaving, we also caught sight of two drake eider ducks out in the estuary. A fitting end to our trip.

The Langdale Beck ran very close to where we stayed, and after dinner most evenings, we had a short walk before turning in for the night. The Beck was home to dipper, kingfisher and goosander and many a happy hour was spent enjoying these birds, the dipper especially. The dippers here were very tolerant of people, unlike the ones back home. The Beck was a very popular area for walkers, so over the years the birds had learned they had nothing to fear and just got on with life. I doubt if many of the walkers even saw the birds and, if they did, they probably did not know what they were.

Another speciality which could be seen locally was the red-breasted merganser, a very unusual bird back home. A pair or two bred on Windermere so a visit to see these birds was always a must; they always stood the chance of being our only sighting of the year.

In the past we had always seen these birds at Ambleside, and once again we were not to be disappointed. Two drakes were just off the jetty and they looked very smart indeed. Presuming we had two pairs on the lake, the ducks were probably sitting on eggs on nearby small islands.

During our week's holiday, we saw ninety-seven species, plus several different orchids and many other interesting wild flowers with the otter being very close to being our top event. At this time, I was becoming increasingly interested in pursuing my writing and I was fortunate enough to get the chance of writing a regular feature for the Birmingham Mail. The newspaper had a corner especially for children 'Uncle Len's Corner' as it was known, and I was given the opportunity of writing a natural history feature for the young readers. It commenced as a three-month trial, and my first efforts went under the heading of 'Bird Table'. It proved to be successful and continued for several years. Once we had exhausted bird topics, we introduced a piece called 'Country Notebook' which covered the broader aspects of wildlife. I was paid the princely sum of £6.00, which may not sound a lot in today's money, but remember this was the '60s; the tax-man also took his bit and I had an artist to pay. I may not have been rich, but I was now a 'professional freelance journalist' – the bug had bitten. I now commenced to look at my interests with the written word in mind. Writing also taught me something and that was how little I really knew, and unlike the spoken word, the written word is not lost. My bit of spare cash was now being spent on building up a collection of books relating to the various aspects I was writing about and my knowledge slowly increased. You never stop learning where nature is concerned: wildlife adapts to the environment continuously, and this is where evolution comes in. Darwin knew what he was talking and writing about. As the '60s moved on; I managed to improve my position at work and with this came an increase in salary; we could now manage two holidays a year, so we started to broaden our horizons. We still had our week in the Lakes and our first holiday elsewhere took us down to St. David's in Pembrokeshire – new countryside and new birds. We were also without Meg on this occasion, she was being looked after by my parents.

I had holidayed in Rhyl as a child – my only experience of Wales –

down in Pembrokeshire, it was wild by comparison. We stayed in a small licensed hotel which was only licensed for people staying at the hotel so it was very peaceful and the couple who ran it knew what they were at. It was positioned just a fifteen-minute walk from the rugged coast and on our first afternoon we took a stroll down. As we approached a call was heard, we stopped and looked at each other, and a piercing 'pcheu' rang out; what were we listening to?

We quickly rounded a corner and there, gliding along the cliff face, were two choughs; you could not ask for a better introduction to St David's than that. Unlike the choughs we were told we had seen when in Cornwall a few years back, we could be more than certain of these two birds, their red bills and legs were clearly visible. As they occasionally stooped down the cliffs with wings arched backwards, they almost looked like a black bird of prey. We enjoyed these two birds for several minutes before they vanished from sight further along the cliffs, and had a feeling we were going to enjoy Pembrokeshire.

Just off the coast of Pembrokeshire lies the island of Ramsey; however, unfortunately, the week we were there no landings were possible, but we did have two boat trips round the island and these were memorable for us. It provided us with the opportunity to see several sea birds which were new to us. Guillemots and razorbills both swam and flew passed the boat, no puffins unfortunately; although, we had been told to keep our eyes open for them. The occasional gannet gave us a fly past and one dived for fish. A most spectacular display as it hit the water, beak first, with wings folded back, looking almost like a white torpedo being fired into the water. This bird must have some neck muscles! Approaching the island more closely, we saw kittiwakes, shags, great black-backed gulls and a passing short-eared owl – all new species apart from the gull.

Whitesand Bay lies just up the coast and a superb beach it is too. Very aptly named as the sand is decidedly pale and here we met up with two charming little wading birds, one of which was a completely new bird for us, the sanderling. This bird appeared to have a life long battle with the tide. It was a lovely day and the tide was just gently rolling in, and the sanderlings, of which there must have been about a dozen, were dashing out following the tide and as it flowed back in again, they just raced off onto drier sand. They never seemed to tire of this and carried on for long periods. They were obviously not doing this for fun, the water movement was no doubt exposing food for them. They just looked a delightful small bird. The other wader was the ringed plover, another bird which seemed to prefer running to flying. We actually found a nest, if you can call a scrape in the ground a nest, which contained two eggs. Needless to say we promptly moved on allowing the bird to return back to her nest. The sound of our favourite bird could also be heard here, curlews were breeding close by, it was almost as though we had not left home – well not quite!

In Ramsey Sound, the stretch of water between the mainland and the island was frequented by seals and on calm days their heads could be clearly seen as they drifted slowly by. They always looked very inquisitive we thought; they almost turned their heads to study us as they passed, probably wondering what we were.

When in this part of Wales, Strumble Head is a must or so we had been told so it was firmly on our agenda. We picked a fine, calm day, for our visit, and we chose wisely.

Strumble has an old lighthouse perched on the rocky islet of Ynys Meicel which is no longer manned; it is automatically operated, and the Head is famed for its sea-watching. June is not the best time for sea-watching, as most of the birds which pass by are now breeding, but we were not to be let down. Out at sea we saw several Manx shearwaters fly past, these graceful birds just glided past with hardly a flick of their wings, superb flying machines. A few scoter were on the water, I did not know whether any bred locally, we were just happy to see them. Occasional fulmars glided past, although I understand they do not breed on the Head as the cliffs are too shallow. Further out at sea many gannets were evident; good fishing out there that day by the look of things. The odd shag and cormorant were also to be seen amongst them.

Back to the Head. The finest member of the crow family breeds here: raven, and their deep croaks, echoed round the headland, buzzards also soared round the headland, their broad wings could almost have fooled you into believing they were eagles – two birds rarely seen back home. Chough were also to be seen once again, we never tired of these, and several smaller birds were breeding there. Stonechats, linnets, yellowhammers, whitethroats and grasshopper warblers could be seen and heard and whilst enjoying these a peregrine falcon came swooping along the shallow cliffs. The small birds quickly became mute at this point, I wonder why? One thing was certain, we would be back sometime.

St. David's is one of the smallest cities in the UK with a superb cathedral which at the time had a very accomplished organist. We were nearby on one day when the heavens opened and we had very heavy rain for a couple of hours or so. We popped into the cathedral, as much as to get out of the rain as anything else, and heard the organ being played. We sat down at the back of the cathedral and had a most enjoyable organ concert completely on our own, the playing was superb. At the finish, the organist walked up from the organ to see us sitting there; needless to say, we complimented him on his playing and had a most pleasant chat. He told us he always practised at that time and people were always welcome. As the rest of the week was dry and very pleasant, we did not take him up on his offer.

Near to the cathedral lay the ruins of the Bishop's Palace, which was just a walled ruin with no roof. In this was the largest colony of jackdaws I have ever seen and the noise which echoed round the four walls was amazing. The birds were very tolerant of people as many visited the ruin, so it was not unusual to have the birds almost running round your feet.

In St. David's itself another unusual feature was the rookery. This was contained in a row of trees which ran along the high street. The trees were not large, each contained just a very small number of nests. Beneath the trees, car parking was available and on one occasion we had just parked up when up drove a superb MG open-top sports car. The driver jumped out, as these sporty types usually did by hopping over the door, not opening it, and started to run down the street. I shouted to him, he stopped and I pointed overhead, the message was understood: back he came and put his hood up. I hate to think what state his upholstery would have been in due to the droppings from the rookery. Your roof was in enough of a mess when you came back, but parking was limited. I have not returned for many years and I have often wondered if the rookery is still there.

Off the coast you have three of the finest 'bird islands' in the UK,

Grassholm, Stokholm and Skomer, home to many thousands of true sea birds. We did not manage to get across to any of these, unfortunately, probably a very good reason to go back.

Later in the '60s another addition to the family arrived, our daughter Sarah was born so holidays went on the back burner for a year or two. This gave us the opportunity to explore more locally with day trips into Derbyshire and southern Yorkshire became more regular events.

We quickly found areas that were pushchair accessible and we managed several walks along the many attractive rivers to be found, especially in Derbyshire and the moors along the borders with neighbouring Yorkshire were also well-studied. Our first experience of red grouse was there and the male birds call 'go-bak, go-bak' rang out on many an occasion. One autumn we also experienced a wonderful sight, a male hen harrier was seen for a short period – a bird I had only ever dreamed of seeing such is their rarity.

Locally, we have a long lane known as Meadow Lane and for years we have regularly walked along there. Curlews nested in the fields and barn owls were to be seen at dusk, it was a haven, rarely visited by car owners, and many of the fields belonged to famers who had given us permission to roam. Now that Sarah was on the scene, we returned to this frequently and one autumn afternoon, we had a real surprise. In the ditch which ran along one side of the lane I saw a brownish bird struggling in the water, when I went to investigate I found it to be a long-eared owl. Fortunately, it was a chilly day and I had leather gloves on. I caught the owl and we made our way home. Even through a strong pair of gloves, the claws of the owl gripped my fingers and when I took my gloves off it had drawn blood. Owls are never grateful!

One of my near neighbours was the local vet and, over the years, I had got to know him well – regularly taking in injured birds to him – today was no different: I called in with my owl. John, the vet, was out on a call, but his wife found an old cat basket and we put the owl in it. I suggested she put a note on the basket saying what was inside, which she duly did, and she said she would get John to give me a call when he returned.

He did, and John was not a happy man! He had walked into his surgery, seen the basket but the note had vanished, lifted the lid and put his hand inside expecting to pull out a cat to find an owl hanging on his hand. He was not amused and his wife came in just as this all happened. Some comment was made about the note, and John being a country vet had a good use of 'olde English', and my name was not popular.

I was called round – or should that be summoned round – and John was, by then, laughing over the situation and wanted to know which owl it was as he had never seen one previously, neither had I for that matter, and how I had come about it. After a good examination of the bird the news was not good, it was suffering from poison and it died overnight. We sent the carcase off to be examined and it proved to be due to DDT. Long-eared owls eat small birds and small mammals, at that time DDT was in common use on farms and small birds and mammals ate creatures contaminated by the poison, and the owl in turn consumed it by eating the birds and mammals. It was some time before the use of DDT was banned. My first ever long-eared owl was not a happy event, although I have never been closer to one since!

Owls that winter proved to be a major event for us in Yoxall. Just outside the village, we have an area locally known as Jerusalem: the reason for the name is the fact it has three old trees growing on the hill. We had not been over for some time and one of our friends in the village called round one evening to ask me what the owls were flying around Jerusalem most afternoons. I had not the foggiest idea, but when he told me they were in double figures I needed to find out.

Two days later we went across, it was only a few minutes' walk from home and we were lucky in it being a mild afternoon so Dorothy was able to carry Sarah the short distance. We arrived to find several people already there, and after a short while, the owls started to appear. It was an amazing sight, we had seven short-eared owls, two tawny owls and three barn owls flying round us in the gathering gloom: I had never seen so many owls together and have not since. Several times that winter we went to see the birds, never quite as many, but still a magical moment. Unfortunately, it was a one winter event, they have never returned, why they came just for that one period we shall never know, but we thank them for it.

If there was one bird I really wished to see at that time, it was the great northern diver, but records of them were few and far between unless you were in Scotland where the odd pair still bred. Imagine our surprise when we visited Blithfield Reservoir to be told one had been seen off the dam that very morning. We quickly drove round, and there to our joy, a juvenile great northern diver was performing. No wonder they are called divers, when this bird submerged you had no idea where it would surface. The distance it could swim and the time it stayed under water was amazing, not that the small fish in the water appreciated it. We enjoyed the bird for many minutes before it flew off up the reservoir, my bird of that winter.

Feeding birds in the garden was now becoming more popular and various foods for them were obtainable. The odd feeder was being produced and the bird species were increasing slowly. Initially it was just blue tits and great tits on the feeders with dunnocks, robins and blackbirds feeding on the dropped seed beneath. Our village had a large rookery, been there for years I was informed, and if scraps were put out the odd brave rook would pop in for them. Collared doves had become widespread by now, not in the numbers of today but they had moved in from the coast where they first arrived during the past twenty years. A new breeding bird for the UK. They too sought out the dropped seed, so we did not need to travel far to see birds, some now came to see us. I also made two nesting boxes which I installed on my fence and we were delighted to find a pair of blue tits take up residence in one of them. They duly bred and raised five chicks and we were at home the day the young ventured forth, the first birds to breed in our garden. We were very proud of them. On cleaning out the box we found two dead birds in the nest, but raising five out of seven was a good result.

The following year we went one better. We lived in a bungalow and a pair of house martins built their nest on our property, a wonderful mud cup, and we had the pleasure of watching these birds raise two broods. For a few months we had to duck as we walked up our drive to avoid swooping house martins. From studying these birds, we realised that the young from the first brood also assisted in feeding the second brood, at times it almost looked as though birds were just streaming in and out of the nest. Magical moments. The only downside was the fact the nest was directly over a window which constantly needed cleaning: we were pleased we lived in a bungalow! We wished them luck when they left us to migrate southwards, hoping to welcome them back next year.

The '60s slowly closed. I had learned a lot and my interest was far from satisfied. There was a world out there waiting to be investigated and I wished to do so.

I had managed to increase my writing, I now wrote a monthly piece for a Staffordshire county magazine, this was a general wildlife article. It was written for the month of publication, as a guide as to what could be seen and where, so it covered a variety of subjects which helped me learn more about the countryside. Although my number one love was still birds, I was slowly becoming a naturalist.

It was at this time I had the opportunity to become a warden for the RSPB at their Coombes Valley reserve in Staffordshire. A couple of years ago I had helped out for a weekend when the warden had to be away due to family illness, and he had now retired. After very careful consideration, I turned the opportunity down. The reserve had accommodation, a very old cottage was on the reserve, but the facilities at that time were very meagre and having a young child I was not prepared to take her into what were almost primitive conditions. Dorothy had suggested why not take the job on, it would certainly have been something I would have loved to have done: still live at home and travel up to the reserve daily – it was only an hour's journey from home. Warden's jobs are not a five day a week job, 9 till 5, so I declined. The fact the RSPB thought I was capable and had the knowledge to do the job, thrilled me greatly. Much as I would have loved the work, I still believe I made the correct decision, and have had no regrets. A short time later I was offered the position of a representative at their Northern Ireland office, but as things in Ireland were at their worst, there was no way I would take my family into that situation which the RSPB fully understood. My two opportunities had passed me by; it was back to bird watching, and bit of writing, and earning my living from buying. Little did I know at that time, but come the next decade things would change somewhat.

THE DECADE OF CHANGE

The 70s came in sadly; Meg, our basset hound, died and Sarah had been diagnosed with an allergy to animal fur so another dog was not available to us walking would never quite be the same.

My freelance journalism was progressing nicely and I now had two national magazines taking my work: the ladies magazine, The Peoples Friend and a glossy known as Choice. In the latter, my artist friend Janet Whittaker was illustrating in full colour and her work was becoming well known, leading to several exhibitions; she was very accomplished, and this obviously helped me.

Time was now right for our first holiday with Sarah. We booked a holiday cottage on the Gower in South Wales, and as soon as we arrived, we knew we had booked well. The cottage was in Llangennith, only a short distance from the sweep of sands near to Whiteford Point; here, Sarah built her first ever sandcastle! The Gower also had several very good bird watching locations, Oxwich Bay and Worms Head especially so.

Our first day there was spent in driving round the Gower to get our bearings as it was new location for us and it was very pleasant countryside. It was early June and we seemed to have caught a decent week's weather, wild flowers were in an abundance. Being a peninsular the sea is never far away so we had great times poking about in rock pools where Sarah was seeing creatures which had only been seen in books previously. She was fascinated by small crabs and sea anemones, and why not; they were all new to her. This was her first real introduction to things natural, we just hoped it would continue in view of our interests.

Back now to some of the birds we saw and enjoyed. Walking across the Burrows towards Whiteford Sand, we saw a large grey, white and black bird in the distance which we first took to be a grey heron. The bird, fortunately, banked and to our great surprise we found ourselves looking at a male hen harrier; a sight to make the heart beat a little faster.

You will remember I mentioned seeing one earlier, this bird was only the second sighting we have ever had; you do not get many to the pound I am sorry to say. The Gower was definitely looking good. On reaching Whiteford Sand the tide was fully in and gannets had drifted in with it and were feeding just off shore and further out the odd auks were flying past, too far away to be sure whether they were razorbills or guillemots, but as they did look black and white – we presumed them to be razorbills. Cormorants were busily feeding and flying off in the general direction of Worms Head where they were probably breeding, and further out, we were convinced we saw the odd shag. Worms Head would most definitely have to be visited.

As the tide receded waders started to appear feeding on the exposed mud, ringed plovers and redshanks initially, but as the water moved further out curlews and oystercatchers appeared. On the drier areas where stones and gravel lay the odd turnstones were feeding, quite an interesting range for us land-locked folk.

Further out at sea, I was surprised to see a small number of eider ducks. I had always understood they did not breed further south than Walney Island, but I have since learned they have been seen here for many years. Whether they have ever bred I do not know. One sea duck which does breed locally is the red-breasted merganser and we were pleased to see some of these.

The Burrows are owned by the National Trust, the first of their Enterprise Neptune purchases, their campaign to protect key sections of the British coastline. It was not only birds which do well here, unusual flowers flourish included amongst these being moonwort, yellow birds-nest, fen orchid, bird's foot trefoil, yellow bedstraw and sea pansies to name but a few. An area to delight both the ornithologist and botanist. Back at the cottage, a local provided us with some very interesting news: bittern had breed at Oxwich Bay; were we aware of it? No. Our next location was now decided.

Oxwich Bay was approached through an extensive area of reedswamp, it covered over 100 acres I had been told, and was probably the largest such area in southwest Britain. On further investigation, a booming male was heard in 1969 for the first time and reports have been made for further instances since then. To see one would be magical, to hear one would be an excellent substitution.

Fortunately, there were several areas where you could pull a car off the road and we spent the morning doing so. No bitterns, but grey herons were constant visitors from the nearby heronry, cormorants were roosting up among the scattered trees and reed warblers were reeling away constantly. Over the reeds, swifts and hirundines were feeding actively on the many flying insects as were several species of dragonflies. Food a plenty here.

Whilst watching all of this Dorothy grabbed my arm. 'Listen,' she said, and in the distance a deep boom could be heard. For a few seconds, the sound resonated round the swamp before silence returned. This was the second time Dorothy had heard the bittern; it was only my third occasion – reason for celebration here – Sarah remained unimpressed!

This was the only time we heard the bird, although we returned to the site a couple of times during the week. Bearded tits had also been reported from here, but we had no sign nor sound of those. Worms Head needed a good warm day and one duly arrived. Rhossili lay at the foot of the Head, which was a rocky promontory connected to the mainland by an extensive rocky causeway, only seen when the tide retreated which allowed access at low water. The Head comprised four small hills which rose like a dragon's back, and there was where the name Worms Head came from. The name 'Worm' in Norse meant dragon or serpent. It was amazing just what you could learn when you went bird watching! Having a young child with us, we did not venture forth along the Head, we settled down and viewed from a comfortable spot.

Sheep grazed the table top of Inner Worm, feeding on, I was reliably informed, red fescue. Other maritime plants to be seen included: spring squill, golden samphire, rock samphire, sea beet, rock sea-lavender, sea stork's bill and buck's-horn plantain. Enough there to satisfy most interests, although it was birds which brought in the majority of visitors.

Unfortunately, viewing of the birds, especially in the nesting locations, was best accomplished from the sea so land watching was only really possible when seen in flight. Kittiwakes appeared to be the commonest birds as they flew round the cliffs calling away, they were rarely silent; the occasional razorbill and guillemot could be seen, and the odd pair of puffins bred here, or so we had been told, none was evident to us. A few gulls were to be seen, lesser black-backed, great black-backed and more common were black-headed gulls.

The most exciting of the birds to be seen for us was the fulmars. Apart from coming to land to breed they were a very maritime bird and, for us from the Midland counties, they were rarely seen. To see these birds gliding round on fixed wings, with rarely a flap, was a wonderful sight. I have often thought that fulmars and shearwaters were the most perfectly designed 'flying machines' we have in northern waters. They glided and soared effortlessly and their speed at times, especially the fulmars, was exceptional. Some bird.

The Head was not just home to sea birds, jackdaws too liked breeding on cliffs, and many did there. On the day we were there, a peregrine falcon put in a brief appearance – always a welcome sight. Two small birds kept dropping down a cliff and it was some time before I realised we had a pair of rock pipits for company. As with the fulmars, these were rare and unusual birds at home, so we enjoyed them while we could.

Our holiday came to an end, and we both considered the Gower to be a little gem. The worst part about things was the number of caravans we came across, many of the roads and lanes were not designed for those, and caravanning was becoming more popular by the day.

Later in the year the opportunity to have a few further day's holiday came along, and this time we decided to visit Aberporth, a small resort in Cardigan Bay. It was mid-September and once again weather conditions were very good, and we were hoping to see birds on passage. This time we lived it up, we stayed at a small hotel which catered for young children so Dorothy had a week away from cooking.

The hotel was close to the beach so Sarah had many an enjoyable hour on it, and as the beach contained many rock pools she was in her element. Seals were also to be seen in the bay regularly so that was an added interest. Our first love, the birds, these were also very evident. Small wading birds were to be seen on the shore, dunlins, many still in their bold summer plumage, flashing their black bellies as they ran, ringed plovers feeding amongst the shingle, oystercatchers and redshank feeding along the shore line with large numbers of our favourite bird, the curlew, feeding in deeper water.

The bird which interested us the most, and amused us to a degree, was the sanderling. This little bird was rushing about following the tide as it retreated and then rolled back again, using vast amounts of energy as it searched for food in the damp sand. They were completely oblivious to us as at times they almost danced round our feet. I wondered if these birds had moved down from the Arctic Circle where many bred. There they would rarely, if ever, see man, and consequently had no fear of us. Whatever the reason, we were only too pleased to have their company.

Another bird which attracted us was the buzzard. We had not seen many buzzards whilst out birding, as at that time they were not a common bird in Staffordshire. Here large numbers were passing through, I had never appreciated so many were migratory, I had always taken them to be residents; obviously, all were not if these numbers were taken into account. There was always something to learn in this game and you could not always believe what the books told you.

Out at sea many duck were to be seen and on one day in particular a large flock of scoters could be seen out in the bay. We studied these in great detail as, occasionally, the rarer velvet scoter could be found tucked in amongst the common scoters. Hard as we worked looking for a black bird with a white wing patch, we searched in vain, no velvet scoters were obvious there. We could, however, appreciate the diving abilities of these birds. They appeared to dive in unison, almost as though one bird gave the command, and all dived together – these birds had Olympic standards when it came to diving!

Tucked away, adjacent to Aberporth, was a large military unit which had surface to air missiles on site and these were occasionally fired out to sea. On one occasion, we were on the beach when a missile blasted off, fired at a moored old boat out in the bay – a bit of target practice was taking place. The birds roosted up on the neighbouring cliffs took to flight in panic, and for a few minutes pandemonium took place. Prior to the missile launch we had not been aware of so many birds roosting on the cliffs. We were surprised by the number of fulmars still to be seen amongst the many gulls; those I would have expected to be out at sea by then. As mentioned previously, we only expected to see them on or near land in the breeding season, not that time of the year.

Our final day on holiday produced the bird of the week for us. The bay was like a mill pond, hardly a ripple disturbed the surface, and two birds caught our attention. They were continuously diving and not providing us with very clear views; fortunately, they were drifting in and we then had the view we wished for. We were watching two red-throated divers, the very first we had ever seen, and both were adult birds, still showing some of their summer colour. What a superb finish to our holiday.

This was one holiday that I did not mind was over. On returning home I found, amongst our post, a letter from the BBC Radio Birmingham. Local radio had commenced in Birmingham a short while previously and they had asked for programme ideas to be forwarded, that I had done, suggesting a general wildlife programme reflecting what could be experienced locally. Unknown to me, Alan Richards, a well-known local birder and then Secretary of the West Midland Bird Club, had also written in with ideas for a bird study programme. We were both invited to Pebble Mill, the then headquarters for the BBC in Birmingham, to discuss our ideas. Although I knew of Alan, I was a new name and face to him.

We hit it off from day one and it was decided we would jointly present a weekly, 15-minute programme called 'Countryside' for which we were paid £2.50; being a radio 'star' obviously paid well! To be honest, I would willingly have done it for free, not that I told the BBC that. The programme ran from 1971 until 1975 and those were very happy and informative years, and I learned a lot from Alan. We have remained in touch although not meeting up regularly, Christmas cards and the like. One of the perks of the 'job' was doing book reviews. The publishers sent copies of their latest publications into Pebble Mill for review on the programme, and we were able to keep these books. Several are still sitting on my book shelves, bringing back happy memories. We reviewed them honestly and always sent copies of our reviews to the publishers so they were able to use these if they so wished. We had several producers on the programme and one in particular, Pete Simpkin, was interested in doing some outside programmes – up to then, all had been studio recorded. Three programmes in particular still remain the highlights of my work with Pete; these being 'Nightingales in Worcestershire, a Dawn Chorus,' this went out live – the only programme to ever do so – and finally an interview with Peter Scott down at Slimbridge, this covered two programmes. Meeting and talking with that man is still my most cherished and proud moment. What a man! At that time, I was also able to just call him Peter. A short while afterwards, he became Sir Peter Scott, and he earned it. Part of the Dawn Chorus programme was also used by the BBC for national transmission, and for this I received a fee of six guineas, fame and wealth at last!

All good things come to an end, our last programme went out on the air on the 16th October 1975, and as Alan once put it: our 'Glory Days' were over.

During this period, bird watching had slightly got on the back burner so to speak. Pressure at work had become intense, the motor industry was going through turmoil at the time and much over-time was being worked – not that the money was not welcomed. My freelance journalism had increased and I was spending much time with my BBC work, so I may have been writing and talking about it, but I was not doing a lot of it.

Fortunately, we did manage the odd holiday and although those were mainly taken on the coast so that Sarah could enjoy the sea and sand, we did see a few very interesting birds. At Weymouth we saw and heard our first Cetti's warblers and on Portland Bill we experienced black redstarts. In Devon, at Prawle Point we saw one of the country's rarest birds, the cirl bunting; near to Slapton Ley, on the shingle bank separating the reserve from Start Bay, we saw a Richard's pipit – a rare migrant from the continent. Prior to seeing those birds, they had just been pictures in books.

Come '76 we decided Sarah was ready for a holiday in The Lakes and we managed to book a cottage at Elterwater; a friend of ours knew the owners and we were able to visit in the spring bank holiday week when the schools were on holiday.

We visited many of our old favourite locations, even managing the golden eagle site; the pair had become well-established by then so seeing them was almost guaranteed, and so it turned out. The female was on the nest and the male was sitting out on a piece of jutting rock, perfect views. As we walked down the valley, we had seen ring ouzels, wheatears, siskins and a solitary common sandpiper along the beck and as we walked back a merlin flew over. Not a bad little collection, even Sarah was thrilled with the eagle.

The unfortunate thing was the weather, apart from the day we visited the eagles, we had rain so Sarah's introduction to The Lakes consisted of many visits to indoor attractions. As she was an avid reader of Beatrix Potter, she was very eager to visit her home Hill Top which we duly did, and I am sure this was the highlight of her week's holiday. Boat rides on Windermere and Coniston Water were done and a cultural visit was made to Dove Cottage at Grasmere – one-time home to the poet, William Wordsworth. It was here he wrote his famous poem about wandering through the daffodils which was hardly surprising due to the number of wild daffodils that apparently thrived there abouts, not that any were visible in June.

Our holiday in The Lakes, due to the weather, did not turn out as hoped for and my return home was greeted by unsettling news. I had made a visit to hospital a few days prior to going on holiday and a letter giving me the results of my tests awaited. It was not the news I wanted, I had cancer of the bladder and was told to contact them immediately, some home coming!

This I duly did; another appointment was quickly made and the options were spelt out to me. There were various treatments available to me, but the general consensus of opinion was an operation to remove the cancer was required, so into hospital I went. It required three visits and three operations to completely remove the cancer and I was away from work for sixteen weeks, so all my bird watching was through hospital windows or in my own back garden. The important thing was the hospital was satisfied it had been completely removed and unlikely to return, and as I am writing this some forty years later, they got it right.

The year did end on a high, I was pleased to say, and it started me on an almost second career: that of a part-time university tutor.

A friend of mine, Charles Brown, who I had originally met through business, had a company manufacturing magnets which I purchased for my company. He was also a well-known photographer/birder whose works featured in many natural history magazines and books, so we had much in common. He had recently moved to live in Yoxall, near to my own home, so we saw each other frequently when out birding. One evening the doorbell rang and Charlie, as we all knew him, was at the door. For many years Charlie had been a part-time tutor for the University of Birmingham, working for their Extramural Studies Department, heading a bird study course being held in Walsall. Due to increased work at his company, he was finding it very difficult to find the time required to continue with his university duties; would I take them over?

I had never considered myself to have the knowledge or experience to do such a thing, and I told Charlie this. As I did little or no photography, I had no equipment such as a projector or any slides, thus I was unable to present any illustrations etc. All I did was go out and study wildlife and write about it, a totally different thing to teaching it.

We discussed the matter for some time and eventually I agreed to attend his next evening class to see what it was all about. Charlie was very complimentary about my knowledge and, as he explained, he was not going to recommend a person to the University if he was not certain they could do the job – this would not do his reputation any good. Dorothy thought the idea was excellent and I should take up the opportunity, as she said: should I fail, all that would be hurt was mine and Charlie's pride. I was not worried about mine, I did not want to let Charlie down. So along to Walsall I went where Charlie had a class of thirty adult students, and I sat and watched him perform, he was good; how on earth could I follow him? Charlie explained to the class who I was and that he hoped I would take over from him shortly; as he explained, the class would probably have to close otherwise. I was received very pleasantly by all, none of whom I knew, and Charlie closed down the class several minutes before time out so we could all get acquainted. Several of the group were keen photographers who offered to bring in their slides if required and a loan projector was also on offer, which would at least tide me over until I obtained my own. Fortunately, slides could be purchased, so apart from cost, I could set myself up fairly quickly.

I was still unsure, I lacked the confidence at that stage, but as Dorothy kept on saying to me: it was too good an opportunity to miss, and who knew where it could lead? The indoor evening classes were fortnightly with one Sunday a month for an all-day field meeting. The pay was good and all expenses were met by the University, so in many respects, it was too good an offer to refuse. I could now be paid to do the thing I loved most, bird study.

After two more sessions with Charlie, I took the plunge and became a part-time tutor for the University of Birmingham and have never regretted that decision. I owe Charlie a debt for sure.

A year which had a very difficult period had now ended on a high. I was now a 'professional' bird watcher, and one thing I quickly learned was that representing a university opened many a door.

After discussion with the members of the course, it was decided we would go through the British birds in systematic order as a way of refreshing our memories of the principal details with regard to identification. This at least simplified things for me and gently introduced me into 'teaching'. I gave them the opportunity of choosing our first few field meeting locations which was appreciated, so we managed to get off on a good footing. This was the commencement of a forty years' involvement in teaching bird study; I still do this today, although currently in a more limited manner.

Our field meetings were originally by coach, which commenced from Walsall, and our first was a trip to Aberystwyth via the Elan Valley. A few pairs of red kites were still to be seen in the Valley and if we were lucky we might catch up with these, and we did. We had stopped at certain locations as we travelled through the valley along a minor road without success, but as we approached Cwmystwyth, a buzzard flew across in front of us so we stopped the coach to watch this bird. We had chosen well, the buzzard was followed by two red kites, the very first I had ever seen and the same for many of my companions. For two or three minutes, these two birds put on an aerial display of pure elegance before they drifted from sight, and to think, I was being paid for this.

Our next stop was to be Devil's Bridge. Crossbills had been reported from there recently so we intended to give it a few minutes prior to moving onto Aberystwyth. Several small flocks of finch-like birds were flitting among the conifers so we concentrated our efforts on these and our efforts were well rewarded. A group of seven crossbills landed on a nearby conifer and proceeded to feed on the cones. We had great views and three of the birds were beautiful scarlet coloured males, looking almost like miniature parrots. We could now drive onto the coast in a very happy state of mind. Conditions at Aberystwyth were well-nigh perfect for our purpose. The tide was going out rapidly which was what we wanted as we had come to look for waders, purple sandpipers in particular.

There was an area of shingle and rock which became exposed at low tide, and there, I had been reliably informed, purple sandpipers were to be seen. Initially, they were not. Ringed plovers, dunlins, plus a few knots, were feeding away happily until one of our group shouted, 'What's this dark looking wader?' and pointed it out. He had hit the jackpot: a purple sandpiper it was, which quickly became three. We were able to enjoy these birds for several minutes before they vanished from sight among the rocks. That brought our first field meeting to its conclusion, and very successful it had been too. The gods had looked after us, that was for sure. On the coach home, some wag commented that I had now set the standard, he hoped it would continue. So did I!

Going further distances for field meetings provided me with the opportunity to visit places which I had never been to previously. Apart from holidays, and my time in Egypt, most of my birding had been close to home; now I had the chance to venture further.

Slimbridge was our final field meeting of the year. No Peter Scott this time, but as compensation the Bewick's swan numbers were very high and they brought back happy memories of my last visit there. A large number of white-fronted geese had also called in and these brought a great deal of attention as we had been informed a solitary lesser white-fronted goose was amongst them. Hard as we worked, we had no luck in finding this unusual species. We did see one or two in the collection, but you could not count those! The problem with areas such as Slimbridge, you had to be very careful to make sure the birds you were seeing were wild and not collection birds. The collection birds were pinioned, but at times, it was not too obvious depending upon which side you were viewing the bird from.

Large numbers of wigeons and teals were to be seen near to the River Severn accompanied by a large number of curlews, well into treble figures, a magnificent sight, with redshanks and ruffs also well represented. A wonderful spectacle.

That brought the year to its conclusion and also helped me gain further experience and confidence. Would it continue into the new year?

Our first meeting was to be a visit to the Point of Air, a shingle spit on the mouth of the Dee Estuary. The habitat there ranges from shingle and sand dunes to vast saltmarshes and at low tide large mudflats became exposed, with the RSPB having about 450 acres as a reserve.

During winter large numbers of waders were to be seen when the tide retreated and when the tide was in waterfowl in large numbers drifted in, a speciality being pintail, the drake one of our most attractive ducks. Further out, large flocks of common scoter were to be seen and the odd eider paid a visit.

Unusual birds were regularly reported from the dunes, having had more than their fair share of pipits and buntings, the question was: would we be so lucky? Time would tell!

We chose a day when the tide would be in our favour, arriving just as it was about to turn. The Dee had many duck spread over the area, common scoter were well attended, several hundred of them in fact. Telescopes up, once again looking for a velvet scoter, to again draw a blank so we concentrated our efforts on looking up the Dee, where the pintails usually congregated and there they had. A rough estimate being at least two hundred of them, equally spread between drakes and dukes. I, personally, had never seen so many together in my life – a wonderful spectacle. We saw no eiders but teal and wigeon could be both seen and heard. Time then to concentrate on the mud which was being exposed very quickly; the tide there moved notoriously rapidly we had been informed.

The first waders to be both seen and heard were curlews and oystercatchers, they were rarely quiet which was no bad thing. Following on, came large numbers of knots and dunlins with godwits, redshanks and ringed plovers accompanying them.

From reports I had read, the wader numbers there reached in excess of 20,000, and looking at those that day, I could well believe that to be correct.

We met up with a couple of local birders who informed us that they had just seen three snow buntings on the shingle near the light house, no need to tell you where we promptly headed off to. Snow buntings would be a 'Lifer' for me and several others in the group.

There was quite a lot of activity on the shingle with several small birds seeking food. Linnets were plentiful and whilst watching these we realised that tucked in amongst them was the odd twite, this started an adrenalin rush. Many of my companions had never seen twite, I had only seen them once before myself. We enjoyed these birds for a few minutes before moving on snow bunting hunting, and there we also hit the jackpot. We saw three birds comprising two males and one female and they were really tolerant of us. Breeding so far north those birds rarely came across man so they had no real fear of us, as long as we kept quiet and moved very slowly, they were not the slightest bit worried by us.

We spent some minutes enjoying these birds before time caught up with us and we made our way back to the coach. A most interesting and enjoyable day with a very wide range of species seen. The Point of Air would no doubt be revisited, I was definitely beginning to enjoy being a tutor, long might it continue.

The one thing we had been unable to do that day was to really study the dunes where small bird activity could be seen. A good reason to return.

When completing my bird list at home that evening, I realised the snow bunting was a bit special: it was my 250th species seen in the UK. Not a great number in many respects; at the time, we had about 550 different species on the British List so I was still less than halfway there. However, if I could continue being a tutor and visiting new locations regularly, who knew where I might finish?

Our next field meeting would be to Lancashire to visit Marshside near Southport and then move onto Martin Mere, another Wildfowl Trust reserve. There it was whooper swans whereas Slimbridge had Bewick's swans. Marshside was an RSPB reserve covering a very extensive area of salt marsh with many waders and waterfowl to be seen. Waterfowl from Martin Mere fed there during the day and pink-footed geese were seen in goodly numbers either feeding there or flying out to the coast if the tide was fully out, to feed on exposed weed. When visiting Marshside, you really did need dry weather; there was only one hide available and one screen and should the weather be bad the wind or rain just rushed in from the Irish Sea, not at all pleasant.

We were fortunate for our visit, it was a cold February day, but no wind, and we had the gear to keep ourselves warm. We made our way out to the sea initially. Redshanks and curlews were to be seen and large numbers of dunlins and knots were following the tide out. Oystercatchers were numerous and their calls were echoing round, no complaints from us, it was quite a sound and rarely heard back home.

A small wader was spotted busily feeding in a shallow channel and that one gave us some work to do. The bird was about the size of a dunlin, but it was no dunlin and its feeding technique was definitely sandpiper, but which? The bird flew off, white rump with very dark upper wing surfaces, almost looking like a large house martin, we had ourselves a green sandpiper. For many of my companions, this was a 'Lifer' so they were delighted. As I was quickly finding out, if we were able to start the day with a quality bird, everyone was happy, come what may!

We entered the hide, which compared with outside, was warm. Pink-footed geese and whooper swans were quickly located, black-tailed godwits were feeding in the shallows and a short-eared owl was cruising over the damp meadow. That bird dropped to the ground and after a short while emerged carrying a small rodent in its beak. The owl had found its dinner for the day. On then to Martin Mere, the Slimbridge of the north.

On making our way to the nearest hide we were conscious of pink-foots and barnacle geese flying in, and interestingly, near a feeder by the hide, a party of corn buntings was seen. Those small birds were rather special. Years before they were a relatively common bird, but due to big changes in farming techniques, such as grubbing out hedges, they had become less common. To see a flock of over twenty birds was a bit special to say the least.

Whooper swans were in good numbers and as a hen harrier gave us a fly past the swans called out very agitatedly, and listening to them, you quickly realised where the name whooper came from – whoop they most certainly did.

In front of the hide several ruff were to be seen and due to their close proximity we could easily sex the birds. The male, the ruff, is the larger of the two, the female, the reeve, being the smaller. Many oystercatchers were to be seen and over a distant field a whitish looking owl was out hunting, a magnificent barn owl.

We became aware that a decided change was taking place in the weather as storm clouds built up over the sea, so we quickly decided to make our way home, and it was lucky we did as snow came in thick and fast, we just evading it. I think our coach driver was rather glad we had made that decision. Another good day was had by all.

To many serious birders, Norfolk was the ultimate location to see rare and special birds so we decided it was time to do so. We decided not to go by coach due to the distance and time it would take, so this journey was undertaken by car, and six cars duly commenced the journey – twenty-five of us partaking. It was an early start from Walsall, 6.00 a.m. in fact, as we made our way to Snettisham located on the Wash. We chose that venue as it held the largest number of waders to be seen in England and early March was about the latest date to experience that. Many of the birds to be seen did not breed in the UK, they just over-wintered there, and we needed a suitable tide to experience it all. On that particular Sunday high tide was at 11.00 a.m.; all the birds would now be forced onto land and in the shallow confines, so they would in fact be coming in to see us. Our journey across was perfect and we arrived with good time to settle ourselves in and watch. The mud in front of us was covered with wading birds, all still scurrying about to obtain food before the waves submerged it all, and the range of species to be seen started with the largest; curlews, ending up with the smallest, a few stints, and the total numbers were probably well into six figures. I, personally, had never experienced a sight like it. What we were looking at was being experienced in several locations in the Wash, not probably quite as dramatic, but it just made you think how many birds did the Wash support each winter? No wonder it was so important to many birds.

Just as an exercise in numbers, peak counts in the '70s have claimed 75,000 knots, 50,000 dunlins, 20,000 oystercatchers, 10,000 bar-tailed godwits with similar numbers of curlews and redshanks, and so one could go on. It was not just waders which congregated there each winter, it is estimated up to 15,000 shelduck have been seen at times. I suggested only one thing: do not go to Snettisham to count birds, just go to enjoy them!

To illustrate the range of waders seen my list for that day was: Curlew, bar-tailed godwit, oystercatcher, redshank, lapwing, knot, dunlin, turnstone, ringed plover, little stint, ruff, sanderling and green sandpiper. Thirteen, unlucky for some they do say, not for us.

One thing was certain, we would be back visiting Norfolk frequently in the future, it is definitely the Mecca for English bird watching.

Having travelled further afield in the last few months, we decided to go more local and visit Cannock Chase to see if any early summer migrants had returned, and to assist us in this we chose the last Sunday of the month to do so.

We met at an area known as Seven Springs, so called as seven springs originated there. It was a very pleasant part of the Chase as most of the trees growing there were broadleaved, unlike vast areas of the Chase which were covered with conifers, grown for their timber. Silver birch and oak predominated and bird song was emanating from those.

No sooner had we got out of our cars than the call of chiffchaff and the song of willow warbler could be heard, two birds which might look similar, but totally different in voice which made life for us bird watchers a little more easy.

Seeing these birds in the UK, always reminded me of my time in Egypt, where I saw these birds on migration every spring and autumn as they passed through on their journeys to and from Europe – delightful small birds.

The drumming of a great spotted woodpecker could be heard, and as if not to be out done, the 'laughing' cry of a green woodpecker joined in. Green woodpeckers rarely drummed which was a good help if you could only hear the birds and not see them, as was the case that day.

A superb male redstart popped up on to the top of a small bush. A real glamour bird that fellow and for a few seconds stared at us through its beady eyes, almost like a technicolour robin. A bird we all loved to see, they are a bit special.

Among the song heard was that of blackcap, garden warbler and whitethroat, plus that of our resident song birds: robin, blackbird, song thrush, wren and chaffinch – almost a dawn chorus. The non-song-birds were not to be outdone, jay, magpie, carrion crow, jackdaw, the various titmice, were all vocal; it was, after all, the time for males to attract the females and let breeding commence.

That was a very leisurely day, and it was the last class of the term. It was a pleasant conclusion to my first term's work, and more importantly, they wished me to continue when we started up again in the autumn. Needless to say, I was more than happy with that.

I then had a few months of bird watching by myself or with the family. As much as I had enjoyed my first experience of 'teaching', doing things for myself or family was something I appreciated; I was looking forward to the summer ahead.

We had also talked much about holidays that year, and we decided to try to book up somewhere for the Whitsuntide break when Sarah would be off school. This we managed to do, and we booked ourselves a chalet in Scotland, on the shores of the Lake of Menteith, which was Scotland's only natural lake: note, not loch.

Prior to that visit we had never crossed the border. We chose this location as the Trossachs and various lochs were nearby, plus should we have any poor weather, Stirling was also close. Our principal reason, however, was the chance to see ospreys which we were reliably informed, regularly visited the lake from their nearby nesting site, plus otters were also to be seen on the lake.

The location was superb, the chalets were in the style of Norwegian log cabins and they were positioned right on the shore of the lake amongst silver birches and the like. An idyllic location.

Venturing forth late in the afternoon of our first day we met up with a local bird watcher who was able to tell us more about the ospreys, and pointed out the direction from whence they appeared. He also gave us some information relating to the fact it was called the Lake of Menteith, and if his version was correct, it was quite an interesting tale. Apparently, the Laird of the day brought in a Dutch oceanographer to produce a map of the area covered by the water. Previously, much of his work had been carried out in England and he was obviously used to the word lake. On completion of his work, he named the map The Lake of Menteith; being Dutch, he had probably never heard the word loch. The Laird did not change it so to this day it is known as the Lake of Menteith', as the Ordnance Survey, Sheet 57, clearly stated.

Prior to our Dutchman's involvement, I understand the Gaelic name for the water was Loch Innis Mo Cholmaig Gavlic, from an Englishman's point of view, the Lake of Menteith is more easily pronounceable!

After breakfast the next morning, we walked down to the side of the lake, only a couple of minutes away, and on the way we disturbed a common sandpiper from her nest. Until she had taken to flight we had not been aware of her, we quickly moved on, just pausing to glance at the three eggs in her nest. We would not walk that way down to the lake again and hoped no one else did.

We had hardly reached lake side before Dorothy pointed; up above us, an osprey was gliding down, wings slightly arched – what a sight. The last time I saw an osprey was in Egypt, to then have my first in the UK was marvellous. We watched this bird for several minutes as it dived into the lake, and we were fortunate to see it actually catch a fish, which after some manoeuvring in its claws, it flew off carrying the still alive trout. It would not stay alive for much longer, the osprey no doubt had its 'killing perch' nearby where the deed would be done. It was not much fun being low down in the pecking order.

Walking back to our cabin we stopped. A small, yellowish looking warbler was singing from just above our head; what had we there? Time to put brain in gear. Then it hit me, we were listening to a wood warbler, not a common bird back home. We spent several minutes listening to this delightful little bird. It was almost as though he had flown many miles from Africa just to serenade us – his efforts were fully appreciated.

Talking to a local birder later in the day, he had a very interesting story to tell me. The ospreys were breeding some little distance away, and at that time only a few pairs had re-established themselves, with the Loch Garten pair being the much publicised birds. The RSPB at Loch Garten had the birds under guard 24 hours a day to keep them safe from egg collectors and illegal falconers who might have been after the chicks.

The Menteith pair were also under full protection, a group of local birders had taken on this responsibility; they were very proud of their local birds. Whether the anglers on the lake thought the same is probably another matter, ospreys were experienced 'fishermen', as watching that day's bird clearly illustrated.

Early that evening, we decided to visit the local hotel for dinner and managed to book a table overlooking the lake, which came right up to the foundations of the hotel. Part way through our meal, Sarah noticed a group of six swans swimming past and when I looked at them, I had the surprise of my life: they were adult whooper swans. I had always looked on whooper swans as being winter visitors to our shores; what were those doing there at that time of the year?

After various enquiries, I learned that odd birds frequently over-summered on the lake and, furthermore, a few pairs had bred in Scotland – the books were not always up to date.

Birds we much wished to see, apart from the ospreys, were hooded crows, a bird rarely seen south of the border and we were informed a very good spot to see those birds was Achray Forest, and you would have no need to leave the car park to do so. That sounded too good to be true, but we would give it a whirl.

We quickly found out why it was called a forest. Looking on the map it covered a large amount of ground; fortunately, you could drive through parts of it and it also over-looked Loch Venachar so if we had the time we could visit there.

Our informant was certainly correct about the hooded crows and these birds had developed a very clever way of obtaining scraps. The car park had several plastic refuse bins and several of the crows had learned how to flick open the lids and pop inside to search for scraps. Unfortunately for some of the crows, their vigorous movements inside the bin caused the lids to fall, trapping the birds inside. Come the morning, wardens came round and extricated the crows from the bins and, I am sorry to say, despatched them. They were considered to be vermin and did much damage to the local small bird population. It was a difficult one this, the crows were numerous, small bird populations were on the slide; I was only pleased the decision was not mine.

Driving round parts of the forest we saw many other interesting birds, especially so for us from middle England. Stonechats were plentiful in the heathland areas, a few whinchats were also seen, a goshawk flew overhead and as we gazed down on Loch Venachar a golden eagle glided through, our first Scottish golden eagle.

On one of the car parks, a rustling from a nearby refuse bin caught our attention. Gently lifting the lid a hooded crow hopped out and, without a word of thanks, flew off. I was pleased no wardens were about to see me do this, but I know one thing, that was the closest I would ever get to a hooded crow. Corvus corone cornix, just be glad it was someone from south of the border who found you!

That brought a perfect day to its end, off home then for dinner and making plans for the next day; Scotland, no doubt, had many other wonders to show us.

The visit to the Achray Forest had brought us right to the edge of The Trossachs and the nearby Loch Katrine, an area good for bird watching we were reliably informed, and as the day was forecasted well that would be our destination.

The ride through the forest was most pleasant, hooded crows were again plentiful and occasional ravens could be seen. We managed to park up on the side of the road overlooking Loch Achray, and as we enjoyed the view, a large, greyish bird of prey, flew through. Our initial thoughts were a male hen harrier, but a comment by Dorothy brought a couple details to my notice. She had seen a black bar on the upper wing of the bird and commented the rump looked grey. I quickly took a second and more intense look at the bird, she had hit the jackpot: this was no male hen harrier, it was a male Montagu's harrier.

Monty's, as we birders called them, were one of the rarest breeding birds in the UK, and although the odd pair bred in Scotland, I was not aware of their breeding in that part of the country. It was a bird we have never seen previously and was going to be our top bird of the holiday without a doubt. Dorothy could be rightly pleased with herself with this one. I would probably have missed the two points she saw, two pairs of eyes would always beat one. The harrier drifted from sight and we continued our way down to Loch Katrine.

We arrived just as a pleasure boat was about to do a tour of the Loch, this seemed an ideal and pleasant way to enjoy the occasion, so we joined in.

On the cruise we saw red-breasted merganser, a pair of great crested grebes which were not common that far north, a family party of goosander and good numbers of hirundines. A large bird of prey was picked up in the distance which we presumed to be a golden eagle and common gulls were plentiful, they were common up there where they lived up to their name. It was a very relaxing couple of hours and the temperature with being on water was ideal. I thought we were beginning to like Scotland. The question then was what to do the following day?

The weather had decided what we did, rain had moved in and looked likely for most of that day, so a visit to Stirling fitted in well – Sarah enjoyed castles. The castle was a bit special, I must say; I understood that Mary Queen of the Scots spent her early years there and it did boast some fine tapestries, and the regimental museum was worth a visit in its own right. Stirling itself was a most interesting town or should that be city? We even had birds to see, jackdaws on the castle walls! Not a wasted day at all, and the next day we understood the sun would be back. Should that prove to be the case, a visit to Loch Lomond would be called for; you could not be close to Loch Lomond without visiting it, or so I had been told!

The forecasters had it right, it was a very bright day and our journey across to the eastern side of Loch Lomond was very pleasant. We called in at Aberfoyle and had a quick look at Loch Ard on our way and arrived at the southern end of Loch Lomond, parking up in Loch Lomond Park. To say the Loch was enormous was putting it mildly, it just stretched as far as the eye could see, a strip of water which almost looked as though it was going straight up the spine of Scotland.

We then had three choices: see the Loch by boat; drive along the western side, which had a main road skirting the Loch for most of the way: or stay east side where we could visit the Loch down minor roads – we chose the latter. We had been told that there were several interesting forest walks to be found along that side so we made our way to Garadhban Forest which also overlooked Inchcailloch Island and provided superb views of further up the Loch with Ben Lomond in the distance, all 974 metres of it according to my OS map. Superb country no matter in which direction you looked.

We had hardly got out of our car before we had an adrenalin rush. An osprey flew directly overhead in transit to the Loch and we spent the next few minutes watching the bird dive into the water. Unlike our friend from the Lake of Menteith, this osprey was unsuccessful and it flew further up the Loch to no doubt try again.

Once again hooded crows were evident, especially round the forest fringes, no doubt seeking out worms and the like to be found on the open ground. In the woodland various titmice were to be found, no crested tits unfortunately; we would have been delighted to have seen one of those, a bird only to be found in Scotland. Flycatchers were very active, especially the pied flycatcher, always a bird we were happy to see – they were not so common in Staffordshire.

Walking down to the Loch we had a very pleasant surprise, a ring ouzel was seen carrying food, a most delightful sight. These birds were very infrequent back home, so we stopped to enjoy the bird for a few minutes. It was very active and made several journeys to where I suppose the nest was located. We did not move any closer, we had no wish to disturb the bird; we were just pleased to be able to share a few minutes with the bird.

On reaching the pier, we were greeted by a very vocal display from a pair of oystercatchers, they did not appreciate our arrival. They were probably the noisiest waders we had, extremely vocal, their loud calls must be very useful in warning other birds of possible dangers, not that any birds had cause to fear us.

A common sandpiper flew through, piping away as it did so, this was a little more musical than the earlier oystercatchers and over the Loch terns were to be seen. They were at some distance but, looking at the paleness on the wing surfaces, we presumed they were Arctic terns, but we could not be completely certain. Arctic terns and common terns could be easily confused, especially when at distance, and birders who appreciated this referred to them as 'commics' so that was what we settled for that day!

Whilst enjoying the terns we became aware of the sky darkening quite rapidly, a storm looked imminent, and as we had no waterproofs with us, we decided discretion was the best thing and rapidly returned to our car. We had made the right decision, a short but very heavy shower followed. It was difficult to judge whether more was to follow, so we thought we would make our way back to base but take a slight detour to see more of the countryside round the area.

We made our way first to Drymen and then took a minor road which skirted the Garadhban Forest and the Loch Ard Forest, heading for Aberfoyle, and we chose well. It was very narrow in places, not a road for speed, very quiet, and as we crossed an area of open moorland, we saw and heard our favourite bird: the curlew. Several pairs were obviously breeding there and their superb calls and songs echoed round.

We just stopped, wound down the windows, and listened. No bird had a call like this, the hair on the back of your neck just rose; as a friend of mine used to say, 'It is just magic,' and I could not argue with that.

Further on, we stopped again. Two golden plovers flew across the road in front of us, these had to be looked at more closely. Although they were birds we had seen previously, that was our first opportunity of seeing them in their wonderful summer plumage; they were not called golden plover without reason. Those two birds were immaculate, their golden-brown upper parts contrasted with their black faces, necks and under parts and they strutted around as though just for our benefit. A wonderful two or three minutes before they were up and away, calling as they did so, a sad-sounding but melodious single note whistle, best described as 'whoo-ee'. In choosing that minor road, we had hit the jack-pot – two marvellous memories. As I said earlier, Scotland was beginning to grow on us, and the local brew was 'nae' bad. Then what to do the next day?

That was to be our last day, unfortunately, so we chose to visit Callander. We needed to buy a couple of gifts to take back with us and then we would move on to Loch Lubnaig where the road ran all along one shore.

Callander was a pleasant town, we bought our gifts without any trouble, had a very pleasant coffee and toasted teacake at a café and made our way to Loch Lubnaig. This was a longish and narrow Loch, with several areas where you could park a car and enjoy walking. From a birding point of view, it was not great – a few ducks, mallards and goosanders – the now almost inevitable hooded crows and warblers. Wild flowers, however, were wonderful and we even stumbled across two species of orchids, so we were not complaining. It was a most leisurely and relaxing day which, in front of the following day's long drive home, was a good thing.

That evening we again went out for dinner, enjoyed the whooper swans once more and made a promise to return. When would that be was the question?

That turned out to be our only holiday of the year due to having an extension built at home which took several weeks to be accomplished. I needed extra space as a part study so I could do my university preparation work more easily and a sun lounge for relaxing in, which was easier than moving house and less costly.

September duly arrived and I was back to my bird study course once again. I was pleased to see that I had hardly lost any of my previous members and we even had one or two new faces. After a general discussion, we decided to alternate our field meeting between a mixture of long distance and local. It was surprising to learn that many members did not know anything about what could be experienced on their own doorsteps so to speak. With winter looming, and the daylight hours shortening, distance was not always the best bet and we had many areas just an hour from home. Most of the course were members of the West Midland Bird Club which meant we could visit their two principal reserves, Belvide and Blithfield Reservoirs where, during the winter, large numbers of gulls and waterfowl visited and the moorlands of Derbyshire and Staffordshire were only a short distance away.

For our first meeting, however, we decided to try the coast in the hope we could experience the passage of sea birds travelling south from their breeding grounds in or near to the Arctic, and the possible arrival of early Winter migrants from northern Europe, so Spurn Point on Humberside was our chosen destination. An area I had never visited, although I had heard much about it. Spurn Point was a long and narrow strip of very unstable land which stretched out across the entrance to the Humber. In parts, it was only thirty yards or so wide and was constantly being re-shaped by gales and heavy seas. At the tip, lay a coast guard station and lighthouse and a rich area of sea buckthorn much appreciated by the migrant birds. From the one side, you gazed out over the North Sea; from the other, you could look up the Humber estuary at large numbers of waders which congregated in the sheltered areas. It also had an Observatory and serious bird study had taken place for many years. The list of species seen was legend and I had always been told it was a place I must visit, so that day I was, or should that be we were?

Ten of us made the journey, three car loads, and we were very fortunate with it being a very pleasant looking day. The journey up was uneventful and as we drove into Kilnsea, a small village on the Point, we came across a large number of cars with many birders milling around. Needless to say, we found somewhere to park and approached some birders to enquire what was going on. Two firecrests had been seen in the church grounds and neighbouring gardens, so we joined the throng.

I had never seen a firecrest, although I was once told I had. One was seen on Cannock Chase and I was told by one of the birders that a small bird moving through a tree was the bird in question. I could see little of the bird, could have been a wren as far as I was concerned so it never appeared on any lists of mine. I did not mind more experienced birders telling me what I was looking at, as long as I could see enough detail to recognise the bird myself.

They were one of our smallest birds and were quite rare. Their nearest relative the goldcrest was very similar and was fairly common and in many respects they were very similar in appearance and behaviour; you did need a clear view to split them. The bird we were seeking had a very pronounced white stripe over the eye and a black eye stripe, the goldcrest lacked these. So it was a question of seeing clearly the head markings on a bird which only measured a little over three inches in length, we had some work to do I thought. Fortunately, there were well over thirty or so birders looking for the birds; the question was, now would someone be lucky?

A bit of excitement was generated. We had a small party of spotted flycatchers feeding away and on the ground two redstarts were to be seen, two beautiful looking males. Those birds were actively feeding up in preparation for their journey southwards to Africa, I quietly wished them luck.

Talking to a local birder I learned that there had been a passage of shearwaters and terns earlier on, so once we had finished there we might have further excitement out at sea as the tide was coming in the birds should be brought in closer for us; well, that was the theory!

We concentrated our attention on the trees once again and after a short while a shout went up, a birder pointed towards a silver birch, and on a bare branch stood our bird. A magnificent male firecrest, a 'Lifer' to start the day with. Whether I had ever seen one or not when on the Chase no longer mattered, I had now. A few seconds later, further movement beneath the bird and the second firecrest popped out, and to make the picture complete, that bird was a female so we not only had two firecrests, we had a pair. The birds studied us for some seconds before once again vanishing into the leaves. We were happy, if that was to be all we were to have that day, we would not be complaining. On then to the shore.

There were not so many people there so parking was not a problem. We set up our scopes and commenced to gaze out to sea. There was certainly plenty of activity out over the waves, and the first birds we really saw were a small flock of eiders flying low over the sea. There were seven of them, all drakes, and in that clear light they really looked smart, they were a wonderful bird much appreciated by birders, especially us inland types; eiders rarely travelled far from the coast, being very much a marine duck.

Large numbers of gulls were out at sea and small flocks of Sandwich terns were passing down the coast, another very marine bird, not seen all that often inland. The occasional auks, razorbills and guillemots were busily flying past; these were not going in any particular direction, probably just hunting for shoals of fish.

One of my colleagues drew our attention to three birds, flying very low over the water, hardly flapping their wings as they did so – perfect shearwater flight. We waited for them to come closer, when they did, we were delighted to see they were Manx shearwaters; we could hardly contain our delight. One of the birds we really had hoped for was there, and they gave us a superb flypast. They were the ultimate flying machine, effortless, they hardly flapped their wings, they just tilted them and gained uplift from the waves. Fortunately, they were not the only ones we saw during the remainder of the day, we probably had almost treble figures; we had been lucky for a passage of the birds.

Wonderful though the Manx's had been, I had a real stroke of luck. Whilst studying some gannets I became conscious of a very dark looking shearwater clipping the waves nearby. I called this to the attention of my friends, we had a sooty shearwater. A far more special bird than the Manx, a bird not frequently seen, and when it was, it was usually a west coast bird, being an Atlantic species, few passed down the east coast – we were very lucky that day. What made it even more special, it was a 'Lifer' for us all. They were aptly named being a very dark bird and at the distance we were viewing the bird it just looked completely black, almost like a cormorant apart from shape and flight. I had thought the firecrest would be the bird of the day for us, not then, it had competition.

As the tide started to turn the odd skua put in an appearance. Arctic skuas were the most numerous, not that there were that many, but out at sea two large skuas were harassing the gulls. A closer look was required and to our delight those birds were great skuas, bonxie's as they were commonly known – a bit of Gaelic there I supposed – they did breed that far north.

Those two species brought our trip to its conclusion, we did not have time to go down to the tip of the Point, but that gave us a good reason to go back – not that one was needed really. Spurn had lived up to its reputation and we had seen several birds which we were unlikely to see back home. Due to the tide and time available, we had done no watching over the estuary, so apart from the odd oystercatcher, curlew and redshank, we had seen few waders but you could not have everything; we were more than happy with what we had.

The following month our field meeting was local and we decided we would visit two venues, Belvide and Blithfield Reservoirs, both West Midland Bird Club nature reserves which were only open to members and we all were. Belvide was a canal feeder reservoir; Blithfield was a South Staffordshire Water Works supply reservoir – both had hides and car parking facilities for members. The range of species seen was very good and during the winter period large numbers of gulls and waterfowls are likely. I know October was not exactly winter, but we chose the last Sunday in the month to make our visit.

The first thing we noted was the large number of gulls present, especially black-headed and lesser black-backed, some of which were already moulting into their winter plumage; the black-heads looking particularly so. A few herring gulls and great black-backed gulls were also present and a birder already there told us to look out for a Mediterranean gull he had seen earlier. That piece of news certainly concentrated the mind, and as the bird was a winter adult, we also knew what to look for.

To the inexperienced eye, adult, winter plumaged black-headed and Med' gulls, look very similar, especially so as both lose their head colour, in the case of the black-headed gull their head is brown (just to further confuse matters), the Med' gull is black. The Med' gull is slightly larger, but unless they are standing close to each other, this is not readily apparent. The big thing for us birders is the fact the Med' gull is what we term a white-winged gull. The majority of our commoner gulls have black primaries when in adult plumage, the Med' gull has white, so this was where we concentrated our efforts. Concentrate we most certainly did, all to no avail; if the Med' gull was still about, he was hiding away well. There was a decent range of ducks, pochards, tufteds, mallards, teals and wigeons with great crested grebe numbers high. A large mixed flock of Canada geese and greylags were also on the water, and closer investigation revealed six barnacle geese tucked away amongst them. Cormorant numbers were high and several grey heron were scattered round the shore line. A decent selection, but nothing to get overly excited about. On to Blithfield.

We made our way down to the hide overlooking Tad Bay, and had hardly got settled in when we had a bit of excitement. A small party of about a dozen swallows provided us with a fly-past, these birds were very late to be setting off on their annual migration. We could only wish them luck, as we waved them on their way.

There were not so many gulls there as previously seen at Belvide, and those which were there were as at Belvide, black-heads and lesser black-backs. The duck selection was similar too, the only difference being the fact the wigeon at Blithfield were very vocal, their soft whistling call was heard. The duck I was impressed with was the North American ruddy duck.

This duck was introduced, be it accidentally, into the UK, and the Wildfowl Trust at Slimbridge seemed to be the location birds escaped from. In several parts of the country, they have commenced to breed in a wild state and are now part of our wildfowl population. The Midlands seems to do well with them, and about twenty or so birds, of both sexes, are visible today. They are a delightful small diving duck with a short stiff tail which sticks up much like a wren's does, giving the bird a rather jaunty look. A delightful addition to our duck membership.

Whilst enjoying those birds, my attention was drawn to a what was believed to be a herring gull with yellow legs; the only problem is herring gulls legs are pink, not yellow. What have we there? It certainly was not a lesser black-backed gull which has yellow legs; the back colour is most definitely a soft grey. Then it hit me, I am back to my days in the Middle East and the Mediterranean. The Mediterranean race of the herring gull has yellow legs and, occasionally, the odd one strays north and ends up in the UK. This was my first occasion of seeing the bird in the UK, when I last saw this bird I was in Cyprus and Malta, and that was twenty odd years ago – and the weather was warmer then!

I was asked the question by one or two of my members, what do they count it as, is it still just a herring gull. I do count races in my own lists, and I do this for two reasons. Firstly, they are different from our own species so they need recording as they are a unusual record; secondly, you never know if and when they may become a full species in their own right. So much work is now being done on DNA, new species of animals are almost being invented! Record this one as herring gull, yellow-legged race I told them. It was even a UK 'Lifer' for us all.

Even as we were discussing the gull, a panic occurred. A mass exodus took place, the gulls and ducks all took to the air accompanied by a large flock of lapwings; we had not been aware of those. We quickly found out the reason for their behaviour: a peregrine falcon had swooped in and was busily chasing a group of lapwings, judging by the size of the bird it was a female (they are larger than the males). She was intent on obtaining a meal, a lapwing made the mistake of peeling off from the group and this turned out to be the last thing this particular lapwing was ever going to do. The peregrine struck the bird from underneath, feathers flew, and the falcon followed the lapwing down to the ground beneath. Seconds later she flew up, carrying the now dead lapwing in her claws, dinner assured. To many people what we had seen was cruel, but it is not. Some birds are meat eaters, just like many of us, others eat insects or seeds; they all have their place in the order of things. Wild creatures do not kill for pleasure, unlike man, this peregrine had killed so she could live, and once she fuelled her hunger, she would not hunt again until hungry.

That day's little escapade brought back memories of a conversation I once had with a couple who witnessed a similar situation, and we spoke about it. A peregrine on that occasion had taken a teal, and the killing had not been quick, so a certain amount of suffering had obviously taken place. They were quite distressed by what they had witnessed and spoke to me about it. To try to put their minds at rest, I asked them if they had ever seen a song thrush or blackbird extract a worm from out of the ground and then pull it to pieces as they ate it. They had and had not even thought about it, but a worm is a living thing just as much as the teal, and does a worm too feel pain? I am not a scientist so I cannot answer that question, but surely there is no difference; the teal and the worm were killed solely for food, not for fun. How many of us are truly vegetarian?

Not a lot occurred after all of that, but we all went home with memories and hopefully had learned a little, and peregrine falcons, yellow-legged gulls, North American ruddy ducks and barnacle geese were not bad birds to see on the same day, and all local.

At our next indoor class, we discussed amendments to our field meetings, in as much as I suggested going out occasionally to look for specific birds. There is a danger in this, if we do not find the birds we could easily end up with seeing little else, but if we wish to experience the rare and unusual a, little gambling has to take place. I did not believe I had convinced all of the logic in my thoughts, but it was agreed we would give it a whirl, and it was decided we would try this idea come our November and December field meetings. The onus was now on me; I probably should have kept my thoughts to myself!

I now had to do some work in finding a couple of good locations, and after making various enquiries and speaking with birders I know well, I sorted out my first location: the Staffordshire Moorlands the home to black grouse, red grouse and wintering short-eared owls and on our return journey we would call in at Stoke to seek out long-eared owls. The grouse and short-eared owls were being seen at Swallow Moss, an area I had never visited so a reconnaissance run was required and the long-eared owls were at Park Hall, where I had been previously. Although unsuccessfully. My group members were happy enough with my ideas, the result was open to question.

We made it the last Sunday in the month again, but after obtaining further information we decided to do the trip in reverse, Park Hall being our first call. The reason for this choice was the fact the owls roosted up during the day and with luck could be found in a conifer plantation. Our chances were quite good, at the last count eleven birds had been seen, and the birders had a secret weapon. When an owl had been located a circle round the tree was made on the ground, so when looking for the owls you looked as much on the ground as up in the trees.

Twelve of us made the trip and with so many eyes it did not take us long to find our first owl. Pressed hard against the trunk, high up in a conifer tree, the bird merged perfectly with the bark of the tree, and if it had not been for the fact the bird was studying us with equal intent, eyes wide open, we might not have picked it up. The curiosity of the owl was incredible, it actually turned its head as it scrutinised the ring of birders round its tree, before getting bored with it all, straightened up its head, appearing to go back to sleep. We would remember this long-eared owl for many years to come, me for ever!

We spent a further half an hour looking for more owls, and we did in fact find seven, and on our way back out to the car park we found a tawny owl sitting out in an old oak tree. Were we going to be so lucky with the short-eared owl later, if so it would be one hell of a day. The strain on me seemed to be reducing slightly – I trust that to be the case.

Our drive to Swallow Moss took us out right into the Staffordshire Moorlands, passing a very interesting piece of natural sculpture known as the 'Winking Man', which is the perfect name for it. The M.O.D. owns a large expanse of the moor, which is used on occasion for military purposes; fortunately, no red warning flags were flying that day which was a good thing.

A party of six red grouse flew across the road in front of us and they landed on an area of grass which provided perfect views. We pulled off the road to enjoy these birds, four males and two females, and although it was wintertime, the males were still looking very smart, they stayed in view for a few minutes before vanishing from sight among the heather and bracken. A very satisfactory start to being on the moors.

My reconnaissance run up to Swallow Moss, previously, had not been very successful; all I had seen then was two fleeting glimpses of red grouse, no black or owls on that occasion. At least we now had the red on our list.

At Swallow Moss, the black grouse were reported from near to Fernyford Farm where they were seen perching in trees or flying in and out of a small piece of woodland which lay near the track down to the farm. We parked up and made our way down the public footpath towards the farm, flushing three red grouse as we did so, the omens were looking good.

We set up our scopes and commenced to study the trees in which the birds were reported to roost, to quickly find our information was not wrong. Five black grouse were perched in a tree, four of which were males and one female, and the males looked magical. They were a new species for me and I was going to enjoy every moment of this. They are a large bird and in many respects they looked a little incongruous perched in a bare tree, you expect game birds to be seen either in the air or on the ground. Not I hasten to add, that I heard anyone complaining.

After several minutes, the grouse took off and vanished into the wood mentioned previously; our experience was over. Now to drive round to where the owl was reported from, near an area known as Reaps Moor. This was only about a mile away and we arrived to find several other birders already in residence, a good sign we had found the right spot.

Talking to the birders, we were interested to hear that a male hen harrier had been seen, not regularly, but a few times each week, that could well be another bird to keep our eyes open for; if not that day, on future visits.

Where we were standing, we had a goodly number of meadow pipits actively feeding so we studied these in case a more unusual pipit, such as a water pipit, was tucked away amongst them. No such luck, they were all meadow pipits, but then things changed. A shout went up 'Here it comes.' We did not have to ask what 'it' was. Gliding, low over the moor, came our owl. With hardly a flap of the wings, it appeared to just float past, just tilting its primaries upwards when it required a bit of lift. Owls, I have considered for many years to be the perfect flying machine. Nothing ever appears to be done at speed, it all looks most leisurely, and even when they drop on their prey, it is done most casually. They gently close their wings and drop silently onto their prey. If there is a 'second life', I would suggest coming back as an owl, not a small rodent!

Although our short-eared owl was putting on a wonderful flying display, it was having no luck with its hunting; unfortunately, it was slowly moving further away from us, which was not what we wanted. After a few minutes; it glided over a ridge to be seen no more. We hung around for several minutes, it did not return, but what a wonderful conclusion to our day out, and for some the owl was another 'Lifer'.

When I first muted the idea of occasionally going out to try to see specific birds, I never dreamed our first venture would turn out like it had that day. When I suggested we tried for four species, long-eared owl, short-eared owl, red grouse and black grouse, I would have considered it to be a success if we had seen two of them; to land a 'full house', plus a tawny owl, was unbelievable. That day must go down as a great day's birding, and as one of my colleagues, bless him, said, 'You have set the standard now, we expect this all the time.' I will not repeat what I said in reply! And as I have mentioned before, I was being paid to do this; somebody, somewhere, must love me.

Now what would December bring? We decided to take our field meeting on the second Sunday of the month, with Christmas looming, the ladies especially, would have other things on their minds. Due to the short hours of daylight we chose Cannock Chase, a few reports of a great grey shrike had been made, so we thought we would try to chase this bird down so that would be a really serious day; one bird only, mind you, some bird.

A day or two before we were due to meet, small numbers of waxwings arrived on the Chase, and a friend of mine saw them and was able to give me full directions of just where he had seen them. The area, which was just off the Penkridge Bank Car Park, apparently had a good number of hawthorn trees with a heavy crop so the birds were likely to stay put. Dorothy had never seen a waxwing so we nipped across on the Saturday to see if we could find them; Sarah was visiting friends so she could not join us.

My informant was right: a flock of twenty-three waxwings were busily engrossed hawthorn berry eating. These birds are very people friendly and you can get remarkably close to them. On one occasion, they were feeding just above our heads, actually dropping the occasional berry on us. Waxwings are also noisy birds, very conversational and I believe they were once known as Bohemian chatterers – listening to those just above our heads, very aptly named.

If you are unfamiliar with waxwings, just have a look at them in your field guide, they are an exotic bird and are probably the one species birders can never have enough of. They breed in northern Europe and visit us during winter, but their movements are not a regular annual migration such as fieldfares and redwings, it all depends upon the success or otherwise of the berry crop back home. Some years they are here in large numbers; other times, we hardly see any – when they arrive in mass we refer to it as a 'Fall'. Twenty-three does not make a 'Fall', but we were more than happy, Dorothy especially so! Hopefully, they would still be there the next day, and where should we start, shrike or waxwings – decisions, decisions?

Eighteen of us met up in Lichfield on an overcast and chilly morning, so we only had to use five cars, parking on Cannock Chase at times can be rather awkward, especially on a Sunday. We initially had a chat concerning our route. I had suggested we went for the shrike first as we might need extra time to locate that bird, and as I had good idea of just where the waxwings were likely to be, time there was not so important. This was accepted, so on our way we went.

The shrike was last reported from the Sherbrook Valley, below Coppice Hill. This, fortunately, was an area I knew well and the bird regularly perched up in a dead silver birch I was reliably informed.

We parked up as close as possible and slowly made our way down into the Sherbrook Valley. There, the valley was principally heather and bracken with scattered trees before meeting up with deciduous woodland of mainly oak and silver birch. The dead silver birch stump was growing from out of the heather and bracken and would provide the shrike with a very good vantage point to look out for its prey. Well, that was the theory; what would happen in practice?

The dead stump was easily located, but not a bird in sight. A movement beneath the tree caught our attention; it was a robin, I suggested it moved off quickly in case the shrike was about. A buzzard soared overhead and a distant green woodpecker could be heard 'laughing' away, was it trying to tell us something?

We hung around for about a good hour and it was quite chilly, when someone exclaimed 'What's that?' Bingo, the shrike had dropped down and was sitting out on the end of a bare stump with not a care in the world. A superb view, and the fact it was a chilly morning no longer mattered, we all had an inner glow. The shrike stood there posturing away as though its sole intent was to show us just how beautiful and magnificent a bird it really was, and it succeeded. Then off it flew, almost as though it thought enough was enough, 'I have got more important things to do,' and I would agree. Although we hung about for many more minutes the shrike did not return, so back to our cars we went; hot drinks were now required and then – waxwings, we hoped!

The drive round to the Penkridge Bank Car Park was only the matter of minutes and we arrived just as light rain commenced to fall, how chilly it was. I was surprised it was not snow or at least sleet, not the conditions we would have selected.

Fortunately, the area where we saw the waxwings the previous day was only a few minutes away so we quickly set off. The shrike may have made us wait, but within minutes, a delightful chatter could be heard. I pointed this out to my friends and you could sense the excitement. Only the odd one or two of us had experienced waxwings previously, and there, just yards away, was a delightful group chattering and feeding away on the crop of hawthorn berries. I counted them, seventeen – six down on the other day's numbers, but who was caring?

For the next twenty minutes or so, we just stood where we were enjoying the waxwings. For those who had never seen the birds before, they could not believe just how close the birds were. I am sure of one thing, they would not forget that day. All good things have to come to an end, the birds erupted as a dog came racing through and our day was over.

As the rain was now beginning to become very heavy, we were not sorry to move on. When we got back to our cars, I asked the 'Wag from the moors', was today's standard OK? He gave me a smile and a nod: I think round II was mine; the question was for how long could I keep it up?

We would not have an answer to that question until the New Year. All I knew was the last year had been an incredible adventure for me, and I had met some delightful people and some magnificent birds.

At our first indoor session, we discussed plans for the rest of the term which would take us up to April. With January being a notorious month for inclement weather, we decided to go local again and spread our wings in February and March. January would be Chillington and Belvide;

February, Slimbridge; finally, March for Rutland Water.

Our reasons for choosing these locations were as follows: Chillington had an avenue leading up to the entrance to the Hall which was lined with many trees including beech and hornbeam; trees much loved by hawfinches, a not common bird within the county. Several members of the course would welcome the opportunity to see those.

2. Belvide has its waterfowl and gulls as previously mentioned and was only a short distance from Chillington.

3. Slimbridge – where we were after the Bewick's swans and white-fronted geese before they returned to their breeding grounds in northern Europe and Asia.

4. Rutland Water was a recently opened, massive reservoir which was already attracting many unusual birds so it was about time a visit was made.

We were correct about January weather. It was already damp as we met at Cannock to share cars once again, and heavier rain had been forecast nearer mid-day. If that turned out to be correct, we might at least be in a hide at Belvide when the rain arrived. In this climate of ours, you either get on with things or never accomplish anything.

Twelve of us that day, just three car loads, and Chillington here we come. The Avenue, or to give it the correct title Upper Avenue, as there are two, was very impressive. The trees were mature and there had been a good harvest of beech mast judging by what was lying on the ground.

There was plenty of bird activity going on, both on the ground and in the air. A large mixed flock of titmice were feeding away in the trees, long-tailed tits were well into double figures – a delightful bird – everyone loves to see. On the ground, it was principally chaffinches and greenfinches, and there we concentrated our efforts. After about twenty minutes, we got our reward: five hawfinches landed and commenced to flick the mast about as they searched for the seed it may contain.

Hawfinches are the largest of our finch family, with a very powerful bill which they use well. They are capable of cracking hazel nuts, so I suggest you never put your finger in its bill, eating beech seeds are no problem. Seeing five together was the largest numbers I had ever seen at once, my few records were all of solitary birds, and there were not many of them. My friends who have never seen the bird before were delighted, and as I jokingly told them, 'So they should be!'

As we turned to leave, a sparrowhawk flew down the Avenue and, needless to say, there was a major eruption with all the birds departing at speed so did we; well, we departed, I would not say at speed. Our timing was right that was for sure, with Belvide being next on the agenda. We arrived just as the rain started with a vengeance. We stayed in our cars and ate our packed lunches in the hope the rain might slacken. It did not, so we were going to get a bit damp; fortunately, the nearest hide was just a few minutes away, so we headed in that direction. We stopped for a few moments to listen to a great spotted woodpecker drumming away and hoping it had found something of interest, it was certainly working at it. A nuthatch was also calling loudly, a strong call for such a little fellow.

Reaching the hide we found we had it all to ourselves, so we can all sit down and get on with our birding. Looking in the hide log we might be in for a bit of excitement – a drake smew was recorded the day before – and the bird was seen from that hide, just off the dam. Up scopes, it was now concentration time.

A drake smew is unmistakable, being a distinctive white and black bird. They are a winter visiting species and we only see an occasional bird so far inland, so to say they are a bit special is putting it mildly. I have only seen six in all my years of birding, and for some of my colleagues it would be a 'Lifer' should we be lucky. They breed across northern Europe into Asia and we get a few on passage and at wintering sites normally near to the coast. That day's bird was obviously worth some effort; although, how the rain was now falling, it would not be easy. They are a diving duck which feed on fish and insect larvae, and when under water, they can swim quite a distance.

After about half an hour we were beginning to wonder if the duck was still there, when a voice said, 'I think I've got it.' We swung round to where he was pointing and several pairs of eyes were now concentrated on that one spot; our colleague was right, the smew could be seen. Even at distance, and in such poor light, there was no mistaking this fellow. We watched him diving several times and, on one occasion, he actually surfaced with a small fish in his bill. At that point, a muted cheer went up in the hide. You do not have to be mad to be a birder, but it does help!

The light was rapidly deteriorating so we decided to call it a day, just staying long enough to enjoy a flock of about twenty North American ruddy ducks which had just sailed into view; a wonderful finale to the day. As we moved out of the hide a voice exclaimed, 'Don't ask, you're doing fine.' This could not carry on. A poor day must be just round the corner. It has been a wonderful start to the year, fortune had really favoured us, providing some magical birds with which to start our 'Year Lists'. Long might it continue.

I know I have only mentioned the special birds seen that day, but on checking my list, when getting home, we had seen fifty-three species – not bad for being so close to home and taking into account the poor weather.

February saw us returning to a site we visited some months ago. The lure of Bewick's swans and white-fronted geese would always draw the birder back to Slimbridge and I had so many happy memories there, thanks to my interviewing Peter Scott.

Five cars left Walsall for the trip down the M5 to Slimbridge and, I was sorry to say, we had clicked for a poor day's weather, rain being forecast for all day. Fortunately, Slimbridge has many hides and very good catering facilities so, hopefully, it would not be all bad.

One advantage with the poor weather was the fact it had kept the number of visitors down and there were not many cars parked up when we arrived, although a couple of coach parties were already there. We booked in and checked up where the special birds were and we were on our way.

You did not have to go far to see the first Bewick's swans, several were to be seen on Swan Lake, where else you may ask? Many of the duck to be seen were captive birds, you would never get so close to goosander and smew in the wild, but it was a wonderful opportunity to study these birds close up. The majority of the swans were wild enough as they flew in and out to the River Severn Estuary, where they would no doubt be feeding as the tide would be out; we understood the geese were out there too. One bit of special information gleaned was the fact there were three bean geese tucked in amongst the white-fronts. Bean geese, now they are something, being one of the rarer geese to visit the UK each winter.

We made our way to the Zeiss Hide, in the north west of the reserve, which overlooks the marshes. It was from there the white-fronts were last recorded, but before doing, so we nipped into the Kingfisher Hide; we had been informed mandarin duck were seen that morning. Mandarin duck are the glamour bird among British waterfowl, they were introduced into the UK many years ago and some escaped and set up feral flocks in the country, and these have been so successful, they are now on the British list.

The duck originated from eastern Asia and I have read recent comments that the British population is now equal or higher to that back home in its native land. If that is the case, we have probably helped to save the bird from possible extinction – now there's a thought.

Nipping into the Kingfisher Hide hit the jackpot. Eleven mandarin ducks were showing well, seven exquisite drakes and four ducks, all with full sets of primaries; these are free-fliers alright, they have not walked out of the collection. According to a birder in the hide, six of the birds were a family which bred there last year, the pair raising four young, now fully grown. We were very pleased to have been told about these birds, they are not common back home.

Now for the Zeiss Hide and geese hunting. The water in front of the hide had a good selection of waterfowl in attendance, and here they all had a good chance of being wild birds. Wigeons and teals were well represented as were north American ruddy ducks, not that the latter where unexpected, it was from here that many escaped in the first place. A comment was made by a birder, he believed he had spotted a drake scaup, now that would be a bit of quality. Several pairs of eyes were now concentrated on the area he pointed out and it is not long before we found his bird, and he was right, a drake scaup it most certainly was. We will certainly settle for him; I saw only one or two most years, and for some of my colleagues it was a 'Lifer'. Now let us concentrate on finding the geese.

The geese took little finding – there must have been three hundred of them in the marsh – and after enjoying them for a time we concentrated on going through, bird by bird, in an attempt to find the three bean geese we had heard about.

Bean geese are slightly larger than white-fronts, show little white at the base of the bill, are darker necked, their bills have dark marks spread over, the white-fronts bills being unmarked pink or yellow and they have dark belly markings. Bean geese are another northern European species which normally migrate southwards on the continent, very few crossing over to the UK.

We had spent some time when one of my colleagues asked, 'Have bean geese got orange-yellowish legs?' Yes, was the answer to that question, and a quick look in the direction he was pointing confirmed things; he had, indeed, found the bean geese.

Light and time had now caught up with us, but we had experienced a very good day with several exceptional birds, and we had only seen but a portion of Slimbridge, always a good reason to return.

After much discussion, we decided not to visit Rutland Water. It is a very large water and consequently the birds can be widespread so we thought we would leave it alone until the autumn when the passage of waders should be at its best. Instead, we thought we would have a serious 'twitch' and go after a rare bird which was being reported from a small pool lying adjacent to the A5 near to Burlington in Shropshire. The bird in question was a spotted sandpiper, a vagrant from north America, a wader similar to our common sandpiper and a bird none of us had seen previously; this was to be a very serious 'twitch' indeed. Although only an hour or so from home it was a journey for one bird, should we not find it the day could be a complete waste, but real rarities are hard to come by so we would give it a whirl!

At least the weather was better than previously, clear and dry, a good start there. Sixteen of us made the journey, visiting an area new to all of us and chasing a bird also new to us all.

Fortunately, I had been given the map reference for the location, so I knew exactly where we were heading, and we arrived to find two birders already in attendance. It was a good job there were not many more, as parking was at a premium, but we managed to park our four cars up safely.

The two birders had been there for about an hour and, although they had seen the bird, it had been fleeting views; as they said, it could easily have been a common sandpiper had not they known differently. We were obviously going to have our work cut out, but nobody ever said serious birding was easy! And work it certainly turned out to be.

Fleeting glimpses it was and after about half an hour the two birders left, we, being made of sterner stuff, hung on. We had come up specifically to see this bird, so if it took time, so be it. Time it took, but we were rewarded. The spotted sandpiper came out onto a small expanse of mud and for two or three minutes gave us all a perfect view. It had certainly been worth the wait and at that time of the year the bird was moulting into summer plumage. Spots could be seen on the under parts and the legs had a decided ruddy tinge. It had been worth the wait, we all had a 'Lifer', now that cannot be bad.

As we still had time, we decided to call in at Gailey Pools on the way back and have a look at the heronry. On a small island on one of the pools, an heronry had been in existence for many years and very good views of the birds could be obtained. Herons are early breeding birds so there should be much activity round the nests, and so it turned out to be. Birds were sitting eggs by now in some of the nests so their mates were flying in with food to feed the sitting birds. That was not just the case of throwing the fish in, the food was handed over with much ceremony, and why not? The catching of the fish had required skill, so a bit of show was fully justified.

That brought our day out to a very pleasant end, and the general consensus of opinion was 'Twitches' should be considered in the future. It was also our last field meeting of the course, so I now had the summer months for myself and family, prior to starting up again come September which was what my group wanted. The early months of summer passed by pleasantly, with trips to the Derbyshire Dales to spend time enjoying the dippers. Cannock Chase to enjoy the nightjars once again, and local walks. The highlight of early summer, locally, was the arrival of an osprey which called in at Blithfield Reservoir on its way up to Scotland. The bird stayed on for a week and certainly brought the bird watchers in.

Time for Sarah to have a seaside holiday again so we booked a chalet on the north coast of Somerset, in a small hamlet near to Minehead. It looked a peaceful site with only five chalets, with the beach but a short walk away, so all we needed was some good weather. We were lucky to get in really as we had left it a little late for a summer holiday booking.

Our journey down was terrible, it was the second week of the main holiday break with many people travelling down to Weston-Super-Mare, Burnham-on-Sea and Minehead itself, all popular holiday resorts for the people from the Midlands, but at least where we were staying was peaceful itself.

The weather on the journey down had been wonderful, but the Sunday came in very wet and quite cool. Sarah got nowhere near the beach, and this was how our week continued. We did get the odd period of dry weather and on the one occasion we made the beach, Sarah managed to a build a castle or two. The most exciting thing we did was find a few fossils lying on the beach, these Sarah still has.

We did see a bit of Somerset, mainly from the car, and whilst driving across Exmoor, we saw the odd red grouse and buzzard. At Dunster we had the highlight of the week. We were walking round the castle grounds, where a small stream ran through, and stopped by a bridge. Imagine our amazement as two large bats flew out from under the brick bridge. These were two greater horseshoe bats, and this was in broad daylight. According to my field guide, these bats are a woodland bat, so what they were doing there I have no idea – not that any of us were complaining, we just enjoyed sharing their company for a short while.

During the week we saw several deer on Exmoor, and one group looked particularly large so we presumed they were red deer, our largest native species. They certainly looked heavier and had longer antlers than the fallow deer we are familiar with on Cannock Chase.

Exmoor also seemed to have a good population of stoats. Driving on many of the country lanes which cross the moor we had several sightings; one which ran in front of us was actually carrying a small animal in its mouth, dinner for the family no doubt.

We at least brought a few happy memories back home with us. You could do little about the weather, we were just sorry for Sarah; you are only young once. Back to the bird study course. Twenty-eight members enrolled including four new faces, so the numbers were holding up well. We planned the species of birds we would cover at the indoor meetings and arranged our field meetings, these being the sessions most course members were really interested in. Learning about birds was fine, seeing them and experiencing them was better, and I cannot argue with that.

In September, we would visit Titchwell in Norfolk; October,

Gibraltar Point in Lincolnshire; and, November, we would try somewhere local that decision could be left until nearer the date. Both Titchwell and Gibraltar Point were new venues for me.

In 1973, the RSPB purchased over 400 acres of derelict farmland, which had been abandoned for almost twenty years since flooded by rough seas which broke through the coastal defences. Over recent years, much work had been carried out and the range of species was very good. For many years, local birders had the place to themselves so they might resent the RSPBs. involvement which is now bringing in visitors, such as us, from further afield.

We arrived in decent weather conditions, I am pleased to say, and walked down the pathway to the shore. You could see just how the RSPB were converting the area and, once completed, it should be a very superb area. We were very fortunate to see two marsh harriers fly across in front of us; we had been informed that they were breeding there and that the odd bittern had been reported. To see one of those would be something rather special.

A very good selection of waders were on the shore, ranging from the largest – curlews down to the smaller sanderling. The latter were doing their usual performance, chasing the tide both in and out, racing as they searched for food, delightful birds. Although we had good numbers of waders, it was not going to compare with Snettisham a few miles north of there, where, as mentioned previously, birds are seen in their tens of thousands.

That day was not just waders, numbers of duck were on the sea, especially common scoters and wigeons, with a few terns passing through; one flock of about fifty little terns was very spectacular. A large bird was picked up, well out at sea, and after careful observation we were delighted to see it was a red-throated diver, that bird went down well for all of us. Little did we know, but red was going to be the colour of the day! A small area of sand was low lying and covered with water, making a small lake, and several of the longer legged waders, redshanks, oystercatchers, two greenshanks and a few bar-tailed godwits were feeding in this so we watched these with interest. I suddenly became aware of a small, longish billed bird, swimming in the water and spinning round in circles – an adrenalin rush commenced. I called to my friends, pointed out the bird, it was a juvenile red-necked phalarope, what a great bird to get. None of my friends had ever seen one before, it was only my second. When we mentioned the name, red-necked phalarope, a stampede started with birders running from all directions; this was obviously the bird of the day for many, and we had found it. Not a bad feeling at all.

Red-necked phalaropes are a very scarce breeding species in the UK, with just a few pairs hanging on in Scotland. Their usual migration route is in a south easterly direction, heading towards the Indian Ocean and the Persian Gulf, where it winters at sea. We were on the right side of the UK to catch this bird in transit to warmer climes. Have a safe journey.

Titchwell had certainly done us proud, many interesting birds to add to our various lists and for many the red-throated diver was a 'Lifer', and as mentioned earlier, the red-necked phalarope was a 'Lifer' for them all. I think it was a safe bet that we would be back at Titchwell again.

Gibraltar Point has long been a Mecca for birders. The list of species seen there include many a rarity never recorded anywhere else. It has a field station and observatory where much bird ringing is carried out. It is managed by the Lincolnshire Trust for Nature Conservation and is now a National Nature Reserve and an SSSI. The reserve lies three miles south of Skegness, so a spot of birding can be accompanied by time at the seaside! Not a bad combination should you have young children.

We arrived on a breezy, but clear, morning; the only problem was the amount of sand being blown about by the breeze, so you had to be a little cautious in which direction you looked. Driven sand and optics are not a good mix.

As we got out of our cars a couple of birders rushed across to us, pointing wildly down the reserve, two common cranes had just departed. In the distance two dark specks were flying southwards across The Wash; at this distance, they could have been any large bird – no way could we count these as a sighting. We just hoped this was not going to be the story of our visit – nearly birds!

It was not. We quickly learned that a male black redstart was performing further down the car park, so a quick stroll was called for. Not many black redstarts breed in the UK and the few that do seem to be favouring larger cities. London and Birmingham have a few pairs. I have seen them in Birmingham myself when I worked in the city, but most of my colleagues that day had not, so we set off to put that right.

A group of twenty or so birders, all gazing intently at a small bird hopping round like a robin, was our guide. Black redstarts are accommodating birds and this one was being feed crumbled up cake, and appeared to be enjoying it. They are a European species and I understand that in their native countries they are quite tame and confiding; this bird was certainly proving that point, as tame as our robins. It was probably a safe bet to presume this bird had come across from the continent and was not a British bird, but who cared, they all count. Missing out on the cranes no longer mattered.

We made our way along the footpath which took us through the Old Marsh to the beach and foreshore which gazed out into the North Sea. Several waders were evident. Much as we saw last month, when at Titchwell, the impressive feature was the many duck to be seen on the sea.

The flock of common scoter was massive, several hundred birds there, and as they did their synchronised diving, they looked very impressive. We managed to shelter out of the wind and set up our scopes, I wanted to work our way through the scoter just in case the odd velvet scoter was tucked in among them. Here we were looking for a black bird with a white wing patch, but I was not optimistic as the sea was quite rough due to the breeze with many white 'horses'. Our luck, however, held; two birds were picked out, and after a few minutes of careful observation, we had our velvet scoter – two drakes – we could now relax.

A few red-breasted mergansers were also to be seen and eider ducks were quite plentiful, always a delight to see, the drakes are very smart birds indeed. Wigeon were plentiful, both on the sea and on the reserve and many gulls were sporting about. I had not seen so many great black-backed gulls for a long time and common gulls were living up to their name. The odd tern was still passing through, mainly well out at sea, and we took most of these to be Sandwich terns judging by their size and Arctic terns, and whilst watching these a very heavy billed tern flew down the shore. I could not believe my eyes – I was looking at a gull-billed tern. The heavy black bill and black legs showed up really well, this was certainly no Sandwich tern. Before today, this tern had only been a picture in a book; I had never dreamed of seeing one in the UK, but here it was. My colleagues could not believe their luck, one or two had never heard of the bird previously, a 'Lifer' for us all. It was moments like this that made a long journey really worthwhile.

After the excitement of the black redstart, velvet scoter and now the gull-billed tern, there was only one way the rest of our day could go, and that was much quieter. Plenty of birds to see, all of which we were familiar with, but no complaints. We reported the gull-billed tern before we left and they were pleased to hear about it as it collaborated an earlier report. So we journeyed home, very contented after another good day, and as I have mentioned previously, I was being paid to do this; I was a lucky man indeed.

Our meeting in November was arranged. Crossbills had been reported from Cannock Chase in sizable flocks. Crossbills are another bird which birders love to see and it does not matter how frequently they do so. They are a magical small bird with a bill which is perfectly designed for their mode of feeding. The two parts of the beak, (the mandibles) cross over at the tip which enables them to extract the seeds from pine cones with ease, very aptly named. The male is also a very attractive bird having a bright red rump, very striking in flight. The female – she also is no slouch – has a greenish-yellow rump. They look a large and hefty finch, although they are only 17 cm in length. In flight they are very vocal which is a good identification aid, this being a metallic 'kip-kip', oft repeated. They are an early breeding species who coincide this with the ripening of the cones which can commence in February. The softer cones of spruce trees being their particular favourite at this time. Enough about the bird, let us go and find it!

The weather was kind to us, a dry and reasonably bright day was forecast. From information gleaned from birding friends, crossbills had been seen for a few days now at Strawberry Hill, an area I was familiar with. They were apparently seen regularly drinking at a small stream which passes through. Crossbills require regular water as the seeds from the cones contain a gluey extract which causes their bills to stick, so this has to be freed frequently.

We parked up at the Seven Springs Car Park, listening to a nuthatch calling, and a great spotted woodpecker drumming, before walking off towards Strawberry Hill. Initially you walk through deciduous woodland before coming out into forestry planted coniferous woodland, mainly a mixture of Norway spruce and larch with the odd old Scot's pine still standing proudly – a wonderful tree and native. Where the pathways divided, a small stream crossed, and it was here the crossbills were seen recently, or so my informant claimed. A good stand of twenty or so Norway spruce were growing by the stream, so we settle in and studied these closely both visually and audibly.

We spent a good half an hour with little to report. Conifer plantations were not the most popular areas for woodland birds being home to the more specialised species, coal tits being one, and we did at least see and hear these. Ravens were calling from up on high and a mewing buzzard glided across, and then we heard what we were waiting for: 'Kip-kip', 'kip-kip', rang out several times – crossbills were about –and to our delight, a small flock of nine fluttered down to the stream and proceeded to bathe and drink. We just stood still and silent as we watched these incredible birds going about their business. It must have lasted a good five minutes before they were up and away, but they did not go far, they flew up into the nearby Norway spruces where we had wonderful views of them feeding; they were a most acrobatic bird, and showed us all their skills.

After half an hour's wait, we had a memorable half an hour enjoying this small group; two further visits were made to the stream before they departed, with stomachs full and thirsts quenched.

We made our way back down to Seven Springs enjoying a party of siskins and lesser redpolls feeding away among the deciduous trees, silver birches appearing to be their particular favourites. Several species of titmice were to be seen – especially blue, great and long-tailed tits, all actively feeding away – and amongst a group of chaffinches feeding on fallen beech mast, two male bramblings were seen. We were doing very well with woodland birds; mind you, there were enough trees for them, it was after all, Cannock Chase!

Time had finally caught up with us; time to make our ways back home. It had been another useful trip out to show just what can be seen locally, and as it was also our last field meeting of the year. I must now think of where we would go and what we could see come the new year.

We would sort that out at our first indoor meeting.

The final year of the 70s is nigh, and I have one or two ideas to discuss when we commence our classes in January. Until then, I had Christmas and the New Year to look forward to.

Back at our second term of that course, the question was raised by members: 'Could we run a summer course, so we could study birds breeding?' That sounded a good idea to me, but would it to the University? There was only one way to find out – ask!

The University were happy with the suggestion as long as a minimum number of students enrolled, this being twenty. I saw no difficulty with that; the biggest problem was the fact we could not commence before the next year, so we would wait and see. Provisionally, the course members were happy to wait.

What to do at the start of that term? We would commence with a visit to the Staffordshire/Derbyshire Moorlands to see the red grouse, calling in at Tittesworth Reservoir in transit. We had been to the moors previously, but it was all back to bird lists, and the chance to start off with some of the more unusual birds. February, we would visit Blithfield Reservoir, and come March, we would wait until nearer the date to see if we had any early migrants coming in.

Tittesworth Reservoir initially looked rather quiet, but this was quickly sorted out when a large flock of Canada geese flew in, and these birds rarely do anything quietly. Going through the flock, we picked out a small number of barnacle geese which were always worth closer study – a very smart bird. A few greylag geese were also scattered through the flock, so that was not a bad start to things.

Concentrating our efforts over the water, we quickly found mallards, teals, wigeons, tufted ducks, North American ruddy ducks, pochards, goldeneyes, goosanders and a drake scaup; a cracking bird to start the year off with. The usual coots, moorhens, cormorants, grebes, the commoner gulls and the normal passerines on the feeders, made up the picture, many of which were 'Year Ticks', needless to say.

A coffee was called for and then off to the moors, on which patches of snow could be seen, it was winter up there!

We turned off to cross Axe Edge Moor in real wintery looking conditions; it was almost completely snow covered with just the thicker gorse protruding through. The first birds seen were a small flock of pipits, we presumed all meadow pipits. They did not hang around to be studied in detail and a pair of raven were circling overhead, not that they found anything, they just drifted off.

As we crossed over the moor, the conditions improved, not so much snow evident. The land there was at a slightly lower altitude than earlier on which no doubt accounted for less snow, although there was still enough.

We pulled in at a spot where we could park up our cars, we were lucky no one else was there, and settled down to wait; we did not have long to do so. Whirring in over the gorse came seven red grouse, crossing the road in front of us and vanishing over a ridge. All in all, I doubt if we saw them for more than half a minute, but short though the time was, we had a wonderful view and could hear their wing beats as they were very close. For those who had never seen red grouse previously, their first sighting was a bit special.

Not a lot else was out on the moors that day, although we did catch up with a few more grouse, and as the weather was beginning to bite, we decided enough was enough and so we made our ways home. A decent start to a new year and on completing my day's list we had seen forty-one species, not a bad total at all.

Conditions at Blithfield Reservoir were not favourable to birding – heavy rain and poor visibility – and, due to the conditions, only four of us turned out. We parked up on the Watery Lane car park where we could at least view from the dryness of our cars. We may well have waterproof clothing, you just cannot view well through wet optics – they may be waterproof, but you cannot look through lenses which have water over them, hence the use of the cars.

Even though the conditions were poor, birds were there to be seen. A flock of about two hundred wigeons were close in, a few teals were along the water's edge, the normal mallards and coots were to be seen and a large flock of geese were further out. After careful scrutiny these proved to be all Canada geese, and whilst watching these they all took off to vanish down the reservoir in their usual noisy flight, Canada's rarely do anything quietly.

A pair of goldeneyes flew in and as we were enjoying these I picked up four swans approaching through the gloom. Something about these four birds made me point them out to my colleagues. The birds looked short necked and their necks were held quite straight, lacking the graceful curve of the mute swan's neck, had we four Bewick's swans swimming towards us? After what seemed an eternity, we obtained the views we wanted, and Bewick's swans they most certainly were. The rain and gloom no longer mattered, Bewick's swans were not common place on local waters and to see them on your own doorstep was certainly more cost effective than driving down to Slimbridge. After a few minutes, the swans had swum through so we decided to drive over the causeway and see if anything could be found in Admaston Reach.

Things were very quiet, a few wigeons and two oystercatchers were all we could find. Further down in Blithe Bay, a few mute swans were barely visible and a small group of greylag geese were grazing the shore. The latter are slowly becoming more regular sightings, they were all no doubt feral birds, bred and released for shooting we presume; true wild greylags were rarely seen locally, the bulk end up in Scotland.

A small flock of dark looking ducks landed close in and we were delighted to see these were North American ruddy ducks, a bird which is rapidly becoming one of my favourite ducks. They may have no right to be here, being feral like the greylags, none had ever flown in from across the 'pond'. These were all the off-springs of escapees, but none of us were worried over that slight detail.

Once these ducks had swum from sight we decided to call it a day; the rain was getting heavier and the gloom even denser, but the Bewick's and the ruddy ducks had made our day for us, so we were not complaining, and we had not got wet!

Our thoughts for chasing after any early summer migrants was rapidly receding, apart from the odd chiffchaff and blackcap little was being reported, so we decided to concentrate on late winter migrants. Reports had been made of a hen harrier and great grey shrike from Beeley Moor in Derbyshire, both birds being seen regularly from an area locally known as the 'Triangle'. I knew of this spot so we decided to travel over the borders into our neighbouring county of Derbyshire once again, although visiting different moorlands from our last trip. We were in 'Twitch' mode. Our day commenced very well, it was a clear blue sky and the forecast was for it to continue until early afternoon when rain was coming in. If that proved to be the case, we would be more than happy. Fifteen of us made the trip, four cars required, and for once I was a passenger not a driver.

The drive up from the village of Beeley village passed the Beeley Plantation, and the Hall Bank Plantation, and we were very pleased to see a large mixed flock of fieldfares and redwings still feeding away; they would not be there for much longer.

Once hitting the moors trees become rather thin on the ground – if you would excuse the pun – we were now in the land of red grouse, or at least we should have been, and their requirements are gorse and heather. We were slowly following another car which, judging by its speed, also contains birders, when it's hazard lights flashed, it stopped, and out leapt two people to look over the wall – we did likewise.

Quartering the ground, no more than fifty yards away, was a magnificent male hen harrier; the first of the two birds we really hoped to see. The bird glided back and forth with little or no effort before it eventually vanished from sight, a lovely few minutes. As I walked to thank the two birders who had made this all possible, I realised I knew them: they were members of the Burton-on-Trent Branch of the RSPB We had a chat and I was more than ever thankful we met up with them.

They had seen the great grey shrike about half an hour before and were able to give me a positive location in the 'Triangle', but even more important than this news: they had also seen a goshawk a little further on, near Harewood Grange. This bird had been seen hunting over Harewood Moor and kept on returning to a specific piece of conifer plantation. The favourite breeding location for goshawks is this type of woodland.

Goshawks currently are among our rarest breeding birds-of-prey, so the chance of seeing one of these was not to be missed. After a few minutes' conversation, we decided to go straight to the goshawk site and call to look for the shrike on our return journey.

Once again, I was fortunate in knowing the area so we made our way without mishap and parked up in a suitable spot to view much of the moor; fortunately, conditions were still good, and there was no rain as yet. You have days when you think someone up there loves you; I doubt if we had been here ten minutes before the gos' appeared. It flew almost over our heads and proceeded to flap and glide its way over the moor, going hither and hither, it appeared to have no plan. A couple of times it dropped to the ground, coming up with nothing, but then it suddenly raced off at speed to vanish from sight. A minute or so later, back came the bird, with a still live thrush-like looking bird, firmly clasped in its claws. 'Madam Goshawk' was going to feast well that night.

We were happy, now for the shrike. The 'Triangle' had a few small areas of trees and we had our instructions of which group to look for. Shrikes regularly perch on bare branches studying the land nearby where they hunt their prey which can vary, but they are red blood eaters in the full sense of the word, and smaller birds are their favoured diet at that time of the year. Birders have had many a discussion regarding shrikes and several consider they should be included among the birds-of-prey. I do not subscribe to this logic, but I fully understand the reasoning behind it.

We found the spot and shared things with a few more birders; the more eyes the better, I always say! A particular silver birch stump was pointed out to us this, it was claimed, was the favoured perching point for the shrike so we settled down to wait, and wait was certainly the name of the game. Forty-five minutes passed and I was beginning to think our luck had run out, and it also commenced to spot with rain. Then a voice called out, 'Here it is,' and true to what we had been told, the shrike landed on its favourite stump and commenced to preen itself. For five minutes or so, we enjoyed the spectacle; it was the longest period of time I had ever been able to study a great grey shrike – normally, a few seconds and the bird has gone. This bird was a real poser, and we were mightily grateful. Preening over, the bird was off and that was that for the day. The rain was also increasing in intensity which was a good sign for us to go home. To say that was a special day is putting it mildly; we had come out for two special birds and had seen three – plus other birds. A fitting conclusion to the end of our course, it would be very interesting to see how things would go come September when we would start a new course. I could now look forward to a few months doing just what the family wanted, and number one priority was to book up a holiday.

Friends of ours own a holiday cottage at Wells in Norfolk, so we managed to book this for a week in August – thanks to a cancellation – so we had that to look forward to; although I had visited Norfolk for the odd bird watching trip, it would be a new area for Dorothy and Sarah. As well as being a top birding area, it also has many other points of interest, so all we wanted now was the weather.

Wells was a few months away, so now we had a few ventures nearer to hand to contemplate, and a walk along the River Dove was worth serious thought; especially as it was less than an hour's drive from home. Dovedale, our chosen venue, could be very busy especially on a Sunday so we had chosen a late April Saturday for our trip out, and a lovely day it was too. Dorothy and myself had long had an affection for Dovedale, we had cycled there many times years ago, and the place had never lost its appeal, and Sarah, fortunately, enjoyed the place as much. It also had an interesting bird population, especially dipper and goosander, so an hour or two could be well spent. We arrived to find Sarah wanting to walk up to the top of Thorpe Cloud, one of the highest peaks at Dovedale. On reaching the top, I thought she wished she had not; in my youthful days, I always looked on this peak as a mountain – mind you, the view was pretty spectacular to say the least.

Back to the river. After an initial two or three crossings of the stepping stones, children do have peculiar ideas of what is fun, we slowly made our way along the river and it was not long before we saw our first dipper of the morning. We had hit lucky, this was the birds favourite feeding spot and it had a nest not far away to which it kept flying with food.

Dipper are amazing birds. They are only about 18 cm in length; they are a passerine, which means, loosely: a perching bird – yet they obtain most of their food from underwater, although they are not webbed footed.

Our bird had a favourite piece of rock sticking up out of the river to which it regularly returned and dropped back into the river to seek food again. This procedure was repeated many times and it kept on flying off in the same direction. We could not see exactly where it finished up, but it was obviously at a nest, and judging by its activity, it must have had young. This has been a magical few minutes and many walkers had past us by with not even a look. I could never be a serious walker, there was far too much to see and enjoy; I would never get to my destination.

We moved on up river. On the opposite bank the rocky crags of Dovedale Castle loomed up, it was no castle, just a superb rock formation and on the weirs beneath another dipper was feeding away. Walking on the Twelve Apostles dominated the view – further rocky formations. More or less opposite these was Lover's Leap.

The story has it that a rejected maiden threw herself off this precipice, but was saved by bushes growing beneath. She then spent the rest of her life in prolonged seclusion. They do say the course of true love does not run smooth!

Whilst enjoying these sights, Sarah brought our attention to a small bird sitting out on a nearby rock, a superb male wheatear. The Dales are the nearest area to where we live for these delightful little birds. They are true posers and do not believe in hiding their light beneath a bushel, they are beautiful and wish the world to know it. Thank you wheatear, we do!

Due to our climbing Thorpe Cloud, time had caught up with us so we commenced our return journey, and quickly stopped – a drake goosander had just bobbed up from beneath the river's surface, and here again we have quite a bird. They are a saw bill and live on fish which they swim after under water, and the odd pair have commenced to live on some of the Dales faster flowing rivers such as the Dove, Manifold and Derwent. I would not think their appearance was greatly appreciated by the local trout fishermen who have to pay for their fishing!

As we approached the Stepping Stones, we stopped: a deep, guttural croak was heard, a raven was about, but search as hard as we could it was not located. We would have liked to have seen the bird, raven locally are an uncommon bird. That day it was not to be, but it brought our trip out to a perfect conclusion. Four cracking birds less than an hour from home, now that cannot be bad.

One thing I made it my business to do when we first came to live in Yoxall was to get to know the local farmers. Many of these farms had been in the same family for generations, and most were grazing of sheep and cattle – not too many acres were cultivated – and the bird life on these farms was wonderful. Skylarks were very common and there can be no better sound in the English countryside than singing skylarks, Vaughan Williams certainly knew what he was on about when he wrote his piece 'The Lark Ascending'. Good as this piece of music is, I do not think he beat the real thing!

I think many of the farmers were quite surprised when asked for permission to walk their land, and without exception this was granted. Many a friendship developed from this, and many a pint of bitter was drunk down at the local pub. Life in the countryside was not all work.

We walked many a mile across fields, seeing interesting birds. Curlews still nested; for a couple of years, we had common sandpiper nest along the shores of the River Swarbourn and cormorants were regularly seen in the River Trent. Some of the meadows had old ponds surrounded by marshy ground, snipe and lapwings were to be found, and we had all of this to ourselves. One year, we were thrilled to bits to find a nesting redshank – a bit special this one. They may not be a rare bird, but they were far from common in our neck of the woods.

Time for our holiday arrived, it was mid-August, and off to Wells we went. The journey to Norfolk was accomplished without any real problems, traffic was quite light. We quickly located the cottage which was a lovely old building, about three hundred years old with car parking space, this spot no doubt was a garden when the cottage was built.

Wells is a delightful small town, not quite on the coast due to tidal changes over the years; its full name of Wells-next-the Sea tells you all you want to know. To reach the sea, shipping had to go out along a channel and then out into Holkham Bay. The tide was in that day so a few small craft were heading out and in the opposite direction the odd seal's head popped up to survey the scene, much to Sarah's delight. Oystercatchers and gulls were very vocal, with the latter being not at all worried by people; the visitors, no doubt, were looked upon as being food providers.

As well as getting to know our way round Wells, we also needed to buy a few provisions; our friends had also told us about a fish and chip shop which they claimed to be the best in the locality, so we needed to find this. We duly did and that sorted our dinner out for that evening; it was less than a five-minute walk from the cottage – I will be back later.

Sunday dawned bright and warm, so we decided not to travel any distance, we would walk down to the beach near Wells. Before I forget, the fish and chips were delicious; the shop used fish caught by local fishermen, so they were lovely and fresh. I think we might be back during the week!

We had a very leisurely stroll down the channel to the Holkham Dunes National Nature Reserve which had very interesting pine woods and the dunes themselves supported an exceptional range of marine plants. I had heard rumours that parrot crossbills had been seen and that the common crossbill was plentiful in the pine woods. Should that prove to be true, this was likely not to be our only visit.

At that time of the year, bird song was less, the breeding season had been completed so the male birds no longer had cause to try and attract a mate; sound was now just a question of calls, with the odd exception. Robins do sing throughout the year, as do a few territory owning birds. Pine woods also have a lower number of species, food is not so readily available as in deciduous woodlands, so they are normally quieter which helped us. If crossbills were about we should hear their 'kip, kip' call. We lived in hope.

We walked slowly along the fringe of the pine woods so we were able to view over the marsh areas as well as the woods. From the woods, the odd call of the coal tit could be heard and from the fringe of the wood where a few bushes grew, chaffinch could be heard calling. Over the marshy areas, several dragonflies could be seen including one very large specimen – too far away to be certain of identification, unfortunately – and butterflies were very evident, a superb sight.

Stonechats could be seen over the marshy area where several small trees were growing – ideal perching posts for the stonechats. The calls of curlews and redshanks were also heard – ideal territory for these two waders. Rounding a dune, we stopped: in an expanse of water, an interesting collection of waders could be seen. The majority were black-tailed godwits with two or three greenshanks and a mixture of smaller waders, these required careful scrutiny. They turned out to be dunlins, common sandpipers and a solitary wood sandpiper, well worth stopping for. Dorothy gave me a nudge and pointed to the pine trees. From out of these came the call we had been waiting; for, 'kip, kip' was ringing out and judging by the volume it was several birds, not one or two. We made our way slowly into the trees and located the group of birds, over thirty of them; one of the largest group of crossbills I had ever seen. They were feeding away on the soft spruce cones and we settled down to study them all closely. Fortunately, crossbills are a fairly tolerant species and as long as you do not make a noise or move violently, they will just get on with things. Both Dorothy and I went through these birds with great care, not once, several times, but they all proved to be just the common crossbill – no parrots where tucked in amongst these. We did at least manage an accurate count, our estimate of over thirty was correct. In fact, we had thirty-four, and some of the males looked beautiful, so scarlet in the sun; you would have thought they were a tropical bird. Even Sarah seemed impressed with these birds, although I think she was more concerned with the thoughts of an ice cream she had been promised.

We made our way slowly back to the car parking area where a café was located; Dorothy and I for coffee and something to eat, Sarah more interested in the prospect the ice cream. This we enjoyed and slowly walked back to Wells, a most pleasant walk, and we did not mind having to go back in the hope of finding the parrot crossbills.

The following day we were back, and this time, I drove down which gave us more time to spend in the woods and on the dunes; once again, the weather was very pleasant.

The previous day, we had walked eastwards, now we were heading west, through the Holkham Meals towards Holkham Gap and Lady Ann's Road – whether we would get that far remained to be seen.

Walking along the fringe of the woods, there was a fair bit of bird activity going on, which was different from the day before. The finches looked as though they were already flocking up, chaffinches in double figures together, and a goodly number of siskins and redpolls were to be seen. Most of the latter were feeding high in the trees, so we just presumed these to be lesser redpolls, although other redpolls could easily have been mixed in amongst them.

As we progressed further, the odd bullfinch was seen and one large old holly tree had a large number of goldcrests feeding on it; there must have been some insect infestation on this tree. Whatever it was, the crests were enjoying their bonanza and probably doing the tree a favour too!

We arrived at Lady Ann's Road far quicker than expected, so we turned off and visit the Dunes and that proved to be the right decision. Just as we were about to come out of the pines, a loud and rather harsh 'cherk-cherk' was heard. It was not a call I recognised, but seconds after hearing it, two birds landed on the ground in front of us and proceeded to peck around the fallen cones, parrot crossbills. We just stood rock still, these birds were less than twenty feet away and gave us not a second glance.

Having seen the common crossbills so well before, there was no way we would mistake these today. They may only be slightly larger, but their black bill is a very powerful looking tool and their head is more rectangular and heavy looking. You would not want to put your finger in this bird's bill. We birders usually have to chase 'Lifers', not have them come to chase us. No complaints there.

The Dunes were very quiet, the odd curlew and oystercatcher, although a small passage of terns took place. These were far out at sea and, judging by their heavy looking flight, we presumed them to be Sandwich terns.

Moving on through the Dunes, we spotted a small flock of linnets and something about two of the birds caught our attention. Dorothy had a better angled view than I did, and as they flew, she noted they had a reddish-pink rump and a pale wing bar; these were no linnets that was for sure. We followed them closely and, finally, obtained the view we wanted. We saw their miniscule pale yellow bill, they were two twite. These birds may not have been a 'Lifer', but they were very thin on the ground those days, so we took them with pleasure.

Back now to the car park for a spot of lunch at the café, and it would be more than ice cream for Sarah, argue though she might, and did!

The pleasant weather appeared to be continuing, so for a change, we had decided to visit Holkham Hall and estate which had been home to the Earl of Leicester's family for many years, and still is. The Hall was worthy of visiting we had been told and the estate also has a large lake – where if my information was correct – Egyptian geese had been released and were now breeding in a completely wild state, and that alone was worth the visit. There was also a very good café on-site, which removed the problem of taking food, so we could just relax.

As we dove through to park near the Hall, a large herd of fallow deer crossed the road in front of us; they were in no hurry and we spent a few minutes watching them file across. Being on an estate such as this, I suppose they were quite used to cars so they did not dash off as a truly wild deer would. Wild or semi-domestic, they were a wonderful sight so close.

We arrived at the car park, made our way to the café for coffee and a soft drink for Sarah, checked what they had available for lunch, and set off.

The pleasant morning was fading rapidly, so it was decision time. Dorothy and Sarah decided to visit the Hall which was due to open shortly; I put on my waterproof attire and set off Egyptian goose hunting.

The rain did come, but fortunately only lightly, so conditions were not that bad. There was a large monument in the woodland near the top of the lake and I had been told that frequently a tawny owl could be seen sitting on the monument or perched in trees nearby. Our old friend the tawny was always worth spending some time on, and there was no difficulty in locating the monument – large it certainly was.

I found I was not the only birder looking for the tawny, several others were there and to my amazement one of them called out, 'Hello Brian,' I looked and saw it was a member of my bird class. Tony, as is his name, had been there for about an hour and he had at least seen a little owl, and he was able to take me to the tree and point the bird out for me. A very good start to the day as far as I was concerned.

A few more minutes passed and a call went up, 'Here he comes,' and gliding onto the monument came our tawny owl; whether it was a him or her was of no significance, what was important is the fact it was a tawny owl, and at its sighting about twenty birders became happier people.

Owls are both fascinating birds and they also seem to be fascinated by people. They will frequently sit quite still just staring down at people beneath, and if there is a line of people they slowly turn their heads as though counting us up. Never seeming to blink and never taking their eyes of us, and what eyes.

To me it is the archetypal owl. Large, almost black eyes set in the centre of two facial discs which stare ahead all the time. Their head movement is such that they never take their eyes off you, they just twist their head and their body remains still. Whenever I see one, I expect its head to screw off!

Our 'Strix aluco', to give our bird its scientific name, was a real poser and it knew it. Off now to find the geese, having said cheerio to

Tony who had elsewhere to go. I had almost walked completely round the lake before I came across my first Egyptian goose; I should say geese, there were twenty-seven of them. Looking further across the slopes of Howe Hill, there were more to be seen, plus a decent flock of greylag geese. Holkham was certainly living up to expectations.

On the lake itself were many coot, a few moorhen, several tufted ducks, my old friend the ruddy duck – I will drop the American tag – these birds have never seen America. The odd oystercatcher walked the shore and a kingfisher flew past on several occasions, no complaints there. Common terns were also feeding on the lake and I would not be surprised if some of these had not bred there.

Time to find Dorothy and Sarah. Lunch called, and then we would go to look around Wells as there were one or two things we needed to buy. I knew one thing: they claimed Norfolk to be the Mecca for bird watching, and they might be right.

The fine weather was continuing so a visit to either Cley marshes or Blakeney Point was on the agenda, both being top birding areas; for Wednesday, we chose Cley. I understood that Cley nature reserve had been run by the Norfolk Naturalists Trust since 1926; originally, much shooting took place locally and literature refers to the fact the marshes had a bloodthirsty history before the Trust moved in. Shooting still occurred in Norfolk, but much conservation work was now carried out by the various conservational bodies who owned or managed large areas of the county.

We parked up by the coastguard station on Cley eye, and we were lucky, there was no one available to collect the parking fee. We decided we would walk along the shingle bank towards Arnold's Marsh, from there we could view both the sea and the reserve. A slight breeze was coming in off the sea making it most pleasant for walking.

Thanks to the breeze, many gulls were drifting past and among them were goodly number of kittiwakes; a gull is not seen often in the part of the country from whence we came. I was also pleased with the number of little gulls that were passing through, some of which drifted into the reserve, they did seem to have a preference for fresh water for bathing in. On the other hand, many of the larger gulls prefer salt water and apart from breeding rarely spend a large amount of time on dry land.

Auks were also on the move, both guillemots and razorbills, very marine these birds. Norfolk is almost cliffless apart from up at Hunstanton, and I was not aware of any auks breeding there so these birds were probably moving down from northern England on their way out into the Atlantic for the winter.

Large numbers of waders were on the marshes: curlews, redshanks, godwits and oystercatchers were easily picked up, and running in the shallow lagoons were dunlins, knots and ringed plovers. The calls, especially from the curlews, redshanks and oystercatchers is quite striking. Living in Staffordshire, we were not used to seeing wading birds in such numbers; it was sights and sounds such as these that made birding so marvellous and special.

We had brought a packed lunch with us so we sat down at the corner of Arnold's Marsh in a sheltered spot to eat our lunch, and whilst doing so, three medium sized waders flew in and landed on a nearby small lagoon. They obviously had not spotted us, and we were pleased they had not – they were three spotted redshanks. Two juveniles and one an adult, who still showed much of his sooty hued summer plumage, and for a few minutes we were able to share the scene with them. Very elegant birds, they do not breed in the UK; these birds were on passage from further north, and we were only too pleased to spend this period of time with them.

On our return journey to the car we saw nothing new, but we all agreed the walk had been well worth the effort and the holiday was certainly proving to be most enjoyable, with the range of birds being seen very good. It would be interesting to see just how many different species we saw in the week, three figures does not look out of the question. And there was still no car parking attendant!

On our short journey home, the weather changed almost dramatically. A thunder storm came in from off the North Sea and for about ten minutes it crashed round with a vengeance, leaving the road awash in places. We were very pleased not to be still out walking that was for sure. It had stopped when we arrived so we were happy with that. Now what to do the next day; according to the weather forecast, it still looked good although it may be duller.

We decided upon on Blakeney Point. We had two options there, the

127

Point was over three miles in length or we could go up to Morston Quay and cross in one of the small motor boats that did the trip regularly, tide depending. A quick check on the tides, they were ideal for what we wanted, so a quick drive to Morston is made. We were lucky, a boat was about to sail with room for us. On the pleasant journey across, we had the company of several seals; one of which, came very close to the boat and almost escorted us across. According to the boat owner, this particular seal had more or less adopted his boat and regularly sailed close in; mind you, he had fed the seal on occasion which was probably the real reason for it being so attentive, not that any of the passengers were complaining.

Blakeney Point was owned by the National Trust, they acquired it in 1912 I had been informed, and if that is the case, it is one of the oldest nature reserves in the UK and was long stoney shingle-ridge. Much better visited by boat than a round trip of about seven miles on shingle – not the best of walking conditions.

At peak passage times, the range of birds which could be seen on the Point were legend; August is not a peak time, but a few smaller birds were flicking about in the vegetation along the channel. Several stonechats were to be seen along with the odd whinchat, wheatears were looking for small insects on the shingle, their efforts being supported by a family party of yellow wagtails. In a small strip of water, a largish wader was probing away which I initially took to be a curlew, but something did not look right.

I was very pleased I studied the bird more closely, this was no curlew, it was its cousin, the slightly smaller whimbrel. When seen in isolation these two birds could be easily confused. That day's bird, however, moved closer to us and the two dark lateral crown stripes showed up well as did the decided kink in the bill. They are a darker looking bird than the curlew and not so well patterned. A very good quality bird to see, not one on my anticipated list that was for sure. Of particular interest was the number of swifts passing through. They are one of our shortest stay birds, arriving mid to late April and usually having departed by mid-September. Back home, we normally considered August to be their departure month and see very few in September. That day, they were hurtling through the sky, most noisily, as was their wont.

In some parts of the country, they used to call them 'screechers', and it was easy to understand why. Some bird – aptly named!

The time to depart had arrived, back to the boat we went, again escorted by the seal, and this time the boatman threw it a large fish which the seal gulped down with relish. Another most pleasant day with more interesting birds seen.

Only one more remaining day and once again the weather was holding. We decided to travel further round the north coast and call in at Thornham, have a meander round the various creeks to be found there, or so I had been reliably informed, and then walk across the dunes to Holme where an observatory was sited. Depending upon how the time went, we could then have a quick drive round to Hunstanton to look at the only cliffs found in north Norfolk.

Two other cars were parked up at Thornham Harbour, which was a wild and exposed part of the coast. Various narrow channels ran through the marsh and curlews, redshanks and oystercatchers could be heard calling. Many gulls were to be seen, and on the exposed mud in the harbour common and green sandpiper were feeding away with a flock of nine spotted redshanks amongst them. To call this a harbour was a slight exaggeration, it was really just a channel along which a few boats were moored up, but picturesque in a way. Whilst looking at one very smart boat a call echoed out, a very agitated 'pleet, pleet', oft repeated; what had we here? I had no idea, it was a completely new call to me.

Dorothy suddenly pointed, and along one of the channels, flew a very distinctive black and white bird with long trailing grey legs as it landed in the water. We could not believe what we were looking at: an avocet. We had seen some real quality birds that week, but an avocet took the biscuit. Then I remembered reading about the return of avocets to breed in Norfolk after an absence of many years. Two years ago they bred at Cley, and had continued to do so, but when we were there a few days before I had forgotten about this and we did not go onto the reserve proper to look for them. The fact that one had come to look for us, and found us, is remarkable. Whether this bird was one of ours or a visitor from Holland we should never know, but this was one bird we would never forget.

We spent many minutes enjoying this bird which was not the

slightest bit interested in us; we were just very careful to remain still and talk in whispers. If ever a bird was perfectly designed, both in beauty, elegance and the perfect feeding technique, this was the bird. The bird was wading up to its knees, and swinging its head from side to side, with the up curved bill scooping the many surface-water invertebrates that were available. The timing of those sweeps could easily be set to music, there was almost a rhythm to it. All good things have to come to an end, off it flew back down the channel.

The fact these delightful birds were back breeding in the UK, after many years of absence, was wonderful. All we could now hope was that they were successful and slowly return back in numbers. I was sure the various conservation bodies in Norfolk would give them every chance.

Due to the time spent enjoying the avocet, we decided to miss out on Holme and drive straight to Hunstanton where we could obtain food and have a walk along the cliff tops. A café was found, and food eaten, so we walked over to the cliffs. As with most of the coast round Norfolk, it was in constant conflict with the powers of the sea, and one or two places had been put out of bounds so to speak. In one particular spot, a very large piece of cliff had fallen onto the beach beneath. With the constant erosion by the sea at the base of the cliffs, the heavy over hangs from above would easily drop. Sitting out on a beach can be a dangerous occupation!

Where we parked up was adjacent to an area of open grass, and on there a large flock of curlews were busily feeding away. With the dryness we had experienced that week, I had no idea of what they were feeding on; I would have thought the ground would be too dry and hard for their beaks, but they were obviously finding something.

Walking on a little further we were pleased to see several fulmars, these were gracefully gliding along the cliffs, as they did so well, with just the odd flap and tilt of the wing as help to rise in the air or change direction. Perfect masters of their environment without a doubt.

Time had definitely caught up with us so we commenced our return journey, enjoying wheatears and stonechats as we did, and with a final wave to the curlews, we were on our way. dinner and packing to do. I thought the dinner would be fish and chips again, and we would indulge in a bottle of wine!

The holiday had worked out perfectly: weather was good, the accommodation most comfortable and many birds and memories; Norfolk, we would be back. Incidentally, when I did my week's list we just failed to get three figures; we died in the hole, as they say, on ninety-seven. Another good reason to return, to get the magic hundred.

Back then to my bird course, and once again numbers were good. A lot of retired folk were getting in on this birding game, and as the University gave them special rates, who could blame them?

At our initial session, we discussed our thoughts on where to go for the three field meetings. One would be a local visit, another to go after any special bird that may appear on the scene, should this occur, and the third to be another visit to Spurn Point. As you will recollect, our last visit there proved to be very fruitful. This will be our first field meeting in late September, when passage should be at its highest.

Spurn proved to be a very popular venue with twenty-two of us making the journey. We met up at the local church where we experienced much excitement last year. We had it all to ourselves, no 'Twitch' on; well, at least not here.

At the next car park there was much more activity. North of the car park, up Beacon Lane, lay the Beacon Lane Ponds and there we were informed was a hoopoe, and in a field opposite, a white stork had been seen. No need to ask where we headed, two very interesting birds there to see; hoopoes, especially, were very attractive birds and for many would be a 'Lifer', so would the white stork.

The stork was easily found, a bird this size and colour could hardly hide itself. It was just 'stalking' about the field among a large flock of lapwings. Apologies for the pun, but when seen walking, stalking was the best way to describe it. The day had commenced very well.

Storks last bred in the UK many years ago. It was rumoured the last pair which attempted to breed did so on the tower of Glasgow Cathedral; whether that was true or not, I did not know, but it made a good story. In parts of Europe they are still treated with a certain reverence and many a home has a platform fitted to the roof in the hope the stork will nest on it. Where this bird had originated from we should never know, but the bird did not appear to be ringed so all the signs were it was a wild bird not an escapee.

As we approached the Ponds we saw a large group of birders, well over thirty, all gazing in the same direction – this was usually a good sign of where to look! There, making its way along the shore of one of the ponds was our quarry, the hoopoe. Hoopoes are like no other bird, just have a look in your field guide; to describe them in words is almost an impossibility, but I will try. It is a basically black and white bird with head, shoulders and crest a pinky-brown, just three colours really.

But who put them together was indeed a great artist. I like the way Lars Jonsson describes the bird – 'In flight, it is a revelation of 'firework-display' proportions, recalling, if anything a gigantic butterfly'. I cannot add to that, and all my friends agreed. Some bird, and we had seen it.

We made our way back to the cars, ate our lunches, and settled down to some sea watching; you did not do much of that living in the Midlands!

A good passage of terns, gulls, shearwaters and waders was taking place, and amongst these the odd skua was up to their piratical behaviour. The mixture of species was as before, but one skua seemed rather long and slim – I pointed this bird out to my colleagues – I had a feeling we had a long-tailed skua here, a more uncommon species.

Eventually we got the view we wanted, a long-tailed skua it most certainly was, and apart from for me, it was another 'Lifer' for all. Spurn was again living up to its reputation.

Out far to sea, a long thin line of geese were flying through, at that distance it was impossible to identify them with certainty, but with the speed of their wing beats combined with the fact they did not look large; I presumed them to be brent geese, but we could not really claim them.

A couple of birders came running up to us, 'Quick!' they said. 'A wryneck has just been seen down the lane on a tree in a cottage garden.' We needed no second bidding. Wrynecks were a very uncommon bird with only a few pairs still breeding in the UK; I had only ever seen two in my life.

The cottage did not take much finding, as with the hoopoe, a group of birders were standing in the lane looking into the front garden of the cottage; what the owners must have thought I did not know, but I need not have worried. A couple of the birders had gone up to the cottage and told the lady occupant what was going on, and she was delighted to know she had such a rare bird in her own garden and did not mind how many people looked at it. When you watched this bird feeding on an old apple tree stump, you quickly appreciated where the name 'wryneck' came from. Like the owls I have mentioned previously, this bird nearly twists it head off!

The wryneck eventually decided enough was enough, and flicked round to the back of the cottage and vanished from sight. The birders still rushing down the lane to see the bird looked as though they were going to be disappointed, but in this game you win some, you lose some. After several minutes, the bird did not show again so we decided it was time to go home. Another great birding day over, and Spurn, we would most certainly be back.

It was only as I was journeying home that I realised we had hardly spent any time at all studying the waders; I could never remember not doing that before. It just goes to show how engrossed we were with the birds we did record; mind you, they were a bit special!

Two birds in north Wales drew our attention, making a 'Twitch' into the Principality very interesting. A little egret was on Anglesey and back on the mainland, a black duck had been reported near to Llanfairfechan. Two interesting contrasts here: one bird pure white, one almost black – well, black in name. The little egret would probably be a bird from southern Europe and the duck a north American species, two birds well worth a bit of effort, and 'Lifers' for all of us. Our October 'Twitch' sorted, all we wanted was a bit of luck and some decent weather.

Five cars made the journey and we decided to go to Anglesey first and call in at Llanfairfechan on our return journey. I had been lucky in having the map reference for where the little egret was last seen, near to the Cefni Reservoir, so we made that our first stop, and straight away hit the jackpot. In a field a small white heron was making its way across the ground, probing away with his long bill into the very damp earth, probably seeking out worms. I understood north Wales had some very heavy rain over the past week or so, and this had no doubt brought worms and other creatures up very close to the surface, making perfect feeding conditions for birds with long bills.

I had last seen little egrets when in Egypt, so this bird brought back very pleasant memories; I had never dreamed of seeing one in the UK. We spent some time enjoying this bird before it vanished over a ridge and we decided to go black duck hunting.

Finding the black duck was not going to be so easy, no map reference this time, it was now down to our own observation skills. The black duck is a close relation to our mallard and we do not even know if the bird is a duck or a drake – the information being very scant. Fortunately, I had been able to find out some details on variances with the plumage of the mallard, so hopefully this information would be of assistance. Time would tell!

We arrived at Llanfairfechan and made our way to the beach, hoping to see some birders as we had no real information as to where the bird is being seen, and the beach stretches a long way in both directions. The tide was also turning and we had no idea of its speed. I was just about to toss a coin to decide which way to go when a voice from behind us said 'After the duck lads?' We swung round, a man was out walking his dog, and carrying a pair of binoculars round his neck – usually a good sign. Obviously we said yes, and he pointed west along the beach. A channel was visible cutting through a grassy area along the beach and apparently the duck was seen regularly there amongst the local mallards. The necessary question was raised regarding the sex of the bird, it was a drake and an adult drake. That made things a little easier, not a lot, but we now knew what we were looking for.

Although the bird closely resembles a mallard, an adult, drake black duck, lacks the black head of our mallard and has a mostly blackish-brown body plumage with a buffish-brown head and face, a dark brown crown along with a yellow bill. Not a lot to go for, especially if only seen at distance where it could be readily confused with an eclipse drake mallard.

Nearing the spot, we saw several mallards being driven along the channel by the incoming tide, so it was up telescopes, and at speed. The one redeeming feature regarding this channel was the fact it was not wide; the ducks were swimming through no more than four or so deep, which gave us a chance.

More mallards arrived and, fortunately for us, they seemed to prefer to swim through rather than fly over; there must be some food advantage there for them. One of my colleagues grabbed my arm and pulled me across to his scope, 'I think I have it,' he muttered. A quick look confirmed this, he had indeed, and what was especially so wonderful was the fact he was a new student to the group and a complete beginner. He would not forget that day, and neither would the rest of us.

The ducks vanished down the channel and the tide completed its journey. After a quick look at the many gulls flying round, we returned to our cars for the journey home. Another very successful 'Twitch' under taken.

Although we had decided to have another local field meeting, reports of a night heron from a park in Cardiff were being discussed; here, we were looking at a bird even rarer than the little egret seen the last month. Discussion time, the group were obviously in 'Twitch Mode', Cardiff it would be and back to Wales we went.

To make a day of it we called in near to Swansea, initially to do a bit of sea watching, and there we were very fortunate. We bumped into a group of birders who pointed out a Mediterranean gull to us, another cracking bird for us all. A few of these gulls had reached the UK and the odd pair were now breeding there. They can be easily mistaken for a black-headed gull, except they are what we commonly call a white-winged gull. Adults, which the one we were looking at was, have white wing tips; the black-headed has black. Even though they were moving through to winter plumage, this bird's white wings were clearly seen, plus the fact there were plenty of black-headeds about for comparison. Definitely, a cracking start.

Out at sea, a large group of scoter were to be seen and, hard as we worked, these birds all looked to be the common scoter; we were hoping for the odd velvet scoter to be hidden amongst them, if there were any, and hidden is the operative word. Several grebes were also on the sea – these all turned out to be great crested grebes – none of the rarer species, unfortunately.

The weather was turning decidedly unpleasant, so if we were going to have a chance with the night heron we must move on. The information on the bird was not good in the respect of the bird's age. Juveniles are a very dark looking bird, whereas the adults are brightly coloured: mainly black, grey and white. They are also nocturnal birds which roost up during the day and become active near dusk. How dark it was getting it might soon be dusk.

We found the park without any trouble just as the rain commenced; fortunately, not heavily, but the sky was getting darker all the time. The park was a typical city park: a lake where people boated and fished, large areas of grass and flower beds, which at that time of the year did not boast much colour!

A couple of birders walked past us, and questions were asked. The bird was roosting up in a tree on the island in the lake, and equally important, we were told the bird was a first winter bird – a juvenile. At least we now knew what we were looking for. To have the chance of seeing these two rare heron species within a month of each other, and in the same country, Wales, was a bit special.

Moving onto the lake, a streaky looking bird standing in a bare tree was not difficult to find. There it was, head tucked in as though asleep, so we could not see the bill, which was quite a powerful tool, although the yellowish legs were visible. They are a characteristic heron with a stocky body and frequently sit hunched up, as this bird was doing.

We studied the heron for a few more minutes – it did not wake up – and as the rain was now coming down heavily, we concluded our birding. Another good day, which brought our year to an end and what a year! Several very rare birds and also it gave me a chance to pull in many a bird, which may not have been rare, but I was unlikely to see near to home. I am pleased to say that I have now broken the three hundred mark, and to think I am being paid for this. Somebody, somewhere, must really love me!

See you next year, in the 80s.

THE 80s, WHEN IT REALLY TOOK OFF

The decade started off quietly, my class membership was round the thirty mark, which was considered to be very satisfactory, with the nucleus of members having been with me from when I first took over. After various discussion with the University, it was decided to run a summer course of twelve sessions; a combination of indoor classes and field meetings to take place on an evening, and Wednesday was chosen as the day. It was going to be a split of six indoor sessions and six field meetings, all of which would be local due to the time factor. To get it up and running, the University decided that it would require a minimum of twelve course members. I put this to my current students and was very pleased when sixteen said they liked the idea. The University were pleased with this, so the new course would run that year, commencing in May. This allowed them time for publicity and me to make a few plans. The main advantage to be gained from this new course would be the opportunity to study our breeding birds and the habitats in which they were to be found. We have many birds which only stay here for a few short months, warblers, hirundines, swifts, the cuckoo, and many wood land species, be great to get to grips with some of those. Although I have enjoyed many of those myself, they would be new to many of my students. Dorothy and Sarah may be able to accompany me on some of these field meetings too. Back to current birding. January was a bit unpleasant this year, so we decided to wait until late in the month before arranging our field meetings. When we did, we decided to go locally. Bewick's swans and whooper swans had been reported from Blithfield Reservoir and Chasewater respectively, so combined with the normal winter waterfowl, they would be our venues and we met up first at Chasewater.

Chasewater is a canal feeder reservoir, not very attractive, but has a very good selection of birds, especially gulls. If you want a rare gull, a glaucous or Iceland for instance, this is the place to see them. Gulls congregate here in their thousands and at their evening roost many gull watchers come to study them. Unless you are a gull addict, gull watching is very hard work: they have so many plumage changes depending upon age and season, and in the poor light of evening, you have to be good.

Gull watchers, fortunately, are confiding people. On the odd occasion, I nipped across and I just approached the few I knew well and they would always show me where the special gulls were – if they were there. I could enjoy my gulls and then go home, not having been frustrated and frozen in the process. We should not be back gull watching that day.

The whooper swans at Chasewater appeared to have a favourite spot and this appeared to be off the dam, so to the dam we went. We were not to be disappointed. Five whooper swans were quickly seen, just gliding along without a care in the world. At times, they swam in a line, looking like the fleet sailing by. They are a slender necked bird and I believe they look more elegant than the mute swan, and their black and yellow bills were clearly seen. Unlike the mute swan, they do not have a black knob at the base of their bills. They are a similar size – although they are slightly wider winged – and most of the whoopers seen in the UK are believed to have migrated down from Iceland, and they will move off during March and April, coming back anytime from October depending upon the ice situation back at home. Teal and wigeon numbers were good, the wigeon's whistling call being heard almost continuously, a delightful sound. Great crested grebes were well accounted for, as were Canada geese and coots, and the usual mallards were waiting patiently near the Visitor Centre waiting to be fed. Not a bad start to a new year.

Now for Blithfield. The whereabouts of the Bewick's swans was not clear, although as eleven of them had been reported, we had a few to look for. We decided to make for the causeway, which crosses the reservoir almost in the middle, from where we could look over most of the reservoir with telescopes.

Bewicks's in many respects are a smaller version of the whooper, with a shorter neck and usually more black on the bill. They visit us each winter from the Arctic tundra via the southern Baltic, some stopping off in western Europe; although the majority arrive here, with Slimbridge being the best place to see them in number. Most years the odd few are seen locally, with eleven being a tidy flock, as long as we can find them.

We parked up in the car park in Watery Lane and surveyed the southern end of the reservoir. A few mute swans could be seen, also many Canada geese – wigeons are as musical as they were at Chasewater – and the odd large gull was seen. A great black-backed gull was standing out on a buoy; an adult, and it really did look large; no wonder they are called the great, they are our largest native gull and definitely king of the pile. Nothing argues with a great black-back, unless it does not want to live.

Onto the causeway where we could study the northern side of the reservoir, this was usually the most productive side, and so it turned out. A large number of the ruddy ducks were quickly seen, a few cormorants, two delightful drake goldeneyes, lovely birds these, and in the distance a large number of swans – fifty or sixty of them I estimated.

The majority of these were going to be mute swans, but tucked away amongst them should be the Bewick's we were seeking. Concentration time. We scanned through the swans, nothing to report, so we started a sweep back through them. Whilst doing this a colleague grabbed my arm and pointed to a field at the side of the adjoining bay, a group of swans were grazing the ground; he had found our swans. We had been studying the swans on the water while all the time the Bewick's had been grazing in a nearby field. Did they have smiles on their faces?

As claimed, there were eleven of them, and even at that distance we could make out the bill markings so there was no mistaking what we were looking at. It was not very often we could see all three of our wild swans on the same day, all in a completely wild state. You may be lucky enough to do so at places such as Slimbridge or Martin Mere, where wild swans will call in and join the collection birds, ours that day were wild alright, and local – very!

For some of our group, these were both 'Lifers'; I was sure they would remember this day for many years to come. A great start to the year, and most of us had not driven miles to do so. I would go home happy enough that was for sure.The great grey shrike and hen harrier were still being reported regularly from Beeley Moor, in Derbyshire, so we decided to go after these as they would be two very good birds to get on our 'Year Lists' so early in the year, plus for some of the new members they would also be 'Lifers'.

The Sunday chosen proved to be a very good choice, it was forecast to stay bright all day, cold obviously, but bright. Five cars started off from

Lichfield and, as we were not travelling far, we decided to call in near to Chatsworth House to see if we could find dipper on the Derwent, where the B6012 crossed the river near to Beeley Lodge. This turned out to be a good decision. From the bridge we arrived just in time to see three goosander fly off down the river – two drakes and one duck – and a grey wagtail was foraging away on the riverbank. We were there no longer than twenty minutes when the bird we really wanted flew down the river, landing on an exposed piece of rock, twenty feet or so in front of us. We could not ask for a much better view. The bird proceeded to drop into the water and swim off after food, which it returned to the rock to eat. How a small bird such as this, which does not have webbed feet, could feed in this manner, I have no idea, but for several minutes we enjoyed it doing so. The bird obviously ate its fill, and flew back up the river.

Now for the moors and, in particular, the area known as the Beeley Triangle. As we drove up through Beeley village it was noticeable that areas of snow remained, nothing particularly widespread, just lying in hollows or where it had originally drifted a little. Near to the Triangle there is a Triangulation pillar (a trig point as they are commonly known), which according to my OS map, is at 367 metres so we were aiming high.

The Triangle is mainly heather and bracken with a few trees, and as I have mentioned earlier, the shrike appears to favour one specific small area of stunted silver birch, or so it had been in the past. There were no other birders evident, so we were going to have to do all the work ourselves, and we drove straight up and parked near this area.

Initially things were very quiet, until a wren woke up, and they are rarely quiet, and a blackbird commenced to forage among the leaf litter. In the distance a raven could be heard croaking away, very strenuously, but it was behind a rise and could not be seen. With the voice they have, sound is almost as good as seeing, probably more so.

We had been there about thirty minutes, much of that time spent sitting in our cars, it was rather chilly up there to put it mildly, when a movement at the base of a silver birch caught our attention, and up popped our shrike. It sat out on the top of the birch for a few minutes before it dropped down onto the ground, to reappear with something wriggling in its bill. What it was I do not know, you would not have thought that any insects were about in that weather, but the shrike flew off and that was that. It did not return, although we hung on for several minutes; time, then, for harrier hunting.

The hen harrier had last been reported from near to Hunger Hill on the edge of Harewood Moor, about a mile or so away from our current position, so we headed in that direction. Things there looked better; we quickly located a small group of cars and several birders all gazing intently over the Moor. We joined them and to our delight the hen harrier, which incidentally was a magnificent male, was quartering the Moor just in front of us. You do not get many sightings this easily or so clearly, and for four or five minutes we had the bird in full view before it drifted over a ridge to vanish from sight. Unfortunately, it did not return so we went off homeward, more than happy with what we had seen.

So far that year things were going well, with several quality sightings to start things off, and within the first two months I had broken the one hundred mark for the year. Nothing new as yet, but the year was young, and we never know what may be lying round the corner. In March, we decided to travel a little further afield and have a day's coastal birding so we headed back to the north Wales coast intending to spend time back at the Point of Air, where we had the chance of gulls, ducks and waders and possible early birds of passage moving through. To accommodate the possibility of the latter, we chose the last Sunday in the month, and weather wise a very pleasant day it turned out to be. I had previously checked the tides for the day and it was due to be fully in as we arrived, which was ideal for our purposes as the waders would be on the marsh and the ducks would be close in as they fed in the shallower waters. As far as the gulls were concerned, it did not really matter, they are at home just as much on the mud as on the sea. Walking across the dunes we noticed a movement of gannets out at sea, that was a good bird to pick up so quickly. These birds were probably moving up the coast to their nesting sites in Cumbria or even as far away as Scotland and to see these birds diving into the sea is always a wonderful sight. They just go in bill first like a dart, they must have good neck muscles and head protection. The odd shearwater was to be seen gliding low over the waves, these were quite far out but I presumed them to be Manx shearwaters as the time was right for their appearance as they breed on some of the islands off Wales and the west coast.

Clearing the dunes, we settled ourselves down to study the water ahead. On estuaries it is amazing just how quickly the tide travels, both in and out, and mud was already appearing. The waders were aware of this and a large number of dunlins and knots appeared, a few hundred of them, they would not be round for much longer as they would fly further north to breed. Curlews were also starting to appear, wading up to their knees in the water as they probed deep with their long, curved bills. These too would be on the move shortly.

Two birds which would probably stay to breed in the area were the oystercatchers and ringed plovers, and these birds appeared to be more interested in probing the exposed ground to wading for their food. Each to their own.

The odd turnstone and sanderling were also to be seen, these too being birds on passage, and wading were redshanks and just four ruffs. A good enough selection of birds, and the majority would be firsts for the year. So we were all happy.

Out at sea are a small number of pintails; the majority of these had obviously left for their breeding grounds further north. The birds remaining were probably non-breeding birds. What I did find of particular interest was the large raft of scoter out at sea – a few hundred there – and once again, hard as we worked, they all appeared to be common scoter. A few small groups of shelduck were also on the water, and these may well be locally breeding birds: a very bright and attractive looking duck.

The tide quickly moved out so we now concentrated our efforts on the dunes behind us. We were probably too late for the snow buntings, but we might find other interesting passerines. Linnets were still in their flocks with a smattering of goldfinches among them, the odd chaffinch could be seen where there are bushes and a beautiful male reed bunting; puts in an appearance, a superb looking bird. Then the bird of the day appeared, and we nearly missed this taking it to be another reed bunting, a lovely male Lapland bunting popped up on the sand. It is not unlike a reed bunting superficially, having the black upon the head and a white collar, but when you study it closely, there any resemblance ends. Facial markings were clearly seen.

Lapland buntings are birds I have always associated with the east coast and the name tells you from where they originate. I did not expect to see one on the west coast, but I was not complaining. Unbelievably so, I was the only one of us who had ever seen a Lapland bunting previously so my colleagues were delighted with the bird, not that I was complaining, I had not seen that many before.

Time for home, but things had not finished yet. Near where we had parked the cars was a small wooded area and from out of there we could hear the call of a chiffchaff. Is summer here? Chiffchaff are one of our earliest returning migrants, although I usually do not expect to hear them until April; although one does hear talk of their over-wintering. Either way, we were all happy and left after having quite a day.

That brought this course to its conclusion, we now waited to see what happened in May when I commenced my summer term. A new challenge and one I was looking forward too.

I attended a Tutor's Evening at the University of Birmingham, and I was pleased I had. Whilst there, I had discussion regarding my summer course where I suggested we could have full day field meetings which we would count as two normal evening meetings. I explained that this would give me the opportunity to take the students to study breeding birds which was not obtainable to us locally. To see seabird breeding colonies for instance. They were happy to go along with this, and also if I wished to change an indoor meeting to a field meeting I could do so, as long as I informed them in advance so that room hire charges could be avoided. I could now draw up my plans in preparation for our May start. It also meant I was not running a class every Wednesday evening, which I must confess suited me better.

I planned the following. In May we would start with a visit to Trench Woods in Worcestershire to listen to the nightingales. In June, Cannock chase for the nightjars; late June to Bempton for the cliff nesting sea birds – here puffins breed. Finally, early July to Walney Island where large numbers of gulls breed, plus eider ducks. That gave us two evening meetings and two all day meetings which covered the equivalent of six classes. When we met for our first session, I would put that forward as my proposal for the course, and then it was up to them as to what they wanted. These courses were not run for my benefit, they were for the students who attended.

I was very pleased with the number of students enrolling; we had nineteen, including four new members. We discussed my proposals for the course and all were happy with this. I found out that few of my members had experienced nightjars and many were not even aware that nightingales bred locally, so our first two evening meetings were arranged. As these would finish late, we decided to hold them on a Friday evening with no one needing to get up early for work on the following day. This was quickly agreed with the University, as were the dates.

Trench Woods, you will recollect, is where I took part in a recorded programme featuring the nightingales, and I had not been back since; time to put that right. Near the woods was a very pleasant country pub, here we met up. Some of us had food and a pleasant drink to go along with it. The owner was only too happy for us to leave our cars on his car park, where they were much safer than being parked in the lane. Just prior to dusk, we set off; we had half a mile or so to locate the areas where the birds were regularly heard.

The evening was very warm and large numbers of insects were on the wing, some of the biting kind, for insect eating birds it was bonanza time – we were not so happy. Chiffchaffs, willow warblers, garden warblers and blackcaps were singing well, but as it got darker these birds slowly calmed down, until all we could hear was a hooting tawny owl and he did not hoot for long.

We had chosen the right night. We had hardly arrived in situ before a nightingale burst forth in song, the world's master songster was no more than twenty feet away and he gave it everything. We could not see him obviously, but you do not go to see nightingales at night; you go to hear them when they have everything to themselves, the only competition being another nightingale. They do sing during the day when you can see them, but then they are competing against all the other country sounds, and brilliant though they are, at night-time they are special! Very!

We stood still, and silent, for almost half an hour until the bird stopped. It did not sing again whilst we were there; it no doubt, had other things on its mind: food seeking probably being one of them.

Rather than walk back down through the now very dark woods, we walked down the lane to the pub. Thanked the publican, and made our ways home; many, like me, full of admiration for this bird's musical prowess.

The evening chosen for nightjar hunting looked ideal. It had been a warm day, little or no wind with a warmish evening which should be ideal for night flying insects on which the nightjars feed. We met at the White House Car Park, full of hope and expectancy. It was 8.00 p.m. so we had ninety minutes or so before we would position ourselves for the nightjars and roding woodcock; the two speciality birds we were after. Prior to that we would walk down into the Sherbrook Valley to see if we could find any tree pipits and cuckoos. As far as cuckoos were concerned, the Sherbrook Valley had an outstanding record: several males could be heard each summer – long may it continue. If two birds epitomise summer, it is the cuckoo and the swallow.

We had hardly entered the Valley before we heard the first cuckoo calling and it was not many minutes before we found one in flight, the evening had started well. A male stonechat sat out on the top of a gorse bush, he was really posing for us, and a real beauty he was too. Tree pipits could be heard singing and we located two different males singing away from their chosen perches, sufficiently apart to avoid any friction. Overhead swifts were hyperactive, there was obviously a goodly supply of flying insects up there, and they were making the best of it.

Although nightjars and woodcocks were top of our list, we then had the experience which would be that of the evening I am sure. A male hobby came hurtling across, narrowly missing out on a swallow, to take a very large dragonfly. We watched the bird clip off the dragonfly's wings, which drifted down to earth like pieces of gossamer as they glinted in the evening sun, before it devoured the dragonfly whilst still on the wing. The hobby then shot off to repeat the process. Any bird which can catch a dragonfly on the wing is an exceptional flying machine. Dragonflies are the finest of insect flyers; one moment they hover like a helicopter, the next they are off like a fighter jet. Then they appear to fly backwards. Some insect, and in the case of the hobby, some predator. It is moments such as these that makes birding so worthwhile. Animal behaviour is amazing.

Dusk was now drawing in, although the cuckoos did not seem to think so, three or four were still calling, but the swifts had departed to higher altitude as we made our way to the nearest corner of Parr's Warren – a conifer plantation.

We were still in transit, so to speak, when the first of the roding woodcock came flying past; this bird was out patrolling his territory, warning off any marauding male woodcock – this area is spoken for! Occasionally, you will get both the male and female roding together, but at that time of the year I think it safe to presume the female is sitting eggs so the male has to do the work itself. Mind you, it looked as though it was doing it with skill and finesse.

We saw the woodcock on several occasions and then the bird we came for. From the edge of the plantation a nightjar flew out, right over our heads, and landed on a dead branch of a nearby silver birch and commenced churring. I do not think I had ever been so close to a churring nightjar before, and to see and hear this bird was superb. They almost have a ventriloquial effect. You can see their throats quivering with the effort, but the sound seems to be coming from another direction. Some sound, some bird, almost a mystery bird, which it was believed to be many years ago. In a matter of days, only, we had moved from exquisite song – thanks to the nightingale – to the sound of mystery and magic.

Needless to say, we all made our ways home in happy frames of mind. Next time out it would be a sea-bird city: come and join us.

Bempton Cliffs, Yorkshire, lies between Flamborough Head and Filey and has some of the tallest cliffs in England, averaging 400 feet. These chalk cliffs are home to probably England's largest seabird nesting colony, thousands of bird congregate here every spring and it must be the finest spot in England to see everyone's favourite bird, the puffin. Also, so I understand, it has the only mainland nesting colony of gannets to be found in England. The few hundred pairs breeding here at present have slowly increased from very small numbers, increasing year on year.

As I said earlier, everyone's favourite bird is the puffin, and twenty-two of us set out to see them; we had a few guests there that day. The drive up took us a little over three hours, but we had set out at 7.30 a.m. because of the distance.

The walk down to the cliff tops was to the accompaniment of the cries of the large kittiwake colony which breeds here. Their call is where the name comes from, 'kittiwake, kittiwake', as with the cuckoo, you could call it nothing else. Although being very common, they are the most marine of gulls, only venturing to land to breed, the rest of their lives spent way out at sea. A truly pelagic bird. In flight, they are very tern-like, and when looking down on them over the sea, returning to their nests, they frequently fly low over the water in lines – no mistaking these little beauties. The cliff ledges were lined with their nests, almost touching each other, with the usual squabbles taking place with their close neighbours. They have a bright black eye, this provides them with a kinder expression than that illustrated by the bright yellow-eyed herring gull. Further along the cliffs is the home of the auks, guillemots and razorbills, especially so; the puffins tend to nest in holes and cracks, not out on open ledges, and with the former, we are again talking of birds in their thousands. Guillemots and razorbills are not noted for their nest building activities, they just lay their eggs on the ledge; they may use a bit of shell as ornamentation, and their eggs are very conical shaped. If a parent left rapidly, a roundish egg would easily roll off the ledge – a conical egg has the chance of just spinning and staying in place. The more I become involved with nature the more I am amazed; nothing it does has no reason.

Down a crevice, we saw what we came for: several puffins were sitting out on narrow ledges, looking as though they were taking in the morning sun. Amazing little birds, looking like miniature waiters in their crisp black and white plumages and their magnificent multi-coloured bills. It was enough to make you believe that 'someone up there', did have a hand in the design of these super birds. People seeing the bird for the very first time, come out with many an adjective to describe how they see the bird, but today one of my colleagues came out with the best: she just simply said, 'Oh my God! He's beautiful.' You cannot put it better than that!

Walking on we came to a broad sweep of cliff and on the ledges, deep down, and looking quite precarious, were some nesting gannets. You do not expect to see our largest sea-bird nestling on a narrow ledge; highly dangerous you would have thought. When you see gannets on natural history programmes, the birds are usually in a tight mass nesting on the top of stacks and rocky islands. Not on narrow ledges, hardly as wide as the bird. At Bempton the top of the cliffs is very grassy, but it is also open to the public and, unfortunately, gannets and people do not mix well.

Fulmar are very active along this stretch of cliff, as they glide, seemingly effortlessly: just a twist of their tail, the tilt of their wing, and with the occasional wing-flap; these birds have it cracked. Watching these birds made me suddenly realise just how close to the birds we can be. I can only presume that because the area is well visited by both bird watchers and walkers, the birds have no fear. To look at a gannet, no more than twenty feet away, is something very special; the size of the bird is like having a white goose fly past.

My attention was drawn out to sea. One of my colleagues had spotted a line of black looking birds flying in low over the waves. I was pleased he had, they were shags, another of the speciality birds here. Unlike their close cousin, the cormorant, which breeds inland, the shag is very much a marine bird, nesting on cliffs and feeding out at sea.

Sea cliffs are also home to pigeons in large numbers. Here, the feral domestic pigeon is a very common sight. These birds are all wild enough, but as their line is directly from escaped birds, they come along in a multitude of colours – some very attractive too. They are descendants of the now rare rock dove and, occasionally, a few feral are dead ringers for the rock, or are they? Local birders claim that several of the birds are pure rock dove and we were looking at five birds there which looked every inch so. These five birds fitted every descriptive detail of the rock dove and the fact the five birds were in a small group of their own and not mixed in with the rest, made me think we had definite rock doves. The question was raised by some of my colleagues, 'What do we list these as?' I tell them, that as far as I am concerned, they are going down as rock doves; nobody here can convince me otherwise. If these birds had been seen in isolation, the question would never have been raised. As well as kittiwakes, many other gulls nested on the cliffs: herring, lesser black-backed, black-headed and a few great black-backed. Out at sea terns were seen, many Arctic terns and occasional small flocks of Sandwich terns could be seen and we also picked up two female eider ducks; obviously, non-breeding birds. Many small birds were to be seen; sand martins, which probably breed along the cliffs in suitable locations, and house martins – swallows and swifts were continually flying past. A very good selection of birds, and before I forget, a peregrine; how can you forget a peregrine? Don't answer that! Time was rapidly catching up with us so we quickly sought out a few rock pipits and stonechats, and home we went. A most interesting day and another location where we would return. We had toted up forty-six different species and several thousand birds. Some bird city!

Our next session was an indoor meeting and there we studied warblers; it was our intention to have our next field meeting on the Chase listening to, and hopefully, seeing warblers.

Seven Springs sits by some old deciduous woodland, a mixture of true British trees, favoured by the many warblers who return here each spring. Chiffchaffs and willow warblers were calling and singing away, and a chiffchaff was also seen busily flying into a patch of bracken; no doubt, the bird's nest was tucked under here – we did not go to investigate.

Garden warblers and blackcaps seemed to be almost competing with each other, and this gave us the opportunity to really study their song as they are quite similar to the untrained ear, especially when heard in isolation. Tonight, we had the wonderful chance to carry out comparisons.

The garden warbler's song is variously described as musical, mellow and quite liquid, and although being similar to the blackcaps, I believe it to be much sweeter and softer with longer phrases. The song of the blackcap on the other hand is a short, mellow, musical warble of rising strength. I often joke that the garden warbler serenades us, whereas the blackcap belts it out. Unfortunately, both birds sing frequently from dense bushes so you rarely see the bird so song becomes a very important feature for identification. Tonight's artists were in good voice and we heard both well.

June is probably the last month to really hear birds sing; things quieten down come July. By then, most birds will be busy feeding their young who are now out of the nest – no time for posing, they have work to do and plenty of it.

The odd whitethroat was still singing well, but they do continue to sing much later than many of their cousins which is a help in identification. Other vocalists included song thrush, blackbird and the robin. The last mentioned is our only bird which sings continuously throughout the year which probably accounts for the fact they are the most territorial of all birds. They basically have two songs: one for the summer, when they have to attract their mate which I find to be a more melodious song; and during the winter months, this changes to a more melancholy song, almost as though it wishes winter away, and who can blame him?

A family party of spotted flycatcher were found, two adults with three young, and watching the adults perform you quickly appreciated why they are called flycatchers. The three young birds were sitting out on a branch and the adults kept darting off this to catch a flying insect, with which they return to feed their young. A very impressive performance; we just hope the young are learning the tricks of the trade as it will not be long before they have to look after themselves.

Night time was drawing in, and a most pleasant and educational evening it had turned out to be. As we were about to drive off, a jay woke up, and a 'skaaak, skaaak' rang out, not very melodious I am afraid, but jays are not noted for clarity of voice, they are just happy to be the most colourful member of the crow family. Thank you, Garrulus glandarius, for your goodbyes!

Time now for Walney Island which lies off the coast of Cumbria, near Barrow–in–Furness: our objective being South Walney, a Cumbrian Wildlife Trust reserve noted for the number of gulls which breed there – estimated at over twelve thousand pairs, which is a lot of birds. I explained to my colleagues that decent head gear would be required as when walking through the breeding colonies the gulls can become very aggressive and a lesser black-backed or herring gull in your face is not the most pleasant of experiences. You will recollect I mentioned this fact previously when a gull attacked me at Walney, drawing blood. You do not forget those incidents when visiting again.

On the water were two family parties of eider ducks; one duck with seven ducklings; the other, had five ducklings. The drakes were nowhere to be seen, which was not unusual with ducks. Along the shoreline were oystercatchers with quite large chicks, they had obviously bred early, and two pairs of redshank also had their families along.

We reached the pathway which branched off through the gull

colonies, donned on our head gear, and bravely went where no one had ever been before, except me that is! We had hardly entered the area before the first attack came. I had mentioned before coming that it may be of use if any of us had walking sticks; if so, bring one along. It was a good job we had. Whirling these over our heads was a very effective deterrent to the attacking gulls, who kept their distance. The only problem was it did not deter their 'poo' attacks with most of us becoming speckled in white. Such are the pleasures and enjoyments of bird watching! It was a good job I had warned them not to look upwards. Being this close to a gull, you can really appreciate their size, and when we met up with a pair of great black-backed gulls, it was like tackling angry geese. Visiting a gull colony really does mean you take your own life into your own hands. We emerged unharmed even if slightly stained, all having not so much as enjoyed the experience, but learned a lot from it. Gulls would be viewed slightly differently from now on. We now had two options. We could walk back along the bay shore, or go along the seashore: we chose the latter. It was a calm day so the sea was relatively smooth, thus any birds sitting out on the sea could be viewed in good conditions. Further up the coast is St Bees Head, there is a sea bird nesting colony, with many auks nesting, razorbills and guillemots. Small flocks of these birds could be seen flying past as they made their ways home; no doubt, with a belly full of food for their young. A few gannets could also be seen, not as we had a few days ago at Bempton, these now were way out at sea. A small group of eiders could be seen, all drakes, so this was where they congregated, leaving the ducks to look after the ducklings – must be a great life being a drake eider.

Occasional terns flew past, the majority looking like Sandwich terns, but one of my colleagues picked out a very pale backed tern, which I was able to get onto quickly. He had hit the jackpot: the tern was a roseate tern, a very special bird with only small numbers breeding in the UK. This is usually a bird you have to make a special journey to see, visiting their few widespread colonies, normally round the coast, with few records in our neck of the woods. We have had some experiences today, but this bird was certainly the bird of the day.

Leaving the shore, we made our ways back to the cars, picking up dunlins, curlews and ringed plovers in transit, plus being abused by a pair of oystercatchers which no doubt had young hidden away in the long grasses. Another most enjoyable field meeting, although the odd comment was made about visiting gull colonies; one suggesting, if we do it again (heaven forbid), it might be a good idea to take a plastic mac' – you can wash them more easily. Point taken!

How things had been planned we now had two indoor meetings, or evening meetings and one all-day meeting remaining; where to go was the question? The all-day meeting was quickly resolved: we would go rarity hunting to try to find one of the UK's rarest breeding birds, the golden oriole. If we failed, we could go after stone curlews which also breed nearby. Not the best of times to go after breeding rarities, July, but I think the group believed they were on a roll with how our luck had been. I did warn them we are chasing after two birds which were going to be very difficult to see, so the day could end up a total disaster. They were all happy with this, so it was arranged.

As we had managed to squeeze the Walney trip into late June, we decided to go after the orioles the first Sunday in July, and seventeen of us made the trip down. We are not visiting a nature reserve this time, we were visiting a poplar tree plantation, grown for the match making industry; these trees, due to their leaf cover, are much appreciated by golden orioles who can remain almost invisible when up in the leaf canopy. Our destination was near to Lakenheath, an area I had never previously visited, but armed with my OS map and the necessary map reference, we were on our way; four cars make the journey and as I was the only one with a map, we were travelling in convoy. I was a passenger for this trip so I could guide my driver to the correct destination, which we accomplished with little trouble. My friend, who had told me where he had seen the orioles, had drawn me a little map so once we parked up, we were on our way. A couple of other cars were also parked, both with bird stickers on the wind screens, which gave us confidence we were in the right area. After about half an hour's walk through the plantation, we heard voices ahead, and sure enough five other birders were standing and looking up the trees; I did not think they were very pleased to see a group our size roll up!

After a little chat, we found out that none of them had ever seen or heard golden orioles before; they were there on a 'Twitch', and I began to realise I was the only person with previous experience of the bird. Visually the bird is no problem, the male anyway, being the only black and yellow bird we have in the UK. The female, on the other hand, could be confused for a female green woodpecker if only a glimpse was obtained. The real cruncher is the voice, and what a voice.

When I was a young lad, I went to see all the Tarzan films and the jungle sounds to us youngsters were as much part of the films as the acting. The golden orioles call is straight out of the sound track of these films, there is nothing remotely similar to it. It is best described as a melancholy, but fast and clear fluting, whistle: 'choo-klee-klooee'. To me it has always sounded more mammal than bird, almost monkey-like, but that is probably my imagination taking over. All we wanted now was for one to call.

We had plenty of other sounds to consider, the various warblers were quite active. A nearby redstart gave us several notes and, in the distance, a great spotted woodpecker was both calling and drumming, but where was the sound we most wanted? Having come this far, we were not going to give up; if it took time, then so be it. Time it did take, three hours passed and even my patience was beginning to wane. I was very pleased I had suggested we took our provisions with us. Then a sound similar to a jay's call was heard, but I thought this was not harsh enough to be a jay. I mentioned this to one and all, and suggested we concentrated our efforts in the direction of the call. After a few minutes it was jackpot time, 'Choo-klee-klooee' burst forth, and out of a tall poplar flew our quarry.

I mentioned earlier the fact it is a black and yellow bird, but to see this thrush-sized bird in flight is a wonderful sight. It has a fast, gently undulating flight, not unlike a woodpecker, having a bright yellow head, chest, belly and back, with black wings and black on the tail as a contrast. Some bird, completely unmistakable. There were many happy birders enjoying this bird.

It seemed to have woken up and we shared several more moments with the bird before it again vanished from sight and silence returned once more.

It was obvious stone curlews were no longer on the agenda; we had spent so much time waiting for the oriole, but no one was complaining. We had come out principally for this one bird, and we had got it, stone curlews can always wait for another day. A very successful 'Twitch'.

Our next two evening field meetings were damp squibs, and I do not mean that humorously. On both occasions the heavens opened and, although a few hardy souls turned out, we were not rewarded with a great deal. These two disappointments did not detract from the fact the members considered it to be a very successful venture and asked that I made sure we could do the same next year. I was more than happy to do so and quickly sorted this out with the University who were pleased with the numbers.

It was now September, and we were off with our twenty-four class winter course. We had twenty-eight members; we had lost one or two of our regulars, some of whom had moved to the south for their retirements. The odd new face had joined so our reputation must have been spreading.

At our initial meeting we had chosen to study sea and coastal birds for the first three months, so we selected the Point of Air for coastal species, and Gibraltar Point for sea passage and left one date for a 'Twitch'. Due to the success of recent 'Twitches', the class had rather taken to the idea – let us hope we can keep producing.

Gibraltar Point became our first venue due to the wind conditions in the North Sea. Strong north-easterlies had been driving onto our eastern coast and Gibraltar Point had been doing very well. The occasional stork and crane had been reported with scaups and long-tailed ducks seeking sheltered waters. An early movement of redwings and fieldfares had also been mentioned, so that being the case we should have much to look for.

Four cars set off, sixteen birders out for excitement. We arrived in almost gale-like conditions, with very large waves breaking on the beach; it was not going to be an easy day for birding, nor for the birds for that matter. Smaller birds, such as redwings and fieldfares, would find it extremely difficult to make land; let us hope they were still the other side of the North Sea waiting for conditions to improve before they attempted the crossing. The sand being blown about was not very good for your optics, so we quickly gave up on the sea watching and turned our attention onto the marsh and lagoons. With the dunes behind us, we at least had some protection from the wind driven sand; although, at times, not a lot. The small birds on the marsh were really keeping their heads down, and those which did attempt things did not fly where they wished

– they just got blown to wherever they could land. We did, however, manage to identify two water pipits which pleased a few members for whom it was a 'Lifer' they already had a good start to their day. A twite was also discovered, this poor bird was almost cowering down to seek shelter. We quickly noted it and moved on, another 'Lifer' for one or two.

On reaching the Fenland Lagoon, we took shelter and studied the water. It was still very choppy, but we did not have waves crashing about and three ducks bouncing about on the water caught our attention. We have two of the ducks we were hoping for: two drake long-tailed ducks and a female scaup. The 'Lifers' were totting up that was for sure, not for me, unfortunately, but these courses, as I have said before, were not run for my benefit – not that I was complaining, far from it. We were about to move on when a large bird-of-prey was blown across in front of us; we were able to look at the bird for no more than five seconds before it was blown from sight. Several pairs of eyes looked in my direction, 'What on earth was that?' being the general comment. I had to admit I could not be certain, but from the bit of detail I had manged to see I presumed it was a harrier – a juvenile marsh harrier to be more precise. As I said, it was a case of a 'nearly bird'; we needed someone else to have had a better view so any new birder we saw, the question was asked, not always answered though.

Moving onto The Mere, and this proved to be the right decision. A large grey and blackish looking bird was stalking through the Old Marsh, almost ostrich-like; we had found the crane, and what a bird. They are much taller than a heron and move with very slow and dignified steps on their long legs – very stately. With their large bustle, they look like something from Victorian times, some bird.

My group were delighted with this sighting; they were a rare bird in the UK with just a very small colony still holding on in Norfolk – our bird was probably a migrant from the Continent. Not that we were the slightest bit concerned with its origins, we were just enjoying a 'mega' bird.

Approaching closer, we became conscious of a change in the weather: the sand was beginning to stick, and rain was in the air. It had been unpleasant before, now it was decidedly so; you could not use your optics in these conditions. Our cars were parked up by the Visitor Centre so we made our ways there as quickly as possible. Once our equipment was safely stacked away, two of us made our way to the Centre to ask about the marsh harrier. We were delighted to hear that two marsh harriers had been on the reserve for a day or so and one of them was a juvenile male. Another good bird added to our day's list. The rain was now falling as though it really meant it, so off home we went. It was a little earlier than expected, but having experienced another great day.

October looked like the Point of Air, but a phone call from a friend of mine, quickly changed that. He had just come back from North Wales where he saw a cattle egret: a very rare bird in the UK. You may remember I wrote about these when I was in Egypt, and at that time they were known as buff-backed herons, but in the passing years they have become accepted as cattle egrets due to their close association with cattle. A quick number of phone calls to my group, and they were one again in 'Twitch Mode'. Should we be lucky enough to see the bird, it would make Wales an amazing country for rare herons; three in one year – unbelievable. The bird was seen in a farmer's field near to Penrhyn Bay, the name of the farm was unpronounceable. He was able to give me the map reference, however, so finding the farm would be no problem; let us hope the same thing applies to the bird. As time goes on in this game, I was becoming more grateful for the Ordnance Survey; I was very thankful I learned to read a map. We arrived at the farm (the name certainly looked unpronounceable), and in a distant field a small white shape was just visible among a herd of black and white cows. What to do now? We could hardly walk all over the farmer's fields so I decided to drive down the track to the farm and ask for permission. I drove down, knocked on the door to be met by, presumably, the farmer's wife who asked what I was after; I must admit, she sounded very aggressive. Before I could say anything, a man pushed past her and grunted the same question; they did not appear very friendly. I started to explain about the bird and could we possible go to see it? Before I got far he exploded, muttering various threats to the birding community. I was sure he was swearing in Welsh judging by the tone, then his wife grabbed his arm and muttered something in Welsh. He stopped, looked directly at me and asked, 'Are you asking for permission to go on my land?'

'Yes,' I replied, and his whole attitude changed. He told me that for days he had been driven mad by bird watchers trespassing on his land and leaving gates open. One birder, he claimed, had climbed over a stone wall and dislodged part of it. 'How many of you are there?' was his next question.

'Five car loads, eighteen of us,' I replied.

He waved at the space in front of the farm, 'Plenty of room for you all to park; I do not have to mention gates?'

'No,' I replied.

'Let me know when you leave, and it is a pleasant change to be asked, instead of just raided.'

I fetched my colleagues down, explained the circumstances of what had been going on, and made our way across four fields to get close to our quarry; needless to say, closing four gates as we did. I do not think I have ever led a more orderly group of birders in my life!

We approached within about fifty yards of the bird where a stone wall provided us with cover, and set our scopes up. Cattle egrets do not probe in mud or water as often as little egrets, they tend to chase after insects being disturbed by the cattle as they feed; very much a land creature. We were really enjoying ourselves and when the egret actually landed on the back of one of the cows, the bird really was living up to its name.

We spent about an hour with this bird – before we moved off, we thanked the farmer – to do a little birding in Penrhyn Bay, but unfortunately, the tide was fully in so apart from a selection of gulls and the odd late tern passing through, things were very quiet. At least it gave us time to have a delayed lunch.

Among the shingle, above the high tide line, a few small birds were feeding away and one of my colleagues commented on how white two of them looked. I was very pleased he had picked up these two birds; they were two female snow buntings, always a quality bird to see. Along with the cattle egret, these birds were also 'Lifers' for some of my colleagues. Although we had not seen a large range of species, two of them were straight out of the top drawer, and things can rarely get better than that.

Time for home, and once again, a group of happy birders.

At our next indoor meeting, we discussed whether we should visit

157

the coast once again, having done so on our previous two field meetings. Due to the success of these meetings, the coast it would be, so our next field meeting would be the Point of Air.

It was a lovely morning when we set out, a clear blue sky, little or no wind and a very pleasant temperature for the time of the year. Fifteen of us made the trip, four car loads, and we all arrived within minutes of each other at our destination.

On getting out of our cars, I realised just how quiet it was – hardly a bird was calling and looking round there were few birds to be seen. We climbed over the dunes and gazed out into the Dee Estuary; the water was like a mill pond, hardly a ripple. I could never remember seeing the sea quite like this. The tide was on its way out but it was hard to notice, with very few waders feeding along the tide line. A few curlews, ringed plovers and redshanks were all we found.

The picture out on the sea was not very different. A few gulls scattered about with the odd pintail and shelduck hidden away amongst them. We turned our attention to the spit, where as you know, we have seen interesting passerines in the past. Not today, the odd linnet and two stonechats, the latter at least brought a bit of colour to the scene. I had never known the Point so quiet, I could only presume many of the birds had remained on Hilbre Island which lies out in the estuary. If the pickings there are good, they have no need to journey elsewhere. That day was clearly a case of after the Lord Mayor's Show; our good run was bound to finish at sometime, and it had. What to do with the rest of the day?

The answer to that question was quickly answered. Two local birders came walking up to us and asked, 'Had we seen the white-fronts?' The answer to that was obviously no. They pointed us in the right direction and told us to look on the water off from the colliery, where they had seen twelve white-fronted geese which were believed to be the Greenland race; although they did not think so. The day had suddenly brightened up appreciably; if we were able to find these birds, it would make our trip well worthwhile.

We had a quick lunch break, as we had about a mile to walk. As we skirted the marsh, a peregrine falcon flew across, disturbing a few snipes and redshanks, which had not been visible to us, and a flock of pipits were not amused by the birds' appearance either. Reaching the point, we set up our scopes and commenced to scan the area in front of us. Quite a few duck were on the water, mainly mallard and shelducks, with gull activity out in the estuary. These birds looked as though they may have found a shoal of small fish near to the surface as they dived and plunged into the water, as is usually the case, very noisily.

Continuing to scan the water a colleague spoke up, 'Hi Bri, what are those birds out on the mud?' I spun round, he had hit the jackpot. The geese had moved off the sea and were walking, very deliberately, up the mud to where vegetation was growing. It was a mixed flock of adults and juveniles, so I concentrated my attention on the adults.

The Greenland white-front has a slightly longer and heavier bill than the white-fronted, and it also is a deeper orange-yellow; I could see no evidence of these differences. I can understand birders presuming them to be Greenlands, they tend to arrive earlier than their fellows, but I could see no evidence of a deeper bill colour. I settled for white-fronted geese; I would have liked them to be the Greenland race, they are much more unusual, but we were all happy. A quiet day had ended with some excitement. True wild geese are always exciting, a bit up market from Canada geese!

That concluded our field meetings for the year, we would now wait to see what '81 brought in for us. More special moments we hope. In future, I had decided to concentrate my writing on the more unusual places and events. I am frequently referring to places which we regularly visit; often with nothing special to report, so I will just briefly mention these if appropriate and introduce you to pastures new – some of which will also be new to me.

The first two months of the year passed by without too much excitement, although I knocked up my first hundred species by the end of February. Amazingly enough, nothing special was among them, apart from two Bewick's swans seen at Blithfield Reservoir; the remainder were the anticipated species. Our first serious trip out was to take us to Anglesey. Here we would do some sea watching in the hope we may see some early auks and shearwaters passing through, and then call in at Aber Falls to see if we could find chough, which had been reported as breeding there once again. The latter would be a class bird to start the year.

We started off early, another 6.00 a.m. start, and drove directly to South Stack Cliffs; here, the RSPB have a reserve and this area I have long considered to be the most spectacular cliff scenery in North Wales. Some areas rise to over three hundred and fifty feet, and are important in their own right as breeding territory for many species. But as stated earlier, we were there to sea watch.

Before we commenced our sea watch, the resident peregrine falcon put on a flying display for us, some bird. There are few breeding sites for these birds at present, although with the protection they are now having, they may increase in number – we can but hope.

We settled in by the lighthouse, where we could obtain some shelter. There was a strong breeze coming in off the sea which could help us by driving passing birds closer in shore. A few shag passed us by, fulmar were cruising round the cliffs effortlessly, and the occasional gannet could be seen out at sea. Small groups of razorbills and guillemots were flying past the Stack. A group of smaller auks passed us, about a dozen puffins – a few still breed on Anglesey I had been informed – these were always a welcome sight.

The usual gulls were out at sea or on the cliffs: herring, lesser-black-backed, black-headed and the odd great black-backed gull. Two terns drifted by, these looked quite large, so it was safe to presume Sandwich terns. We had collected one or two quality birds here to start off with, then a shout goes up 'What's that?' A quick look, and three Manx shearwaters were gliding past, with hardly a flap of their wings as they almost rode the waves. They were poetry in motion, as they glided past on their widespread, slender wings, just tilting tail and wings to keep them above the waves. Their flight is so economical, it is no wonder they can travel such long distances and spend so much of their lives at sea. We had got what we really came for, and to say we were delighted is putting it mildly.

Time for lunch, and Aber Falls called. If you should be looking for Aber Falls on any maps, turn off the A55 in Aber village and follow a minor road through the village. You will find a car park (at map ref: SH663719, OS Map 115) from here, a nature trail takes you to the falls. When walking along the river, look out for dipper and grey wagtails, and siskins have commenced to breed in the conifer plantation, or so I had been told. We did not see or hear any that day, but we did see a drake red-breasted merganser on the river, which was more than adequate compensation.

Approaching the Falls, we could hear chough calling so we quickened our pace. We spent a lot of time trying to locate the chough, but we were not fortunate enough, so it would have to go down as an audible not a visual record, but that was better than nothing.

On our return, we saw both dipper and grey wagtail but no siskins. The walk, however, had been very pleasant and it was a good ending to the day. Over the past few months, you must be beginning to think that Wales is the only country to have birds so it is time to put that right. Next month we decided to visit Chew Valley Lake and Bridgwater Bay.

Chew Valley Lake was flooded in 1956 and has slowly built up a reputation in the bird world, and currently has a red-necked grebe in attendance – a bird well worth chasing – and Bridgwater Bay should still have a good selection of waders. I had never visited Chew before, so I was looking forward to visiting this location.

I had not realised just how large Chew Valley Lake was. It has an eight-mile perimeter, so we certainly will not be walking round it. The grebe had been reported most frequently from off the dam, so we managed to park close by, and quickly got down to business.

Fortunately, it was a calm day and little or no sailing had commenced, so we had things pretty well to ourselves and six scopes were scanning the water. We quickly picked up great crested and little grebes and the air had a goodly number of hirundines flying after the emerging flying insects. Red-necked grebes are the second largest of the grebes seen in the UK, and are principally a winter visitor to our shores, so a record in April is quite late; although summer birds are being recorded more frequently. I had read of claims they have commenced to breed in Scotland, but whether this is true I do not know.

One of my colleagues grabbed my arm and pointed. He had found a very dark looking grebe with a pale grey looking face, and a very dark neck. We quickly looked in the direction he was pointing; we had our red-necked grebe. The bird is almost in full summer plumage, I had previously only seen juveniles or winter plumaged birds, this bird was an absolute beauty. More thick-necked than the great crested, coloured in a dark rust-brown and has a black bill with a yellow gape – quite distinctive. Seeing the bird among several great crested grebes, there is no confusion; the great crested have areas of white visible, the red-necked little or no white. If it had not been for the clarity of the light and our optics, you could almost be forgiven for thinking the bird was all over black.

We spent many minutes enjoying the bird – watching it dive frequently – and, on one occasion, it came up with a largish fish, which it swallowed with difficulty. You would have thought the fish was more than enough, but no, the grebe proceeded to dive for more, not that we saw it catch anything else.

Bridgwater Bay awaited us, so we moved on; if we saw nothing else of excitement, we were all happy for many they had started the day off with a 'Lifer'. It was almost a 'Lifer' for me to see it in summer plumage.

We drove towards Steart along a minor no-through-road and parked up near the end. We had lunch and made our way to the shore. The tide was racing out and the waders were chasing after it, so we settled in, set up our scopes, and commenced to wader watch.

Close in were two busy turnstones, dashing about, turning over larger pieces of shingle and moving bits of weed as they sorted out food. These birds never seem to stand still and are a bird watchers delight as they seem completely at ease with us. The odd ringed plover was also to be seen; these birds were not so confiding as the turnstones, however.

Further out, the larger waders were feeding away. Curlews, oystercatchers, bar-tailed godwits and redshanks, not in large numbers; these were late stragglers still in transit to their breeding grounds further north.

The odd knot and dunlin could also be picked out dashing along the edge of the tide, and a bird flew in which completely amazed me. A superb adult, fully plumaged grey plover; just one, but what a bird. I have frequently said to people, this bird should not be called a grey plover, it is more silver. Just have a look at them in your field guide, and I am sure you will agree with me. A glamour bird if there ever is! It did not stay for long before it flew off, but thank you for popping in.

It was getting near to the time to depart, when one of my colleagues pointed out a small looking wader feeding in a nearby pool. I was very pleased he had; he had found the wader of the day regarding rarity: it was a little stint. It may not have the glamour of a grey plover, but you do not see these very often. It is a bird of passage, making its way further north in Europe to where they breed. They are the smallest wader to be seen regularly in the UK and small in number too. I frequently go a full year without seeing one; I would not have that problem that year!

The little stint brought the day to an end, and another good one too. We all could travel home happy and contented.

That brought our first term to a close; we now had our shorter summer course to look forward to, and we had sixteen members for that course.

Our first two evening field meetings, once again, took in evenings on the Chase for the nightjars where we were successful and a further trip out for nightingales, who performed mightily. I think these evenings will become regular annual events, and why not? Both birds are a bit special. Time now for our Sunday trips further afield and we decided to visit Radipole and Portland, first, then we would go down to the Brecks for golden oriole and stone curlew.

Our trip down to Radipole was an early start once again, and three cars left Walsall at 6.00 a.m. on a bright and sunny morning. Radipole has one speciality bird which many in the group had never seen or heard, and that is the Cetti's warbler. The bulk of the small UK population was found along the southern coast of England, and there is at least one feature of the bird: its voice. If it was there, we would most certainly have heard it, even if we did not see it.

Radipole Nature Reserve is almost completely surrounded by the urban development of Weymouth, so here you can combine nature with the seaside. It is a relatively new reserve having been taken under the wing (no pun intended), by the RSPB as recently as 1975; although Weymouth Borough Council had designated it as an official bird sanctuary way back in 1928. Some foresight shown there I think you will agree. The reserve is always open and entry is free, being mainly public footpaths and there is a large pay and display car park adjacent. The RSPB facilities are available between 9.00 a.m. and 5.00 p.m. at this time of the year.

It is a wetland site comprising goodly areas of reed, several lakes of varying sizes and being next to the coast attracts a wide range of species. Although we will be taking note of all the species, we were there mainly for warblers, with the Cetti's warbler being our number one attraction. Once we moved on to Portland Bill we could concentrate on sea birds.

We had not been here long before we had a very enjoyable surprise. From out of a reed bed came the call of a bearded tit; I was not even aware that they were to be seen and heard here, what a super start. Although it is called a tit, it is not a true relative of the blue tits etc., it is just that it is a tit-like bird should we see it. They may be a most attractive and colourful bird, but during the breeding season, they spend most of their time deep in the reed beds when sound is the best way to know they are there. The call is a twanging 'tying' and 'ping' note. I have always thought it was like a single note heard from a banjo or guitar, and this we were listening out for, but the bird did not show itself, although we saw the odd rustle in the reeds.

Moving on, we heard the soft purring of the turtle dove and finally caught sight of the bird on some overhead wires; another quality bird for the day. We finally arrived near to the spot, where we had been informed, Cetti's warblers call regularly, and settled in to wait. The area looked right: a tangle of bramble and small bushes, close to water; the former providing all the cover the bird loves, and the water producing many flying insects.

To try to describe the Cetti's call is very difficult. Every field guide you read has a different interpretation; all I will say is it is very loud. An explosive outburst of abrupt and bubbling notes, and mixed in all of this has a drawn-out rolling 'pling', which sounds almost like a clock-work toy being wound up. We were listening to a reed warbler singing away when we almost all jumped with shock. A call of a Cetti's warbler burst forth just feet behind us. It was in a very thick tangle and really let rip – no mistaking this fellow – the noise made your head swim. For the many who had never experienced the bird's call previously, they could not believe the volume and intensity of what they were now listening to. As with the nightingale, you did not have to see this bird to identify it. We hung on for many more minutes and as much as the bird called, it had no intention of showing itself, so it was time to move on to Portland Bill.

Before we moved on, I must mention the fact the Cetti's warbler is a true residential warbler along with the Dartford warbler; all other warblers are principally returning migrants – although a few reports are made for odd birds over-wintering, chiffchaffs and blackcaps mainly.

The sea was very calm off Portland and, in consequence, the birds were very distant apart from the cliff nesting species which were constantly flying to or flying off the cliffs. Out at sea, gannets could be seen diving into the water, shags were flying low over the surface and way out a solitary shearwater was seen flying through; presumably this was a Manx shearwater, although we could not be 100% sure.

Closer in fulmars were gliding past, as they do so well, and guillemots were very active as they flew in and out on whirring wings, looking like a big black and white bee. The odd cormorant was sitting out as though enjoying the sun, wings widespread as is their wont. Lower down on the rocks near the sea, two small dark looking waders were dodging the tide, we needed to look at these more seriously. We got the view we wanted; they were purple sandpipers, a bit of real quality there.

Once again, time had caught up with us so we made our way back to the cars, and as we did so, a small flock of curlews flew overhead – calling as they went – the perfect ending to a super day. And it was all put down to the birds – thank you Aves!

I have been told of another site for golden orioles, this does not necessitate so much time and efforts as experienced last year, when we tried to have a similar meeting. We decided to put this to the test. An early start once again, but on a very pleasant morning, we were on our way to Santon Downham; four car loads of eager birders. Santon Downham was another new location for me, but I was once again armed with map references and details of best place to see the orioles. All we now required was for the golden orioles to respond.

Santon Downham lies in a large area of forest, mainly planted by the Forestry Commission which comprises conifers principally. Fortunately, areas of broad leaved trees have survived and some of these skirt the banks of the Little Ouse River; although it is far from little.

We made our way to a bridge over the river, where we had been reliably informed, orioles frequently flew across the river. It would appear they are nesting on one side of the river, but obtaining much of their food from the other. We settled in and wait, along with some other birders who were also oriole hunting.

A shout went up, but a brief look quickly dispelled any excitement, a green woodpecker flew across and broke into a 'yaffle' as he landed – obviously laughing at us. During the next hour or so, this woodpecker repeated his efforts, and on one occasion both the male and female flew across together; these birds were doing their best to torment us. Then it happened.

A bold yellow and black bird flitted across the Ouse, flying silently and gentle, he was in no rush. It really was a case of 'what a pretty boy I am', and almost as though he thought we had suffered enough and deserved something for our efforts. We did not dispute that. During the next thirty minutes or so, the bird repeated this process, and on two occasions it looked as though he was carrying food. Our patience had been well rewarded and the views were far better than those of last year when we visited Lakenheath. Time now for stone curlews; Weeting Heath, here we come.

The journey was only minutes and we arrived, parked up, paid our entry fees, found out where the stone curlews had been seen, and off we went. The reserve is not large and in transit to the hide we stopped to admire a hunting spotted flycatcher going about its business. The bird kept on returning to the same tree so it was safe to believe it had a nest there.

The hide was very busy and only a few of us were able to get in. Fortunately, I knew of a small track which led to a gate which overlooked the field, so I took the rest of us to it. This we had to ourselves, so we set up scopes and got down to work. We had not been there long before one of my colleagues said he had an unusual looking skylark in his scope, and as I moved across to have a look, it hit me.

I had completely forgotten that woodlarks nested in the Brecks, and had done so for a few years here at Weeting Heath. Looking through his scope, I was right: it was a woodlark he had in view, a 'Lifer' for most of my companions, and a totally unexpected one. Back now to stone curlew hunting.

The reserve is a small wooded area surrounded by sandy heathland, the habitat much favoured by the stone curlew. Rabbits are probably the commonest animal here and the stone curlews probably use their old scrapes as nesting sites. To call them curlews is, I believe, a misnomer. The curlew is a large bird with long legs and a long de-curved bill, and in every sense of the word is a true wader. The stone curlew on the other hand is a bird of dry terrain, with a heavy bill more suited to eating ground insects, snails, slugs etc., and, at times, even mice, young birds and frogs. You do not need a long probing bill for such food. It has a big head with bright, almost bird-of-prey-like eyes, and frequently stands completely motionless. It is more active at dusk and night when its startling range of calls are likely to send a shiver down your back. In flight it has a call which is curlew-like, a 'ke-e-uhw' best describes it, and I sometimes wonder if this is where the birds name originates. Anyway, let us get back to looking for one.

We had several false alarms as rabbits popped their heads up from behind mounds, but large eyes the stone curlew may have, it does not have long ears. Our patience was finally rewarded, over a mound walked a stone curlew with slow and ponderous steps to stop and survey the surrounding countryside – the large eyes showing clearly. The bird stood completely still for a few minutes before it again slowly moved on, to vanish over a ridge and that was that. We stayed for over half an hour but the bird did not return, but we were happy: we had experienced a wonderful view of the bird and added to the oriole and woodlark. The trip had been well worth the effort.

The remainder of the summer course comprised indoor meetings and local field meetings, which although very pleasant did not produce any birds of real excitement. At the ending of the course, we managed a family holiday which brought us back to our first love 'The Lake District', where we rented a cottage near to Windermere.

We chose the perfect spot in many respects. It was very quiet and peaceful and, on occasion, we were joined by deer in the garden. The garden backed onto open fields and the owners had been feeding the deer for a long time, so they were regular evening visitors; we carried on doing so and fallow deer were seen frequently.

As it was a few years since we last visited The Lakes, Sarah was older so we were able to venture further afield. In doing so we saw many interesting birds and renewed our acquaintance with the golden eagles once again which we understood had a youngster almost fully grown –

who was expected to leave the nest over the next few days – which it did so successfully we were informed.As well as the eagles, we saw many other birds: buzzard, goshawk, peregrine, red grouse, golden plover, kittiwake, raven, wheatear, whinchat, redstart and pied flycatcher. These were the pick of the bunch so to speak; we actually saw eighty-six species in total, plus the deer, and several stoats on our travels.

The weather excelled itself, which does not happen all that often in The Lakes, so several boat trips were made and a very relaxing holiday it turned out to be.

Back now to my bird course, where we had twenty-five members, so the numbers were holding up well – with a few new faces. We decided to only have two long distance field meetings prior to Christmas; one in October; one in November; and in December, we would have a local morning only meeting. This we would repeat in the New Year, a local meeting in January travelling further afield in February and March. This made a lot of sense with the short hours of daylight during mid-winter.

For our October meeting, we decided to visit Exmouth and Dawlish Warren where we had learned avocets were now over-wintering, a good enough reason for the journey. Not only did we see the avocets we chalked up eighty-two different species, the pick of which were the following: gannet, pintail, common scoter, eider, red-breasted merganser, brent goose, peregrine, grey plover, golden plover, black-tailed godwit, greenshank, knot, dunlin, sanderling, ruff, Sandwich tern, rock pipit and a lesser redpoll. A very good start to a new term we all thought.

November saw us visiting Southport and Martin Mere, and the weather was rather bleak. Fortunately, both the locations we were visiting had hides, and we were going to need them as persistent rain was coming in from off the sea accompanied by a strong wind. Certainly not the weather to be out in trying to use optical equipment. Bad as the conditions were, a goodly selection of waders was seen at the RSPB reserve at Southport, Marshside as it is known. The reserve overlooks the Ribble Estuary and is an interesting site to visit at any time of the year, although I prefer the winter when the geese and wild swans have come in. I understand that depending upon the tides these birds in particular commute between Marshside and Martin Mere, so if they are not at one location they are likely to be at the other.

We had timed our arrival to coincide with almost high tide as this was the best time to see the waders. The tide would have driven them onto the reserve, and this was exactly what had happened. The selection of waders was very good, and once again I will only list the more interesting seen. Grey plover, golden plover, turnstone, curlew, bar-tailed godwit, black-tailed godwit, knot, purple sandpiper and ruff. There were few geese or swans so we anticipated these would be at Martin Mere. So on our way we went.

Martin Mere is a Wildfowl Trust reserve and has many captive birds on view, so you have to be very careful of what you list; full sets of primary feathers are all important, and if seen in flight that does solve the problem. Pinioned birds cannot fly. Once you move from the collection area the chances of only seeing genuine wild birds increases.

We had deliberately chosen to visit Martin Mere on the last Sunday in the month in the hope the wintering geese and swans would have started to move in, and as we moved round, so it turned out.

Initially, it was the swans. At least two hundred or so whooper swans were to be seen, and tucked away amongst them a small group of seven Bewick's swans were picked out. Seeing them together; the size difference was easily noted making identification very positive; no need to concentrate on bill differences that was for sure.

Making our way further into the reserve a largish flock of geese flew in; listening to these they were obviously pink-footed geese, so we awaited their arrival. They did not disappoint, they landed on a damp meadow quite close to where we stood, so we could study them easily. One of my colleagues touched my arm, and pointed, stating, 'Those five geese are not the same, look at their breasts?'

I quickly looked, and he most certainly was correct. He had picked out a small group of white-fronted geese; these had not been anticipated that is for sure. This made us study the flock more intently; was anything else tucked in among the pink-foots? There was: two barnacle geese were located, these were probably escapees and not truly wild, but as they had flown in, we would have them.

Light was beginning to fade as we had one last look over the marshy meadows surrounding Martin Mere, and we were very pleased we had. A short-eared owl was quartering a meadow, always a marvellous sight, and in the distance another large bird glided into sight. A harrier, but which one? As it came in closer, we could see it was a female hen harrier, and she proceeded to hunt close to the owl; what a wonderful pairing and what a way to complete our day out.

Our last field meeting of the year had been superb, and on the day we had recorded seventy-three different species, and my total for the year closed on one hundred and eighty-six. No complaints there. What would '82 bring? We chose to visit the Gower for our first field meeting, this being late February, and as far as the weather was concerned, we had chosen well. Bright and clear, although cold, but we had the clothes to protect us against that.

We made our way directly to Worms Head, for sea watching. Thanks to the calm weather, there was only a slight breeze coming in from over the sea, so any passage birds should have been seen quite easily; no crashing waves and 'white horses' to distract us.

The tide still had some way to go before it was fully in, but several duck species were drifting in on it. The pick of these being common scoter, eider, red-breasted merganser and shelduck. Further out, a small flock of brent geese were flying through – all of these birds not being common birds to us in the Midlands.

In the distance, the odd gannet and shag could be seen and on the sea fringe, escaping the in-coming tide, many waders were running across the beach; the pick of these being ringed plover, grey plover, turnstone, curlew, greenshank and sanderling – not a bad little selection there.

Time to move inland to see what we could find. Things there were just as interesting. We had peregrine, merlin and marsh harrier, three rather special birds-of-prey these. A few raven were also heard but not seen, and skylarks were very vocal, the sun must have awakened them from their slumbers.

We had a few minutes left, so we had a quick look out to sea once again, where we saw three Manx shearwaters pass through plus the odd fulmar. All in all a good selection of birds which were part of the fifty we saw that day.

We chose not to have a distance field meeting in March, we would go local and have our meeting in April when we would once again visit

Bempton Cliffs to enjoy the sea bird colonies. We knew we were unlikely to see anything there not seen on previous visits, but birding is not just about obtaining new species – enjoyable though that may be – it is the opportunity to study bird behaviour, and there are few better places than Bempton to do that. Then, should we have the time, we would call in at Hornsea Mere on the way home. Bittern and bearded tits were seen there, or so we have been informed.

When we arrived at Bempton, we parked next to a mini-bus with Dutch plates, little realising we would catch up with the occupants during the morning, but more of that later. Bempton Cliffs was as busy as usual. From the car park, the calling kittiwakes could be easily heard. Walking along the cliff tops we heard and saw the various auks and once again stood spell bound watching the gannets soaring by. It was a very calm morning and large numbers of birds could be clearly seen on the water, the only unfortunate thing with this was that many of the passage birds would be far out at sea, not being driven close in shore. They do talk of the ill-wind, or as was in our case, no wind at all!

We did manage to pick up the odd tern progressing further north, these were Sandwich terns. Small flocks of shags were flying out to sea hunting and, of particular interest, a flock of eleven drake eider ducks were drifting slowly by – just being driven by the tide– definitely in relaxed mode!

Fulmar numbers were very good, and these birds were displaying their usual flying skills. As I have mentioned before, they are in a class of their own. One bird came in so close I could almost have shaken its wing. The tubular nostril tubes very visible which quickly showed this bird was no gull, it was a member of the group we refer to as tubenoses. The dark eye and head shape were also clearly seen at that short distance, apart from seeing the occasional nesting bird, this was the best view I had probably ever had. Some bird, some occasion.

Nearing the viewpoint known as the Grandstand, we saw a group of birders who were all talking in rather excited Dutch; we had met our visitors from Holland. We moved over to talk to them, and needless to say, they answered us in perfect English – our friends from the Continent never fail to amaze me. I was talking to one of them and asked him why come across to England when Holland has so many interesting birds;

British birders regularly went the other way.

He taught me a quick geography lesson, they have no cliffs in Holland so if they wish to see cliff nesting birds they have to cross the North Sea. Their only experience of many of the birds we take for granted, is when they are storm blown onto the Dutch coast. Whilst we were talking one of my colleagues told us he had spotted a 'cracking' bridled guillemot as he termed it. Our new Dutch friends instantly asked where is it? It appeared this was the one bird they really wanted to see.

Bridled guillemots are not a separate species from the guillemot, they are just a bird with a slight plumage variance. They have a white ring round the eye and a white line moving backwards on the head, almost as though it is wearing spectacles, which certainly makes the bird look rather special. Anyway, back to our new Dutch friends.

I quickly got the bird in my scope and called them over to look at the bird; I must confess, I was very impressed with their orderly queue. The bird was a real poser and just stood there being admired. I thought this 'bridled' was the most photographed ever, and no doubt is still deep in the heart of many a Dutch birder!

Many birds were just standing out in full view, almost as though they were enjoying the sunshine as much as we were, some of the razorbills looked as though they had their eyes shut. The puffins, particularly, looked like they were contented with things, and two of these in particular, who were perched quite close by, seemed just as interested in studying us as we were them. When a person moved off they turned their heads to follow for a short time, before coming back to stare us out. Seeing animals behave like this does make you wonder how well-developed their brains are. No animal does anything without a reason, their survival depends upon their understanding of a situation and how they interpret things, it cannot be all down to just instinct.

If we were to have time at Hornsea Mere, we really must move on, so bidding our new friends goodbye and wishing them a safe and comfortable journey home, we were on our way.

None of the group had visited Hornsea previously, me included, so we really did not know what to expect. The Mere is the largest natural lake in Yorkshire and is only a mile or so from the sea. In the space of an hour or so, we have descended from cliffs four hundred feet high down to sea level. Quite a change. The Mere is a mile and a half long by half a mile wide, and has extensive reed beds, hence the talk of bitterns and bearded tits

We booked ourselves in, asked about the bitterns and bearded tits, only to be told these were only occasional visitors during autumn and winter – so that at least saved us looking for them – so we could concentrate on other things, and two of them were most interesting. They had three bean geese and two pink-footed geese and those birds were recently reported as being on the open water of the Mere. No second bidding required, we were off; two top birds there to finish the day off.

We found ourselves a decent viewing spot where we could study a large area of the lake and it was not long before we find a small flock of grey geese; unfortunately, those turned out to be all grey lag geese – a decent enough bird, but not what we were hoping for.

Many minutes passed before five grey geese sailed out of the dense reed bed into open water, we had them, three beans and two pink-foots. Two superb species of grey geese brought our day to a marvellous conclusion. Yorkshire had been good to us that day and, as we left a reed warbler serenaded us from the reed bed. That gave us sixty-six birds on the day, not a bad total that.

Hornsea brought our term to a close. We would now prepare for our short summer term. It would be interesting to see how many members we would have that year.

Fifteen turned up so we were up and running once again, and as in previous years we would concentrate on field meetings with only occasional classes indoors. Before we commenced with the field meetings, we had a holiday to look forward to. We had booked a cottage in Thurlston, Devon, and we clicked for a very pleasant week on the weather front. The area had some very pleasant walks, a few good quality inns and restaurants so we did not go hungry, nor thirsty for that matter, and the bird selection was more than favourable.

During the week, where we knocked up eighty-four species we saw a few choice birds, included amongst them the following: Hobby, peregrine, turnstone, purple sandpiper, curlew, roseate tern, turtle dove, raven, stonechat, whinchat, wheatear, Cetti's warbler, tawny pipit (the bird of the week), rock pipit and finally the cirl bunting – another quality species. Both the tawny pipit and cirl bunting were 'Lifers' for me; it could not get much better than that.

Time for a visit to the Brecks again, especially as I had been given details of where a red-backed shrike was breeding at Thetford. In close proximity, we had three of the rarest breeding birds in England: golden oriole, stone curlew and red-backed shrike – to see those three birds on the same day would be something extra special. We had decided to give it a try, and because of this, we made an extra early start, leaving Lichfield at 5.30 a.m.; four cars made the trip, fifteen birders all ready to go. Once again, I was a passenger being the only person who knew exactly where we were going for the shrike – map and map reference to hand. As the shrike was going to be a 'Lifer' for everyone but me, we decided to make that our first port of call, calling in for the stone curlews and golden orioles on the way back.

The shrike was breeding in a small area of hawthorn right on the edge of a car parking area and the RSPB had set up wardens to watch over the bird to protect it from egg thieves. The area was taped off and no one was allowed in. Fortunately, shrike are birds which sit out well so seeing the bird was not going to be a problem. In many respects it was the craziest place for a bird to breed. England's possibly rarest bird was breeding right next door to children playing football and shouting away, with many dogs joining in the fun. The big consolation was the fact that with so many people about the bird was probably safer from egg thieves there than it would have been if breeding somewhere extra quiet. We had barely got ourselves ready before a shout went up. Sitting out, on the top of an hawthorn bush, was the male red-backed shrike. He just sat there, posing, with cameras clicking away, and a smart bird he certainly was. After a few minutes, he was off; no doubt, hunting for food. Talking to a warden he informed me the eggs had actually hatched; well three of the four laid had, so it was even more important to protect the birds.

After about a further half an hour we decided to move, we had had several superb views of the shrike, some bird. Out next stop was Santon Downham, would the oriole behave?

It did, eventually. After nearly an hour if flew across the river, just as it did the previous year, and for about ten minutes repeated the process. We were happy. On then to Weeting Heath. Walking through the wooded area to the hide, we had a very pleasant surprise. A woodcock flew out, flying across the pathway directly in front of us, that bird had not been on our hit-list. As with last year, spotted flycatchers were again evident and turtle doves could be heard purring softly, a delightful sound.

Entering the hide, the only person in there, a lady, put her fingers to her lips and pointed just in front of the hide. A stone curlew was strutting across the ground feet from the hide, what a corking view. It continued on its slow, deliberate pace, for a minute or two, before taking to flight and vanishing in the distance. It was hard to imagine a clearer view than that, you would have to had the bird in the hand to see it better.

We waited in the hope it would return, it did not, but our time was not wasted. We heard woodlarks and saw several wheatears; they brought our day to a very pleasant conclusion, and some day it had been.

Time for pastures new – Minsmere. Here the RSPB have recreated a fragment of the once extensive marshes and reedbeds of Suffolk, and in doing so Minsmere was probably their premier reserve, so it was well overdue for visiting. Quality birds such as bittern, avocet, beaded tit and marsh harrier now bred there, those four birds alone made a journey worthwhile.

The gods had favoured us again, the weather was just about perfect, clear, bright and only a cooling breeze, which was very welcome. Minsmere was a large reserve, we would not have time to cover all of it, so we concentrated our efforts on The Scrape, and if we had time we would pop up to North Marsh.

The day commenced perfectly; a bittern gave us a flypast before vanishing deep in the reedbed. I doubted we saw the bird for thirty seconds, and little did we know at the time, it was to be our only sighting; there's luck for you. We made our way to the North Hide, as I believe it is now known, which over-looked both shingle and reed bed so, hopefully, we would have a goodly range of species there. On entering the hide, our hopes could be fulfilled. We were informed that a spoonbill was foraging in the reedbed and a water rail was calling frequently; although we did not see it, as the reedbed was so thick. We will take an audible water rail, there is no way of mistaking their call; the spoonbill is different, and we wanted to see it.

In the hide a volunteer was holding 'court', and the only bird which interest him was the marsh harrier. Every time one takes to the air, which was frequent, he shouted and pointed it out. The bulk of us were not the slightest bit interested, we were concentrating our efforts on a large white bird with a preposterous spoon shaped bill, hoping it popped out of the reeds. One birder was heard to comment, 'Is the marsh harrier the only bird he knows?' This was probably a little unkind, although there was a notice in the hide regarding being quiet; birds have ears – it clearly stated!

A bit of activity occurred on the edge of the reedbed, almost as though a fight of sorts was taking place, and out flew a small party of bearded tits which rapidly vanished further along the reeds. A couple of us had a chuckle between ourselves; the marsh harrier fan never even mentioned them, now who was being unkind?

We had been in the hide for almost an hour by then, a very interesting and intense time in many respects, when a birder pointed and whispered, 'Look,' he had obviously read the notice. In a channel between the reeds, a large white bird was slowly walking along it, swishing its large spoon sideways as it was doing so. We had the bird we really wanted, and a superb view it really was; none of the birders in the hide was interested in marsh harriers now, apart from the harrier man. He was obviously a dedicated person.

The spoonbill remained in sight for two or three minutes before it made its way back into the reeds, and that was the last we saw of it. We were happy, it had been a magical few minutes; I thought Minsmere was beginning to grow on us.

Time to concentrate on the shingle bed in front of the reeds. There were several waders feeding upon this, and one in particular drew our attention. One or two birders were claiming it to be a curlew, but some of us were having none of it. The bird was large and had a down-curved bill and, although we did not have any other birds to really compare its size with, it did not look long legged or long billed enough to be a curlew; we needed the bird to turn to face us so we could study head markings. After what seemed ages, the bird condescended and turned to look straight at us, it was a whimbrel – well worth the wait. Two dark lateral stripes on the crown and the long bill with a decided kink towards the end, was conclusive enough. I love curlews, they are my favourite bird, but a whimbrel is a bit more special; what did I say about Minsmere growing on us? Another bird with a down-curved bill ran into sight, this one was rather small – no confusing this fellow – it was a curlew sandpiper and it still had much of its red summer plumage; a most attractive small wader when seen in this condition. Another smart looking bird was a full summer plumaged spotted redshank. It was a sooty black covered with silvery stars, quite spectacular. This bird looked like a male to me, and it was a real beauty. Most waders are just brown looking birds. To have had two of the more colourful species close together was a bit special. I hasten to add, they are both only colourful during the summer.

Among the waders, which totalled seventeen species, the pick of the remaining birds were turnstone, black-tailed godwit, bar-tailed godwit, green sandpiper, knot, ruff and avocet. I thought that day's waders were the largest range of species I had ever seen at a single site, quite a record. After one last pan from the hide, before going to visit North Marsh we picked up a little tern and a Sandwich tern – a very good addition to our day's total. Now what will North Marsh have for us?

Marsh harriers were gliding about, and it was a pity our friend from the hide was not there as he would have enjoyed himself, and the odd Cetti's warbler could be heard, but as is their wont, not seen. The occasional wader was flying over and a red-legged partridge was heard calling, but due to the thickness of the vegetation, we could not see it. Two snipe put on a flying display for us, and even though the breeding season was over, one of the birds was drumming away; he was obviously practicing for next year!

Time to depart after a wonderful day. We had toted up eighty-six species and all of my colleagues went home with 'Lifers' I did not, but I added eight to my 'Years List', so there were no complaints from me. I thought we would be back, Minsmere certainly had much to offer, and we had only seen a bit of it.

To finish the year off, we decided to go across to Norfolk and visit Cley; this reserve to Norfolk is what Minsmere is to Suffolk – another location where birds are legend. To date, over three hundred different species have been recorded. Due to the short daylight hours of winter that required another early start and we again left Lichfield at 6.00 a.m. I was rapidly coming to the conclusion that the males amongst us had very tolerant spouses!

We again made good time, and met up on the Coastguard Car Park. That day, no one was collecting parking fees, so there were no complaints from us. That was my first visit deep into winter so I was very interested in what we would find. Fifteen of us had made the journey, and we had all arrived within minutes of each other; there was no need to drive in convoy, we all knew where we were going.

One advantage of Cley is the fact we could sea watch as well as look for birds on the reserve, so we quickly climbed over the dunes to look at the sea and shore, where a stiff on the sea breeze was blowing; good for bringing the birds in closer, but not so good for staring into. We managed to find a more sheltered spot, and set up our equipment. Again let us concentrate on the special species we saw, and we commenced with two jackpots. On the sea, and close in were two red-throated divers and four black-necked grebes – we were delighted, what a start – one of each would have been more than enough! A small flock of seven scaup were bouncing about on the waves, the largest number I had ever seen together. Out at sea, skeins of brent geese were to be seen – some of these skeins were in their hundreds, which always a tremendous sight – a wonderful goose; It's a pity we only see them in the winter. Among the gulls were several common gulls and the odd razorbill flew past. Close in a drake red-breasted merganser swam past – always a wonderful sight – and as we moved off to go back into the reserve, three snow buntings popped up out of the shingle: a superb looking male and two juveniles. If we saw nothing else we had already had a bumper day.

We entered the reserve, paid our dues, and made our way to the first hide. There, we were sheltered from the sea breeze so conditions were much improved. Many waders were present; the pick of the bunch for us being grey and golden plovers, a solitary jack snipe, and our old friends the turnstones. Curlews were very well represented, now that was a bird which always excited me. A little owl was sitting out on the roof of the neighbouring hide. People did not seem to upset this bird, and judging by the photographs being taken, it would be well recorded. A water rail is letting rip from the reeds nearby, much to everyone's pleasure. As I have mentioned before, you may not see this bird, but there is no mistaking its voice.

While all this was going on, two local birders came into the hide, or to say burst into the hide would describe their appearance better. 'Look over to East Bank, a rough-legged buzzard has just flown over Arnold's Marsh and on into East Bank, and it may pass in front of us.' We required no further comment to concentrate our efforts.

A rough-legged buzzard would be very special to say the least. Just the odd few visit the UK in winter – and it is a few – probably in low single figures, and if seen that day, would be a 'Lifer' for us all. Fortunately, common buzzards were not a bird seen in Norfolk very often, so any buzzard species was likely to be the one we wanted.

A female hen harrier put in an appearance, gliding low over the reeds, that caused an adrenalin rush, but only momentarily. Marvellous as she was, she would take second place to a possible rough-legged buzzard.

Time passed by, no buzzard until someone shouted, 'This is no harrier,' and he was right. Gliding, low over the reeds, came our rough-legged buzzard, no mistaking that bird. A much paler bird than our buzzard, longer winged and with a very distinctive white tail showing a black terminal band to the tail. This bird hid nothing, it even soared up and hovered on a few occasions, telling us what a pretty boy he was; no one was arguing that was a fact. All good things come to an end, and it vanished in the general direction of Blakeney Point. The bird of the day for everyone. Light was now beginning to fade, so we called it a day and made our ways home, in a very contented frame of mind.

That brought the year; to an end, and I had reached a grand total of two hundred species over the year, a milestone of sorts. Now we waited to see what '83 could bring in?

For the past two or three years I had also been running a general wildlife study course for the University of Birmingham. This had ended up more a study of wild flowers, and these have two distinct advantage: they do not move off and you can take your field guide to the flower. I became very interested in the wild flowers to be found in my local village church, St. Peter's, Yoxall, and from this an idea grew in my mind. Dorothy and I started to visit churchyards to see just what flowers thrived there; this study eventually developed into a book I wrote, titled: *English*

Churchyard Flora. This was published in 1983 by Curlew Countryside Publications, a proud moment for me.

Now back to birds, the subject of this publication. Our first serious trip out was to Rhos-on-Sea and Aber. The black duck I had reported on earlier was still being reported; I would welcome the opportunity of a better view myself, and it would be good to get the chough onto our 'Year Lists' so early in the year. Some of my current members had seen neither bird, so, if lucky, they would be in for something a little special. Plus, with our usual luck in North Wales, who knew what else we could see?

Since our last visit a few gales had transformed the coast somewhat and the black duck was now being reported from a different location and appeared to be spending more time at sea; that being the case, we might obtain a clearer view than previously. We could but hope.

We arrived in light drizzle, not the condition we wanted, but out at sea the sky was lightening so we might yet be lucky. There were several groups of ducks on the water, the inevitable common scoters, with once again no obvious surf scoters in their midst, and mallards and wigeons were well represented. We concentrated our efforts on the mallards, the likely chosen companions for the black duck. It was not proving easy, but at least conditions were improving; the sky was breaking up and the sun made fleeting appearances. Two great black-backed gulls came to our assistance, quite unintentionally, needless to say. They dropped in amongst the mallards and put them to flight, and to our delight they flew in closer to where we were positioned, landing back onto the sea no more than fifty yards away. Up telescopes, concentration time!

It did not take us too long to find the bird, he was in good plumage condition and once located it really stood out amongst the mallards. He might not be black, but he is most certainly very dark.

We realised we had spent over an hour seeking out this duck; they do say time flies when you are having fun. Many of my colleagues had commenced the day with a 'Lifer', so they would be happy come what may. Quickly looking through the waders along the shore, the pick were golden plover, turnstone, curlew, knot and purple sandpiper.

Approaching Aber, we pulled over and stopped. A bird of prey was gliding round in circles over the roadway, and although it was fairly large, it certainly was no buzzard. We jumped out of our cars, quickly realising the bird was a goshawk, and these were not common, far from it, they were more than a bit special. Some of my colleagues had never seen one before. Their day was just getting better by the hour, and I was not complaining, as with the black duck, it was my first for the year and could well be my only one. The gos' slowly drifted away, giving the impression he was just out for a bit of fun, not seriously hunting! I am a firm believer that birds of prey do fly for just pleasure and exercise. They are not always hunting and their aerial skills have to be continually honed.

The birds continued to fall out of the sky for us (excuse the pun, it's not intended). We had only just parked up when the rich, deep croak of raven was heard, and a pair flew directly overhead, a superb greeting.

We slowly made our way towards the Falls when the call we really wished to hear broke out. 'Krau, krau' echoed out and flying across the valley ahead of us came our chough, this to everyone's delight, especially the few who had never seen the bird previously. We were certainly picking up some very good birds to start our 'Year Lists'.

It was now decision time, due to our fortune that day we now had some time to spare. Should we go further down the valley there at Aber, or call in somewhere else on our journey home. We chose the latter. It was now up to me to make the decision, so I decided we would finish off with a bit of sea watching which we could do, looking over the Abergele Roads as this stretch of Colwyn Bay is known.

Driving back from Aber we stopped to enjoy three buzzards loafing about in the sky, and then made our way to Abergele Roads, where we were able to park beach side which we had to ourselves and was free. Conditions were quite calm so we just set up our scopes where we were, and panned the sea and shore. Once again several species of duck were on the water, among which were small flocks of shelduck with the odd red-breasted merganser and goosander visible. Most of the expected gulls were evident: herring, lesser black-backed, great black-backed, black-headed and common gulls, with cormorants out at sea. Nothing too exciting, but I should not have said that. One of my colleagues grabbed my arm and pointed. 'What's that large pale looking gull out there?' I swung round to look where he was pointing, and this fellow had hit the jackpot: he had located a full adult glaucous gull, a visitor from the

Arctic, a rare gull in Britain. I had seen glaucous gulls previously, only two or three, and they had always been biscuit coloured juveniles – not a full winter plumaged adult. This view was almost as though I was seeing the bird for the first time. For the remainder of my group, it was the first time.

The light was rapidly deteriorating, so we had to call it a day, but what a day. If I should ever leave Yoxall, I would have to live in North Wales; the birds up there are quite something. That day we saw seventy-four species, many of course I have not mentioned, and combined with what I had seen locally previously, it had put me over one hundred for the month which was some figure for me.

For our February meeting, we decided to visit Great Linford and Willen, near Newport Pagnell; new locations which had been recommended to us. Unfortunately for us, they were not so good. If we had not seen a barn owl, a short-eared owl and an early chiffchaff, the latter probably an over-wintering bird from northern Europe, it would not have been worth the effort. We only had forty-nine species on the day, but the three mentioned above were good quality birds so early in the year. The journey at least had not been long, and how we had been doing on recent trips, you would have thought this birding was easy; at times, it is not. It can be hard and very frustrating. Birding is very similar to the expression, 'If you cannot stand the heat of a kitchen then keep out'. To be a birder, you have to be a supreme optimist!

During March, we made two local visits to Belvide Reservoir and Blithfield Reservoir, where we did not see anything unusual; although at Blithfield, we had a late flock of twenty-one Bewick's swans and the numbers of grey lags seemed to be on the increase. Come April, we decided to try somewhere new and visited Bradgate Park and Swithland Woods in Leicestershire. Dorothy and I have visited this area frequently; it is very good for woodland and open country birds, and both fallow and red deer are to be seen, which are very tolerant of people. I remember how on one occasion, Dorothy and I had sat down on a bench, opened up a pack of sandwiches which we placed on the bench whilst we got our drinks out. Before we could do anything, a red deer had come up and stolen the pack, paper and all. Fortunately, we had another pack of sandwiches, but our supplies that day had been drastically reduced.

Needless to say, I warned my group of this.

It was a very pleasant day, birds were everywhere and although we had nothing rare, we did see all three species of woodpecker: green, great spotted and the lesser spotted. The days you can see all three in one area you can count on the fingers of one hand, so that was a bit special. We saw eighty-eight species on the day included among them were the North American ruddy duck, cuckoo – an early record for this bird and another early record – a yellow wagtail, plus plenty of deer, but no sandwiches were stolen! It was time to take my group up to The Lakes to see the golden eagle. These birds were very special being the only pair breeding in England, so this became a very specific 'Twitch'.

Thanks to the motorway, a journey of this distance was no longer a problem and fifteen of us made the trip up to Haweswater; in four cars. The largest problem there was that the area was popular with walkers, car parking could be difficult on summer weekends, but we were lucky, we beat the ramblers to it.

The walk down the Riggindale Valley, along the Beck, was always most pleasurable and I was introducing fourteen newcomers to it all. The golden eagles were nesting at the end of the valley; at Short Stile, as I believed this spot was known. We should not be allowed past the wardens who were protecting the birds, but if my previous experience was anything to go by, this would be no problem.

It was not. The female could even be seen sitting on the nest, or standing on it was probably a more accurate description. I could only presume the chick was quite large and the temperature was such as it did not need to be brooded. The male was sitting out in full view, the weather being particularly bright and warm.

Our attention was momentarily distracted. A pair of wheatears landed on the stone wall nearby and both vanished into it with food, there was obviously a nest with large chicks if both birds were busily feeding away. We turned to concentrate on the male golden eagle to find it was now airborne, and lying down the valley directly towards us. It flew past in all its splendour, providing my friends with a most wonderful view; we were talking of the bird only being a cricket pitch length away. Over the years I have had some wonderful views myself of this bird, but that days was the best ever. Those seeing a golden eagle for the first time, certainly know they have!

The eagle vanished over Haweswater, off hunting somewhere I supposed, so we could now seek out other birds of the valley. Common sandpiper were again breeding – well, at least one pair was – we had already mentioned wheatears; we saw several more pairs; a male peregrine falcon flies through, this bird apparently was also breeding locally so we were informed. A cuckoo could be heard calling away and a few pairs of tree pipits are joining in with their melodious song, then one of the wardens shouted and pointed. Up the valley came the returning male golden eagle, and he was due a very good reception. I would have thought, he appeared to be carrying a rabbit in his claws. The eagles were going to feast well it would appear. As if to show the eagle he was not the only large bird to be seen in the valley, a buzzard cruised down, although it was noticeable it did not fly down to the bottom; it was keeping well away from the golden eagle. I wondered why?

Time to slowly move back to our parked cars and in transit we saw and heard curlews, flushed a redshank along the Beck, saw two male ring ouzels and heard raven croaking away; although, we did not see the latter. Passing the small wood we saw spotted flycatcher and just as we cleared this we had a very pleasant surprise, a tawny owl flew into the wood. I could only presume the bird had young to feed and was having to hunt more frequently.

On Haweswater itself we found shelduck, goosander, and mallard, many with family parties of ducklings, and a real big surprise: a drake eider was out on the water. Something about this bird did not look right, the way it was holding one of its wings made me believe the bird was injured and probably was unable to fly hence his being there on his own. Our trip to The Lakes was over, and we all agreed it had been worth every effort. When I did my day's list, I saw we had seen or heard sixty-six different species and included among those were some 'crackers'. Wales is not the only place! The New Forest was chosen as our next full day field meeting, and as with our previous meeting, we were hoping to find a very special bird once again; not quite as rare as an English breeding golden eagle, but still very special and it only bred in a few specific locations in England and that bird was the Dartford warbler.

I had learned of two locations in the New Forest where birds had been seen and heard that year, so once again armed with map references, we were on the hunt. An early start once again, it went without saying, and twelve of us were on our way. Our first spot was near to Beaulieu Palace, not the type of location you would have expected a rare bird to breed successfully, but having said that, I suppose birders did not visit stately homes and motor museums; well, not when birding. To be fair, when we arrived on-site, it was a good mile away from the palace and the only people there were us. We spent a good hour examining the area, all to no avail. Once we thought we had heard the bird, but our experience of this bird was such, we could not be sure, and as with a few birds previously, I again was the only person to have ever seen the bird. Fortunately, we saw many other birds so the hour was not a complete blank.

On to our second site. This time we were visiting the area around Burley. I, at least, was familiar with this area having previously visited with Dorothy; although we were not Dartford warbler hunting on that occasion. We arrived to find a very large area of gorse, it looked like acres of it, and we expected to find one small bird in that lot. What did I say earlier about 'heat in the kitchen?'

We spilt ourselves up into three groups of four, and in military fashion, we slowly made our way through the gorse – that was where we could – you did not batter yourself through gorse! Whitethroats were quite common there and they created the odd adrenalin rush, and a hobby flew across, which did not help much; everything went into cover. Normally, we would have been delighted to spend time with a hobby, but not that day!

Things were not panning out, or so we thought. A slight rustle from deep inside a gorse patch caught our attention, we could not see anything but we could hear the movement. We wanted the bird, presuming it was a bird, to sing or put in an appearance, preferably both. After what seemed an eternity, a 'tr-tchiarr' rang out, and repeated several times. We had our Dartford warbler, but hearing it was not good enough for my colleagues, seeing it was necessary for them. The bird stopped calling, a sudden movement near the top of some gorse, and out popped a long-tailed dark bird which promptly cocked his tail like a wren. Everyone was happy now, they had their Dartford warbler and this bird was a superb male. The long wait and the time and miles travelled were now worth it. Our bird did not stay for long, twenty seconds or so later, he popped back in the gorse and did not even say goodbye! That was that, our New Forest adventure was at an end. We had not done badly though, among the birds seen but not mentioned were pied flycatcher, wood warbler, lesser redpoll, redstart, stonechat and grey partridge – all quality birds. We had fifty-four on the day, and we would all remember the Dartford warbler, and so we should!

The New Forest brought our summer course to an end, and now for what some of my members call, 'the serious stuff': our two winter terms commenced. Numbers were holding up well, with twenty-eight members, four of whom were new.

At our initial meeting, I was able to inform the group of a very rare bird which appeared to have settled in at Ingbirchworth Reservoir near to Sheffield. The bird was a spotted sandpiper, a rare vagrant form North America, a relative to our common sandpiper; did they wish to have a go for it? No need to ask the question really, they most certainly did. The date was fixed, all I now had to do was find out exactly where the reservoir lay; it was a complete new place for me, I had never even heard of it. Fortunately, knowing it was near to Sheffield, out came my old friend Ordnance Survey, and I found the area; where we could park up would have to be sorted out when we went.

Come 18th September, and we were on our way; five car loads of twenty-three eager birders. I must confess I was a little bit concerned, no reports of the bird had been made over the past two days, but we decided to take the chance. Birds can only be reported if birders report them, it does not mean they are not there; well, at least, we hoped that would be the case. We arrived to find a car parking area very quickly, although only two or three cars were parked up, not a good sign when rarity chasing. The question was which way to go. This was sorted out for us by a dog walker. We spoke to him about the bird, which meant nothing to him, but he was able to tell us that he had seen a couple of birders who seemed very interested in something and he pointed us in their direction. That being the only information we had, off we went. I was very impressed with the selection of waders to be seen along the shores of the reservoir, considering there was not a lot of mud visible. We had snipe, green sandpiper, common sandpiper, greenshank, ruff and spotted redshank, but where was our spotted sandpiper? At the end of the reservoir, we spied our two birders, quite a distance away, so we quickly made our way towards them. Part way towards them, we stopped: a cracking drake pintail was out on the water; you do not pass these birds by, rarity hunting or not! At this time of the year, the bird was in good condition and looked every inch the bird seen in field guides. Worth the trip on his own. The surprising thing about the pintail was the fact the only other birds visible on the water were mallards and Canada geese; no need to say who was the star of the bunch!

After a much longer time than I thought, we arrived at the birders, asked the obvious question, they just pointed, and twenty yards or so away was our target. Spotted sandpiper, specially birds in this plumage condition, it was a juvenile and needed to be studied closely. I had only ever seen one spotted sandpiper previously, so I had studied my various field guides to see what the subtle differences are, and they seemed to firm upon but a few. Fortunately, with this bird being so co-operative and feeding so close, it was a little easier than it could have been. It had quite plain upper parts and the coverts were more boldly marked. Our locals also pointed out the bill colour which was yellowish with a dark tip, on a juvenile common, the bill is more uniformly dark. Added to this the pale legs and less distinct eye line concluded the obvious differences. To say we were happy birders was putting it mildly. Whilst enjoying the bird, we noticed heavy cloud was building up from which rain was visible. We had a long walk back to the cars, so discretion won the day, and we left the spotted sandpiper to itself. The rain also won, it poured down, we were thankful for our waterproofs which, fortunately, we had put on.

That brought our day to its conclusion, a little earlier than we had expected, but we were not complaining.

When I did my list we had only seen thirty-two birds, but thanks to the pintail and the spotted sandpiper, it had been a very good day. To put the spotted sandpiper in perspective, I have previously mentioned seeing 'Lifers' such as cirl bunting and Dartford warbler for instance. These birds are rare breeding birds in the UK, but if you wish to see them, you can, all you have to do is spend time where they breed and you will. The spotted sandpiper is in a different category. This may be the only one in the UK this year, some years we may have none. It is a true vagrant, completely lost, having probably been blown across the Atlantic by strong winds, and unfortunately, it will never return home. A rarity in every sense of the word, completely lost however. Our next trip was to the Exe and Dawlish Warren. It was not so much a quiet day, it was just a day when all we saw were expected. The waders were in good number, amongst these were ringed plovers, turnstones, grey plovers, curlews, black and bar-tailed godwits, common sandpipers and sanderlings. On the water, common scoter and eider were seen. The surprise of the day was a kingfisher flying along the shore, we do not usually associate these birds with salt water, although as this one had illustrated, they did; we had fifty-eight birds on the day. The last meeting was a complete disaster. We had planned to visit Marshside and Martin Mere. Part the way up the M6 was blocked by a serious accident, and whilst sitting in the stationary traffic, the heavens opened up and we had very heavy rain. When we finally got off the motorway, we decided to call it a day, and that brought 1983 to a close. The total of birds I saw during the year had reached one hundred and eighty-two, not as high as last year, but quite a bit of quality. We now looked forward to '84.

The year came in for me in a big way, I changed my employment. Things at Joseph Lucas had changed a lot so I sought employment elsewhere, and obtained the position of Group Purchasing Manager at Armitage Shanks, the sanitary ware and bathroom equipment manufacturers. I had left one large manufacturer for another. This company was close to home and, for the first time ever, I had the services of a company car – something I had never dreamed of.

Back to my bird study course. Our first couple of meetings were again half day local events, and nothing unusual was seen on those. Come March, we became a little more adventurous and travelled further afield. We decided to visit Hest Bank, and Leighton Moss. The latter we had visited previously. Hest Bank, however, was new to us all, but I had heard of some very good sightings being made there.

Hest Bank lies just north of Morecambe, and overlooks Morecambe Bay, so once again we had to arrange a date with a suitable high tide so the birds would be brought in closer. There we were after water birds, the odd great northern diver had been reported and several species of duck had been seen – all of interest to us so early in the year, the diver especially so. That bird for some of my colleagues would be a 'Lifer'. Leighton Moss, with its large area of reedbeds, was offering us the chance of bitterns and bearded tits should we be so lucky.

Tide sorted, sixteen of us made the journey up north, and did so without any troubles, unlike our last trip up the M6, and at Hest we parked up in an ideal spot to study the Bay. The tide was almost fully in and large numbers of birds were either on the sea or flying over it, so we quickly set up our scopes and started to pan the area. The light was good and being on the west coast, the sun, which just happened to be out, was behind us so colours on the birds were highlighted.

The range of duck species was spectacular, the pick of which were pintail, goldeneye, red-breasted merganser, goosander, teal, wigeon and shelduck; all birds it was great to get on your 'Year List' so early in the year. Waders were fleeing the incoming tide and among those were curlew, dunlin and knot, we were obtaining some class birds that day. Then a cry went up, 'What are those two large looking birds?' I looked to where he was pointing. Our colleague had hit the jackpot: he had found two great northern divers, not bad going for someone who had never seen the bird before! The divers were both adult birds, moulting through into their adult summer plumage, and they looked magnificent. It had been a year or two since I last saw a great northern, and that day it was almost as if I was seeing them for the first time.

They are a thick necked, heavy looking bird, with a large head, steep forehead and a very heavy bill. The band of white stripes on the side of the neck were showing well and the white markings on the back looked almost silver-like in that day's sunlight. Another feature which was noticeable was the heavy bill held very horizontally; you would have thought that a bill this size would droop somewhat! A superb bird to see, and should we see nothing else, we will still go home happy.

The divers eventually sailed off out of the Bay, and we decided we too would move off. Leighton Moss, can you beat this?

The Moss tried its best, and probably just about sneaked it. We had only been in the hide a few minutes before we saw a small party of bearded tits and brambling were feeding away on a nearby bird table;

189

two birds there we were more than happy to see. Yellowhammers were very active and I was surprised by their numbers. On the water were several fresh-water ducks, mallards, tufteds, gadwalls, shovelers and pochards, plus a decent flock of greylag geese. There were several wader species, additional to those already seen at Hest: redshanks, oystercatchers, ringed plovers and snipes.

Then to put the icing on the cake so to speak, out of the reedbed stalked a bittern, and binoculars nor scopes were needed for this bird; it was less than twenty yards away – what a view. You really do appreciate their size when seen this closely and clearly, along with the superb markings on the bird. No wonder they are almost invisible when standing still in the reeds. The bird stabbed its bill into the water, did not seem to catch anything, and then as though it thought it was not worth the effort, stalked off back into the reeds to vanish from view. What a magical few minutes; we certainly travelled off home happily after that experience.

On that day, we toted up sixty-four species, many of which were 'Lifers' for some of my colleagues and 'Year Ticks' for us all. A superb day.

After the success of trying somewhere new when we visited Hest Bank, we decided we would try another new venue, Blacktoft Sands, an RSPB reserve near to Goole in Yorkshire. This reserve boasts some of the largest tidall reedbeds in England, home to marsh harriers, bearded tits and occasional owls, well worth a try.

This was to be an early April trip to avoid Easter and the school holidays. It was a journey of a little over one hundred miles from Lichfield and we accomplished it in just over two hours. Most of the journey was dual carriage or motorway, so this was achieved with little or no hold ups. Fourteen of us made the trip, and the venue was new to us all.

Blacktoft turned out to be a very compact reserve, with several hides spreadout over a mile or so, little walking was required – the hides were very close to each other as you can imagine. We booked ourselves in, being all RSPB members entrance and parking were free and asked about the best birds likely to be seen. We learned that a small flock of brent geese was on-site, a most unusual species for the reserve. Both hen and marsh harrier had been seen, two early little ringed plovers had arrived the previous day, a barn owl was showing interest in a nest box and a short-eared owl came out hunting mid to late afternoon. Bearded tits had already paired up and were probably breeding. We concluded more than enough to keep our interest going! We had only just left the Visitor Centre when we heard geese calling, and looking up the brent geese gave us a splendid flypast; enough to bring a fillip to any birder's heart! What a start.

We decided to make our way to the furthest hide, the Ousefleet Hide, and then make our way back to our cars for lunch, and then we would do the other section of the reserve during the afternoon.

Ousefleet turned out to be the right decision. Several waders were on the mud, including curlew, redshank, snipe, dunlin and ringed plover. Whilst enjoying these a muffled shout mentioned some small birds that were foraging in a gravel bank. We quickly swung our attention to the gravel, and we were pleased we had, two male shore larks were feeding away. No one had mentioned these being on the reserve, and they were a bit special that was for sure. I have only ever seen shore larks twice in my life, and none of my colleagues had ever seen one. We thought the brents were a great start, I doubted anything would eclipse the shore larks.

In the distance, over the reedbed, a marsh harrier could be seen hunting away and the lapwings were not pleased about that; they constantly harried the bird as they tried to drive it away.

We made our way round to the Marshland Hide. Here there was more water and a decent range of ducks were seen: the pick of these being red-breasted merganser, a solitary drake and a small number of shelduck. While we were enjoying these, the brent geese emerged from behind an island which had been hiding them from our view. We could now enjoy these at our leisure. The quality waders here were black-tailed godwits and curlews once again. The water looked too deep for the smaller waders, they were hopefully round the corner at the Xerox Hide. Initially, things looked very quiet at Xerox. The lagoon had several small islands which restricted the view somewhat; this was best viewed from upstairs in the hide, but this was full so we had to stay put.

From behind one of the smaller islands a jack snipe appeared, which was unexpected, but very welcomed. A pair of oystercatchers flew in, noisily as is their usual way of arrival, they rarely do anything quietly. More ringed plovers and dunlins were scurrying along the shores of the islands and two of these caught my attention. Turning to my colleagues I asked, 'Can any of you see the colour of the legs and bills of those two 'ringies' on the corner of the island?' The answer came back; the bill looked black and the legs looked as though they were covered in mud. I believed we had our little ringed plovers so it was now time to concentrate on a clear view of the birds' heads. We needed to see if the eye had a yellowish ring round it, that would be the clincher. The birds kept on walking ever closer to us, but as they approached a harrier came across and put everything to flight. 'Look at the wings, is there a wing bar?' I shouted.

'No,' came the reply.

We had our little ringed plovers, its close relative the ringed plover has a bright white wing bar. That was my earliest record ever of a little ringed plover; they are a summer migrant – not very common – they only became a regular breeding bird in recent years.

Blacktoft was doing us proud that day. On our way back to the cars for lunch, we called in at the Visitor Centre and informed them about the shore larks. The news was new to them and the last thing we saw were two wardens racing off towards the Ousefleet Hide.

Lunch completed, we made our way to the Singleton Hide, intending to call in at the Townend Hide on our return journey. Singleton is the extreme eastern end of the reserve; from here on, only reedbed is to be seen with no access. Near here, the rivers Ouse and Trent converge which no doubt accounts for the large reedbed at Blacktoft.

We had the hide to ourselves, which was rather surprising, it could be the fact news about the shore larks had got out. A movement in the reedbed near the corner of the hide caught our attention, and out of it emerged two bearded tits, a pair as it so happened, and these were in full view for several seconds. They retreated back into the reeds and that was that; we did not see them again.

A harrier was picked up in the distance which we initially took to be the marsh harrier when one of my colleagues commented on how pale the bird looked; I looked more closely and got the bird in my scope. This bird was very grey, it was no marsh harrier. We had, in fact, found the hen harrier – a superb male bird. It quartered the reeds for several minutes before it drifted from view. That bird would not stay here for much longer, a few breed in Scotland, and it is a few, many of our winter visiting birds come from much further north. Time was catching up with us; if we intended to visit Townend Hide, we had to get a move on. Walking down we had company, the short-eared owl was out hunting and this bird had no fear of man. It just cruised the pathway in front of us as we stood still and silent watching the bird go about its business. It glided backwards and forward along the path several times before it flicked up and vanished over the bushes. What a finish to our day. Blacktoft Sands would most certainly be visited again.

We managed an early holiday. Sarah had just finished school and was due to start work in a few weeks' time, and The Lakes were again our destination. A cottage was again rented for the week and the weather was kind to us. Among the more interesting birds seen during our week were red-breasted merganser, snow goose, whooper swan, golden eagle, peregrine falcon, lesser spotted woodpecker, raven, dipper, wheatear and redstart. It was not really a bird watching holiday, we spent most of the time on seeing the sights and countryside of The Lakes; it was after all, a bit special. Plus, we did not know for how many more years Sarah would wish to holiday with us. She was maturing and making new friends. The summer course did not produce anything new, much as we enjoyed ourselves. We had our usual nightingale and nightjar evenings, visited the Brecks, where we again saw golden oriole, and stone curlew and went golden eagle hunting. Some of the course members had never seen the bird previously, so this visit became a must.

We combined it with a visit to Leighton Moss on our return journey. Here we were surprised to see early returning winter birds such as wigeon and pintail; I did not expect to see these birds in July. They were free flyers so they definitely were not collection birds.

Our first field meeting for the winter course was to Rutland Water. This was taken in early September and sixteen of us made the journey. The weather, unfortunately, was not the best. So we were very pleased to have hides to view from. The weather may not have been good, the birding was very good. We had sixty-nine birds on the day, the pick of which were red-necked grebe, pintail, scaup, ruddy duck, little ringed plover, green sandpiper, greenshank, ruff, little gull, black tern, little tern, tawny owl and spotted flycatcher. A few 'Lifers' or 'Year Ticks' there for everyone. We could safely count that as a very successful visit.

We had a family holiday arranged for mid-September; this time, we went down to Dorset, which was not the first visit we had made to this part of the country. We stayed, once again, in a cottage and had a very pleasant week; the weather was delightful.

The birding was up to the usual standard found in the county. The pick of the eighty-one species we saw were white-fronted goose, black swan, hobby, roseate tern little tern, Sandwich tern, turtle dove, kingfisher, wheatear, stonechat, whinchat, redstart, black redstart, Dartford warbler, wood warbler, rock pipit, white wagtail and twite. Some quality among those birds.

A 'Fall' had occurred at Spurn Point I was told, many small passerines had been reported, so we quickly organised a field meeting for the last day in September; we were just hoping the birds remained. The possibility of a 'Lifer' or two for all of us was the draw.

Fifteen of us drove off, in 'Twitch Mode', and made our way to Spurn. We stopped by the church at Kilnsea, where you will remember we saw firecrest. That day we had the churchyard to ourselves, which is never a good sign if a 'Twitch' is on. We did, however, see both spotted and pied flycatchers, which are not birds to be sniffed at, before driving off to the Point. Here things looked more promising, there were several birders in attendance.

Unfortunately, it was a very calm day, the type of conditions when the birds were likely to move on. Earlier in the week, we were informed, gale conditions had brought in many birds across the North Sea, but these had now mostly dispersed so we were going to have to work hard to find anything.

We gave the sea a few minutes, where we found common scoter, eider, pintail and brent geese – not a bad start – and then moved on down the Point. We stopped on the Narrow Neck to look for waders in the Humber Estuary as the tide was slowly coming back in. This proved to be a very good spot; waders were close in and amongst these were grey plovers, golden plovers, ringed plovers, bar-tailed godwits, greenshanks, knots, curlew sandpipers, dunlins, sanderlings, ruffs and two little stints.

They were not on their own, there were also the commoner waders to be seen; in total, we had fifteen different wader species. The Point now called; what would we find among the thick area of buckthorn? If any passerines were to be found, that should be the place.

As we approached, a pipit foraging along the track side caught our attention and we managed to pull off and park up. I had never seen such a pale looking pipit before and the bird was standing quite erect. My colleagues in the car looked at me, they did not have to speak, their expression was enough – what had we got here? I had not the foggiest idea so I had to quickly put my brain into gear. Whilst one of my colleagues was struggling to get his field guide out of his pocket, not easily accomplished when sitting in a car, then it hit me. The bird was a tawny pipit. The book was extracted, a quick look, and I was right; a tawny pipit it, indeed, was. A colleague managed to get out of the car and made his way back to the cars behind us to pass the information on. There were fifteen very happy birders sitting in those four cars. A magnificent 'Lifer' for all my friends, and for me it was only my second sighting. If we see nothing else, the day was already good.

Reaching the car park, we found a bit of excitement going on. A group of birders had located a red-backed shrike which was sitting out on a stump, just preening away. As I may have mentioned before, you do not ignore shrikes of any type, red-backed in particular, so we enjoyed this one for a few minutes. We told the birders about out tawny pipit, they instantly lost interest in the shrike, and drove off. We proceeded down to the Point.

Fieldfare and redwing numbers were good, and they were feeding on the buckthorn berries with relish. A few wheatears were chasing small insects across the sand and two male whinchats were sitting at the entrance to the bird trap, having the sense not to go into it. Although they would have been ringed and released quite quickly, I must confess I am not a ringing fan; although I did some in my younger days when in Egypt. Since then I have formed the opinion that ringing is not justified, especially when it is the commoner birds which are ringed most frequently. Surely, we know all there is to know about those.

Off into the denser buckthorn, you certainly did not venture from the pathway here, it is not called buckthorn for nothing! Goodly numbers of goldcrests were seen; hard as we looked, no firecrests were tucked in amongst them. Several willow warblers and chiffchaffs were feeding on insects which were on the buckthorn and whilst enjoying those a small bird flicked up which I initially took to be a another goldcrest, but the bird had two yellow wing bars which showed up well, plus a long yellow supercilium. We were looking at a yellow-browed warbler, a first winter bird; the bird of the day was here as far as I was concerned, as it was my first ever sighting. It fed very actively for a few minutes before vanishing into the thick buckthorn. Some bird to finish up with, one or two of my newer members had never heard of the bird before, they had now. We had fifty-nine birds on the day; Spurn Point had done it again.

At our October indoor meeting, the members who had not been able to make our last trip to Spurn raised the question of going up again that month. I had no objection, although I did explain that nothing was guaranteed and the chance of two very successful meetings in succession were unlikely; they would take the chance.

So it was that twenty-four members made the trip; six car loads left Lichfield that morning. We stopped at Kilnsea, the church was very peaceful, nothing there to get excited about. Our next stop was to do some sea watching. Here we again had common scoter, eider, red-breasted merganser, shelduck, goosander and brent geese. Enough there to get your teeth into. Next came wader hunting. The pick here were grey plovers, curlews, turnstones, black-tailed godwits, greenshanks, knots and sanderlings, out of total of thirteen species of waders, no one was complaining.

Moving on down the Point we again found many fieldfares and redwings and as we slowly drove down a small, very darkish little bird, flicked out ahead of us. Stopping we found ourselves looking at a smart, adult male, black redstart, we were more than happy with that.

On the Point itself, the warblers had by now all moved on, although we thought we heard a blackcap, but it only gave us a short burst. Goldcrests were still seen albeit in much smaller numbers than in September. A yellow wagtail did surprise us, so late in the year this was totally unexpected. Whilst enjoying him a merlin came flashing across; fortunately, for the wagtail, it did not appear to be in hunting mode.

Coming out of the buckthorn, onto the water's edge, we were

delighted to see a Lapland bunting feeding on the sandy ground. What he had found I did not know, probably some small insects – such as ants – were on the move. We just stood still and watched him go about his business; he was not aware of us I was sure. Eventually, he moved on having eaten his fill by the look of things.

As we turned to make or way back to the cars, one of my colleagues pointed, saying 'I think I have a diver on the sea.' We quickly turned, it was now a case of up scopes, and a diver it most certainly was. The bird was showing bright white under parts and neck, which was quite thick with a dark back; it was an adult, winter plumaged, black-throated diver. This was a 'Lifer' for many of my colleagues and a 'Year Tick' for me. It also gave me my third diver species of the year, not something that happened very often.

A good bird to end up with. Spurn may not have quite compared that day with our last visit, but I did not think anyone was complaining; well, not to me anyway. Fifty-five birds on the day.

With the short hours of daylight, we decided not to travel a great distance so we chose Rutland Water for our final meeting of the year, and seventeen of us made the journey.

The red-necked grebe seen a month or so back was still in attendance, which was appreciated by those who missed out last time. Among the ducks were several quality birds, the pick of which were goldeneye, common scoter, goosander, ruddy duck and a superb drake long-tailed duck; he alone being worth the journey. Waders were few, with snipe and greenshank being the most interesting.

As we moved on, we bumped into two birders whom I knew and they informed us of where a long-eared owl was roosting and also where a short-eared owl regularly hunted.

That news put a spring into our steps.

The long-eared owl was quickly located. The bird was obviously asleep and did not look at us at all; we quietly crept away. We made our way to the hide from which the short-eared owl was reported; fortunately, we all managed to get in. We were told the owl was about hunting the shore line and its favourite area was pointed out to us. It was just a question of time we were assured. They were right. After ten minutes or so the owl appeared and slowly quartered the ground, just feet above it.

The bird dropped down on three occasions, but did not catch anything. After a few minutes it gave up and flew off and out of view.

Time and light caught up with us, so home we went. Another successful day on which to end the year. With that day's help, I had reached one hundred and ninety-four for the year. Now we waited to see what '85 brought?

1985 started very well. The University asked me to lead a party of birders to the Camargue, in southern France; I needed no second bidding. A friend of mine, Gerry Griffiths, had recently visited the Camargue, and he was also a tutor for the University so I approached him and he agreed to join me in leading a party to the area. The University were only too happy to have two leaders for such a venture, and it also gave us an increase in the number of likely participants. We quickly obtained the necessary numbers and arrangements were finalised for us to visit in May, staying in Arles, which lay just on the edge of the Camargue. As well as birding, many planning meetings had to be held, both between the two of us and with the University. A busy time lay ahead.

Getting back to the current. Our first field meeting of the year was Clumber Park. This is National Trust and our interest lay in the parkland itself. It has a large lake, areas of woodland, both deciduous and coniferous, and its main claim to fame on the bird front are the hawfinches which bred there. It is a short distance from home, just over an hour, and Dorothy and I had visited it on many an occasion so I at least knew my way round it, and where the birds might be found.

That day we concentrated our efforts on a walk round the lake and the wooded area near the church, where the hawfinches were regularly seen. In January the hours of light are limited so we had no chance of visiting other areas of the park, and we also wished to make use of the café facilities; a warm drink and warm food are very beneficial on a cold January day, and that day it was cold. The temperature did not rise above freezing, so a turnout of fourteen was very good in the circumstances.

We commenced with a coffee before making our way to the lake. The principal ducks seen were tufted ducks and pochards, and these were well represented. Canada geese numbers were high and these birds chased after anyone who ventured near in the hope of food, they were unlucky with us. I was surprised at the low numbers of mallards, these are usually the commonest duck to be found. Gull numbers were also low, just a few black-headed gulls, the omens did not look good.

Walking on, a large mixed flock of thrushes brightened up the scene. There must have been several hundred fieldfares and redwings in that flock, it was certainly the largest I had seen for a few years.

A little later on we had a very pleasant surprise. From off an island swam a pair of mandarin ducks, the male bird looking simply magnificent. One or two of my colleagues had never seen mandarin previously, they were going to remember this pair. We spent some time just enjoying those birds before they took to flight and vanished down the lake. At least we knew they were not pinioned! Not a lot else occurred as we walked round the lake and we reached the wooded area by the church. Here it was concentration time, but there is one advantage about trees in winter, not many have foliage so birds cannot hide away so easily unless they vanished into the several yew trees that grew there.

There was a great amount of titmice activity, with several small flocks working their ways through the trees. Here we actually saw all the titmice to be seen in England: great, blue, coal, marsh, willow and long-tailed tits. The only titmouse missing was the crested tit which only breeds in Scotland. That was the only occasion I had ever seen them all in one place, a unique little record really.

We were watching a mixed flock of siskins and lesser redpolls when a colleague shouted, 'I think I have a hawfinch.'. We quickly turned, indeed he had – well not quite – it was not a hawfinch it was three. Unfortunately, they were on a yew tree, and in the matter of seconds they vanished into its interior, never to appear again. We were very pleased our colleague had spotted these birds, all of us at least saw them, short though the viewing was.

The cold by now was beginning to bite. A warm drink and some warm food were called for – this we had and thoroughly enjoyed – and then decided to call it a day. When I completed my list that evening, we had seen fifty-one species, not a bad few hours' work, and the mandarin ducks will be remembered by many, that is for sure. I had also reached eighty-six for the month so far. I might reach one hundred before the month was out.

Our February meeting was back to Wales, the Elan Valley and

Devil's Bridge. A bit of a 'Twitch' really, we were after red kite and crossbills, plus anything else that cared to show itself. Before I forget, I failed with my one hundred in January – I died in the hole on ninety-eight – I was looking forward to reaching it in the Valley.

The main reservoir there in the Elan Valley provides water for the city of Birmingham and the architecture on the dam is most impressive. I quickly reached my hundred with goosander and buzzard, I could now relax and enjoy myself!

Whilst we were watching a kestrel hovering over the water, and hoping it did not dive in, a largish bird of prey flew low across the water – it was a superb female goshawk. She flushed a couple of lapwings who were very fortunate to escape her attention, they no doubt flew off with pounding hearts. A heron flew across rather ponderously and the odd mallard and shoveler could be seen on the water. Time to drive off down the valley.

I knew of an old quarry working we would be passing where peregrine falcon had bred for a few years, so we made a quick stop, and we were lucky. The tiercel (the male falcon) was out gliding round the cliff face and we just stood there appreciating the bird's grace. For several minutes it glided back and forth before settling on a ledge, as if saying, 'That is it for the day.'. We did not complain. We continued on our way down the Valley towards Devil's Bridge. Nearing Devil's Bridge we drove through Cwmystwyth, and on leaving the village, we saw three large birds of prey flying low over a field. We stopped and quickly got out of our cars. Those birds were three red kites, one of the rarest birds of prey in the UK, and this part of the country is their last breeding area. They are not seen in any other part of the UK, and here we had three of them putting on a magnificent flying display just for our benefit. I know there are one or two locations locally where people put out food for the kites in an effort to help them; I just hope they are successful.

All good things must come to an end, and our kites vanish over the horizon. One of our top birds accounted for, will we be lucky with the crossbills?

Pulling in at Devil's Bridge, we disturbed a sparrowhawk which was feeding on the ground of the car park; it flew off with what looked like a blackbird in its claws. This hawk made me suddenly think, what a day we have had for birds of prey; buzzard, kestrel, goshawk, peregrine falcon, red kite and finally sparrowhawk. Six in one day, what have I said about Wales previously?

Devil's Bridge is principally conifer trees, commercially grown, and they are not great woods for small birds. Their insect life is minimal so at this time of the year it is mainly seed eating birds which may be found, and as you will remember from a previous visit here, crossbills are big seed eaters. They break open the cones of the Norway spruce to extract the seeds, and a few hundred of those trees are grown here.

We were not doing very well, so after a late lunch we proceeded further into the woods. We stopped at a clearing where trees have been felled as there was activity in one of the standing trees. 'Kip. Kip' rang out, we had crossbills at last. A small flock of half a dozen or so birds were busily attacking the cones, and they were doing it with zeal. Pieces of the cones were flying off as they attacked the seeds inside. What was interesting was the fact all the bird were males, but they were a very early breeding species, and the females were no doubt sitting eggs. We enjoyed these birds for a good ten minutes before they all flew off, no doubt to find water which they needed to wash off the resin from their bills – otherwise, they would get 'glued up'. Another very successful day drew to its conclusion, exactly fifty species seen that day, amongst which were a few gems.

Our final trip would be to the Ladybower Reservoir and Milldale, Derbyshire. Ladybower is famous because it was here that the RAF carried out much of their training for the Dam Buster Raids carried out during the War. No Lancasters would be disturbing the peace that day, it was other flying objects we were interested in – birds.

Sixteen of us made the trip and things were very peaceful when we arrived, few visitors which suited us admirably. We were not being anti-social, it was just that crowds and birds did not mix. It was a very calm day with hardly a ripple on the water, so conditions were ideal. The only problem was the fact birds were few and far between; the pick being a small flock of goldeneye and a solitary red-breasted merganser. Three curlews flew over calling away, which brightened up the scene and a redshank could be heard calling, but not seen. We decided to spend more time at Milldale. Driving across, we improved things somewhat. We saw a short-eared owl, red grouse, grey partridge, skylark, and stopping at a small wood we knew, we saw crossbills and lesser redpolls. Arriving at Milldale, we were greeted by a little owl perched in a tree in the car park, a very pleasant welcome that. We made our way down to the River Dove. A pair of grey wagtails were sporting about in the shallows, always a delightful sight; I have long considered the male grey wagtail to be one of our top glamour birds. Walking along the river we met up with a couple of birders who pointed out a roosting tawny owl to us. It was tucked away among some thick ivy which was growing up an old oak tree. If they had not pointed it out to us, we would probably not have seen the bird. We thanked them, accordingly, and carried on.

A flock of small birds was moving through a patch of silver birch trees. We stopped to study them and it turned out to be a mixed flock of titmice and siskins, and very active they were.

Further on, a movement on some stones in the river caught our attention: it was a dipper and for several minutes we enjoyed its company. It was actively feeding and jumped into the water frequently, and regularly surfaced with some small creature wriggling away in its bill. This bird was certainly doing well.

Several fieldfares and redwings were still to be seen, although it will not be long before they are returning to their Scandinavian homes; they could well be the last I would see until the autumn again.

One of my colleagues made a comment about rain and pointed skywards. He was right, a thick black cloud was slowly moving across, so discretion being the better part of valour; we hastily made our way back to our cars and, fortunately, beat the rain.

That was the final meeting of the term we now had the summer course and the Camargue to look forward to. That day's total was sixty, not bad considering we were only fifty miles or so from home. It just illustrates the fact you do not have to journey miles to see birds. The birder numbers were still holding up for the summer course, two of whom expressed interest in visiting the Camargue and I was able to get them included at that late stage. They closed the bookings which stood at twenty-eight, plus Gerry and myself. We now had less than two months to finalise the full details. The air travel, transport in France which would be by coach and the hotel arrangements, were all done by the University.

Gerry and myself, we had to organise where we were going and when, and this needed to be done prior to our leaving so that the coach costs could be worked out and paid for. We did manage to get agreement for changing our venues if required, as long as there was no great difference in mileage. Thanks to Gerry's previous knowledge of the area and the amount of studying I carried out, we came out with our plans and the University gave us their approval. We would fly out of Heathrow to Marseille, where the coach would pick us up and then onto Arles.

Anyway, enough of the future, exciting though it was, let us get back to the summer course. We did our nightingales and nightjars once again, both visits were successful. Visited both Blithfield and Belvide Reservoirs and made a trip down to the River Severn, near to Pershore. Here I had learned that marsh warblers were being reported, that was a bird we had to have a go for, and the fact they were being seen so close to home was wonderful news. They are one of the rarest breeding warblers in England, so a date was set, and off we went. This was to be our last trip prior our Camargue adventure.

Several cars were parked up near the bridge over the river, the majority of which had RSPB stickers on their windscreens. Birders were obviously about and a quick look found them, so off in their direction we went. The news was good. A marsh warbler had been seen moving about in an area of reed and bramble, but we were told to be careful as a sedge warbler was also being seen. Although the birds would look totally different, to our untrained ears, their calls were very similar at times, and as the marsh warbler is a great mimic, to see the bird was the only way we would be certain. We could be in for a long evening, but as the bird would be a 'Lifer' for everyone, we were happy to wait. And wait we did. For well over ninety minutes we patrolled the area, saw and heard the sedge warbler, on many occasions, and we were informed by our new friends that we had heard the marsh warbler. Then it all happened. Our marsh warbler popped up and stood out on the top of a tall reed, and for about twenty seconds it let rip. I would not say the bird sang, it just shouted a jumble of phrases at us; the bird certainly was no nightingale, but we heard him out in delight. The bird vanished back deep into the undergrowth and although we heard him a few times, and were happy to know we were hearing him then, he did not put in another appearance. I think it is safe to say we all drove home happy.

Now for the Camargue, where I understand marsh warblers are more common, if that is the case we may actually be able to recognise them – now there is a thought!

Another thought had occurred to me. I will close this chapter here as I believe the Camargue will require a chapter of its own. It will all be new. Apart from Gerry, none of us had visited previously and when Gerry was there, he did not have any responsibility for other birders. It will be a test of both his and my knowledge and experience especially as we will be meeting birds never seen or heard previously, and our colleagues who have paid for this will expect us to know. The Camargue will be a challenge, let us hope we are up to it.

LA CAMARGUE

Our flight was only slightly delayed but I saw something I never expected to see in the UK. A flight from Israel had landed and armed police were escorting the passengers through the terminal and we were all pushed to one side to allow them to pass. Armed police, I never believed this would happen to us. The world was changing, unfortunately, and was only likely to get worse.

On our arrival, the coach was waiting for us and the driver spoke very good English and even better still was a keen birdwatcher. I sat near him on the journey to Arles and he had several suggestions of where we should go and he even suggested that as we would have a few hours available that afternoon; he would take us to a local heronry where several species of herons and egrets bred and good views were guaranteed. I put this to my colleagues and the answer was a unanimous 'Yes'. Having been cooped up on a plane and coach for several hours, the thoughts of a bit of fresh air and some exciting birds to start with, sounded too good to miss.

We quickly booked ourselves in, deposited our cases in our rooms, sorted out our optics and cameras and back into the coach we went. I do not speak French so I cannot tell you the name of the place we were taken to, apart from the fact it was unpronounceable, but it was less than half an hour from the hotel. It was a narrow strip of deciduous woodland alongside a small river and reedbed and I was very pleased we were here early May, the 3rd May in fact, as this was an area which looked likely to be mosquito infested. We had deliberately come early in the hope we avoided those as the Camargue is a very large marshy area and mosquitoes were part of the picture. That day we had it right, they were few and far between although the odd bite occurred. Anyway, back to the birds, they were, after all, what we had come for. Jean Luc our driver, was not wrong, if this was anything to go by, he was going to be very useful to us during the week. We quickly picked out the grey herons, we knew them of course, but the two or three purple herons among them were a totally different thing, our first 'Lifers', that is apart from Gerry who had seen the birds elsewhere on his previous visit. Little egrets, cattle egrets and squacco herons were constantly flying in and out; bitterns could be heard booming from the reed beds, the odd night heron was starting to leave the heronry and over the reedbed marsh harriers were seen. From the reedbed great reed warblers could be heard and seen, what a start to our week, and I had been assured by both Gerry and Jean Luc it could only get better.

Back to the hotel. The wine and meal was going to be good that night, and we planned our trip for Sunday, along with a glass of brandy, what else could you drink in France? We were going to visit Cacharel which overlooks the Etang de Gines where there was a large flamingo colony, then down to Saintes-Maries-De-La-Mer where slender-billed gulls bred, that was on the coast. Then, if we had the time, we would call in at Gines where the Centre d'information du Parc Naturel Regional is located. Just in case you are thinking I have suddenly developed a French tongue, I have not, I am just referring to my notes and my 'parc naturel regional du camargue' map!

In transit to Cacharel we saw several flamingos, greater flamingos to be more accurate, as they flew over the road ahead of us. Several hundred pairs were breeding on the Etang, and to see such long-legged and elegant birds sitting on their mud nests, which appeared like mud chimney pots, looked almost incongruous. When seen walking through the water they are some bird and here, in the bright French sunlight, they certainly had a pink hue to them. We now knew we really were in the Camargue. Back in the coach and off now to find, we hoped, the slender-billed gulls. We understood these were to be seen at the Baisse de la Blancarde, from a sea wall which overlooked the area. Neither Gerry or Jean was familiar with the area, it was just something I had gleaned from another birding friend of mine, and he had omitted to pass on some very important information!

We found the spot without too much trouble, and being a Sunday the beach was quite busy, but our interest lay in the sea. Telescopes set up, we lined the wall and commenced to gaze seawards, then it hit us. We were staring across a nudist beach, through telescopes; what would people think we were doing? I must be honest, some of the scopes did dip a bit, and for some reason these were all being used by men! Fortunately, the occupants of the beach were not overly concerned, some jumped up and waved at us, shouting something in French, which when translated was an invitation to go down and join them. We 'resisted' the temptation, and Jean shouted down to the nearest, explaining who we were, where we were from, and what we were doing. They seemed happy with this; we wiped the sweat from our brows and got down to gull seeking.

This part of France is about as far west as the slender-billed gull breeds; it is more of an eastern Mediterranean species, so it was a bit special in France. We spent some time going through the various gulls along the sea fringes, then Gerry spotted a small group of six of the birds flying in a line, low across the sea. This is where experience comes into play, he was the only one among us who had seen the bird previously and I for one was very pleased he had. We all had our slender-billed gull. On leaving we gave our 'nudist' friends a cheery wave, to which many responded, and back to the coach we went, with, I must confess, many a smile. As one wag said, 'They do call it bird watching after all.' I will not repeat what his wife said to him! After all that excitement, our visit to Gines was going to have to be brief, and so it turned out. We did, however, see more interesting birds; greater flamingos, purple herons, marsh harriers and in a small wooded area a pair of hoopoes. Every birder wants to see hoopoes and that pair put on a splendid show for us. The male was actually displaying to the female, and some performance it really was. His crest at times was fully opened and it seemed to stretch past the tip of his long de-curved bill, looking like a magnificent pinkish fan in the bright light.

Whilst we were enjoying our hoopoes a shout went up, 'What are these birds of prey coming across?' A quick look and Gerry and I answered almost as one 'Black kites,' and plural it certainly was; we had nine of them. This took me back to my days in Egypt where flocks of black kites were regularly seen, but these are the first I have seen in over thirty years. They are a fairly common bird in this part of Europe, but your first views are the ones you remember, and we shall be taking many a memory home I am sure.

A final view over the Etang produced black-winged stilts and avocets which brought the curtains down on a superb day. The question now was, can we keep this up? Or as Jean assured me, it can only get better.

One final event of the day. As we drove back to Arles, Jean stopped the coach so we could look at some of the famous black bulls of the Camargue. A herd of about twenty were splashing their way through the marsh, and majestic beasts they certainly were. Bull fighting is carried out in this part of France, but unlike the Spanish bull fighting where the animals get killed, this does not happen here in France; the bull is the important part of things, and their top animals are very prized indeed.

We decided to give the Camargue a rest for our next trip out. The weather forecast looked very settled so we decided to go mountaineering, not on foot, but by coach. About one hundred kilometres north-east of Arles lies Mont Ventoux, at 6263 feet; now you know why I mentioned 'not on foot'. Here we were after some of the larger birds of prey, eagles and vultures, plus rock thrushes and a few of the interesting warblers found on the lower slopes. Also, when Gerry was here last, he had found a small conifer area where crested titmice were seen so we had a good selection to seek.

Gerry's memory was good and he directed the coach to the crested titmouse location, which also sported a small café, where very pleasant coffee was obtained. Crested tits, as I have mentioned previously, only breed in Scotland so this would be an opportunity for many of us to see the bird for the first time – me included. The wooded area was comparatively small, so we spread ourselves out and slowly walked through it. We had not walked far before a purring trill was heard. I looked at Gerry, he nodded, we had a calling crested tit in the vicinity. We gathered close together as we tried to track the call down; we need not have bothered, the bird came to see us.

A sudden movement and the bird landed on the low branch of a nearby tree, and proceeded to stare us out. It was as if the bird was challenging us as to what we were doing, and as if in anger, the crest appeared to be raised stiffly. What a view and the first view for many of us. The bird stood its ground for a minute or two before it was off, never to be seen again. We heard birds trilling away, saw the odd movement, but that first sighting was the only bird we really saw; it was our lucky day. The question now was will it continue?

The drive up the mountain was most impressive and Jean handled it as though he was a man born to mountain driving. We parked as near to the summit as was permitted, quickly ate our lunch, and were on our way. A golden eagle was soaring away near the summit. looking very spectacular as they normally do, and looking down into the valley beneath us a flock of about twenty honey buzzards was passing through, some sight that. Continuing on our way, we noticed what appeared to be a large nest in a crack on a sharp rock face. Looking at it carefully through our scopes, there appeared to be movement on it – a nest it most definitely was – probably the eagles, we thought. We settled down to watch it and to our absolute delight and excitement, an Egyptian vulture flew in; we just could not believe it. Here was another bird like the hoopoe, my only one ever had been in Egypt. The adult vulture appeared to feed the nestling and then settled down to brood the young bird.

At this altitude things can be rather quiet, not many small birds are evident, so we drove down to look over the rocky outcrops which covered the lower slopes of Mont Ventoux. Here as well as rocks, scattered shrubby trees grew, and a few patches of orchids were visible; unfortunately, no one could identify these, they were not species seen in the UK.

One or two lesser kestrels were seen, very active birds these, another memory from my days in Egypt and I was pleased to have experienced them previously as they could easily have been dispatched as kestrels.

Some activity was occurring on the ground beneath a small area of scrub and a thrush-like bird popped out, thrush-like it most certainly was; it was a male rock thrush, an incredibly attractive looking bird. It is a combination of grey blue and rosehip red, with a brilliant white panel on the back. I cannot really describe the bird, just look in your field guide and I think you will agree with me that it is some bird. The bird appeared to find a small grub or caterpillar and flew off with this in his bill. Sadly, he did not return, leaving us once again with just our memories! Two small, pipit-like birds caught our attention. A closer look confirmed they were water pipits. If ever a name is an anomaly, this bird's name is. For many years it had been considered to be a race of rock pipit until it was decided it was a species in its own right. The bird was mainly seen in the UK as a winter visitor, invariably near to water, lakes, reservoirs, pools etc., so it was christened as a water pipit. Unfortunately, where the bird originates from is mountain slopes and rocky outcrops, such as we were among then, no water to be seen for miles, so if a bird was ever incorrectly named this is it. Whatever my thoughts may be, as a water pipit it went on my list.

On now down to the café where as we had some time we would go warbler hunting. As well as the crested tits' wood there was agricultural ground, hedges and a few gardens there abouts, so after a coffee we went walk about.

From a wildish looking garden, a brief burst of song emerged. I looked at Gerry, he looked back at me, and Jean was no help either – he just muttered something in French which may have meant something to him, but not to us. I was pretty sure I had heard this song before, and I thought I had heard it in Malta where I spent a couple of days on my return from Egypt. Then it hit me; could it be a melodious warbler? I asked Jean the question, but the name in English meant nothing to him, so I got my Collins Field Guide out of my backpack.

I had brought this field guide with me just in case this type of situation arose. Jean's English may be very good, but you cannot expect non-English speakers to know all the English names for various birds. In the Collins field guide, they also have the names in four languages; French being one of them. 'Hypolais polyglotte,' I say. Jean breaks out in laughter at my pronunciation, but nods his head; melodious warbler we have and, as if to prove the point, the bird popped up onto the top of a bush. If he had done this earlier it would have saved us a lot of confusion, but we had got there even if the route was a little devious.

A goshawk flew through as though it was interested in whatever had been going on – at least we had no problem with this bird – the melodious warbler vanishing back deep into its bush. He was no fool! A small yellowish-green bird burst out of the nearby conifers and proceeds to preen itself. We were mightily pleased it did; the bird was a citril finch, a bird I did not expect to see there. According to my field guides, they rarely breed below 5000 feet. Mind you, we were still quite high there and the bird may well have been just on passage to higher ground.

Whatever the reason, we were delighted the birds just kept on coming; if we had seen any of these back home, we would have gone crazy. To think, they were probably just the norm there.

It was not all unusual birds for us, many of the birds we saw and heard back home were just as common here. Chiffchaff and willow warblers for instance, swallows and house martins; we had been seeing or hearing these whilst on our travels, not necessarily at that altitude, but lower down most certainly.

Time to start our homeward journey, but as we approached lower levels we passed a small area that back home we would consider to be a quarry. It had a sharp, steep face and martins were flying to and from it. We stopped, and were pleased we did. The martins were crag martins, not sand martins as we first thought, and flying amongst them were a few Alpine swifts – a much larger swift than those we are familiar with back home. For the next few minutes, we enjoyed watching these masters of the air as they hurtled back and forth, the swifts especially had rocket boosters fitted. A fine end to our day out.

The question was, once the brandy was poured, where would we go next?

The decision was made – after about the third brandy – we would go back to the Camargue and really give that a good going over. There was also a small quarried area where Gerry had seen bee-eaters. Now that is a bird to consider, a technicoloured swallow if there ever was. The only thing which worried Gerry was the thought we may be just a few days early for their arrival; when he saw them last, it was later in the month. We had to give it a try, and we did seem to be on a roll!

The place in question was close to Gageron, down a minor road, where we should have no problem with parking the coach. Jean Luc knew the area well, although he was unaware of the bee-eater colony, so he was looking forward to it as much we were. Gerry was right, parking no problem and we had a short walk of about ten minutes to the quarry. Part way there I stopped and pointed, 'Listen, I am sure I can hear bee-eaters.' This was a call I had lived with for weeks at a time when they were passing through Egypt on migration; a call I had always dreamed of hearing in the UK. France may not be the UK, but it is a bit closer than Egypt! We were listening to a call which books variously refer to as a 'schrru'. Whatever that may mean, to me they have a penetrating bell-like ring which carries long distances, several hundred yards, and that was what I could hear then. 'Gerry, don't worry, your birds are here; I had been waiting thirty long years to hear that call again, and I am not going to get it wrong now,' I told him. And I had not. Over this quarry, about twenty or so bee-eaters where flying furiously; some birds were even excavating their nesting burrows. We just sat down and took it all in, they may not be the rarest birds to be seen in the Camargue, but they were certainly the most colourful. The bird of the holiday so far for me, I had waited a long time to see them again. Time to journey on further into the Camargue. Having shown us the black bulls, Jean now wanted to show us the white horses for which the Camargue is equally famous, and it did not take him long to do so. Galloping through the marsh, with water spraying up behind them, came a group of the horses. They are an eponymous breed of white horses known as Camarguais, and are believed to be one of the oldest breeds of horse in the world. They are ridden by the cowboys who rear the equally famous black fighting cattle. The bulls are raised in semi-rural conditions and are allowed to run through the Camargue as free-running herds, as we had seen a day or so back. I did not think I would wish to stand in front of either the bulls or the horses!

That bit of background dealt with, let us get back to the birds and the Camargue wildlife. The Camargue was only set up as a national reserve in 1970 I believe, but has already received international approval as being one of the most important wildlife areas in the world. In Europe, it is probably the most important.

Considering the amount of water in the area, waterfowl numbers were not large. A few great crested grebes, mallards, shelducks and red-crested pochards, plus the odd mute swan, and that was about it; surprising really. Add to those coots, moorhens and water rails and that was about it. We might have been low on waterfowl, birds of prey certainly made up for it. Additional to those previously mentioned that day, we chalked up sparrowhawk, Montagu's harrier, osprey, hobby, peregrine falcon, red-footed falcon and kestrel. We actually had nine different species as we travelled round the Camargue that day, unbelievable.

We were interested in seeing some of the warblers which were not regularly seen in the UK, so we went off seeking those. As with any piece of countryside the landscape varies and, although the Camargue is famous as a wetland area it too has pockets of woodland and scrub and these we headed for. Many of the locations are not named on any maps, they were just spots known to Gerry and Jean and they provided us with a goodly selection of birds. Fan-tailed warblers, spectacled warblers, Cetti's warblers, Sardinian warblers plus melodious and great reed warblers already seen. Warblers we were familiar with such as reed warbler, sedge warbler, willow warbler, chiffchaff, blackcap, whitethroat, lesser whitethroat, garden warbler and wood warbler were plentiful, and those caused us no identification problems.

In one particular scrubby area, a great spotted cuckoo put in an appearance, and I was really surprised at the size of the bird. Much larger than our cuckoo, it lays its eggs in the nests of magpies. This gives you some idea of the size of the bird. It is a long tailed bird with bronze coloured primaries and a black cap with a slight tuft. Although not resembling our cuckoo, the flight is very much that of a cuckoo. Another interesting fact, which I have read, is that the bird will lay several eggs in the same nest. Little did we know this was to be our only sighting of the bird, they were much rarer than we thought.

Journeying back to Arles we called in near to Mas D'Argon at a roadside marsh where, according to Jean, many herons and terns were to be seen, and he was not wrong. It was almost like a repeat of our first day, except it was too early for night herons to be putting in an appearance. It was the selection of terns which grabbed our attention, I had never seen so many species of tern in one place. As the pool was a marshy pool I expected to see black terns; there we had black, white-winged black and whiskered terns, but additional to those we also saw gull-billed terns – admittedly only two, common terns, little terns and Sandwich terns. An incredible selection with which to finish off the day. Arles called, more food, wine and brandy, then decision making. This was not going to be difficult; one area I had been interested in from the moment the Camargue had been suggested, was La Crau. This is an area of semi-arid plains, or so my information informed me, which is home to little bustards, stone curlews, pin-tailed sandgrouse and a bird I have only ever seen once previously, the roller. Various birds of prey were reported from the area and the best place to head for was the old airfield of Piste de Vallon. You have to be careful there as it still is a military zone, but there are locations nearby where I had been assured you would not get involved with the military. Then, if we had time, we would visit a large rubbish tip at Entressen where many birds of prey congregated. You cannot beat a bit of quality to finish off your day; here I mean the birds, not the tip!

Jean Luq knew the area well and he parked up near to an old military tower which made an excellent viewpoint, and within minutes of our arrival we had seen both little bustard and pin-tailed sandgrouse. The bustards were in display mode so they were not hiding away as is their usual state; therefore, we had marvellous views, and as only Gerry and Jean had seen these birds previously, it was jack-pot time for most of us. It was easy to see where the name pin-tailed originates from, it certainly has a pin-tail, and what was extra pleasing is this bird was a new species for all of us.

Whilst all of this was going on the odd skylark had been singing, when we became conscious of a larger looking lark running on the ground, and we were glad we had; this bird turned out to be a calandra lark. Another bird, which prior to that day, that had only ever been a picture in a book. La Crau was doing us proud.

As things quietened down we spent some time gazing skywards. As well as skylarks, the odd crested lark was airborne and high in the sky above them a very pale looking bird glided across. In the hazy sunlight, we at first thought it was a gull of some sort probably going to the tip, but as the bird came ever closer we realised it was a bird of prey, not a large bird. It did not look much larger than a kestrel, but it was its colour which drew our attention. It was very pale with dark primaries and as it tilted in flight it showed black patches on the secondary coverts. I could not believe what I was looking at, neither could Gerry; we had a black-shouldered kite, a bird I had not even considered we might see. Our field guides did not show the bird to visit this part of France, what it was doing I did not know, but we were mighty glad it had.

Whilst we were discussing this bird a group of birders arrived, rather out of breath, and in French of a sorts asked us about the bird. We burst into laughter; they were obviously English and, in fact, were Londoners. Of all the places to meet up with some fellow countrymen. Back to our native tongue. They were interested in the bird we had just seen, which they had only seen from a distance. When we were able to confirm their thoughts they were delighted to have met up with us. They stayed with us for another hour or so before they were off into the Camargue. They were only there for three days so they were not hanging about.

We were just about ready to move off ourselves when a larger bird of prey came across, a buzzard, but wait a minute. This bird was very long-winged and rather pale and at times hung, almost motionless. My first thoughts were rough-legged buzzard, but it did not have the pale tail and black terminal band. Fortunately, the bird came in lower and slowly flew past us and the bird looked very buffish and rusty-red in colour. Nothing else for it, but out with our field guides and as we were looking I suddenly thought, if it was not a buzzard, or a rough-legged buzzard – and the head was too large for an honey buzzard – there was only one left! 'Look at the long-legged buzzard,' I told my friends. Long-legged it was, another bird I had not even considered, as with the kite previously; what it was doing there, I did not know. I just hoped we did not meet up again with the 'Londoners'; I would have hated to have told them what they just missed.

Walking back to the coach we disturbed a small group of stone curlews which simply ran across the ground in front of us; I can only presume flying was not their top priority. We had a priority, however, the tip at Entressen.

But La Crau had not finished with us yet. Driving across, a bird dropped off some wires and landed on the ground. It looked dove-like but no dove acted like this. We stopped and the bird flew back up onto the wire, what a bit of luck, it was a roller. Had it not dropped off to the ground as we passed, we may easily have taken it for a dove. Telephone and power lines are particular favourite lookout posts for the roller, as this one proved that day, and they are very much a roadside bird – when you see them that is, which we had. The day was getting better by the hour. We made Entressen without any further adventure. As tips go this is a monster, but the birds to be seen were quite something. Back home most tips or landfill sites as we prefer to call them, are normally home to large numbers of gull; there, it was birds of prey. Many black kites were to be seen, well over twenty, and they were very active. A young Egyptian vulture, looking like a first year bird, probably a bird reared last year up Mont Ventoux, was tearing away at some meat or other. Several lesser kestrels were in attendance, no doubt waiting for some small rodent or insect to appear. Gulls were also active, the yellow-legged variant of the herring gull was common there and several Mediterranean gulls were to be seen. All in all, a scene of great activity which was suddenly disturbed and many birds flew off. A large bird of prey descended onto the tip – obviously, an eagle of some sort – and the only bird not really concerned by its approach was the young vulture. It was just about a similar size and did not feel over awed by the eagle. The question for us now was which eagle had we, a golden eagle it obviously was not.

The bird had a large dark area on the under wing and it had glided in on slightly arched wings. Prior to coming to the Camargue, I had read upon the various bird of prey likely to be seen and I was very glad I had: this was a Bonelli's eagle, and as I said so, Jean Luq laughed and nodded his agreement. He had known all along and was just putting me to the test; I must try and get one back on him, I did not know the French had a sense of humour!

Things quietened down, the birds commenced to return and the eagle just sat there watching it all. He was not hungry by the look of things, but he had finished the day off well for us.

Back to Arles to decide where we go the next day.

The week was now beginning to race away, only two full days left. Having seen the rock thrush earlier in the week, many were interested in seeing a blue rock thrush; it being more spectacular than the rock thrush. Jean Luq knew an area where they were pretty much guaranteed, this could be combined with an area Gerry was familiar with where some of the more unusual passerines of the area could be seen – such as crested larks and short-toed larks. The decision was made and Les Baux, followed by La Caume, were our next destinations. Les Baux is a great place for wallcreepers in the winter, not the summer unfortunately. A steep rock face below a ruined Roman fortress was the place to go according to Jean, and he was proved right. Below the fortress Alpine swifts were scything their way through the air, Sardinian warblers were serenading away from the vegetation, and the bird we were really after was out on the rocky ground seeking food. Had Jean brought the bird with him I wondered?

I think everyone agreed with me when I thought the blue rock was the more spectacular bird, and he was not named blue without reason. The male bird is totally blue, and it was he we were studying. Unmistakable. Jean could relax now, his job was done, it was now over to Gerry. We had a bit of walking to do at La Caume where a TV relay station is on the top of the summit, but we were not going up there. Walking through maquis, we found it full of subalpine warblers; I am pleased we were able to see them. Their song was completely new to me. Nearing the mountain, where the vegetation thinned out, we had a pleasant surprise. A great grey shrike popped out and stood on a piece of rock for a few seconds; fortunately, we all managed to see it. A little later, Gerry proved his worth, a crested lark walked across the pathway in front of us, and it appeared not to have a care in the world – and why should it, it was his patch, we were only visitors! Over the mountain a large bird of prey soared, it was an adult Bonelli's eagle, that gave us two different Bonellis eagles in two days. As eagles do, it put on quite a display. Almost as though it was playing to the gallery! We almost gave him a round of applause.

Things did not end there. Right above the TV station an Egyptian vulture glided across, hardly a wing beat as this majestic bird did its best to outshine the Bonelli's. I decreed it a draw!

Turning to walk back we had further excitement, a woodchat shrike this time. This bird had actually caught something. Whether it was a small lizard type animal or a large insect I did not know. Whatever it was it was wriggling away in the bird's bill. According to the field guides, larger insects are its prime food. The shrike studied us for a few seconds before flying off with his catch. Two different shrikes on the same day and in the same place, takes some beating. Nearing the coach, there was more to see. In a rocky area, a wheatear was foraging and this was no common wheatear. We waited for the bird to provide us with a better view. When it finally did, we were delighted to see we had a black-eared wheatear. This was another bird which had never crossed my mind that we might see. These type of surprises are always most welcome.

Our birds that morning had been seen quite quickly so as we had time available. A quick visit back to the Camargue was called for, and we left it up to Jean Luq where he took us. As we had already seen two shrikes, he thought we should see number three and he was taking us to an area where he believed the red-backed shrike was breeding; there were no complaints with that.

Approaching Arles, when I happened to be sitting in the front of the coach, two small birds were seen having a dust bath on the side of the road. I did not recognise them immediately so I asked Jean to stop. He did and we had a real stroke of luck, they were two short-toed larks. We may have missed out on them at La Caume, but if you are meant to see them you will, and we obviously were! They were intent on their dust bath and a coach parked up nearby was not going to distract, which was perfect for us. When seeing a bird for the first time, a good view makes all the difference, and my friends had that. The bird was smaller than a skylark, quite pale, with a pale supercilium, a dark stripe behind the eye, and a rather pointed, finch-like bill. All visible at this short distance. We should all remember our first short-toed lark, and I certainly will.

On for red-backed shrike. That may not have been a new bird for many of my colleagues, but to see three different shrikes on the same day would be very, very special. Over to Jean, I did my bit with the short-toed larks!

The shrike had been seen near to Barbe d'Ase on the banks of Le Grand Rhone, a few miles south of Arles, and Jean managed to park the coach up on a small piece of open ground. I did not think coaches came down there very often! Jean walked us up to an area of scrubby ground, and there we waited.

Half an hour passed us by and we were thinking our luck had run out when it all happened. A red-backed shrike burst out – burst being the only word to describe it – to take a large flying insect on the wing; you would have thought it was a flycatcher not a shrike. These shrikes are the original butcher bird. When food is in good supply they will catch it and spear it on thorns or branch ends, laying up supplies for days when food is not so plentiful. Jean and Gerry between them had given us a good day, but hopefully my short-toed lark was noted.

The next day would be our final day. It had rolled round very quickly, but I was sure none of us would forget it. Where to go? We had decided to visit La Camargue again. We might not see anything new, but it was what we came for. The wine and brandy that evening had a bitter sweet flavour to it.

One thing I had forgotten to mention was that Jean Luq had made enquiries regarding the status of the black-shoulder kite and long-legged buzzard in France, and had found out they were very rare birds. As such, all records should be reported to the French Rare Birds Committee and he brought in two forms for us to fill in, in French. Fortunately, among my friends was Hilary Guy, who had spent many years in France and spoke the language like a native – and like Jean Luq himself – so over a drink or two we filled in our reports and off they went. Whether we would hear anything was another matter, but we had done our duty.

Our destination that day was the extreme tip of the Camargue at Station de Pompage de Beauduc, not too far away from Saintes-Maries, but before reaching there we had the Camarague to travel through. We again enjoyed the greater flamingos, which appeared to be flying everywhere, numerous egrets, herons, marsh harriers aplenty, and near a café stop, we again saw hoopoes, and that was not the end of it all. Driving along the edge of Etang de Consecaniere, a bird of prey flew through. Buzzard sized, but very pale, with black primaries and trailing edges to the wings; only one eagle is this small and so coloured, the booted eagle. We managed to park and watch the bird for several seconds before it vanished from sight. What a cracking start to our last day.

A few of the commoner waders were to be seen along the shores of the Etang: common sandpipers, redshanks, greenshanks, curlew sandpipers and grey plovers; all birds we were familiar with back home. At least we did not need to get our field guides out for these birds!

Driving through a small arid area, a group of starlings caught our attention. Stopping the coach once again, we found we were looking at a small group of spotless starlings; a new bird for all of us, apart from Jean Luq, needless to say. Another bird I had not really thought about. Whilst enjoying the starlings we had a most pleasant surprise, a golden oriole dropped in and joined them. After our struggles back home to see this bird, here we had one just yards away collecting small insects from the ground. Things were just getting better by the minute. Not a new bird to many of us, just the best view we could possibly have.

We stopped outside Saintes-Maries for a coffee break before proceeding on to our destination where we would have our snack lunch before birding.

Here it was bird of prey time. A large bird came gliding past, very pale and long winged, obviously an eagle, but which? The undersides of the wings was almost solely white, with just a few dark markings and dark primaries. Gerry and Jean were as much in the dark as I was. As I struggled to remember my bird of prey studies, realisation dawned: it was a short-toed eagle. It had a contrasting dark head, and I remembered this. Field guides were got out and I was proved to be correct; it was very nice to win one as they say. Some coffee-stop that! Four different eagles in a week, that would take some beating.

Eagle watching over, now for our final destination. As we drove in, another delight awaited us. Walking along the edge of the Etang de Galabert was a white stork; the last bird I expected so far south in Europe at that time of the year. I would have expected them all to have passed through on their way to their breeding grounds. We did not complain, that was a fact.

Lunch over, concentration time. Round the edges of the various small islands, where sand and gravel was showing, were a few ringed plover types – mainly little ringed plovers and the odd ringed plover – but one bird in particular kept attracting our attention. It was certainly paler than its fellows and did not show so much black on the face and the black neck-band was broken. Gerry and I looked at each other. We nodded. We had a Kentish plover, a new bird for several of us.

We turned our attention to the shingled shores of the Golfe des Saintes-Maries ou de Beauduc. According to Jean, there was usually a good selection of yellow wagtails at that time of the year, and among them many of the variants of that particular species were recorded. There are eight races of the yellow wagtail, with the yellow wagtail, Motacilla flava flavissima being the race most commonly seen in the U.K. They are a summer migrant, and are among our most colourful birds. Jean was correct, several wagtails were scurrying amongst the shingle; no doubt, seeking out small flies which were emerging from the ground. They are very active feeders and in the brilliant light of that day, they looked strikingly yellow; one would have thought one was looking at long-tailed canaries! Jean was right, they were not all 'flavissimas'. Concentration time, and out came the field guides; I thought we might require some assistance. After much effort, we managed to identify four races positively, and believe we may have had a fifth. The larger proportion were our yellow wagtails, followed by the blue-headed and grey-headed, both of those being the races found in Scandinavia. We located a single Sykes wagtail, he was way off track, being on his way to south east Russia and a probable Spanish wagtail. We just could not get the view we wanted of him. But with Spain being next door, so to speak, it might well have been.

A very informative exercise that had been and we had all learned a lot with regard to yellow wagtails species. Should we come across some of those races in the UK, that experience would be most useful.

Whilst all this yellow wagtail work was going on, Gerry suddenly spoke up, 'Three slender-billed gulls flying past,', and he was right. Quite close in those gulls provided us with very good views, and we did not have any distraction this time!

Just as we were about to depart, dropping onto the ground came a superb male black redstart, which we enjoyed for several minutes as it chased small flying insects across the ground. He was not interested in us, he had a family to provide for, and that was that. Time to return to the hotel; we now had our packing to do, settle our accounts after we have finished for the evening, and prepare to depart. We had experienced a great week. The weather had been kind to us, not a drop of rain, and the birds had been magnificent. Our driver, Jean Luq, had done a wonderful job and his local knowledge had helped us tremendously; he had earned his tip and the brandy was 'nae' bad.

Our drive down to Marseille gave us our final chances to see the greater flamingos, and they did not disappoint. We even stopped for a few minutes to look at a hoopoe, and whilst we were there, we heard a woodlark singing; our first of the week and our one hundred and thirty-third species of the week. Not a bad finale that!

Well not quite. As we taxied to take off, three black kites flew past us, France's final throw. Who knows, we may be back.

BACK TO THE '80s, COULD THE UK EVER BE THE SAME?

Our first field trip was to Anglesey, a place I love, but it did not seem the same after the excitement of the Camargue, but hopefully the birds would soon change that.

Seventeen of us made the journey, and we arrived on a very pleasant morning, making our way straight to South Stack. We had hardly got out of our cars before we heard the 'kyah, kyah' call of the chough, and two flew over our heads. What a start to the day, and we got none of those in the Camargue!

We watched them fly down towards the cliffs and followed them on their way. Razorbills and guillemots could be seen flying low over the sea and to our great pleasure two puffins were also seen. Those are no longer a common bird on Anglesey, although there is an island off the coast called Puffin Island, which I suppose told us something.

Further out at sea the odd Manx shearwater was flying past, as were gannets and a mixture of gulls. The peregrine was sitting out on a cliff ledge studying all of this, but he did not seem very interested, he had probably done all his hunting for the morning.

Time to move on to Cemlyn Bay for an hour or so of tern watching and then, hopefully, we were going off to search for one of the islands special birds: the black guillemot. One or two pairs bred near to Llanbadrig along the cliffs we had been told, whether we found them would be another matter.

Cemlyn was fairly quiet as far as people were concerned. It was a different story on the bird front. Terns are rarely quiet, especially when several hundred are congregated together; believe me, you would not want terns nesting in your own back garden, beautiful though they are.

It was the usual mix of Sandwich terns and Arctic terns, with many of the nests having quite large chicks waiting to be fed. Scattered in amongst the terns the occasional black-headed gull's nest could be seen, not the most ideal of neighbours one would have thought. Hard as we worked, we did not locate any roseate terns, but you cannot win them all. As compensation, however, we did spot the odd little tern so we were happy with that.

On the water in the Bay we had red-breasted mergansers, with more guillemots and razorbills. A pair of angry oystercatchers were chasing a carrion crow away which was intent on stealing one of their young, but the parents were having none of it. Two buzzards were mewing away overhead, which combined with the odd singing skylark, brought the scene to its close. Leaving, if we were lucky, time to hunt down the black guillemots.

Whether we would be fortunate or not to get the 'guillies', it was a beautiful area with many orchids gracing the scene. We made our way to the cliff tops to study the sea beneath. This was obviously the place for fulmars and kittiwakes with many birds in the air and nests visible along the cliff face. A pair of raven were nesting nearby, with the male coming out on an occasional sortie.

Pleasant it might have been, we were not getting what we were there for, the Camargue had changed all of that. But hang on, two very dark looking birds had just dropped onto the waves, we had them, two black guillemots were bobbing on the sea beneath us. Our first trip out had brought us all a 'Lifer', it could not get better than that. We drove home happy in heart. The UK was not so bad after all. Although I had been away on holiday, Dorothy and Sarah had not, but now Sarah was at work we could be more selective, so we chose to have a week away in June and booked ourselves a cottage in Shere, not too far away from Guildford. Here, as well as doing some birding in the Thames Valley, we could visit London and take Sarah to the theatre; she had wished to see the play 'The Mousetrap', so this we would do.

We had booked our accommodation mid-week to mid-week, which avoided the heavy weekend traffic conditions which increased as the summer advanced, so on Wednesday – our first day in Shere – we decided to visit Box Hill. This is an area not famous for its birds, it is named after the box tree which grows there, not a well-known tree in England and the butterfly population is very good; finally, it is a chalk escarpment on which several orchids flourish. Enough there to keep us occupied.

The wild box trees were easily located, areas totally dominated by the tree. In the Midlands many people have box hedges which they keep trimmed neat and tidy, I just never realised they could grow over fifteen feet tall if left to their own devices; some of the trees seen there must be very old indeed. The woods sounded strangely quiet, little or no bird song or calls. Just the occasional coal tit let rip and I saw movement high in the trees, which I took to be goldcrest activity. On walking out of the wood, a buzzard graced us with its presence as it gently glided overhead. We met up with a couple of botanists who pointed us in the direction of some orchids, bee orchids, now that was something a little special; I had not seen many of those in the UK, Dorothy and Sarah – never. We quickly found the spot, and were delighted to see a small patch of the orchids, about forty or so, and the majority were in full flower. We enjoyed them for a few minutes before we saw a party of walkers trampling through and thought best move on; some walkers never look at where they are planting their feet!

During the following hour or so, we found three more orchid species in flower: the common spotted, no problem in identifying that one, a patch of fragrant orchids and on the fringes of a woodland area, a patch of common twayblades; they more than compensated for the lack of birds. The day was very bright and warm. With the many flowers and grasses out in full bloom, the butterflies were very active. Amongst the commoner species, there were a few specials to keep our eyes open for. The first real find was marbled whites, not a butterfly seen back home, but here they were plentiful. Their larvae feed on grass, or so I believe, and there was a good variety of species to be found. An occasional bright yellow brimstone flew past, their broods were just about beginning to emerge, and you cannot mistake them. Small coppers were also coming onto the wing and a few of these were to be seen. A blue butterfly caught my attention which, I at first took to be a common blue, but the blue colour looked so vivid that I had my doubts. I managed to get close to one and noted that the edges of the upper wings were chequered black and white, the common blue I always thought had plain dark margins to the wings. I am no butterfly 'boff,' I only know the commoner species, but I had brought my butterfly field guide with me, and it was in my car. On getting back to the car, we commenced to study the blue butterflies.

Although there are many different species of blue butterflies, we do not have all that many in the UK so it was not such a ponderous job as might be thought. After a few minutes, we had cracked it: the butterfly was the Adonis blue, a locally rare butterfly principally seen in southern England, with Box Hill being one of its locations. When combined with box trees and orchids, those more than made up for the lack of birds. The butterfly, incidentally, was the first I had ever seen. As we commenced to drive back to Shere; the sky started to darken and a thunderstorm followed shortly. The rain really fell sharply, accompanied by thunder and lightning, a typical English summer storm; the roads were quickly awash with water. When we got back to base and put the TV on for the weather forecast, the news was not good. It looked as though the next three days, at least, were going to be complete washouts. Birding and the countryside were unlikely to be on the agenda so we needed to look for other forms of entertainment. A quick phone call to Guildford railway station to enquire about trains to London, then the theatre in London and three seats were booked for The Mouse Trap; that was the following day sorted.

The play was most enjoyable, and it has been running years I understand; for some of the actors, it looked like a permanent job. We enjoyed a meal, did a bit of sightseeing, and caught a train back to Guildford; a very pleasant day it had been. A final comment on the day, it did not rain, well not in London. Having driven into Guildford for the train, we thought it looked well worth a visit so we decided that would be our next trip out. The weather was bad on this occasion so we had chosen wisely, and Dorothy and Sarah enjoyed themselves around the shops. On arriving back at Shere, we decided to have a look round the local church and Sarah was very interested in the bells. She rang at our local church and was very enthusiastic, and by coincidence, a member of the bell ringing team happened to be in church. Seeing our obvious interest in the bells he asked were we ringers. Sarah obviously said yes. he talked to her about her experience and when he learned she had rung at Lichfield cathedral, he seemed suitably impressed. It appeared that there was a ringing practice that evening and he invited Sarah to join them. Needless to say, she accepted the offer. After our evening meal, we walked down to the church, claimed to be one of the most attractive and interesting in Surrey, whether that is true or not I do not know, but I must agree on its attractiveness. Sarah was only interested in the bells, and after meeting the ringers, Dorothy and I took ourselves off for a walk and a drink at the local pub.

When we got back to collect Sarah, she had been asked if she would like to ring for Holy Communion on Sunday; she was only too pleased to do so. We would have been going to church on Sunday in any case, so she could combine both. Bell ringers collect bell towers they have rung in just like birders collect the names of birds we have seen. Each to his own they do say!

The weather situation had not really improved, although longer dry periods were promised so we decided to take a chance and visit Hampton Court, where, should conditions not be good, we would at least have the Palace to visit.

Checking train times and connections etc., I decided we would take a chance and drive there; we at least would not have to drive into London, and we did not have to race there. So on a very dull looking morning, we made our way, and I am very pleased to say the journey was very good. When we arrived, conditions had improved and the sun was trying to break through.

Hampton Court Palace was certainly an impressive looking building, but unfortunately, it was girder strewn; restoration work was being carried out so certain architectural features were obscured, but as we were more interested in the gardens and park land, this did not concern us greatly. One thing which did impress us was the huge grape vine; I understand it is claimed to be the largest in the world, and it looked it.

Many of you who are a similar age to me will probably remember the 1966 film 'A Man for All Seasons' which was shot here at Hampton Court Palace. That is a bit of nostalgia for you. Life is not all birds!

The weather stayed dry for us and we had a pleasant time at Hampton Court where the gardens were most impressive. With the weekend now upon us, and no real improvement in the weather, what to do? We decided to go north and have a drive in the Reading area and then call in at Windsor Great Park. Virginia Water had always interested me; as it was so close, now was the chance to visit.

We had been informed that near to Reading were two locations that seemed to be the type of areas we were interested in, so we decided to give them a try. The first was Black Swan Lake, an appropriate enough name and Moor Copse, we would then motor across to Windsor Great Park. Before starting off we phoned a restaurant in Shere and booked a table for an evening meal, which would enable us to have more time out if required. Map references sorted, and we were on our way. Black Swan Lake is part of a country park complex and is obviously more of a recreational lake than a wild lake, but it does have a few birds present, although nothing of great interest until a kingfisher flew across; that bird brightened the morning up considerably. I had been told it was a very good place for dragonflies, but the weather that day was against most of the flying insects, even the swallows and swifts were having to work hard. It may be called Black Swan Lake, but the only swans we saw were mute swans and they are not black. They were doing work with artificial holts in an attempt to entice otters back, which had been reported from time to time – not that day, needless to say. It was an area with great potential, but further development was required.

On to Moor Copse. This lay alongside the A340, a couple of miles south of Pangbourne, and as the name indicates it is a woodland area, a mixed woodland area. The River Pang runs through part of the Copse and the first part you enter, Hogmoor Copse, is a wet wood of willows, oaks and ash trees. A few warblers were singing away, amongst them, willow warbler, blackcap and garden warbler. Being a wet wood, small insects no doubt were abundant, hence the warblers. Crossing the river, we entered an area known as Park Wood. This was an area of ancient woodland of hazel, alder and several very tall and straight old oaks, very impressive looking trees. The hazel and alder looked very much as though they had been coppiced in the past as quite lush vegetation was growing and the seed heads of primroses and bluebells could still be seen. A few months previously that would have been a most attractive area. As it looked as though we would have to walk back to our car the same way as we came, we turned to return. As we did so, a sparrowhawk came crashing through the twigs of the trees; it was in hot pursuit of a blackbird. The outcome of the chase we did not see, but the hawk meant business. A delightful spot, now for Virginia Water. We were very fortunate in being able to park very close to Virginia Water, and made our way to the shores. It was obviously a popular area, not that we were likely to meet royalty there, we did at least see two birds mentioned by name but not seen when at Reading – 'black swans'. Both clipped and most certainly collection birds.My real interest in going to Virginia Water was the chance of seeing mandarin ducks. I understood that many of these exotics ducks lived there and had been free flying birds for many years. The story goes, I cannot vouch for its accuracy, as follows. Mandarin ducks had been in the royal collection for many years prior to the Second World War. With conscription, many royal employees were called up and, in consequence, the mandarin ducklings were no longer clipped and became free flying birds. Over the years, they increased in number and are now a bird firmly on the British list. It was not long before we had what we came for. A small flock of about a dozen birds, both sexes, flew in and landed on the lake. They did not exhibit the slightest bit of interest in joining the mallards, geese and swans being fed by other visitors; I think it is safe enough to say those birds were wild. They are on my list as such anyway.

Once again the climate chose to curtail our day, heavy cloud was building up, rain was very imminent so we proceeded homewards.

The rain did not follow us and as we journeyed we passed a watercress pond. I had forgotten that this part of the world was famous for its watercress, although now foreign imports of more exotic foods seem to have knocked it on the head. We pulled in to have a look at it all. Apparently, it was the pure spring water found there which made the growing so popular, and was for many years big business, this grower was at least still in business. As we surveyed the pond, Dorothy grabbed my arm, 'Look at that yellow wagtail, it has a blue head.' I swung round, she had hit the jackpot. Amongst the cress beds a magnificent male blue-headed wagtail was chasing flying insects. This took me back a few weeks to the Camargue, what a bird to find in the UK, and as Dorothy quickly told me, 'She had seen one before I had.' She was right, it may only have been seconds, but she recorded her first blue-headed wagtail in the UK before I did, and I was sure I would be frequently reminded of the fact! Home now to smarten ourselves up for the restaurant, we could hardly go there dressed as we were. The restaurant was French which gave us the opportunity to try some of their 'famous' cooking. We had a most enjoyable meal and some very pleasant dry French wine – what else in a French restaurant – and it was just going dark as we walked home, and what a walk! We had not progressed far before we heard a whirring sound. We stopped and turned, and were amazed to see a great number of large beetles flying through the air. Two landed at our feet and we were thrilled to see they were large stag beetles, an incredible looking insect. They are our largest insect, and judging by the size of their antler-like mandibles, those two were both males. Until that night, this beetle had only ever been a picture in a book, there we were being 'attacked' by many of them. Their radars were obviously not operating well judging by the number which flew into us, it was as though someone was throwing large stones at us. That walk home still rates as one of the most exciting we had ever taken.

Sunday dawned, dull but at least dry. Sarah enjoyed her bell ringing, both prior to the service and afterwards, and she was asked if she would join them for Evening Song. She obviously wanted to so that curtailed our activities that afternoon.

We walked home from church down the same road we had walked the previous night and we were very disappointed to see many dead and squashed large stag beetles. They had obviously collided with cars as they flew searching for a mate, a very sad observation and an equally sad ending for the beetles.

When we arrived back at the cottage, we were met by the owner who had called in to see if all things were OK. We told her about our experiences with the stag beetles, and she told us an amusing story.

The year prior, at a similar time, she had rented rooms out to a honeymoon couple from Lancashire. At that time, she was still living in the cottage, and late one evening she heard loud screams coming from their rooms. She ran to see what was the matter and found the young lady sitting on the bed in an almost state of shock, and her husband was not much better. The lady, was pointing at the curtain on which sat three large stag beetles, frightened out of her wits, by them. The owner just collected a small box, knocked the beetles into it and took them out into the garden for releasing, and then returned indoors to console the occupants. She was able to tell them they were harmless, but she got the impression they would not return south for holidays in the future! After lunch, the rains commenced; we had a ride out locally to see a little more of the surrounding countryside, which pleasant though it was, the rain did not help. We returned for an early dinner so that Sarah could complete her bell ringing exploits.

Only one day more remained and that was subject to the weather which, fortunately, looked reasonable; it was dry at least. Where to go? The weather made the decision for us, we woke up with gales suddenly forecast and very heavy rain was already falling. We breakfasted and, after much discussion, we decided to call it a day and go home a day earlier than expected. We phoned up the cottage owner, explained to her what we were doing, which she fully appreciated. She called round to see us so we could settle up the few extras, and by mid-morning, we were on our way home. It had not been the holiday we had hoped for; the weather sorted that out, but we had many happy memories – especially the large stag beetles and Sarah had another church to add to her list of churches she had rung in. Dorothy of course, had her blue-headed wagtail to crow about, and did!

Early July saw the University group off back to Wales, not the coast this time, just over the border into Wales. We were visiting Pistyll Rhaeadr waterfall in the Berwyn Mountains near the village of Llanrhaeadre-ym-Mochant, Powys, 12 miles west of Oswestry – very much the Welsh Borders. The Falls were very spectacular we understood, and the bird watching there is also alleged to be good. The drop was, apparently, about two hundred and fifty feet in three stages, falling into the river known as Afon Rhaeadr.

Although it was no great distance, we made an early start as we understood parking could be a problem as the area was very popular with walkers and day-trippers. As things turned out, we all managed to park comfortably; there were various pull-ins along the lane approaching the Falls.

We decided we would visit the Falls first to admire their beauty prior to seeking out the birds of the area. We concluded the Falls were a bit special and fully understood why people would wish to visit them. A pair of croaking ravens soaring over the Falls certainly added to their charm as far as we were concerned. The ground there was rather harsh so good footwear was advisable, pumps and open-toed sandals were not recommended; we were suitably attired, so off we went. Birding there was not easy but it produced some quality. Birds of prey obviously thrived in these conditions and we saw buzzard, goshawk, red kite, peregrine and kestrel, enough there to keep any birder happy. Along the river we saw dipper, kingfisher and grey wagtail, and in the various wooded areas many warblers were still singing, which was a help in identification as we saw few. Amongst these were blackcap, garden warbler, willow warbler and wood warbler, accompanied by both spotted and pied flycatchers, plus redstarts. A very good selection indeed. In the open and rather rocky terrain, especially above the Falls, wheatears, stonechats with a pair of ring ouzels the prize birds to be seen.

Walking back to our cars we had the bird of the day. A pipit popped out on the track just in front of us, one or two of my colleagues muttered, 'What on earth is that?' It hit me, I was back in Devon with Dorothy. Three years before we saw our first ever tawny pipit, and there that day, I had my third and I was able to share it with eleven of my colleagues. For all of them it was a 'Lifer', you could not end a day better than that.

Pistyll Rhaeadr had proved to be a marvellous spot, not only for the birds, but scenically too. I have bird watched at many a grotty area, in ports, power stations and even back streets, this part of Wales had none of that. On the day we saw fifty-three birds, many of which were pure quality. I knew one thing, I shall have to bring Dorothy there, she would love it.

The following evening, I received a telephone call from Dr Graham Martin. He was the person at the University of Birmingham who was responsible for the many courses being run, both extra-mural such as mine, and full-time university degree courses covering the natural sciences. Apparently, he had received letters from members of the Camargue experience complimenting the University on how well the week had been run and the knowledge of the two leaders. Several had asked would there be any further visits to the Camargue as they would like to go back. Graham wished to strike as the iron was still hot so to speak, and he wanted to know if I could lead another group the following year. I was available, but Gerry was not, he was off to South America. Graham said that was fine as he wanted to join me so he and I could lead the group.

Graham is very much a scientist, not a bird watcher in the sense I am. He was completing a book on the visual and audible perception of owls; you cannot get more serious than that so, as he kindly put it, he would be my Number 2. Nineteen eighty-six was going to be another exciting year, but back to the current. The remainder of the summer meetings passed by quietly without any great events to report. Most of the meetings were local and our tawny pipit was the last quality bird of that summer. Back to our six months autumn/winter session. Once again, the numbers held up well – twenty-seven members enrolled – and questions were already being asked about the Camargue the next year. I was able to tell them that I would have all the information in about a month's time.

We sorted out our three meetings for the remainder of '85. We would visit Spurn Point, the Point of Air and finish off at Gibraltar Point, all coastal venues. Sixteen of us ventured forth for our trip to Spurn and I was a bit concerned. The weather conditions were not favourable, not bad weather just the fact there was a strong off-shore wind forecast, and those winds tended to keep the birds far out at sea. It was too late to make alternative arrangements, so we just had to make the best of it.

The tide was on the way out as we arrived and a goodly selection of waders was to be seen. We had fourteen species; none, unfortunately, unusual, but a few of our favourites were amongst them. Grey plovers, golden plovers, curlews, turnstones, spotted redshanks, knots and sanderlings particularly. Flying in came small flocks of teals and wigeons, those were migrants coming from further north to spend the winter with us. Also a few early fieldfares and redwings were to be seen and further out at sea the odd gannet was passing through.

A small flock of very dark ducks suddenly flew in and landed on the sea, common scoter, just seven of them, but they were a quality addition to what we had seen. Bird numbers and range of species was turning out to be better than I expected.

We made our way down to the Point, but things there were very quiet, although we did spot a couple of early bramblings and further fieldfares and redwings were feeding on the buckthorn berries. Then we had a bit of excitement. Just off the point a battle was taking place, two Arctic skuas and one great skua were harassing a flock of gulls, mainly black-headed, and the gulls were not happy about it. Unfortunately, they drifted away very quickly, but we had experienced a few most enjoyable seconds.

That brought our day to its conclusion, and as it had turned out the day had been both pleasant and productive and you cannot ask for much more than that.

We had clicked for good weather again for our trip to the Point of Air, the question now was: would Wales once again prove to be good? Our last few trips had been remarkable in many ways?

Pintail numbers were good, about fifty birds were out on the sea, a small number of red-breasted mergansers were also visible and shelducks were well into three figures. Three ducks there which were always good to see.

On the wader front, it was the usual selection that I have mentioned previously, and on the sea a solitary guillemot was visible; that was a little bit unexpected.

Moving back to the land. A good mixed flock of fieldfares and redwings were visible and in a small wooded area we had a very pleasant surprise, and probably the bird of the day, a lesser spotted woodpecker. On the shingle a large flock of pipits was seen, but hard as we worked on those, we could only see meadow pipits.

Apart from the woodpecker and the guillemot I suppose we did not have a lot to get overly excited about, but we did chalk up fifty-four species on the day. A pleasant enough day, but not particularly memorable.

How would our final trip for the year work out? Gibraltar Point, it was up to you. Once again, we clicked for off-shore winds and many birds were far out to sea. Fulmars and gannets were drifting through, accompanied by several small flocks of brent geese, and the expected gulls were very much in evidence. It was the latter which brought a diver to our attention. Two lesser black-backed gulls were diving after the bird which was having to plunge deep to avoid their attention. The lesser black-backs eventually gave up and we were pleased to see it was a red-throated diver which eventually surfaced peacefully. A good bit of quality there. The tide was almost fully in so few waders were to be seen, apart that was for the longer legged species such as curlews and bar-tailed godwits, which we were more than happy to see. Whilst enjoying these, two Arctic skuas flew past. They were not hunting, this obviously pleased the smaller gulls, which could happily go about their business. Back on the dunes, meadow pipits were busily feeding away and a solitary skylark rose into the air and actually provided us with a bit of song. I think he had his calendar mixed up a bit! Whilst enjoying this a large brown bird came gliding over the dunes, very low with hardly a flap of its wings, a short-eared owl was out hunting. For about five minutes, we just stood still and admired this bird's skill and beauty. Owls are fascinating birds anytime, but to see one in broad daylight just gliding slowly backwards and forwards, low over the sand, was more than a bit special. This was worth the journey alone.

After the owl, things quietened down appreciably and with the light fading rapidly, we made our ways homewards. Not a bad finish to the year; we had seen fifty-six species. I closed the year on one hundred and seventy-six species, not a bumper year, and when you compare this with one hundred and thirty-three in one week when visiting the Camargue, you can draw your own conclusions! The first few days of '86 were very dreary – winter was here – and due to the short hours of daylight, we chose to go to Rutland Water for our first field meeting. As things turned out, it was not a bad decision.

Fifteen of us made the journey and we all met up on time, and luckily for us the day was quite bright and not very cold. We booked ourselves in, paid our fees and went our way. Within minutes, we had clicked. Right in front of the Visitor Centre hide, a great northern diver was to be seen; what a start to a new year. It was an adult bird in winter plumage and you could really appreciate the size of the bird, so heavy billed and thick necked. No mistaking this bird for anything else.

Duck species we had been informed were very good, and as we started to tick off the commoner species, others came slowly into view. Goldeneye and goosander were quickly ticked off and then a comment from another birder in the hide made me look closely at the duck he was talking about. He was not sure what he was looking at, but he had hit a beauty; it was a female long-tailed duck, another cracker to add to the diver. Rutland was shaping up well. We moved on to the next hide where we added on ruddy ducks, shelducks and grey lag geese to our lists, and then one of my colleagues picked up two very dark birds; he had found two common scoters. Quality ducks were falling out of the sky for us. A few waders were also visible, lapwings, a ringed plover, golden plovers, a snipe and a dunlin.

Five species of gulls were in situ, and amongst the passerines were skylark, meadow pipit, pied wagtail, treecreeper, fieldfare, redwing, linnet, bullfinch, brambling and reed bunting. All in all we had sixty-five species on the day; a very satisfactory start to a new year.

The Elan Valley called again, I still had the odd member who had never seen red kite so it was time to try to change things. Therefore, our February meeting was to the Valley and Devil's Bridge. Wales was a white world, they had experienced a little snow. Fortunately, the roads were clear, the snow only lay on the fields etc., there it looked quite picturesque, although it was obviously cold. We pulled in on the dam which separates Caban-coch Reservoir and Carreg-ddu Reservoir, and there due to the closeness of the water it was very cold. However, I understood no matter how cold it got, the reservoirs there never freeze. Be that as it may, they could have done so that day!

If it had not been for a few goosanders, mallards and a solitary drake goldeneye, the reservoirs would have been deserted. The hills, or should I say mountains, surrounding the reservoirs were a little more productive. A few buzzards were circling the heights and a goshawk flew through at speed; it did not appear to be chasing anything, probably just hurtling around in an attempt to keep warm. Gull numbers were also low. Just the odd lesser black-backed, herring and black-headed gulls – it was probably warmer at sea.

Driving through the Valley towards Devil's Bridge, we had a fleeting glimpse of a peregrine falcon – plus the odd kestrel was hovering – searching for food beneath. A few carrion crows stood out against the snowy background and a small flock of lapwings flew through. It looked as though we were heading for one of those days! Nearing Devil's Bridge things bucked up. Two red kite came gliding across in front of us and for two or three minutes they proceeded to hunt back and forth over a nearby field, putting on a superb show. A raven joined in, although the kites did not seem to appreciate its appearance, they flew off.

Even though Devil's Bridge was higher ground than that we had driven through, the snow was not evident, and there was activity among the smaller birds. Titmice were very active, fieldfares and redwings were feeding in the holly trees, and a treecreeper was busily working his way up the trunks of the trees.

Feeding on the fallen beech mast were chaffinches and three bramblings, and a greenfinch could be heard calling, although we could not locate it. Nearing the conifers, we heard the call we wanted: the 'kip, kip' of crossbills. After several minutes searching, we located them; a party of twelve birds of both sexes, and they thrilled us with their acrobatics as they searched the cones for seeds. For several minutes, we stood there just enjoying them until, 'whoosh', they were off.

That was our final highlight, as things had turned out not such a poor day as I one time thought. We had seen forty-eight different species with among them, a few quality birds. Fourteen birders made their ways home contented, and for a few they had seen their first red kites and crossbills; they had to be happy with that.

Our final field meeting of the term took us up to Southport and as the weather turned out, we had not chosen wisely. We arrived in almost gale-like conditions and as the winds were easterlies all the birds were either being blown out to sea, or in the case of the passerines, keeping their heads down. The sea was just a mass of white waves with any birds on the water being well-nigh invisible. Fortunately, we managed to get into the hide, being the only idiots there! Birding was very poor, the only two birds of real note were a peregrine falcon being blown through and a small flock of bar-tailed godwits on the marsh. Conditions really deteriorated as the day progressed so we wrote the day off and made our ways homewards.

With La Camargue looming up, I spent much time on the arrangements for that. Twenty-six of us were going, that figure included Graham and myself, and we had ten new participants who would be complete strangers to me. We were staying at the same hotel as the previous year and Graham was going to do his best to get Jean Luq as driver once again. Due to Graham's commitments, we were travelling a few days later than before which meant I would be spending my birthday away from home, which would be the first time Dorothy and I were not together to celebrate. As she said, it gave me something to look forward to when I came home! The summer course commenced in April with our first two visits being Clumber Park and early-May back for our nightingales. On the 8th May, we were on our way back to La Camague; how would things turn out that year, and were we returning too soon? Fourteen of my colleagues were among the party, and they had no doubts they were going to enjoy themselves; I hoped they were right.

We arrived safely at Marseille and as we walked out of the airport a cheery voice called out, 'Bonjour Brian.' It was Jean Luq. I was delighted to see him again and, in good Gaelic tradition, he gave me a hug. I introduced him to Graham, who showing his reserved English qualities, shook hands!

I have been giving serious thought as to how I write up this holiday, so much of what we have done is repetitive of my previous chapter on the Camargue, so I have decided to only report upon the major and unusual events and summarise on the week's completion. Needless to say, we commenced exactly how we did in '85, and I still had no name for the spot; it was just a green area on the map. The members who had not visited previously, were just amazed by the range of species seen. As Jean Luq and I told them, it could only get better.

One thing I did not mention last time was the fact the hotel was located on a very large island at a major road junction and was surrounded by a tall hedge. Here Cetti's warblers were well represented, and for some it was their first opportunity to see and hear the bird. Also, as the evening drew in, a small green tree frog came out and croaked away. It was not very large, about as big as the top joint of your thumb, but it certainly had a voice and was a very attractive looking creature. Bats were also common as they hawked insects round the outside lighting. A very pleasant way to while away a few minutes at night whilst supping your cognac!

If the French weather forecasters were any good, it looked as though we were again in for a very pleasant week's weather; I presumed it must rain at times in this part of France?

The birds were again performing for us. Bird of prey numbers were very good, marsh harriers were plentiful and at the tip at Entressen we saw three Egyptian vultures. That was something more than a bit special, especially as they were all adults. The black kite numbers on that day were incredible, it made you wonder where they had all come from; well into treble figures I would have thought.

There was much activity at the bee-eater colony. Being a few days later, more birds were being seen and many were already excavating their tunnels in the sand. I understood they could tunnel in as far as ten feet, if that was true, they must excavate several pounds of sand with just a slender bill and small feet to do so. Nature is simply amazing at times.

Whilst driving through the Camargue, we stopped near to a small bird sanctuary where the owners took in injured birds in an attempt to aid their recovery. Jean Luq had told us a very interesting story, which probably accounted for the white stork we on our last visit.

Two years ago, when the storks were passing through on migration, one stork flew into some overhead wires, injuring its wing. The bird was taken into the sanctuary and after three months was fit for release. The owner was undecided whether to do that or not as the stork would be completely on its own and might have no idea of where to go, so he kept it in captivity. It had been kept in a large aviary so it had room to fly. Come autumn, when the storks were passing through, he released the bird, which quickly joined in with its fellows and he thought that was that.

Imagine his surprise when he woke one morning the following year to see two white storks roosting on the top of the aviary, which he had housed the stork the previous year. He had ringed the bird and there it was, with a companion, standing on the top of the aviary with not another stork in sight. He just expected them to fly off, eventually, but they did not and over the next few days proceeded to build a large nest on the roof of the aviary, and raised one young bird. The stork we saw last year was no doubt the male from there.

They were back again, and as Jean Luq parked the coach up on the side of the road, a white stork walked past the coach in a ditch which ran right alongside us. The bird was less than six feet away from us and it looked, almost amusingly, at all the faces staring at it as it walked on by. What an incredible sight, unbelievable really.

We were not going to visit the sanctuary, but the large nest could be clearly seen from the roadway, with one of the storks standing, sentry-like, on top of a mound of sticks. A few photographs were taken of these two birds, and those of us who did not, we will have the memory for ever!

A visit was made for the slender-billed gulls, but Jean Luq had found a more accessible location, so we were not going to be distracted on this occasion. I was not sure this was a favourable decision for some of the members with last year's memories, but Jean was correct, the views were far better and some of the birds were sitting eggs. One obviously cannot visit the Camargue without going to see the greater flamingos at their colony. Graham, using his University of Birmingham background, had obtained permission to go further into the colony than normally allowed; we were no longer bird watchers, we were scientific ornithologists. From a closer proximity the noise was incredible. As the birds marched along in a vast convoy, they were calling to each other continuously, and there was also an aroma in the air which I would not class as really pleasant! An amazing hour was spent there in the company of those tremendous birds, and there were several thousand I estimated – some sight.

As I had mentioned previously, my birthday was occurring during the week and my fourteen colleagues plus, Jean Luq and his girlfriend had prepared a surprise for me. On the evening of my birthday, I had got myself prepared for our evening meal etc., when Graham came to my door, telling me I was wanted outside. He could not or would not tell me who wanted to see me, so I duly went outside. Imagine my surprise when I was greeted with a rendering of 'Happy Birthday' from my friends, Jean and his girlfriend. Jean had a friend who owned one of the best restaurants in Arles, he had booked a table for the evening for us all, and I was guest of honour. Jean had managed to bring the coach along so we could all be driven in comfort.

What an evening we had, a superb meal, wine and brandy, and we even ended up in a 'competitive' singing evening with the local restaurant visitors; this really was another side to France. The restaurant echoed with the refrains of Ilkley Moor Bar Tat, Frere Jacques and the like. I do not know who won, we just all had a great time, and the 'entente cordial' remained intact. Back to the birds. La Crau had to be re-visited. Those of us there last year had the memories of the black-shouldered kite and long-legged buzzard still, but as I explained, not to expect a repeat that year because miracles rarely occur twice!

Of that I was proved to be correct, but we still had a wonderful visit. Stone curlews, little bustards, pin-tailed sandgrouse, crested larks, black kites and a Bonelli's eagle all put on a show. We drove across to the site where we saw the roller the previous year, and almost in the identical spot, there it was – unbelievable. This certainly did not damage either Jean Luq's reputation nor mine, at times when on a roll, anything could happen.

A visit to Mount Ventoux was also called for, apart from my colleagues who had seen the crested tits last year, the remainder of the group had not and the chance of seeing an Egyptian vulture at its nest was also another attraction they did not want to miss. I was happy enough about the vulture, Jean Luq had already confirmed this, I just hoped the crested tits would perform for us.

As we climbed Mount Ventoux we called in at the small quarry to see if the crag martins and Alpine swifts were still to be seen. They were, much to the pleasure of those who did not see them before, and on up to our coffee stop. The coffee was as delicious as last time and the crested tits were far more accommodating, we saw them as we entered the woodland.

Making our way back to the coach one of the party said to me, 'I did not know a swallow had a pale rump?'

I turned quickly, 'Where?'.

He pointed, and I could not believe my eyes, we were looking at a pair of red-rumped swallows. We did not see those the year before, our first new bird for our Camargue List. Unlike our swallow which tends to be a bird associated with habitation, the red-rumped is more a bird of open rocky country, mind you there was enough of that nearby. We spent several minutes enjoying these two birds before continuing on up the mountain.

We had our lunch before moving on for the vultures. Our lunches, I must confess, were very good and they were always accompanied by a bottle or two of wine. Whilst enjoying this, a lady shrieked out and pointed. I have never seen a millipede so long, it looked almost like a small snake with legs as it sped across the ground to vanish under a large rock. It was almost totally black and did look a bit nasty, although I supposed it was completely harmless to us. Jean did not see it, unfortunately, so we have no idea of what species it was; we were very careful where we sat in future!

The vulture was in situ and we saw it returning to the nest on a few occasions, carrying food, and it looked as though it had two chicks on the nest; although, we could not be absolutely certain. The golden eagle was still in residence and it gave us a flypast or two, and two honey buzzards flew through the valley beneath, not the spectacle of the last visit, but one bird is enough for your 'List'! On our return journey down the mountain we again spotted a rock thrush, or to be more accurate – three different ones – which put on a show that was for sure. Our visit to Mount Ventoux had been most productive, now what would the next day have in store?

Graham had been doing some work many weeks before, and he had organised a visit for us to the Parc Ornithologique at Pont de Gau. Here serious ornithological work was carried out, much like that of our B.T.O. and B.O.U. It would be a serious insight into how our friends on the Continent did their work. On our arrival, Graham took part of our group into the offices. I remained outside talking to a group of ringers, who spoke very good English, and had just returned with three nightingales they were going to ring and weigh etc., prior to their release. Although I am not a supporter of ringing, this was too good a chance to miss of seeing nightingales close to hand, or even in the hand as this proved. Whilst all of this was going on a nightingale was singing away from a nearby thicket, contrary to what their name implies, they do not only sing at night!

One of our colleagues came out and told me I was wanted in the office, so I joined Graham who was talking to a bearded Frenchman. He stopped talking to Graham, walked across to me with hand out stretched, and shook my hand most vigorously. It turned out he was the leader of the ornithological group responsible for maintenance of the French Bird List. He wanted to talk to me about our two submissions from the previous year.

He had intended to write to me but on learning of the visit by students from the University of Birmingham, he had checked and seeing my name as a leader, he came down to see me. He asked me a couple of questions with regard to the black-shouldered kite, which I was able to answer and he told me that this report would be accepted and that it was the first record in that area of France for over fifty years, and that the previous record had questions about it. Now the long-legged buzzard. He had three questions to ask about this bird, questions of minor details on the bird's plumage, and I could not answer these, it was detail I had not picked up on. I told him that colleagues of mine were outside, who had also seen the bird, would he like to ask them? He did, the results were as mine; no, they had not picked up on those details.

Our long-legged buzzard failed the test, although he did say it would be recorded as a probability, and he thought we had in fact seen the bird. So we won one and drew the other. To make a special journey to see me and ask a few questions, showed how seriously the French take their birding.

Our visit had turned out to be most interesting and I was very impressed with the French ornithologists I had met up with. The birds seen had also been of great interest. As well as the nightingales, we saw great reed warblers, Cetti's warblers, heard a melodious warbler, several black kites and marsh harriers and a pair of black-winged stilts with a juvenile, most impressive. Our week finally concluded and everyone agreed it had been a great experience. We did not do quite as well as the last year, where we had seen one hundred and thirty-three species; this year, we saw one hundred and twenty-nine. But we did get one or two species not recorded before, so there were still many wonders of La Camargue to be seen; will it be by any of us, who knows?

I was certain of one thing, after my two visits to France I have to get Dorothy abroad. Possibly not the Camargue with the likelihood of mosquito attack, but there are cooler climes.

The following two to three months passed by very quietly. Although I visited many of my normal haunts, the number of species seen was unusually low. Come July, however, we decided on a family holiday to Guernsey – the Channel Islands – new territory to us. It was also the opportunity for both Sarah and Dorothy to experience flying, or in Dorothy's case, to do so again. When courting, we had flown down to London to visit Covent Garden where we saw Carmen.

For Guernsey, we flew from Bournemouth, so it was a night time drive to catch the flight at 08.00 hours. I parked up an hour or so from the airport and the three of us obtained a few hours rest. I did not sleep myself, and whilst in the car had a wonderful experience. As dawn approached, and it was still fairly dark I heard a nightingale call, not sing, too late in the year for that, and as I enjoyed this a nightjar joined in. I only wished I had my tape recorder with me so I could have recorded it all. The memory, however, still remains.

Our ten days on Guernsey were most enjoyable, pleasant weather and hire cars were very cheaply priced – not that you drove that far, the island is quite small and compact. The hotel was very comfortable and the food was good. The birding was much as that experienced back home, although to be fair, it appeared to be more concentrated here; Guernsey does not have long expanses of coast or beach. The pick of the birds were short-toed treecreeper, black guillemot, Dartford warbler, purple sandpiper, rock pipit and cirl bunting. I was very pleased to have been in the Camargue earlier that year, there I had seen short-toed treecreeper and that was a big help in identifying this little fellow.

The quietness of the year continued and although I visited Spurn, Rutland Water and Leighton Moss, I only totalled one hundred and forty-three species in the UK; my poorest year ever in the U.K. Hopefully 1987 will be an improvement.

Fortunately, my course members were more than happy with things, so we continued much as we had done before. Although the numbers of birds were small, many of them were being seen for the first time, so no complaints were made.

The early part of the year provided us with mixed weather conditions and, because of this, our first field meetings were all local: Cannock Chase, Chillington, Blithfield Reservoir, Belvide Reservoir, Gailey Pools and Chasewater. There we saw the expected species, plus a good selection of the more unusual waterfowl, among which were scaup, common scoter, smew, ruddy duck, red-crested pochard, pintail, pink-footed goose and whooper swan. Enough there to kindle anyone's enthusiasm, especially after a year such as the previous year. By the end of January alone, we had broken the one hundred mark; we still had almost a full year to go.

The previous meetings had all been short. Late February provided us with the opportunity of a full day's meeting, so we chose to visit

243

Rutland Water and Eyebrook Reservoir. We chose well. Added to some of the waterfowl mentioned previously, we saw red-necked grebe, red-breasted merganser, bean goose, barnacle goose and Bewick's swan. In total, we saw sixty-seven species including a kingfisher which put on a wonderful fishing display for us. This bird had a fishing perch on a bush right near where we had parked our cars at Eyebrook, and for several minutes we saw the bird diving into the water and catching small fish. These it stunned on a branch before swallowing. If we had seen nothing else, we would still have had that wonderful memory to take home. Nineteen eighty-seven looked like it could be a memorable year. As one of my colleagues said 'Brian, just keep them coming'. Easier said than done!

Late March saw us return to Wales. Red kites were again calling, so back down the Elan Valley we went. There are certain birds you always wish to include in your 'Year List', and the red kite is most definitely one of those. I had also been told of an area where a rough-legged buzzard had been seen. I informed my colleagues that this must not be declared to anyone, should the bird be breeding, which was suspected; it was of mega-importance as it was probably the only pair in the UK, and egg collectors must be kept away. I further understood the nest was being guarded so we would have to keep our distance and be prepared to be moved on if necessary. Hopefully, the information I have to hand will not make that necessary.

Thirteen of us made the trip in four cars, and although the weather was cold, the conditions were not too bad. At least it was clear and dry. The reservoirs provided us with goldeneye, common scoter and goosander, buzzards were plentiful and the peregrine was still in his quarry. We did not have to venture quite so far as previously down the valley to see our first red kite, a solitary bird was gliding round the lower slopes. Now came the serious work, rough-legged buzzard hunting.

We drove off down a rough track that looked no more than an entrance to a farm and proceeded to park up near to an old barn-type building, it was here I was told to park and not proceed further. Needless to say, we were the only people there and I began to look for a particular shaped group of trees, which we eventually found. My informants had told me one of the birds regularly perched on those trees, particularly one with a broken branch, this was easily found. It was now just a question of setting up our scopes and waiting, and wait we certainly had to do. My colleagues attitudes were similar to mine, if you hope to see a mega rarity then you have to put the time in. An hour or so passed us by, we did not see a lot, although a solitary red kite glided through, which is always most welcome. One of my colleagues suddenly called, 'What is this bird coming in from the right, it is probably only a buzzard? It was not only a buzzard, it was the bird we were after, the rough-legged buzzard, we had our bird. This bird looked very pale and the dark carpal joint, (the wrist of the bird, forming the bend on the wing) really stood out, as did the black terminal band to the white tail. No mistaking this bird. It also hovered frequently, and put on an hovering performance as it landed. A superb experience for many of my group, it being a 'Lifer' for most of us.

We still had time available to us and the light was holding well, so a quick visit to Devil's Bridge was made. No crossbills that day but, whilst we were studying a small flock of goldcrests, out popped a male firecrest who sat out for several seconds before it vanished from sight never to return again. It had justified our calling in at Devils's Bridge, that was for sure.

We had not seen a vast number of birds that day, only forty-seven, but we had picked up some quality. And to finish things off, as we neared home a tawny owl glided over the road ahead of us, beautifully illuminated in our headlights. What more could you ask for?

Spurn Point called, so late March saw us on the east coast once again where we were hoping for a last stab at our winter visitors before they departed our shores and also the hope of a few early summer migrants.

A goodly selection of waders were in attendance, included amongst those were golden plovers, turnstones, curlews, a whimbrel, spotted redshanks and sanderlings; in total, we had twelve different wader species. On the sea were common scoter and shelducks, a good selection of the commoner gulls and two Manx shearwaters drifted slowly through as they proceeded northwards. As we were enjoying the latter, a shout went up, 'What have we here?' I quickly looked in the direction being pointed out, and I had the surprise of my life: a crane was flying in, low over the sea. The bird landed on the shore, not fifty yards away from us, and stalked along the tide line looking almost ostrich-like. It is a very tall bird, elegant I believe, with quite a bustle, almost Victorian. This bird had never been on our radar, they are few and far between in the UK, although a small colony still existed in Norfolk I understood. A cracking new bird for all of us, a 'Lifer'. We also saw a small passage of Sandwich terns making their way north, swallow, sand martins and house martins were also seen. Chiffchaff, willow warblers and blackcaps could be both heard and seen, a real touch of approaching summer there. The odd stonechat, whinchat and wheatear were also moving through, and a solitary ring ouzel really made our day. Fieldfares and redwings were still there in small number; in a few days' time, they would be back crossing the North Sea as they went home. Just as we were about to leave, a pair of yellow wagtails landed. Summer certainly was looming, and our range of species was very impressive. In total we had seen seventy-seven. Spurn was our final meeting of the winter course, and it brought to the end another very successful session.

Now we waited to see what the summer had in store for us. The numbers enrolled on the summer course were again good. Our initial field meetings were all local, nightingales, nightjars, the warblers on the Chase, and a trip one evening to Elkington Bridge to seek out the marsh warblers, as this was a new bird to some of my summer students. We also visited our local reservoirs to catch the wader movement through and we had the thrill of an osprey spending a couple of days at Blithfield, en route to Scotland no doubt. Sarah was now at work and she was also attending college on a Secretarial Course, so she would be unable to join us on any holidays in the immediate future. This gave Dorothy and I the opportunity of holidaying on our own, so we took this, and booked a week in The Lake District.

Although the week was most enjoyable, it was a bit of a disappointment on the bird front, we did not see the golden eagle. We were told one of the birds had died and the partner had left the valley; if that was correct, England had lost its only pair of breeding golden eagles which was very sad news.

The birds normally expected from The Lakes did not disappoint and the walking was most pleasant. We did not climb the heights, we were valley walkers, although we once did tackle Helvellyn. The view was wonderful, but our muscles told us never again and we were many years younger then – they do say you grow wiser with age!

During the week we totalled sixty-eight species, the pick of which were peregrine falcon, ring ouzel, raven, dipper, common sandpiper, redstart, wood warbler, corn bunting, spotted flycatcher and pied flycatcher. The latter was actually breeding in a nest box in the hotel grounds, and we could see them from our room window. We passed many an interesting few minutes studying them. We finished off the summer course with a visit to Leighton Moss and Hest Bank. Although we saw sixty-three species nothing of great note was recorded, we were probably just a little too early for the real autumn movement. Always a good reason to go back.

Course numbers were holding up well, twenty-nine that year and five of them were new faces; could our reputation be spreading?

As an introduction to the new members, three of whom were beginners to the noble art; we chose to visit Spurn Point. Early September usually has a decent selection of passage birds and although I did not anticipate anything extra special, a goodly range of birds was guaranteed.

I had heard stories that the crane we saw earlier was still in the locality, should this put in an appearance then we would have something extra special. We had a good turnout, twenty-three of us made the trip, meeting up at the church at Kilnsea. Things were rather quiet, although we did pick up two spotted flycatchers and a redstart, which pleased our newcomers.

We moved on the short distance to the coast where we could study the North Sea. There was much movement out at sea, flocks of birds were flying past continually and among these were many gannets, those birds certainly pleased our newcomers. The odd skua was way out at sea, much too far to make positive identification and a small flock of red-breasted mergansers drifted past.

A shout went up, 'Brian, look down the beach.' I did, and there was the crane. The day now really woke up. Many of that day's meeting were not on the meeting when we last saw the crane, so for many it was a cracking 'Lifer'; the newcomers could not believe it. Cranes were just pictures in books, they never believed they could be seen in the UK, they did now.

The crane continued to walk along the shore line, with us slowly following it, then it took off, with neck extended and long legs trailing; you could not mistake this fellow. It may pay to mention here, herons, which could be confused with cranes in flight, fly with neck tucked in, not extended. The crane flew over the Point to vanish in the general direction of the Humber Estuary.

Back to studying the sea. Whilst all the excitement with the crane had been going on, many of the birds in the North Sea had started to slowly drift nearer to land. The tide had turned and was now coming in, and here it did come in quite fast. The skuas which had been far out at sea were now much closer providing us with a good opportunity of identifying them. Up scopes!

Our efforts here were rewarded; we had three different skuas, Arctic, great and a solitary pomarine skua, the pick of the bunch and a 'Lifer' for many. Sandwich terns were also moving down the coast, heading south for their winter quarters, and these were passing by in decent numbers, and it was good to see many juveniles amongst them; seems as though they had had a good breeding season.

Hirundines were on the move, especially sand martins and swallows, accompanied by the odd late swift. A willow warbler was seen in the nearby bushes and a sedge warbler could be actually heard; anyone would have thought it was the breeding season. Whinchats and stonechats were also moving through, along with the odd wheatear. Time to move on as the tide was almost at our feet. Spurn Point had done it again, a very good selection of birds with a few choice species: the crane, pomarine skua, Arctic skuas and great skuas to name but a few. We totalled sixty-one on the day, a more than satisfactory number. The newcomers had had a good introduction and were eager to seek more!

Our next field meeting was to the Cheddar Valley and Chew Reservoir. We had heard rumours of a wallcreeper at Cheddar, that would be something very special, a bird we class as 'Mega'; a once in a decade species. Should we miss out we would then have Chew Reservoir as a back-up with its good selection of water birds.

That decided, twenty-four of us ventured forth on a rather damp and dreary morning, hopes were not high. These proved to be correct, no wallcreeper and the locals told us it had not been seen for a couple of days. So that was that, could Chew save our bacon?

At least as we drove to the reservoir the weather slowly improved, the rain finally stopped and the clouds commenced to disperse; was someone on our side after all?

The range of duck species was quite incredible and hidden among them was a real cracker, a substitute 'Mega' in fact. I will list them so you can get an idea of what I am saying: mallard, teal, gadwall, wigeon, pintail, shoveler, tufted duck, pochard, goldeneye, red-breasted merganser, goosander, ruddy duck, shelduck, and finally the duck of the day – a ring-necked duck; a rare visitor from across 'The Pond', this bird was certainly a few thousand miles off track. Many of my class had never even heard of the duck, and few of their field guides even had an illustration of the bird. A 'Lifer' for us all, and the bird luckily had been a drake which made identification easier; fortunately, the bird was illustrated in my field guide. Missing out on the wallcreeper no longer mattered.

The reservoir was quite full, with little or no shore-line, so waders were difficult to find, and the pick of the few we did see were four ruffs. Large numbers of fieldfares and redwings were to be seen, feeding away on the nearby hawthorn hedge. Judging by their numbers, the berry crop there would not last many days.

The cloud was slowly drifting back and the light was reducing quickly, so we gave the gulls which were coming in to roost – one good last look, and could not believe our eyes. Landing on the water close in, almost as though it intended to be seen, was another cracker: a ring-billed gull, another rarity from North America. Two 'Yankees', at the same place and the same day, was positively unbelievable – another 'Lifer' for all, apart from me because I had seen one previously. It was a good job I had, few field guides had illustrations of this bird which, to make matters worse, was a juvenile. Fortunately, my previous sighting was also a juvenile so I was able to explain why the bird was a ring-billed and point out one or two distinguishing features which were not evident on the gulls of a similar size which accompanied it.

Chew had been amazing, it had more than compensated for the disappointment at Cheddar, and we all motored home happy and contented. Two 'Mega' ticks on one day, that was a day we would all remember. Incidentally, we had sixty-one species on the day, but who was counting?

For our October meet, we chose Rutland Water; the numbers of waterfowl should be very good, and if the weather was inclement, there were plenty of hides to shelter in. Sixteen of us made the journey and we all met up at the Visitor Centre from which a very pleasant surprise was observed. A bar-headed goose was visible, probably an escapee, but none the less a most interesting bird to see. I understood they were breeding in Holland in a wild state, just like Canada geese here, so we would never know the answer to that one. It went on all our lists anyway.

I was certainly right about the waterfowl. We saw sixteen different species, including the goose mentioned above. The pick of which were pintail, red-crested pochard, ruddy duck, snow goose and another escapee, a Bahama pintail; the latter was most definitely an escapee!

Due to high water levels waders were not very plentiful with green sandpiper and ruff being the best of those. Grebes, on the other hand, were well represented – as well as the commoner great crested grebes and little grebes – we also saw two Slavonian grebes, a bit special these, and three black-necked grebes. Those went down very well with a few of my colleagues, as they were 'Lifers'. A kingfisher also put on a display for us, and they are always a welcome addition to a day's birding, being probably our most colourful native bird. A bird to rival any bird on the planet I believe.

As dusk descended a barn owl came out to hunt, and it did so right in from of the hide we were in. At times it flew directly in front of the hide, as silent as a ghost, which it almost mimicked being so white. Barn owls are some bird and to be able to almost shake hands with one has got to be a bit special.

No further excitement occurred, but once again we made our ways home satisfied with our day. Birds seen totalled fifty-seven.

Our final trip of the year was to be up to the Staffordshire/Derbyshire Moorlands, just an hour or so from home, where we would at least be able to use the few hours of winter daylight.

We called in at Tittesworth Reservoir first, a warm coffee would set us up for the day, and here we saw a small herd of white-fronted geese, eleven of them. It was a great start to the day, and the coffee was not bad.

On to the Moors. It was rather bleak up there that day a stiff breeze had popped up and it was driving in sleet, not at all pleasant. Our birding was now to be done from the comfort of our cars. The weather did not affect the red grouse, fortunately, and we saw several small coveys of those, but not a lot else.

As we still had some time and the light was not too bad, we decided to nip across to Swallow Moss to see if we could be lucky with the other grouse found on the moors, the black grouse. Grouse hunting could not be done here from the warmth of the cars, the weather had to be faced up to.

We were fortunate, we only walked as far as the old barn where we sheltered to see three male black grouse in the field in front of the barn. I do not suppose we saw them for more than a few minutes before they flew off into the nearby woodland. But compared with not seeing them at all, a few minutes is an eternity.

We might not have seen a large range of species, but some were quality, that was for sure. The total for the day was forty-four.

That was the final meeting for the year. During which I saw a total of two hundred and ten species in the UK, a vast improvement on the last year's figures. The question now is what will '88 bring us?

Before '87 was over I received a telephone call from Graham, he was interested in any experience I had with Mallorca. I told him none, but I had studied the birdlife as I intended to have a holiday there in the near future, and because of this I had prepared plans for when I did go there. The next question was, 'How did I feel about going next year?' my answer was obviously yes.

Graham was planning a joint study tour for both bird watchers and botanists and he was interested in whether I was happy to lead the bird watchers, and did I feel enough members of my two courses would be interested. I was certain they would be. A meeting was arranged for the New Year and could I have my thoughts ready for discussion by then. I only had three weeks to prepare them, but much of this was already available for me. What a Christmas present, and even better, Dorothy would be able to accompany me. She would obviously have to pay but as I did not and I also was paid a fee to lead the party, at the very worst we had a half-price holiday ahead. No complaints there. The first field meeting in '88 was to Crosby and Seaforth, new areas to us all. One of the reasons for visiting there was the fact that an adult ring-billed gull was being regularly seen. Our previous experience of this bird was seeing a juvenile, so the chance of seeing an adult could not be missed.

We met at Cannock which lay close by the motorway and four cars made the journey in convoy, not being familiar with the location, we had no idea where we could have met up. Fortunately, the motorway was not overly busy and the journey was accomplished comfortably enough.

A group of birders was quickly spotted, so we went to join them. We had chosen well, they were looking at the ring-billed gull, and in its adult plumage there was no mistaking this bird. Knowing we were hoping to see this bird, I had brought with me my Field Guide to the Birds of North America, so we were actually able to compare the bird with the illustrations in my book. The black ring on the yellow bill was instantly noted, hence the name of the gull, the greenish-yellow legs combined with its larger size, and interestingly, in flight it sounded very similar to the herring gull. If anyone had questions over the Chew Reservoir ring-billed gull, they had not now.

We had only been there the matter of minutes and we had knocked off the main bird we came up for, things are rarely that easy, so we had a chat with some of the local birders. They were able to give us some very interesting information, some of which related to birds recently seen at Seaforth.

Seaforth has a large marina we were told, and as recently as the day before, both Lapland bunting and snow bunting were reported on the shores of the lake, and a long-tailed duck, a drake, plus three barnacle geese were also to be seen. Four wonderful species with which to start off the new year. You cannot beat local knowledge that is for sure.

The journey from Crosby to Seaforth was only minutes and the lake was quickly located; would our luck hold for the birds?

No water activities were taking place, January is not the time to go sailing I suppose. A few gulls were present on the lake, the inevitable Canada geese and it was on these we concentrated our initial efforts. If the barnacle geese were anywhere they would be tucked in amongst the Canada geese; fortunately, there were only about fifty of them. Our idea proved to be correct, we quickly found the three barnacles, so that was one down three to go!

We were starting to think we would draw a blank on the long-tailed duck when the bird sailed out from behind a buoy. It had probably been resting behind this and our view had been obstructed, not any longer. The duck may not have been in full adult plumage, but the length of the pin-like tail was still most impressive.

We could now concentrate our efforts on the buntings, and looking at how the clouds were building up, combined with an increase in the strength of the wind, time was running out. Our informants had told us the birds, three snow buntings and one Lapland bunting, had been associating with a flock of chaffinches, so that at least gave us a starter, look for chaffinches not buntings.

We managed to find a sheltered spot where we were able to erect our tri-pods and scopes, and start panning the shores of the lake. After some time and a few maybe's, we located a group of about fifty small birds running along the shore, some of which were chaffinches. We quickly located the snow buntings, two of which were glorious males, but the Lapland was proving more difficult. At last, one of my colleagues, and one of the new boys, shouted over 'You did say they looked a bit like a reed bunting did you not Brian?' I nodded, he pointed, rather excitedly, and he had hit the jack pot. There was the Lapland, feeding away on the ground without a care in the world, neither had we now.

A very pleasant ten minutes or so followed as we watched the bird's progress along the shore, until enough was enough, they all took off and flew across the lake. We were more than happy to wave them goodbye!

As we still had time, and the conditions had worsened, we spent half an hour sea watching over what I suppose was Liverpool Bay. Plenty of duck on the water including pintail, scaup, red-breasted merganser and shelduck. A few waders were also present, but not many and the pick of those were curlews and bar-tailed godwits.

Time to head off home, another great day's birding. If anyone had said to me, 'Go to Liverpool for a good day's birding,' I would seriously have doubted their sanity. Liverpool only had football and The Beatles. I now know that to be wrong, it also has some cracking birds. That day we saw sixty-two of them.

My meeting with Graham arrived and I was able to inform him I had fifteen interested birders, all they wanted were dates and costs. We were due to stay at San Vincente which was close to the Formentor Peninsular; here Mallorca's most special bird, the Eleonora's falcon, bred. The numbers were perfect as far as Graham was concerned. Unlike the Camargue, many of the locations were not available to large vehicles so for this tour we would use hire cars. This raised the next question, had I ever driven on the 'wrong side of the road'? I had not, but I did not see that as a problem, so that was sorted. My fifteen interested parties, plus me, made it just four cars required for the birders. From what Graham said, there were twelve interested botanists, so they needed three.

I gave Graham my plans so he could work out the distances we were likely to travel so fuel costs could be dealt with. Unlike being on coaches, we would have to fill up our cars as required and money would have to be made available to cover those costs. Graham would have to have all of this with him, I hoped he had a strong money-belt! I had already sorted out my other car drivers, all of whom had previous experience with driving in Europe. All we now awaited were the costs and dates, which we would have shortly.

It was back to Wales for our next field meeting, calling in at Ludlow to seek out the hawfinches which bred there. We hit the jack-pot almost immediately. Three hawfinches were feeding on the ground beneath some beech trees, beech mast being one of their favourite foods; we just remained quiet and still, watching them feast on, which they did with noticeable relish!

They were joined by goldfinches, chaffinches, bramblings and siskins fed in the trees above. A good selection of some of our most colourful birds. A sparrowhawk unfortunately chose that moment to fly through, and that was the end of that. On then for the Elan Valley, red kite hunting again.

The red kite were not as cooperative as the hawfinches had been and we had almost reached Aberystwyth before we caught a glimpse of one; well, to be more accurate, of three. We only saw them for a few seconds, but at least all of us had.

On reaching Aberystwyth we found the outgoing tide was just perfect. The shingle spit which stretches out into the Bay was rapidly appearing, and the waders were flying onto this as they searched for food.

The three waders we were really after were ringed plover, turnstone and purple sandpiper. The first two were very obliging, they appeared as soon as an area of shingle was made visible. It took many minutes before the dark shape of a purple sandpiper put in an appearance. Against the background of the shingle, and the many small rocks now becoming visible, the sandpipers were almost invisible. If they stopped moving, you had great difficulty in picking them up again, and it took several minutes and many attempts before we all had the satisfaction of seeing them.

Time now to concentrate on some sea watching before the sea retreated too far, although I had been told it did not go out that far. Two red-throated divers were quickly spotted, which was a very good start to the proceedings. Cormorants were busy and the odd shag flew across, providing us with the opportunity of studying a few differences in the plumages of two very similar birds. A very large flock of common scoter were slowly drifting out on the tide – well, into three figures – hard as we searched we could only identify common scoter, none of their more interesting relatives were to be seen amongst them. A surprise occurred. Chough were heard calling and two flew across heading in the direction of the remains of Aberystwyth Castle, I should not think they bred there. Raven were also heard, but not seen unfortunately.

It had been a quiet day for bird numbers, but amongst them we had picked up one or two choice species for early in the year. Our total for the day was forty-eight. We decided we would hit Wales once again, so to finish off the winter course we visited the North Wales Coast, from Llandudno to Rhyl, where a lot of viewing could be done from near the car. At Llandudno things started brilliantly. On the sea, and not far out, a great northern diver and two black-throated divers were seen, and beyond them were gannets, fulmars and cormorants, heading towards the Great Ormes Head. You could not wish for a better start than that. Our next stop would be overlooking Penrhyn Bay and Rhos-on-Sea, and there too the birds were out to impress. At Penrhyn we added another diver to our list, the red-throated, and among the duck was a ring-necked duck and a red-breasted merganser. The ring-necked duck, as you will remember from earlier reports is a rare north American species, a 'Lifer' to several of my colleagues. Also, to see our three native divers just a short distance apart,

255

was also some record. Rhos-on-Sea was not going to miss out on the fun and excitement. There we saw two red-necked grebes plus several great crested grebes on the sea, with two drake scaups also enjoying the day. The tide here was just beginning to turn and this brought several shelduck from out of the dunes, and in that day's decent light they looked very smart.

A few waders were on the shore with some of the knots looking very smart as they were moulting into their red summer plumage. The curlews were very vocal, they must have the most evocative call of any bird, a real send a shiver down your spine call – as long as you have a soul!

After all this excitement there is only one way the remainder of the day could go, not exactly downhill, but quieter. Then I remembered a place Gerry, my Camargue colleague, had mentioned to me some time ago: a location for the very rare Lady Amherst's pheasant, and that day we would be driving very near to the village. I trust you will excuse me for not telling you exactly where. A few birders had been trespassing onto private land to try to see the birds, upsetting the land owner and the local church goers by creating noise and nuisance in the church grounds.

Fortunately, for us, all the church services had been completed that day so we were unlikely to upset anyone; when required, church mice have nothing on us. We parked up and quietly made our way to the back of the churchyard to the wall that separated the church grounds from the adjoining estate. The wall had a few gaps where the stone work had collapsed over the centuries, providing good views over the estate, and there were plenty of pheasants visible. This was understandable as it was a pheasant shoot, but apparently the shooters had strict orders to leave the Lady Amherst's alone, and this they were managing to do.

Before getting on with the pheasants, one of our group brought my attention to a bird perched on the church, a tawny owl was sitting out, enjoying the remaining light prior to going off hunting. By now the owl probably had young in the nest to feed and could, quite easily, be breeding on the church. We left him to get on with things; we now had other thoughts on our minds. Several minutes passed us by, many pheasants were seen, and then, from underneath a clump of rhododendron bushes walked a female pheasant with a very long tail, heavily barred. This was no common pheasant, only the golden pheasant and the Lady Amherst's pheasants have tails so marked, and only the Lady Amherst's has one so long; we had our bird. Whilst enjoying her we had the ultimate pleasure, out walked a male. This bird defies any description, it is so exotic as to be almost unbelievable. Just look at the bird in your field guide, no wonder the shooters have their orders, shoot this bird and you deserve to be shot yourself! It is a bird which prefers to walk rather than fly, and this may be a help in its survival. In other parts of the country, shooting of the bird may be tolerated, as most pheasant are shot on the wing – to spend most of the time on the ground would have certain benefits.

Anyway, be that as it may, for a few short minutes we had the pleasure of studying what is probably the most beautiful and wonderful bird on the British list; what a way to finish off our trip to Wales. The Principality had done it again. That also concluded the winter course. Early next month, we would commence the summer course and come the end of April – Mallorca called. The summer course numbers still held up, twenty-five this time, and seven of them would be coming to Mallorca with me. We managed two local field meetings before leaving for Mallorca, visiting Belvide Reservoir and Blithfield Reservoir where not a lot was seen.

The 30th April saw us flying out to Mallorca. We landed at Palma where a coach took us to San Vincente and our hotel. After booking ourselves in, the seven nominated drivers collected our fleet of cars, and went on a short drive to get used to things; especially me for my first experience of driving on the right. After dinner, we made our plans for the next day.

The botanists went off orchid hunting, we, the birders, made our way to the Formentor Peninsula after the Eleonora's falcons. If we saw those what a start to our stay. I had been fortunate enough to obtain a copy Eddie Watkinson's 'A guide to Bird-watching in Mallorca' and our birding would be based on his suggestions. Eddie was a big name in Mallorcan birding circles and it was very helpful to read a book written by a British birder whose first language was English. Nothing lost in translation.

The drive to Formentor was most enjoyable, peaceful and through some most attractive countryside and as we approached the car park by the lighthouse, we pulled over to enjoy a superb male blue rock thrush. Although I had seen this bird in La Camargue, I had never heard one singing; believe me it is not called a thrush for nothing, his voice is as beautiful as he is. We all thought Mallorca was going to be great after such a wonderful start. From there, we took the pathway to a rocky plateau for some sea watching and also hoping to see the falcon hurtling round the cliffs. We did not see the falcon, but we had great views of rock doves, ravens, crag martins and pallid swifts, whilst out at sea black kites and harriers were passing through.

I must confess I was a little bit worried about the Eleonora's falcons as they are a very late breeding bird. They do not arrive back in Mallorca until late April and do not breed until August/September. Breeding this late coincides with the migration of many passerines which pass through on their migration southwards. As a large percentage of these small birds will be juvenile birds, just weeks/months old they are easy pickings to such a skilful hunter as the falcon, their nestlings do not go hungry that is for sure. The more I learn about wild creatures, the more amazed I become. I had not said anything to my colleagues about my fears, I just hoped the falcons did arrive back for us to appreciate them.

We enjoyed our lunch and made our way to the viewpoint suggested by Eddie, where you could see the falcons flying past when returning to their nesting sites later in the season. Would we be lucky that day, I wondered?

They do say fortune favours the brave, not that I am brave. A voice broke the silence, 'Brian. what's that very dark bird of prey flying past just down the cliff?' I swung round to look and our day was made. Flying past was a dark-phased Eleonora's falcon, the bird we all wanted to see the most. I doubt if we had the bird in sight for above twenty seconds, but I am sure it would be twenty seconds remembered for life! I know one thing, I was very pleased I had purchased a copy of Eddie Watkinson's slim paper back, it was going to be worth its weight in gold. The falcon did not return, but before we continue with the birds seen, let us botanise. On Formentor wild peonies grew, if you were lucky, and they have a short flowering season in April. A few were still in flower, something to tell our colleagues back at base. Back to the birds.

The pick of the bunch for us were Marmora's warbler, subalpine warbler, rock bunting, crested lark and turtle dove, plus the passage of large number of hirundines, swallows especially, plenty of food there for the falcon.

We had plenty to talk about during the evening, and we planned to visit Albufera Marsh and saltpans. This was one of Mallorca's prime birding locations, although for how much longer was another question, as development was being carried out with an area of infilling by the shores of the canal which ran through the area. Fortunately, work had been slowed down due to the financial situation current in Mallorca so we would enjoy it whilst we might.

It was located right on the main coastal road from Alcudia to Arta, so we had two options on the day. Should things be quiet on the Marsh, which was highly unlikely, we had the sea to study. The Marsh covers 4,000 acres according to Eddie; somehow, I did not think we would be seeing all of that!

We managed to park up near to the English Bridge to make our way into the Marsh. The whole area was buzzing with birds and we had hardly moved from the cars when Dorothy shouted and pointed. Overhead, two black-winged stilts were flying, their 'kyeep, kyeep' ringing out as they passed us by. A wonderful start to the day.

The area south of what I believe is called the Main Canal, was a most interesting area of scrub and marsh with a wealth of birds to be seen or heard. Further on lay an area of tamarisks, more scrubby marsh and some thick reed. I will not mention all the birds seen, but just list a few to give you a flavour of the place. Osprey, marsh harrier, crossbill, serin, nightingale, Cetti's warbler, fan-tailed warbler, hoopoe, woodchat shrike, little egret, purple heron, moustached warbler, great reed warbler and among the tamarisks a skulking wryneck. I think you will agree, enough there to create an adrenalin rush. Here was an area much loved by Eddie, and he recommended you visit. The 'Lone Pine' as he calls it, which grows on a small mound which provided excellent views of the area. He was right about the views. Birds, however, did not support him on that occasion, although we added a hen harrier to that day's list. In a wet ditch, we also saw a snake of unknown vintage and a terrapin of again unknown origins. We ate lunch before driving on down to the saltpans, where we hoped to pick up a few interesting waders, including better views of the black-winged stilts seen earlier.

Luck was again with us, we managed to park close by. In a scrubby area, we saw a pair of stone curlews rushing through and the odd short-toed lark was visible and heard, a bright enough start to the proceedings.

There must have been at least three pairs of hoopoes there, more short-toed larks, tawny pipits and quail were heard but not seen. Amongst the waders were ringed plovers, little ringed plovers and Kentish plovers, the last two very rare birds back home; although, the little ringed plover has commenced to breed I understand. Greenshanks and redshanks were quite common as were common sandpipers and a late little stint was a most unexpected sighting; I would have expected this bird to have been in northern Europe well before now. Several pairs of black-winged stilts were to be seen, a most elegant bird as they walked through the water, and the odd avocet was found. A more than decent collection there.

Walking back to our cars a collared pratincole gave us a fly-past, here was a bird I had not considered so that gave us a real bonus, and the odd ruff was beginning to show his magnificent summer plumage, some bird that. Alberfera Marsh had been well worth the visit, I just hoped it would not get spoilt with any future development. One bird which all wished to see was the black vulture, if ever a bird could be called a 'flying bedstead' this was it. The black vulture is classed as Europe's largest bird of prey and the northern mountains of Mallorca did seem to attract this bird. I explained to my group that although the black vulture was very likely, we could quite easily have a quiet day for other birds. They were happy with that, a day 'Twitching' for a bird of that calibre would be a day well spent.

Our plans for Day 3 were made. The High Sierras here we come. I trust you like my bit of Spanish there. A radar station is on Puig Mayor, some 4,740 feet high, that is a bit taller than Ben Nevis, and here food was discarded which was much appreciated by the vultures and occasional eagles too. I quickly assured my friends we would not be walking that high. We would do our viewing from a car park near the reservoir Embalse Gorg Blau, a few hundred feet lower, not a problem when looking for a bird with a nine-foot wingspan.

The drive was not for the feint hearted. I think this was where hairpin bends were invented and round some of these bends it did not pay to look at the drop just feet away from your car. Definitely it was a case of 'keep your eyes on your driving and your hands on the wheel', to quote the words of a pop song of years ago.

We parked up, enjoying blue rock thrushes once again and watching a few crag martins wheel their way through the sky. Also of interest was a large dung beetle seen pushing a ball of dung, the size almost of a golf ball, in front of it. They are a big beetle but this must have been pushing its own weight, nature is wonderful.

Whilst all this was going on a voice suddenly shouts, 'Hi Bri, I think I have a vulture.' At this, we all swung round to look in the direction being pointed. He was right, a vulture it most certainly was; unfortunately, not the black, he had found us an Egyptian vulture, which I hasten to add, no one was complaining about. Time to get scopes and tri-pods out, this vulture watching was serious business. The radar station was not exactly an attractive piece of architecture but if the operators fed the birds of prey, and we saw them, the black vulture especially, we would not be complaining.

It looked like no food had been thrown out that day, a couple of red kites were soaring about and not once did they drop onto the ground beneath; the staff had not eaten their lunches yet by the look of things. Talking about lunches, time we thought of our own.

To brighten up our lunch, a calandra lark dropped in; it kept us amused as it chased ants across the dried floor. Some of the ants seen in these warmer climates are not small like ours back home. The size of these probably meant the lark did not need that many to satisfy its appetite.

Things suddenly started to happen at the radar station, the kites flew down to the ground – food had obviously been thrown out. Within what appeared to be only minutes, three large black looking birds glided across; we had our black vultures, and three of them proceeded to put on quite a display. Without a doubt, they are a massive bird, and they fly effortlessly, or so it appeared. With hardly a flap of their giant wings they just glided down to snatch up food in their talons, with which they then flew to a suitable rocky face to eat their meal before repeating the operation. It was obvious which was top bird there, every time a black vulture landed near the food the other birds moved off.

An eagle joined in the fray, a booted eagle briefly called in but did not seem to appreciate the black vultures' activity, which was probably understandable. The vultures may not have attacked, but their very size is most provocative, and three of them would be enough to frighten anything, even an eagle. Whilst enjoying the birds of prey, my attention was drawn to a small group of large looking swift; we were being visited by a passing number of Alpine swifts, nine of them in fact, and we had but seconds to enjoy them. Seen this closely you could really appreciate their size, looking more like a small falcon than a swift.

Raven were calling almost continuously and when you study the surrounding vistas you can fully appreciate why. The various peaks fully justify the area being known as the High Sierras; it was a wonderful area to visit. If you do so, just be careful with the driving in parts. All good things must come to an end, so time to make our way home. Over dinner, accompanied by the odd tot, we sorted our next trip out; could it possibly be better than that just experienced?

We decided to go to the south east tip of Mallorca where one of the quality birds as far as we were concerned was the Audouin's gull. At that time of the year, we should also catch some passage birds, and stone curlews and hoopoes were regularly seen according to Eddie that is. Cabo de Salinas here we come, and this would be our longest journey of the week. Part of the area is a very private and heavily guarded estate called S'Avall; no admittance and, according to Eddie, should you try you will be politely, but very firmly, told to leave. We did not challenge this. The land is well cultivated with a goodly number of smaller passerines, especially warblers. A bird which did surprise me was the number of red-legged partridges to be seen plus hoopoes, there we saw many, and no one was complaining. Stone curlews and Thekla larks were also well accounted for, but our principal attention lay on the coast, so we walked the short distance to the lighthouse and set up our tripods and scopes to study the sea.

Shearwaters were out at sea, we certainly had Manx shearwaters and Cory's shearwaters, not birds seen that often back at home. Several gulls were active; among these were the yellow-legged variant of the herring gull, which is common in and around the Mediterranean, the Mediterranean gull itself, but the Audouin's gull was not co-operating.

We decided to partake lunch and concentrate our efforts during the afternoon.

Whilst eating our lunches, two British birders arrived on the scene and they were able to tell us where they had just seen the Audouin's gulls. Needless to say, lunch was quickly eaten. The gulls had been seen about half a mile further along the beach so we made our way along the tide-line. The odd tern put in an appearance to keep up our interest until we arrived at the suggested location.

Here there was quite a bit of gull activity so time to settle down and look at them more closely. When you are looking for a bird, and especially a gull, which is not a bird you are familiar with; minor detail can be very important. The Audouin's is not dissimilar to the herring gull, being smaller and much paler and has a dark red bill, black-tipped, unlike the yellow bill of the herring. The legs are also grey, not pink as is the case with the herring gull. Also, which should be noticeable when seen in flight, it shows very little white on the black primaries, and also has a white trailing edge to the wings. It also has a dark eye where the herring gull is bright yellow. Enough there for us to concentrate on.

It took us several minutes to find one; fortunately, it flew very close in so we had very good views. No mistaking this bird, all the detail mentioned above was clearly seen; we had our bird. In fact, we had several, our informants had not been wrong. It is always a bit special when the one bird you really wished to see, is seen, and seen well. We spent half an hour or so enjoying those gulls, before we had to start off home; we had a long journey, but it had been well worthwhile. The question now was: where to the next day?

Only two days left and we had chosen Albufereta, where we once again had two options, Albufetera itself or sea watching. The area, we understood, was good for passage migrants as well as breeding warblers.

We made our way to Albufetera and over the lake we were happy to see several Eleonora's falcons hunting large insects over the water and three spoonbills were feeding in the shallows; a good enough start that. Several little egrets were to be seen and the odd purple heron was stalking the shore line. Over the marshland, marsh harriers were very active and the odd bee-eater was to be seen.

On the adjoining scrubland, subalpine warblers could be seen and heard and a few wheatears were still passing through; one of these caught our attention. It appeared longer-tailed than its companions, and was showing more black on the wings and more white on the tail. The bird turned sidewise on and we clearly saw the smaller black area on the face; we were looking at a black-eared wheatear – we were more than happy now. Hirundines were numerous and this was understandable, flying insects were equally so and many were of the biting variety.

An osprey graced us with its company, as we watched it take a fish, fan-tailed warblers and Marmora's warblers were also showing well with turtle dove purring away from a nearby willow; always a delightful sound. A nightingale was not going to be outdone as he gave us a brief burst. A woodchat shrike put in a brief appearance, but did not stay for long.

As we still had time we drove the short distance down to the Tucan Marsh, but we were a little disappointed there. Firstly, the road through Puerto Alcudia was a nightmare and also there was a large built-up area near the marsh itself. We did, however, see and hear moustached warblers and the odd Cetti's warbler could be heard. Eleonora's were again seen and water rail were heard, so it was not all bad. Back to base, with more decisions to be made. We were now approaching our final day; would it be a repeat of a site previously visited, or would we choose somewhere new? We chose somewhere new and decided to visit Casas Veyas. Here you will find a mixture of cultivated land, woodland and fig tree fields and the range of species to be seen is exceptionally good, particularly when a northerly blows during passage, and that day we were lucky. It may not exactly have been a northerly, but what wind there was came from that direction. The day was going to be a day for passerines in the main, and we were not disappointed. A full list of the species seen is out of the question, but amongst them were subalpine warblers, Sardinian warblers, stonechats, wrynecks, spotless starlings, bee-eaters, nightingales, a golden oriole, hoopoes, wheatears, a whinchat, pied flycatchers, turtle doves and redstarts. We were also lucky with a pair of firecrest and crossbills. A goodly enough list there to satisfy the keenest of birders.

A peregrine falcon also gave us a fly-past, although it frightened many of the birds and the area became strangely quiet after its appearance, which was quite understandable.

Driving back to our hotel, we hit the jackpot of the day. We were approaching Puerto Pollensa through some rather scrubby ground when a companion in my car suddenly pointed and shouted, 'What on earth have we here?' I managed to pull off the road into an area which would take several cars, so my colleagues could follow me in safely. Walking across the field was a long necked game-like bird, showing a very pronounced black 'mane' on its neck with a slight crest on the head. I could not believe what we were looking at, it was a male Houbara bustard. Here, at the end of our stay almost, we had the bird of the week. This bird had never been considered as a possible, they are a rare bird at the best of times, a migrant to central Asia, resident only in north Africa and the Middle East. This bird had probably been blown off course from Africa, what ever the reason, we were not complaining. All I know is, a few complimentary tots of a certain brew were consumed that evening.

It was now all over, we had seen one hundred and eleven birds during the week, not quite as many as we had in La Camargue, but for many a good number of 'Lifers' were included in that number. Their 'World Lists' had done very well. Mine had not done too badly either. Back now to birding in 'dear old Blighty'.

Having returned from Mallorca, I had one or two things to think about. My previous two visits to La Camargue had proceeded far more easily and pleasantly than Mallorca, not that Mallorca was not very satisfactory, but there had been a few misunderstandings along the way. I was of the opinion that this type of tour was not suitable for all, having a mixture of botany and bird study may have sounded a good idea, but when put into practice was not as successful as first thought, and I voiced my opinion of this, which was not appreciated. I was the junior partner in all of this, Graham and the botany expert were full-time employees of the University; I was only part-time. So thinking more about this, I decided that in the future I would go solo and organise my own tours. I would no longer be paid or get free holidays, but that was not important, and I could continue as a tutor with the University.

The year 1988 continued in the usual fashion. We visited the usual haunts, enjoyed Bempton once again – it is always pleasant to share time with the puffins – and had a pleasant weekend in Norfolk where we saw marsh harrier, woodlark and stone curlew once again. Come September, we managed a family holiday in Guernsey, where we had a very pleasant time. Nothing special on the bird front, although we did renew acquaintance with Dartford warblers once again.

Things livened up in the autumn, however, picking up a Forsters tern in the Dee estuary – this being a rare bird from North America – and topping this we had an Alpine swift locally at Sandwell Valley Reserve. This bird had been found on the floor in a local warehouse and taken to Sandwell Valley for both identification and care. The swift survived and was flown to Spain where it was released, a good piece of publicity for British Airways. That bird most certainly put Sandwell Valley on the map, a cracking 'UK Lifer' only minutes away from home. And to think I had only been seeing this bird a few months ago on Mallorca, I need not have gone!

Dorothy and I managed a weekend in the Lakes where we enjoyed a pleasant break and shared our time with a few choice birds. Black grouse, red-throated diver, goshawk, lesser-spotted woodpecker and raven particularly so.

The year finished off on a high at Martin Mere. Here the group had a green-winged teal, a rare duck from North America. Not a bad way to finish a year off. During the year I had two hundred and nine species in the UK, combined with birds seen on Mallorca, I topped the two hundred and fifty-two species mark.

We now waited to see how the decade would finish.

As events turned out, '89 proved to be a rather quiet year as far as birding in the UK was concerned, with only one hundred and fifty-eight species seen, although a few choice species were included amongst those. Avocets, bitterns, bearded tits, brent geese, glaucous gull – just the one – golden eagle, Iceland gull, once again only one, mandarin duck, Mediterranean gull, red-necked grebe, ring-necked parakeet, short-eared owl, spoonbill, waxwing and southern/continental cormorant. We were not complaining.

The highlight of the year, as far as Dorothy and I were concerned, was a holiday in Switzerland; after Mallorca, the travel bug had taken over. We stayed at Wengen for ten days during June/July, and had a wonderful time. The countryside is magnificent, the walking was superb, the service at the hotel was first class, and the birding was completely new and exciting. We were staying right in the Alps with the mighty Eiger towering above us, all 13,015 feet of it. Although Switzerland was an expensive country to visit, we knew we would walk a lot and only used the local train services as necessary; plus the Swiss Travel Card, for tourists, helped a lot.

You may well have heard of Wengen, it is home to one of Switzerland's major ski events, not in June needless to say, although there was plenty of snow viewable higher up; the Eiger being snow-capped all year I understand. The hotel had quite extensive grounds and the bird-life was most interesting. On our first day there, we had a walk round and was delighted to see a nutcracker in the garden; the perfect start to our holiday as far as we were concerned. Alpine swifts were screaming through and black redstarts were very common. Outside the village every chalet appeared to have a pair in residence, and they were as friendly as robins back home, a delightful little bird.

We were obviously in for some very interesting bird watching and some very unusual mammals lived on the mountains; all we required was the weather to enjoy it all in.

We decided that on our first day we would get to know the area round Wengen really well, and studying my Wanderkarte map of the Lauterbrunnental Jungfrau-Region, we quickly sorted out a pleasant looking walk where the inclines did not look too strenuous; although, they were far from flat. It would appear that a day or two prior to our arrival, the cattle had been brought up by train from the valley below to spend their summer feeding on the rich Alpine meadows. As we walked from Wengen, the musical tones of their many bells could be heard; if ever a sound epitomised Switzerland, this was surely it. Delightful was the only word for it.

We headed towards Isenfluh from where we understood superb views could be made. The walk was through very pleasant woodland areas, a mixture of broadleaf and conifer where many birds could be seen, and magnificent Alpine meadows with super arrays of wild flowers; we did not appreciate just how many species of orchid types existed. One thing was quickly apparent, butterflies were everywhere; I have never seen so many different blues together in my life. We will never have the time nor the knowledge to sort all of these out!

The reports of the quality of the views obtained from Isenfluh had not been exaggerated. Numerous high peaks towering above the many valleys beneath. A golden eagle obviously bred there, it was to be seen constantly and black kite glided through regularly. From the many wooded areas, various song birds could be heard; chaffinch numbers were very good – almost on a par with back home – as were robins, although the latter were not as friendly.

Whilst enjoying these, we broke off to study a pair of raven when a series of weird trills burst forth. We swung round. On a nearby piece of rock sat an Alpine chough, and the bird was really letting rip. Binoculars were not required to see this bird – I doubt it was twenty feet away – completely oblivious to us it would seem. For two or three minutes it continued calling and then another chough appeared, presumably its mate, and off they flew. Switzerland was growing on us by the minute. Back to listening to the birds. Many were completely new to us and without actually seeing the birds, identification was going to prove difficult; we were listening to birds rarely, if ever, seen in the UK.

Warblers were very vocal; fortunately, the majority of these were familiar to us, as was the song of greenfinch, goldfinch, linnet and the chaffinches mentioned previously, but from amongst this cacophony of sound was a call we were not familiar with. It was a rather bouncing 'Chit, it it' not un-linnet like, but it just sounded something different to us. The vegetation there abouts was very thick, almost impenetrable to the naked eye, but luckily for us, a bright coloured small finch flew into it, 'Chit it it'ing' as it did so. It was a magnificent male citril finch, a real beauty; what a find on our first day!

Time had caught up with us, it was a longish walk back to the hotel, most of which we had the company of a calling cuckoo (we could at least recognise him!), where after a shower and change, dinner called. Dinner was most enjoyable and we also found that Swiss wine was also very pleasant.

Our next venture would be taking the train up to Kleine Scheidegg. From here the most beautiful views of the Eiger, Monch and Jungfrau and down into the Trummelbach Valley are to be obtained, and as we intended to walk slowly back down to Wengen;, this was our prospect.

At Kleine, you are at 6762 feet; you can see why we took the train up the foothills of the Mannlichen range. You certainly know you are in the Swiss Alps here. We enjoyed a coffee and cake at Kleine, where we ate outside and were assisted in doing so by a black-eared wheatear, which had a distinct liking for a certain sponge cake we were enjoying, so much so we had to go and buy another slice!

After a walk round Kleine, where we were thrilled to bits to see our first Alpine accentor, as well as more superb views, we commenced our slow descent back down to Wengen. The climb up to Kleine is stated as a 2hr 45 min walk; all I can say is you would have to be mighty fit to manage that. You would certainly not have much time to enjoy the views in transit. It took us nearly twice that time to make the descent, but what a descent!

We had barely left Kleine when we stopped. On a grassy slope several Alpine marmots were sitting outside their burrows, many bolt upright, taking in the sun no doubt. What an incredible little animal, they seemed full of curiosity as they appeared to be studying us as intently as we were them. Then a black kite glided over, and down their burrows they went, we continued on our way. A little further down we stopped again. On a steep mountain slope a small group, five in fact, of chamois were congregated. These animals proceeded to drop down the mountainside, at speed, showing their extreme skills as they jumped from rock to rock. How they managed to stay upright I do not know, one slip and they would have plunged several hundred feet to their death. An amazing animal. In a matter of minutes, we had experienced two of the Alps most special creatures.

The Alpine meadows were absolutely splendid, the range of flowers were superb and one false orchid caused some amusement, especially as far as Dorothy was concerned. I was busily photographing the flowers and as I was doing so Dorothy kept trying to catch my attention and was getting very frustrated in the process. Eventually, I looked at where she was pointing just in time to see a black woodpecker fly off a tree. This bird was one of the birds we wished to see the most, and thanks to my photographing a flower, I nearly missed it. Dorothy had enjoyed this bird for probably a couple of minutes, I had it for about ten seconds; I think I will put my camera away, it was not as though I even knew the name of the false orchid! Dorothy will have my undivided attention in future.

Alpine choughs were plentiful and a pair of golden eagles was seen continuously as they soared high in the mountains; I had a feeling we would be accompanied by these birds on many an occasion when out in the mountains. You can never have too much of a good thing.

About halfway down, we came to a belt of trees and feeding on these was another woodpecker: a spotted woodpecker on this occasion. The bird was obstructed from view and I initially took it to be a great spotted woodpecker, but it moved slightly and I saw the bird had a red crown along with a white face. This was no great spotted, we were looking at a middle spotted woodpecker, that gave us two cracking woodpeckers in the space of a matter of minutes and I had found this one. I felt a little better after this.

A bird of prey came gliding across, slowly and laboriously and very low. It was a very broad-winged bird, pale and small bodied, not instantly recognisable and the bird seemed to hang on the wind frequently. It circled round slowly, almost as though it intended us to get a very good view of the bird. The bird was most certainly an eagle of some sort, but which I quickly got my field guide out of my back-pack, and I was very pleased I did; the bird was a short-toed eagle, three superb birds almost in succession of each other. This of course is the beauty of being abroad, many of the birds to be seen are not observed back home, they are residents abroad, and rarities back home.

Nearing Wengen, we came to a very rocky outcrop on which a small bird was flitting about; it was sparrow-size and a very streaky looking bird with a small yellow area on the lower throat – what had we here? A field guide job again, we soon sorted this bird out: it was a male rock sparrow, yet another new bird to us. The call of the bird certainly sounded very house sparrowish, a call to listen out for whilst in Switzerland.

That completed a perfect day, Switzerland was proving to be a good choice and we still had a week to go. The next day we would go down into the valleys, visit Lauterbrunnen Valley and walk up to the Trummelbach Falls which we understood were well worth a visit, being very spectacular.

The short journey down by train was very pleasant to say the least, spectacular in parts would be a more accurate description. We left the train at Lauterbrunnen and walked off along the valley bottom. With the Alps towering up high on both sides of the valley this was a most spectacular walk, and once you left the confines of Lauterbrunnen things quietened down, appreciably, with just a few scattered chalets and the odd vehicle travelling down the valley. We were told that if we wished to catch a bus for our return journey, keep our eyes open for the postal service as this was delivered by the bus. Should we walk the full length of the valley to Stechelberg, the postal motor coach station was located there.

We had the full day ahead of us, the weather was perfect, so we bought our supplies and set off. The valley was very flat with just the odd undulation so walking was not going to be a challenge and headed towards the hamlet of Buchen, where we understood a very pleasant café was located.

The locals were very friendly, the majority commenced to speak to us in German, but most quickly turned to English when they realised where we were from, and the odd person learning of our interest in birds was even able to point us in the direction of the odd speciality. One lady invited us into her garden – she had a red-backed shrike breeding there – and she was as proud as punch over this. The bird had three young in a nest and both adults were actively feeding them. Nesting in a garden they were obviously used to people, so our appearance did not disturb them at all. We were able to tell the lady that red-backed shrikes back home were an exceptionally rare bird and we were lucky if we saw one a year; to have a family in your own garden was just unbelievable. We thanked her profusely and even more so when she poured us a glass of home-made lemon juice. Switzerland was most certainly growing on us, as were its inhabitants. We cleared Buchen, saw the café, but having enjoyed the lemon juice did not need to visit, and turned off for Trummelbach Falls and these did not disappoint.

They are a series of unique glacial waterfalls which fall deep inside the mountain thundering and roaring as they do so, a series of foaming and churning glacial water. Access is by tunnel, and well worth the effort and cost. To take a pair of ear defenders down with you may be a thought. An experience not to be missed, we thought.

On coming out into daylight, Dorothy was up to her tricks once again. Sitting out on a sharp pinnacle sat a large bird of prey; obviously an eagle, but which? Fortunately, the bird appeared to be sitting comfortably so we could view well. A pair of Alpine choughs glided past, which was a big help. The bird was not as large as first thought, more buzzard size; although, it was obviously not a buzzard species. It looked a rather dirty-white bird with a contrasting grey-buff head and breast, then it hit me. We were looking at a booted eagle, what a cracking bird for the day; visiting the Trummelbach Falls had been a superb diversion. We could now journey on to Stechelberg with a real bounce in our step.

Warblers were plentiful there abouts; fortunately, for us, the majority were birds we were familiar with, although on two occasions I became very frustrated. I could hear the birds singing, but could not locate them to get a good view, and their song reminded me of melodious warblers, but it was no good, I could not be sure. In this birding game you do miss a few, but if you are not certain of your observation, there is little point in pretending. We jokingly call them, 'Nearly Birds'!

After a pleasant lunch, and with the weather still being well nigh perfect, we decided to walk back down the Valley along the opposite side to that just completed. We had suddenly remembered that along part of this walk wallcreepers were occasionally reported; now that would be something really special. They tend to favour sheer rock faces where they will breed in a crack in the surface of the rock, and there were several suitable looking rock faces along there.

We stopped at one such location, where a large amount of aerial activity was taking place; we had found a crag martin colony. Many birds were flying across the rock face chasing airborne insects, and amongst them was a small number of Alpine swifts, easily identified by their larger size. No complaints there.

Black kites could be seen circling over the mountain tops and a golden eagle disturbed them on occasion. As with the crag martins and the Alpine swifts, the size difference was obvious.

Walking through a flower meadow near to Lauterbrunnen, Dorothy suddenly stopped and pointed, we could not believe our eyes. A large, pale looking butterfly was flitting, low over the flowers, in a very heavy, flapping flight; we were looking at an Apollo butterfly. This was an insect we had never dreamed of seeing: it is a butterfly of mountainous regions, seen as high as 2,000 metres, and although we were in a valley, we were probably many metres above sea level. What a find, and Dorothy had done it again.

We reached the railway station, no wallcreeper unfortunately, but what we had seen and experienced more than compensated for that. The Apollo on its own was more than enough, an incredible insect.

As we travelled up to Wengen a rock thrush landed on a small tree alongside the track and, as the ascent was very slow, we were able to enjoy this bird for several seconds; a super end to a superb day. And to make things even better, I spotted this one, not Dorothy!

The good weather appeared to be continuing, so we decided to have another local walk next day, thus we spent some time studying our maps. Visitors at the hotel, walkers I must admit not birders, told us the view from the viewpoint at Leiterhorn was spectacular and although not interested in birds, they did say that they saw many in the area and the same with orchids. Also, depending upon our fitness, a little further superb views of the Gundlischwand Valley could be obtained, and this apparently was well worth the effort. Part of the walk was on narrow pathways, but we were assured they were perfectly safe and gradients in the main were moderate, and there was no need to worry about food – several small cafes were on route.

Decision made: Leiterhorn, here we come. Our evening meal was again superb and I must confess we were appreciating Swiss wine.

The day came in beautifully, bright blue sky with hardly a cloud visible and to keep the temperature comfortable; a very pleasant breeze. Our informants were correct, although the land was rising all the time, it was not a slog, and if required there were plenty of pieces of rock to sit on. Birdlife was plentiful, and there were many small plantations of deciduous trees and here several woodpeckers were seen. Amongst these we had black, good views for me this time, middle spotted, grey-headed and three-toed woodpecker; the last two being 'Lifers', needless to say.

Alpine choughs were again plentiful and Alpine swifts were busily hunting flying insects, certainly two birds of altitude. Chamois were leaping about with what looked like gay abandon, as they launched their way, precariously, down steep gradients. What a way to earn a living, they must have feet covered with 'Blue-tac'.

We arrived and quickly made our way to the view point and it was worth it. According to my map, we were at 1250 metres, that is only 95 metres less than the height of Ben Nevis, and towering above us was the Mannlichen at 2342 metres. Fortunately, oxygen masks were not required.

Turning back to look in the direction we had walked, the mighty mounts of the Eiger, Monch and the Jungfrau could be seen in all their snow-capped splendour, some view.

Back to the valley beneath us. This was the continuation of the valley we had walked the previous day, with the river joining up with Lake Brienz, near Interlaken. The town of Interlaken is unique in many ways, especially as it lies directly between two lakes, Thun and the Bienz; could a town be more aptly named? The river in the valley deeply below is, I believe, called the Weisse Lutschine, and at that time of the year unlike rivers back home being clear, rivers in the Alps look more like milk as they are full of snow melt. Cattle bells could be heard all round us as the animals fed on the lush meadows, and as if in accompaniment, bird song was also high on the agenda. Once again mainly warblers of various species, some known others not so, although the occasional thrush joined in – rock thrushes especially so. Mind you, it was very good to hear the odd blackbird and song thrush, we could at least recognise those. Then Dorothy was up to her tricks again. She picked out a largish, black headed warbler singing away from the middle of a bush; I could not believe what we were looking at, she had found us an Orphean warbler. I do not know how she did it, but long may she continue to do so!

A café was visible a short distance further on, so we made our way towards it where, after coffee and cake, we would journey on over the Schneitmald to the village of Usser and view the Gundlischwand Valley beneath. The coffee and cake were again delicious; the Swiss certainly know how to look after you. 'Journey' turned out to be the correct terminology, it was some journey, but well worth the effort.

Various woodpeckers were to be seen, skylarks were very vocal and things could not get much better than that and several ring ouzels were also seen. A pair of short-toed eagles were displaying, this appeared to be very late in the year. Whether they had lost a brood and were attempting a second time we would never know, but it was some display.

Two butterflies caught our attention. I, at first, just brushed them off as small tortoiseshells but these two did not seem to have their brightness of colour. Further investigation was required, and the effort proved well worth it. These were large tortoiseshells, an unusual butterfly back home, so we just sat down for a few minutes to enjoy them. Unlike the small tortoiseshell which lays its eggs on nettles, the large tortoiseshells are tree butterflies; elm, willow and poplar, and several of the first two species were to be seen.

The walk was well worth it, the view was rather special to say the least, and as we arrived we were greeted by a small flock of Alpine choughs; you cannot beat that type of greeting. We enjoyed the view right up the Lutschental Valley, watched a golden eagle dash across the valley towards Grindelwald: another place, we have been told, we must visit. A coffee was called for en route, thoroughly enjoyed, and then back to Wengen. The following day more transport will be used as we intend to go up the Mannlichen, walk the high ridge to Kleine Scheidegg and take the train back down to Wengen. The journey up the Mannlichen was, I am pleased to say, by cable-car. The steep angle of ascent made the journey up very exciting at times. When passing a car on its downwards journey, it was most exciting. A pair of black kites escorted us for part of the journey, and the sure-footed chamois jumped about beneath us as we rose. The nearer the top more snow became evident some of which looked rather deep. Amongst the shallow, thawing snow, many wild flowers were to be seen and against the white back-ground they certainly looked very attractive. Once we got out of the car, we would spend some time looking; at them, these most definitely were Alpine flowers.

We disembarked, a most exciting ride that, and the views across the Lauterbrunnen Valley had been magnificent. Now let us have a look at the wild flowers. Crocuses were the commonest wild flower, both the white and purple varieties which were common near to snow patches. By the side of a small stream of tumbling snow-melt, a medium-tall downy plant caught our attention. It had heads of reddish-purple flowers which really stood out against the snow nearby. This was most certainly something we had never seen before. After many minutes searching away in the field guide, we eventually found what we were looking for, and it was a plant neither of us had heard of previously: it was an adenostyles, a flower which grows up as high as 2700 metres; we were right on its limits there. A superb patch of fragrant orchid was located, we at least did not need the field guide for that one! A very dark, almost black, small orchid was spotted; I will not say by whom, but I am sure you can guess. Here we had a tight, small patch of the black vanilla orchid, a new one for us both. Common spotted orchids were also doing rather well up there at altitude. A few musk orchids had poked their small, yellowish-green spikes of delicate flowers through a snow patch. A small group of lesser butterfly orchids did surprise me. I had always supposed these to be flowers found on the moors, although I suppose the grassy slopes of a mountain could easily be classed as a moor. Not a bad selection of orchids all in one place. We could easily have stayed there all day, but Kleine called, and so did our stomachs; coffees and cakes were calling. The walk along the ridge was spectacular to say the least, with the snow at times still being several feet deep. In one location, the snow plough had actually just cleared a pathway through the snow, and there we were halfway through the year. It may be lovely here, but living here would be another matter. Part of the way along the ridge you came to a ski-lift, which obviously was not being operated now, as the valley down to Grindelwald only had the odd drift of remaining snow – nothing skiable. At the ski-lift station, a very white looking bird flew out of a hole in the brickwork, what had we here? The bird was no doubt nesting in the brickwork, so we settled down to wait, our patience was quickly rewarded: back it came with an insect in its bill, and popped back into the hole. The bird was a magnificent male snow finch, a true bird of the Alps, and one of the birds we really wished to see. The bird came out of its hole once again, flew off up the mountain, and although we waited with bated breath, we did not see its return. On to Kleine, our coffee requirement was getting stronger by the minute. The coffee and cake were up to the standard expected, and this time we did not have to share it.

The snow on the lower slopes of the Eiger there had cleared, so we decided to walk across to Eigergletscher. Here the famous Jungfrau Railway tunnel commences which takes you to the summit – well almost – of the Jungfraujoch, on the slopes of the Jungfrau. Near the tunnel was a large colony of marmots. In Switzerland, I think they refer to this as a 'rockery', considering the landscape adjacent, a very apt name. The marmots were up to their usual tricks, dashing about like crazy and standing erect on the hind parts, an incredible animal. You cannot but believe these delightful animals obtain as much pleasure from studying us as we do them.

Bird life was rather quiet there that day. Alpine choughs were plentiful, the odd black-eared wheatear was to be seen and linnets were in abundance. As we approached Kleine, things bucked up a bit – black kites glided in, black redstarts appeared on the chalets, a citril finch showed briefly, a pair of serin put on a show and white wagtails were seen near the railway station. A more than satisfactory conclusion. A further coffee and we were on our way down to Wengen, by train.

As we got off the train, a nutcracker was heard and in the hotel grounds we saw spotted flycatchers and a song thrush feeding a juvenile. Not a bad welcome home in fact.

We chose to cross the Lautertbrunnental Valley to visit Murren, that would be a day of three different trail journeys. The first down from Wengen into Lauterbrunnen, then up to Grutschalp and finally the train to Murren. Thanks to the expected Swiss efficiency, all the transfers were made without delay. Swiss Railways pride themselves on their time keeping and everything had been smack on time.The journey across to Murren was absolutely delightful. They actually had two locations where the train stopped for a few minutes and you could disembark to enjoy the view. One particular stop provided you with a view commencing with the Eiger and taking you through to the Tschingelhorn: nine peaks ranging from 3454 metres up to the Jungfrau at 4158 metres. A breathtaking sight, and remember there we were talking metres, not feet. No wonder they were all snow-capped! As we boarded the train a pair of lesser kestrels gave us a fly past and a rock thrush a brief burst of song. I thought they were even enjoying the view.

We arrived at Murren to be greeted by a noisy group of crag martins whose sole intent appeared to be to wake up anyone still in bed. Judging by the volume of noise I think they would be successful; an incredible welcoming to Murren.

Part of our reason for wishing to visit Murren was now accomplished, the train journey across would stay in our memories forever. Now can we find the one or two special birds we are after?

The area between Murrenberg and Birg had water pipits breeding, or so we had been informed. We had seen water pipits in the UK on several occasions, but we usually only see this bird during the winter months, there we had the chance of seeing the bird in its summer plumage; well worth some effort. The whole area is overshadowed by the mighty peak of the Schilthorn, another spectacular mountain.

Initially, we followed the Murrenbach brook, working on the assumption where there is water there are usually birds. This theory proved to be correct: white wagtails were active along the shores, and the odd dipper appeared in the frothy, milky water. These dippers were not the race we are familiar with in the UK, so although the differences in plumage were slight, we were more than happy to see those birds. Irrespective of race, they are delightful birds whose feeding habits defy logic as they dive into the water to chase their foods. Some bird.

We left the brook and made our way over what could best be described as mountain moor with many rocky outcrops, a bleak and wild place without a doubt. The odd raven could be seen and in the distance a pair of kite were approaching. These I presumed were black kite so I did not study them as closely as I should. Dorothy, fortunately, was up to her old tricks. 'Look at their tails Brian,' she shouted. These were not black kites, they had superb, deeply forked tails, these were a pair of red kites, and they gave us a superb fly past. Seeing them so close proved them to be a far more elegant flying machine than their black cousins.

Approaching a rocky outcrop, we disturbed a small bird, a pipit of some species, so we settled ourselves in for closer study. This bird had a grey look to it, not the normal streaky brown of meadow pipits and the like. It also sported a distinctive pale eyebrow and the chest and under-parts were decidedly pink; it was no meadow or rock pipit, we had a superb looking male water pipit. We had hunted our quarry down. The bird was busy seeking out small flying insects from the lump of rock, and we were able to enjoy it for several minutes before it dashed off deep into the outcrop. We were more than happy.

Moving on round the outcrop, we stopped. An area of what could be best termed damp grassland lay behind the outcrop, not visible from where we had been previously standing. The area was covered with many large mushrooms, enormous creations, time most certainly to put brain in gear. I had not brought a mushroom field guide with me, it was now down to the little experience I had if we were to crack this one. At least mushrooms do not fly away so we could get amongst them.

Then it hit me, they were a species of parasol mushroom, so I had at least been right in calling them mushrooms and not toadstools. They were like large, upturned dinner plates, very edible I understand, and many of these had been nibbled away round the rims by some animal or other. Whether marmots ate those I did not know, but there was a 'rockery' quite close, and their calls could be heard well.

Time now to start the walk back. We had not gone far when we heard a bird of prey calling from above us. Looking up a booted eagle was gliding across, almost as though it was wishing us bon voyage in 'eagle-talk', we thanked it and travelled on.

A most pleasant day was drawing to its conclusion and the sad thing was, so was our holiday, just a day or two left – what were we to do with them? We decided we had done very well with the birds and wildlife of the country, time for a bit of sightseeing.

Bern attracted us, not only as it is the capital of Switzerland, the chance to see its famous bear pits could not be passed by. The lakes at Interlaken needed to be visited, particularly Brienz where a visit on its world famous steam rack railway; the Brienz Rothorn Railway was something not to be missed, or so we had been informed by railway boffs I know, one of the railway wonders of the world they claim. Plus, it has one or two famous waterfalls well worth a visit, and most lake cruises included visits to these.

Our decision was made, the weather was absolutely gorgeous, perfect for cruising we thought, so Lake Brienz was our destination and to experience the contrast between waterfalls and mountain railways was our intention. We just made the cruiser by a few minutes, and a marvellous old vessel she was too, smoke bellowing forth from her funnel, we set sail.

We wanted this particular sailing as it included a stop to view the Giessbach Waterfalls, which are claimed to be very spectacular; we were about to see if that statement was correct. Spectacular is probably not quite the right word, but I cannot think of a suitable alternative. The milky white water thunders down seven steps, spray literally flying everywhere, before crashing into the lake beneath. The amount of water falling is impossible to calculate I would think and how anything can live at the point of contact I do not know, the water just positively erupts. An incredible experience.

We sailed on to the Brienz Rothorn Railway, for hopefully, another special experience. Looking at the railway stock, I thought we were due for something a bit special. Most of the mountain railways we had seen had been electric powered. This was still a narrow gauged steam railway, opened in 1892 so it says and took two years to construct, and looking at the engine of our train, it looked almost original. The journey up took about an hour and we climbed over 2000 metres. Fortunately, another lake cruiser would be available on our return.

The journey up was quite something; at times, the climbing was so steep you imagined you would drop backwards, this steam train had some power for its size that was obvious. It was a route of many tunnels cut through the granite of the Alps with several deep cuttings. The views over the lake were something special that was for sure, as was that of the local countryside. The drivers had to be careful of marauding cattle in places which were not quite so impressed with the train as we were. As with most of Switzerland's mountain railways, it was single tracked with passing loops, and when passing one of these amazing steam engines the noise from the engine was quite impressive. These trains were tough little brutes!

Our stay at the top was for an hour so we set off to enjoy the views and the birding was not too bad either. Alpine accentors were fairly well distributed, a pair of black-eared wheatears were active – no young visible – and black kite seemed everywhere which was not unusual; a golden eagle circled round high above, and crag martins were widely spread. Our lunch over, time for our return journey. Travelling downhill on so steep rails, was at times almost scary, you just hoped the train did not lose its power – to race down these hills would not be funny! We made it all safely, and my railway boff friends were right: this had been something not to be missed. We caught our cruiser for the return journey over the lake and had a most enjoyable journey. On the journey, we passed another small waterfall the name I do not know, and there we saw a black kite take a dead fish from the surface of the water. The bird just glided low, across the water, and plucked the fish off the surface; it did it with such ease it was obviously a regular occurrence for the bird. It ended our day off perfectly that was for sure.

The next day would be Bern, sightseeing and bear hunting, that is a mixed agenda. The bear hunting did worry me a little, the idea of bears in pits does concern me somewhat.

Bern we had been told was a city of two faces, and as our time was limited to one visit, we should make our way to the old city which was full of medieval architecture and was situated on the banks of the River Aare, and it was near these where the bear pits were located. They were right about the architecture, an incredible area and the view from the cathedral tower was magnificent. As with most places in this country, cafés were everywhere, and Swiss cakes are something rather special; don't ask me what they do for your calorie count! Just enjoy them while you may! A walk along the River Aare was called for, and here we enjoyed many red-crested pochards. These birds were being fed similar to our feeding of mallards on park pools; I have never been so close them. They are a rare duck back home, to see flocks fighting for bread was completely unexpected. Gulls also joined in the fracas, especially black-headed gulls, a bird we had not seen too many of previously, with the odd coot and great crested grebe floating past which reminded us of home. Mind you, a couple of black kites swooping past soon brought us down to earth, in the UK we were not! Now for the bears.

The pits were located nearby so we made our way to them. They were attracting a lot of attention, being a major tourist attraction, and I am sure Dorothy and I were among a very small number of disappointed viewers. I must confess the idea of seeing such a noble creature confined to so small a place did not fill us with pleasure. These creatures may be well fed, looked after, and have all their medical requirements catered for, but they were not put on earth to be so confined. I understand they were regularly taken from the pits to a nearby park, but bears are meant to roam, they are creatures of wild open places. They may not live as long, do not get medical treatment, but they are above all wild and live life as they should.

I am sorry, Bern may be a wonderful old city, but it is unlikely to see us again, the bears have spoilt all of that for us. We have never liked zoos, but the hole in the ground is far worse than any cage as far as we are concerned; no matter how well its inmate is cared for.

The Bern bears were the one big disappointment for us as far as Switzerland was concerned, everything else had been wonderful, and one thing was certain: we would be back, most definitely. There was much more of this wonderful country to see, and the wildlife was something special.

You will recollect that when I came back from my Mallorca Study Tour, I expressed my thoughts that I would not be involved with university study tours again; I would instead try to organise them privately. Finding Switzerland so successful, I arranged a talk with the hotel proprietor to see if he was interested in group bookings and what terms were available. He was. Discounts were available depending upon number; if we allowed him to book the air travel, further discounts were available and as leader of the party I would get a further discount – these were all generous. I explained that it may be a couple of years before I was able to organise a visit, but he was happy with that, and needless to say, so was I.

Our final evening at the hotel was most enjoyable after this, and our last bottle of Swiss wine was pleasanter than ever; it was a gift of the hotel Wengen, we should definitely be back.

Now how do you follow that? With difficulty, although we did get some quality birds, so I will pick out the highlights. Late August saw us at Spurn Point, here the pick of birds seen were pomerine skua, Sandwich tern, and sooty shearwater. September saw us at the Point of Air, the best birds being Arctic skua, black guillemot, curlew, gannet, great skua, pintail, razorbill and spotted sandpiper. October, Spurn and Stoney Creek. Arctic skua, black-throated diver, Brent goose, curlew, firecrest, little gull, merlin, red-throated diver, rock pipit, short-eared owl and a sooty tern; a very good day. We also ran in a late-October trip to Southport and Martin Mere. Here we had barn owl, bar-tailed godwit, hen harrier, ruddy duck and an early three whooper swans. November, we made a trip across to Norfolk where we had a bumper day. Barnacle goose, bar-tailed godwit, black-throated diver, Brent goose, Egyptian goose, glaucous gull, guillemot, hen harrier, merlin, pink-footed goose, pintail, shorelark, snow bunting, snow goose, tawny owl and woodlark were the pick. We actually had ninety-seven birds on the day; you do not get many better than that. We finished the year off down at Cheddar and Chew Reservoir, where we had Bewick's swan, ferruginous duck – a bit special this one – mandarin, pintail, ring-billed gull, ruddy duck, ruddy shelduck, Slavonian grebe, smew and whooper swan. Another good list to finish the year.

Over 1989, I saw 217 species in the UK and 241 abroad; a very good year by any standards. Long may it continue. The next question was – what had the 90's in store for us? Read on to see!

A CENTURY DRAWS TO A CLOSE – WHAT HAD WE IN STORE?

Course numbers were still good, twenty-six start off in January, so we had no complaints. During the next few years, I will only report on field meetings and special events. You have read enough concerning regular events; these will obviously take place, birding is a very repetitive hobby, but I will not bore you with repeat information.

Our first field meeting of the year took us down to Portland Bill, Radipole and Roath Park, this was late January, and we had an exceptionally good day; a wonderful start to a new year. We had eighty-seven birds on the day, which put us all into over a hundred for the first month, so no complaints. Then pick of the birds seen were: barnacle goose, bearded tit, black-throated diver, Brent goose, Cetti's warbler, gannet, guillemot, kittiwake, mandarin, Mediterranean gull, night heron, puffin, razorbill, rock pipit, shag and a snipe. Not a bad start to the year I think you would agree.

February saw us off on a bit of a twitch across to Rutland Water and Eyebrook Reservoir; we were after two birds really, but they were species which could not be guaranteed, so to knock them off early in the year would be good.

We called in at Rutland first for a drake smew, after a bit of trouble we located the bird and also added corn bunting and water rail to our lists, we were more than happy with that. Now for Eyebrook, where we were after a red-crested pochard (memories of Switzerland here). We were very lucky at Eyebrook. A group of birders were studying the bird right where we pulled in, we were obviously meant to see this one. The bird was a superb drake and the view we had of it was very clear and distinct, worth the trip alone. We had sixty-four species on the day, if the year carried on like this we were due a decent range of species. Our next meeting was local, Chasewater, not a lot was seen although we had our first two summer migrants, chiffchaff and sand martin, so we were more

284

than happy with those. Later in March, we ventured further afield, the Dee Estuary called. We had a good selection of birds to enjoy, the pick of which were: bar-tailed godwit, black-throated diver, buzzard, crossbill, fulmar, goshawk, great northern diver, greenshank, kittiwake, peregrine falcon, raven, red-breasted merganser, red-throated diver (that gave us three divers on the day – some event), shag, velvet scoter and whimbrel. A very good selection and they were only part of the total species seen. A cracking day. April saw us try a new venue, Kenfig, and there we added several summer migrants to our list, including amongst those, swallow. I know one swallow does not make a summer, but as we saw several, we were hopeful. The bird of the day there was white-front goose, six of them in fact.

May collected our usual nightingales and nightjars, these had become annual species, and made two very pleasant evening meetings.

Mid-June saw us visit the Moors and Tittesworth Reservoir, red grouse and ring ouzel were the birds we were after that day. Calling in at Tittesworth first, we hit the jackpot for the day: three lesser white-fronted geese were in attendance, these were rather special to say the least, and many swifts were feeding over the water with a pair of grey wagtails active round the shore. A turnstone flew through calling as it did so. Now the Moors. Red grouse were quickly accounted for and as we drove across Axe Edge Moor, we saw wheatear and whinchat; two quality species there. We arrived at the chimney (we are in Cheshire here), and set ourselves up for ring ouzel seeking. They were not very cooperative and it took us well over half an hour before we saw one, but see one we did. So we were more than happy. We had been concentrating our efforts so much we had not realised how dark it was becoming. Heavy cloud was building up and rain was visible in it, time to call it a day. Within minutes,rain was falling bringing an end to another first class day.

During July and August, we decided to hold local meetings; half day ones so we managed to have four meetings. We saw many birds but nothing of great interest apart from a trip to Kingsbury Water Park which provided us with four 'escapees'. Here we saw two bar-headed geese, a swan-necked goose, an emperor goose and a black swan. We were happy enough these were escapees, they were all being fed by young children. I feel sure the black swan would not be long until it is included in the

British bird list, so many have escaped they would soon establish themselves in the wild.

September saw us off to Spurn Point once again, including a visit to the Anglers Country Park, a new location for us, near to Wakefield. This was a bit of a diversion, but a two-barred crossbill had been reported among a flock of crossbills and was showing well. This bird would be a 'Lifer' for everyone, so a quick visit was called for.

The Country Park was a very interesting looking location, and was put into the memory bank for future investigation. We quickly located the crossbill flock, a group of about fifty birders were gazing intently at a group of Scot's pines in which were the flock of crossbills. After just a few minutes our quarry appeared, and it proceeded to put on quite an acrobatic display as it attacked the pine cones. This lasted five or so minutes before the bird vanished, which incidentally was a male, and did not reappear. We had been very fortunate, although really, it had been the easiest 'Twitch' you could wish for. All over in the matter of minutes. Spurn Point, here we come, and how do you follow that.

We arrived at Spurn in not very good conditions, it had clouded over and steady drizzle was falling, not good weather for birding. We managed to get ourselves into a hide where we were at least dry, and one thing the weather had done was drive many birds closer in shore, so it was not all bad.

A steady stream of Arctic skuas were passing through and several waders were feeding along the shore common sandpipers, curlews, two curlew sandpipers which were still looking quite red, and a good number of dunlins; many still sporting their black bellies. Some of the golden plovers were also showing their summer plumage, they are always worth a second look. Not quite two-barred crossbill standards, but we were happy enough.

Further out at sea, a passage of gannets was taking place, many of these birds were dark juveniles. Amongst them were a few little gulls, kittiwakes and the odd sooty shearwater. Not a bad selection at all. It was actually the 9th September and swallows, sand martins and house martins were passing through in large numbers, plus a few swifts – I think they were telling us summer was over!

The weather was starting to tell us something now, the rain

commenced to fall very heavily; time for a quick dash to our cars and home. A disappointing end to our day, but we could not really grumble, the birds had been high quality in the main. The weather did beg the question: how did small birds such as swallows and the like, survive and fly through it? We had a couple of local trips out early October and started to pick up some winter migrants, fieldfares, redwings and siskins in particular and the totals of winter visiting duck were slowly building up, especially pochards, teals and wigeons with a pair of ruddy shelduck at Belvide Reservoir.

Later in the month, Chew Reservoir came back into focus, another 'Twitch' loomed. A green-winged teal, drake, had been reported, and as I believe I have mentioned previously, these American species are most unusual birds and it appears that good views of this bird had been made and it was not ringed. That meant the bird may be a genuine wild bird which had flown across the Pond. When ringed there was always the chance they had escaped from a collection somewhere, and Slimbridge is not too far from Chew.

The day dawned very damp and grey, but after a few phone calls, six of us decided to make the journey; the teal was a bit of a draw. The weather also started to improve and we arrived in dull but dry conditions, although we had a stiff wind to contend with. This was in the wrong direction for us and it had driven most of the birds to the far side of the reservoir, so we had some walking ahead. As I have said on several occasions previously, no one ever said birding was easy!

Winter waterfowl were very well represented, several hundred birds were on the water, which was not going to help us in sorting out just one. Fortunately, as the bird was a drake, that would help us considerably.

A kingfisher was feeding actively in the shallows near where we were parked, so that was a great start and a great spotted woodpecker could be heard drumming away most aggressively, but not seen. Goodly numbers of winter thrushes were to be seen, a small flock of a dozen or so goldcrests were busily feeding in a small clump of trees and three buzzards were soaring high overhead. A grey heron was plodding along the shore accompanied by a little egret, the size difference being really apparent.

Arriving ever closer to the waterfowl we picked out a small flock of approximately twenty teals, so we set up our scopes to concentrate of those. The main feature we were looking for on our bird was the pair of white stripes which run down the side of the breast, one on either side. Not a lot to look for on such a dreary day, but there were six pairs of eyes looking for it, and eventually, six pairs of eyes were successful. Well to be accurate, one pair was initially, five quickly following.

We spent several minutes studying this bird before turning to walk back to our parked cars. The walk back was most unpleasant, we were head on into the wind and rain was slowly moving in, fortunately we had the gear for these conditions. We had our bird, nothing can take that away, and we had seen fifty-seven on the day. The cars also had heaters, what more could one ask for?

November saw us off to Norfolk, making Cley our destination. By now there should be a good selection of winter visitors, geese especially so. Due to the shorter hours of daylight we made an early start, leaving Lichfield at 6.00 a.m., nine of us making the trip, the hardy souls.

We had a good journey, arriving well before 10.00 a.m., which would hopefully give us five hours or so's birding. A small flock of barnacle geese greeted us on arrival and the sound of brent geese could be heard. Many hundred of these came gliding into Cley, always a superb bird to see, one of my favourite birds, a reason always for visiting Norfolk. Common scoter were out a sea, a large flock of them and the occasional common tern was passing through. A small flock of shag were actively feeding out on the sea, always a pleasing bird to see, we do not have many inland, their cousin the cormorant is the bird we see back home.

Concentrating on the geese, we added Canada, Egyptian, grey-lag, pink-footed, snow and white-fronted to the list, not a bad total. Whilst looking through the geese, we had the two birds of the day as far as Cley was concerned, two red-throated divers and the pick of the day – a 'Lifer' for us all – a white-billed diver. We had a group of local birders to thank for that one. Apparently the bird had been reported two days previously, and the birder who reported it had claimed it to be a first year great northern dive. Later observation by some of the local 'experts' proved the bird to be a white billed diver, a mega bird in comparison, and we had walked in to see it. A bird never considered by any of us and a bird unknown to one or two of my companions, a bird of top quality. I must be honest the white billed diver was a bird I never considered I would ever see in the U.K, but we did that day.

Amongst the waders were many curlews and these birds were very vocal. Presuming you have a soul, the call of the curlew will send shivers down your spine or at the very least raise the hairs on the back of your neck. Many birds have delightful calls and beautiful song, but to me the curlew is in a complete class of his own, making the most perfect and evocative calls of any bird. I can listen to them all day. Bar-tailed and black-tailed godwits were in good numbers and among the smaller waders dunlins and knots were well accounted for.

We were enjoying two hen harriers out at sea when our white-billed diver friends came back. 'You are Brummies aren't you?' Not strictly, I am, but most of my friends were Black Country Folk, but we nodded assent. 'You will probably be driving back home via Burnham Overy Staithe, near there a black-bellied dipper has been seen for a few weeks, well worth the slight diversion.' It certainly was. I had my map in my back-pack so this was quickly taken out and the location was noted. We thanked our informants and quickly decided that was where we would go. The black-bellied dipper is the race of dipper I mentioned seeing when in Switzerland, and they are a most unusual bird to migrate so far; I am not too sure they have ever been recorded in England previously, this was one bird we must have a go for. Our race, the white or pale-bellied is an unusual species to find in Norfolk; in any case, the counties streams and rivers are not favourite hunting spots for this bird. That day, all that mattered was that they suited a black-bellied specimen!

We found the location without any problems, but unfortunately there was not another birder in sight, if we were going to find this bird we had to do it ourselves. With no competition if we could see the bird we would instantly know what it was we were looking at, so it was a question of 'seek and yea will find?' we hoped!

It took us several minutes before, a small and rotund dark bird, came whirring down the stream, perching up on a half-submerged tree stump. We had him, well almost, within five seconds or so it was off and continued on its way down the stream. We waited many minutes, it was not coming back. We would have liked more, but we were not complaining. Once again, we had seen some quality birds, all had 'Lifers', a minimum of two in all cases, and chalked up seventy-two on the day. The 90s were doing alright.

The dipper brought our trip to Norfolk to its conclusion the county once again lived up to its reputation.

December saw us in 'Twitch' mode. A parrot crossbill had been reported from near to Kirby-on-Bain in Lincolnshire, this was not a bird to be missed, so we were off east again.

Eleven of us made the trip and the weather could not have been worse. Thick mist so our journey initially was rather slow, but, fortunately, conditions did improve and we arrived in clear conditions – very overcast and chilly – but nether-the-less, visibility was fine. I had the map reference for the small woodland in which the bird was last seen and we quickly located this. A small group of birders were in attendance, always a good sign when on a 'Twitch', and they were able to report the bird had been seen a short time earlier, it was associating with a small flock of crossbills, so we knew what to look for. Parrot crossbills are so called because of their large, parrot like bill, and when added to their larger head, we knew exactly what detail we had to concentrate on. They are fairly common birds across Scandinavia and northern Europe where they have a preference for pine trees, our crossbills prefer spruce, but rarely travel far south of their range. We were all eager to see the bird as it was a 'Lifer' for us all.

We saw several flocks of small birds, finches and the like, particularly enjoying a largish flock of siskins, when we heard the 'kip, kip, kip,' calls of the crossbill. Concentration time, we had to find the flock. After a few minutes they came to find us and our quarry was quickly located.

Although similar in size to our crossbill, the heavier bill and larger head stood out, and the bird looked a dumpier bird than its companions. Its food back home may have been pine cones, it was quite happy here eating the softer spruce cones, pieces of cone were flying in all directions. We were able to enjoy the bird for several minutes before they vanished deeper in to the wood, and although we waited some considerable time, they did not reappear. We were happy, it is always nice to get what you came out for.

Of the remaining birds seen in the wood, the best were green and great spotted woodpecker, nuthatch, treecreeper, sparrowhawk and a large mixed flock of redwings and fieldfares. We journeyed home happy enough, we had seen the bird we came for, and good views of it too. That was our final visit out for the year, and we had seen some quality species, clocking up 217 birds in the year. By coincidence, the same total as the previous year.

A more than satisfactory start to a new year, a new year which starts the last decade of this century, now there's a thought. We managed an early trip locally in January. Which included a visit to the Staffordshire Moorlands, which proved very productive. The top birds seen on the moors were crossbill, red grouse, black grouse, hen harrier, brambling and little owl. Calling in at Tittesworth Reservoir we added pink-footed goose, red-crested pochard, great northern diver, dunlin, goldeneye, goosander, pintail and snow goose. When included with the expected species we totted up 70; not a bad start to a new year. We were beginning to think we were on a roll – time would tell.

Later that month, a 'Twitch' called. A hoopoe had been reported from near Mansfield and a snowy owl, a mega bird this, from just south of Gibraltar Point, on the Wainfleet Sands, an early start was called for. It was once again a question of map references, and these I had. Looking at the map the biggest problem that I could see was parking at Wainfleet, few roads covered the area.

We quickly located the hoopoe site, and it was most unimpressive. It was in the middle of an old factory area, a real brown-area site, where much demolition and building was being carried out. Hardly the location for such an exotic looking bird midst all this grime, not that we were complaining. The bird was soon found, and many of my friends started the day with a 'Lifer', a beautiful 'Lifer' too. On now for the snowy, should we be so lucky?

The journey was uneventful and as we neared the spot it soon became obvious we were heading in the right direction. Cars were parked all over the place, any suitable piece of land had cars on it. Further on a group of about sixty birders were all staring intently over the marsh. We drove as close to them as was possible and joined the throng. Before we talk about our snowy owl, a bit of information may not go amiss. Snowy owls are the rarest owl breeding in the UK, and their record is just the occasional bird breeding, mainly in the Shetland Islands, and these records are few and far between. It is an Arctic species in the true sense of the word, and its colour tells you all you want to know: snow white is only of use where it is white, and as it is a ground nesting species this camouflage is necessary.

Back to our bird. In the far distance a white fleck was visible, looking like a small white plastic bag, this we were told was the owl. Up scopes, and focusing in, on full magnification, you could just about make out it was a bird. Better than nothing, but rather disappointing, the bird just looked as though it was a sleep.

It must have been a good half an hour with no movement, and then the R.A.F came to our rescue, Five jets, tornadoes I believe, flew over at zero feet and flushed every bird on the marsh, many of which we had not even been aware of. The owl took off, and joy of joys, flew steadily in our direction to give us a wonderful fly-past; I doubt if it was twenty yards away, a few cameras clicked that was for sure. We swung round to watch it sedately fly away, and that was the end of our snowy owl, it did not return. Several birders arrived, just seconds too late, and there was much disappointment, but as we frequently say: in this game, you win a few and lose a lot! We had won.

On to Gibraltar Point. We had clicked, birds were everywhere, we were obviously in for a good climax to our day's excursion. I think I will list here all the birds seen that day which will give you some idea of the kind of day we had. It may also surprise you to learn that days such as this could happen in 'Dear Old Blighty'.Barn owl, bar-tailed godwit, Bewick's swan, blackbird, black-headed gull, black-tailed godwit, blue tit, brent goose, Canada goose, carrion crow, chaffinch, collared dove, common gull, common scoter, coot, cormorant, corn bunting, curlew, dunlin, dunnock, eider, feral pigeon, fieldfare, fulmar, gannet, goldcrest, goldeneye, golden plover, goldfinch, great black-backed gull, great crested grebe, great tit, greenfinch, grey-lagged goose, grey partridge, grey plover, hen harrier, herring gull, hoopoe, house sparrow, jackdaw, jay, kestrel, knot, lapwing, lesser black-backed gull, linnet, magpie, mallard, marsh harrier, meadow pipit, merlin, mistle thrush, moorhen, mute swan, oystercatcher, pheasant, pied wagtail, pink-footed goose, pintail, purple sandpiper, redshank, redwing, reed bunting, ringed plover, robin, rock pipit, rook, ruff, sanderling, shag, shoveler, siskin, skylark, snipe, snowy owl, sparrowhawk, starling, stock dove, teal, tree sparrow, tufted duck, turnstone, twite, wigeon, woodpigeon and wren. Total 87

We had also chalked up well over the hundred mark for the year so far, an exceptional start to things, long may it continue.

Early February saw us take a trip down to Wales so we could start the year off with a few choice regulars, red kites, buzzards, goshawks, ravens, crossbills, hawfinches, peregrines, a selection of waders and a few quality species – red-necked grebe, red-throated diver, shag, and red-breasted merganser. All obliged, another good day.

Later in February, we went swan hunting. Chew Reservoir had all three swans in attendance, plus a good selection of other waterfowl. We located mute swans, Bewick's swans and whooper swans without any trouble. The Bewick's were in a sizable flock, thirty-four of them, they had no doubt flown in from nearby Slimbridge. Several species of duck were seen as expected, and a flock of nearly one thousand golden plovers made frequent visits to the shores of the reservoir. No complaints here, another satisfactory day.

March saw us again in 'Twitch' mode. A ferruginous duck and waxwings had been reported from north of Preston, so a visit to Lancashire was called for. Once again, it was a map job; I managed to obtain the necessary map references and realised it was not that close to Preston. We were to journey up as far as Seaforth, where we have been previously, but the two birds mentioned were well worth any effort. To say we had a good day is putting it mildly. We had sixty-three species on the day, the pick of which were – barnacle goose, bar-headed goose, a 'Lifer' for many, ferruginous duck, another 'Lifer' for most, fulmar, little gull, Mediterranean gull, ring-billed gull, sanderling, scaup, tawny owl and the waxwing. A good day by any standards.

A visit to Switzerland was again called for, and I managed to put together a group visit for twenty of us. The hotel was only too pleased to receive us and I managed to get very good terms for a group holiday, so come the 19th June, Wengen, here we come.

The end of March saw Dorothy and I having a short break in the Lake District. Friends of ours lived near to Windermere and they invited us up for a few days; needless to say, we were only too pleased to accept their kind invitation.

We called in at Leighton Moss on the way up, and what a stop this proved to be. We had hardly reached a hide before we heard a bittern booming, and going into the hide we had a superb view of the bird. Bittern are usually hidden away among the reeds, this one had obviously not read the script. It was standing in open water booming away loudly, we just could not believe what we were seeing and hearing, what a start to our few days break.

The bittern was not going to be the end of it. Moving on into another hide, two ladies greeted us, almost rocking with excitement, they were looking at a bird which they could not identify, and they pointed it out to us. For seconds I was as confused as they were, then it hit me, we were looking at a great spotted cuckoo: a bird I had last seen in La Camargue those years ago. What a bird to see in the UK, the two ladies could now become really excited. A UK 'Lifer' to start our holidays with, you cannot have a better start than that.

During our stay it was not all birding obviously, but amongst the birds we did see were buzzard, our first chiffchaff of the year, crossbill, curlew, garganey – a superb drake this bird, lesser redpoll, raven, red-breasted merganser, sand martin, another first of the year, and tawny owl. Away from birds, the finest sighting we had was a roe deer which visited our friends garden regularly each day, they had been feeding this deer for several weeks and it had become very confiding. If food was not available it walked up to the lounge windows and looked in, leaving grubby marks where its nose had pressed against the glass. We had never been so close to a wild deer in our lives.

It was a wonderful few days, really setting us up for spring, now what will that bring in for us?

By mid-May, the summer returning migrants had really started to roll in, some older type field guides call these birds summer visitors, which they are not. They are birds returning home to the land in which they were born, hence I call them returning migrants.

May saw us visiting Bempton Cliffs once again, this has now become an annual event; you cannot miss out on seeing puffins, they are like a drug! Additional to the seabirds we had wheatear and whinchat on passage and a flock of five whimbrel gave us a fly past which was most unexpected. Seventy-one birds on the day. On 26th May, we entered a Bird Race which was raising money for charities; the charities were of your own choice. Teams of four were entered and the race commenced at mid-night and ran for 24 hours. The race was confined to one county and we chose Staffordshire as our area. Both audible and visual records counted but at least three members of the team had to observe the birds. We were after one hundred in the day, which would be quite something for Staffordshire; it had been done on occasions in the past. Although we really worked hard and covered many miles, we died in the hole, closing with ninety-eight. Three other teams did break the hundred mark, well done to them.

Come June we decided on pastures new, where we hoped to catch a 'Year Tick' for many of my colleagues – Dartford warbler. Normally, to see this rather special bird, you had to travel down to the south coast, but the bird has slowly spread further north; no doubt, due to things warming up slightly, climate change as they are starting to call it. Now a few pairs are breeding in Somerset, at Aylesbeare Common, near Exeter, far enough, but not the south coast.

Aylesbeare Common is another rare area of lowland heathland. Spend the evening and nightjars are almost guaranteed and due to the very good dragonfly population, hobbies are regularly seen, so although we would not be staying late enough for nightjars, there was going to be a good selection available, but the Dartford was what we were after.

Once again I had been given the map reference of where Dartford's were being seen, and we managed to park up very close to the area. Very thick gorse prevailed which was ideal for the Dartford's, as they tend to spend their life tucked away in this. Secure nesting, an abundant food supply which feeds on the gorse, protection from bad weather – snow, and seclusion from predators, it is a brave or stupid hawk which will fly into a thick gorse bush in pursuit of its prey. The only problem is for us birders, the birds can hide away too easily, let us hope today was not the day they chose to do so.

The first birds we saw were stonechats, several of them. The marvellous males were sitting out on top of the gorse, singing away, and flashing their simmering colours, a wonderful sight. They are a magnificent bird and to see many of them was indeed a bonus.

Things suddenly went quiet, the stonechats vanished from sight as if by magic. A merlin came flashing across, almost flicking the gorse with its wings, the bird was so low, but it was not going to catch its breakfast this time round. After a few minutes, the odd stonechat reappeared and we could once again enjoy them.

We had been there over half an hour, when a dullish looking bird popped out onto the top of a gorse bush. Compared with the stonechats, dull it may look, but we had our quarry. A male Dartford warbler may not be colourful, but to us it was indeed a little beauty. It flashed its longish tail and sang its little ditty and for about five minutes put on quite a show, before it popped back into the gorse, and that was that. Not that anyone was complaining, those who had never seen the bird had had spanking views, and you cannot better that.

After about an hour we decided to move onto Prawle Point to see what the sea had to offer. Not a lot I am afraid, a few of the expected coastal gulls, two Manx shearwaters gave us a fly past and a turtle dove could be heard purring away, but could not be located. Home called. Not a great number of species, but a few special ones. We travelled home happy enough.

We now had Switzerland to look forward to and, for Dorothy and I, a lot of responsibility; the question was, had we taken on too much? When leading University parties, my responsibility really was just to find them the birds, all the other arrangements were done by the University. Plus, if any problems arose, a representative of the University was on hand to deal with them. Any problem now was mine, from all the arrangements to anything that may occur in Switzerland. Time would be the judge. The 19th of June saw us on our way for ten days and thanks to Swissair; the flight was most comfortable and we all arrived at the hotel together. The hotel quickly got us to our rooms and a light tea was put out for us, which was appreciated. Prior to unpacking a quick look round the hotel gardens was taken and two birds in particular started our stay off well. We had a pair of nutcracker in the garden and a black woodpecker gave us a fly over, two immediate quality birds for my colleagues.

After a most pleasant evening meal with some superb wine and over a tot of spirit we made our plans for the following day, when we would cover the local area; a quiet start after our journey. Then our excursions would be much as Dorothy and I had done on our previous visit, even to the inclusion of a couple of days free to do their own thing.

Once again we were fortunate with the weather, bright and clear with hardly a cloud in the sky and the only rain we experienced lasted barely thirty minutes. Somebody, somewhere, must really love us.

Most of what we saw was a repeat of our previous visit, and the peak birds were black-bellied dipper, black-eared wheatear, black kite, black redstart, citril finch, crag martin, crested tit, firecrest, golden eagle, golden oriole, marsh tit, nutcracker, red-backed shrike, rock bunting, Sardinian warbler, serin, short-toed treecreeper, water pipit, white wagtail, and birds not currently on the British List – black woodpecker, middle spotted woodpecker, snow finch and Alpine chough. We totalled 97 in the week, so everyone went home happy having seen many new species for the first time, and from my point of view, no problems were experienced thanks to Dorothy's assistance and to the service of the hotel. My colleagues thoroughly enjoyed themselves, and the question was, when could we do it again not necessarily Switzerland, any pastures new. I would have to set myself up as a tourist agency!

July and August were quiet months and we saw nothing extra special; after Switzerland a bit of an anti-climax I suppose, but a few 'Year Ticks' were added to our lists.

Come early September a family holiday was called for and we had a week in Scotland, and this was to be a complete break, not a week's bird watching. We chose a coach holiday and stayed at Glen Shee, a very attractive spot, where we intended to do much walking. Having said that, birds are never far away. We saw the odd osprey passing through on their journey southwards, and wonderful herds of red deer – well into their hundreds – coming down to the burn to drink. Golden eagles were regular sightings, with the odd goshawk putting in an appearance. Red grouse were well spread and we learned of a small area where black grouse were to be seen, this we duly did on one of our walks.

There was one day, however, when birding was on the agenda. Further along the valley, I had been informed ptarmigan could be seen and we had not come all this way to miss out on a 'Lifer' for both of us.

It was about a three mile walk along the side of the burn where we would find a farm which did snacks, and the ptarmigan could be seen close by. Well that was the theory; we would now put it to the test.

We had several encounters with dipper and grey wagtail as we walked along. The farm provided us with a delightful ham sandwich and a mug of coffee, and the owner confirmed where the ptarmigan could be best seen. He was right. Several ptarmigan were busily feeding away, less than one hundred yards away, providing very good views through our binoculars. We managed to get much closer, using a stone wall as cover, ending up with superb views.

That was the highlight of the week as far as we were concerned. Coach tours were definitely not for us. We were very pleased we had decided to do our own thing at Glen Shee, as the majority of the other holiday makers were intent on racing round on the various organised events. We obviously lost money in one respect, as many of these events were included in the initial cost, but we did see some beautiful Scottish countryside and we did not have to do any driving. Plus, we had the ptarmigans and you cannot put a price on those!

Later in the month, Spurn Point again called and for this trip we had four members of the group who had never previously visited, so they were in for a treat.

The day was bright with a steady breeze coming in off the sea which, hopefully, would have helped birds to drift inshore. On the water a goodly selection of ducks and gulls were to be seen with seabirds also very evident, especially fulmars and gannets which were well into double figures. Fieldfares and redwings were coming in over the sea. No doubt pleased with the help the breeze was giving them; a following wind always helps when on migration.

The total species seen that day was eighty-six with the pick of the bunch being, Arctic skua, common scoter, corn bunting, fieldfare, fulmar, gannet, greenshank, grey plover, merlin, redwing, Sandwich tern, whimbrel and wood sandpiper. Enough there to keep us going. Spurn Point really never fails.

The end of September saw us off on a 'Twitch' up to Filey Brigg in Yorkshire. A little bunting had been reported, a 'Lifer' for us all, and as the bird seemed to be quite settled in, we decided to go for it. We called in at Flamborough Head for an hour or so sea watching. There we had eider, fulmar, gannet, great skua, guillemot, red-throated diver, rock pipit, and several waders. A good enough start to the day, now for the serious stuff.

At Filey things were very busy, not only was the bunting showing well, over-night a red-breasted flycatcher and a yellow-browed warbler had also drifted in; a 'Twitch' had now become a mega 'Twitch; with the ringing fraternity very evident. Although I do not agree with ringing, I must confess they gave us our first 'Lifer' for the day. They re-caught the little bunting in their net, so we had very good views of this prior to it being released.

Some excitement was evident from a nearby gorse patch. Sitting out on top of the gorse was the yellow-browed warbler, the second 'Lifer' of the day for many of my colleagues. Further along the shore, a group of birders waved to us. As we approached they shouted, 'We have the flycatcher,' and there on the sand was the red-breasted flycatcher. Minus the red breast, unfortunately; the bird was a juvenile, not that we were grumbling.

In the space of less than half-an-hour, the majority of us had chalked up three 'Lifers'; I had two. This was birding made easy, with the large number of birders there that day; you did not have to look for the birds, they were found for you.

That day Yorkshire hit the jackpot, and eighteen birders returned to the Midlands very happy indeed. October saw us having two trips out, the first locally to Belvide Reservoir where the two top birds of the day were a little stint and a pair of ruddy ducks. Later in the month we visited Chew Reservoir, where the pick were Bewick's swans, green sandpiper, kingfisher, pintail, ruddy duck and a small flock of seven shelducks, which looked like a family party. Nothing new for the year, but some quality.

In early November, we again visited Blithfield Reservoir. There we had our first brambling of the winter, a drake ferruginous duck, a bit of real quality here, a small flock of grey plovers, six of them, and a green-winged teal, another quality bird. Whilst at Blithfield, I met up with a friend of mine who had just returned from near to Stone, where he had seen a nutcracker. We were off.

The nutcracker was in the garden of a house, the owner was allowing people in to see the bird on the payment of a small fee for her favourite charity. No complaints there. We paid up and had several minutes enjoying a most unexpected mega 'Tick'. Although I had seen this bird in Switzerland, as written about, this was my first experience of the bird in the UK – a 'Lifer'. And in my own county to boot. As we had time and the light was still good, we made a quick trip up onto the Moors, where we saw red grouse. Not a bad end to our day out.

In December, we were off to Rutland Water where large numbers of wintering waterfowl were congregating; always a most interesting sight. The pick of these were eight Egyptian geese, a snow goose and a pair of ruddy shelducks, well worth the visit. Rutland finished the year off, and a successful year it had been. I had 212 species in the UK and 117 abroad. What had '92 in store?

The New year brought in a change for me. I retired from my tutorship with the University of Birmingham and transferred to Keele University. Many of my current students came with me so I was sure of good numbers to start with. My courses would now be held in Cannock and Tamworth, so I had a busy time ahead.

We had a few new faces so my first field trip was a local one which included Blithfield Reservoir, Park Hall Country Park, near to Stoke, Tittesworth Reservoir and the Staffordshire Moorlands, and our choice proved most successful.

Blithfield had the usual good numbers of wintering waterfowl. The Canada geese flock was most impressive; we usually had a good sized flock, but that day it was well over five hundred, with several greylag geese also in attendance. Great crested grebes and little grebes were also in decent numbers, gulls were also well represented with the largest number of great black-backed gulls I had seen there for a very long time.

The pick of the water birds were definitely Bewick's swans, red-crested pochards, a Ross's goose, a species of snow goose, and a very large flock of ruddy duck. 'Lifers' on their first field meeting for some of the newcomers. Our next stop was Park Hall, where we were after owls; yes in the plural. For several years, long-eared owls had a winter roost there – up to double figures on occasion. It was believed the owls migrated down from Scandinavia, although the odd pair had bred at Park

Hall. If we only saw a single bird, we would be happy. Near the Visitor Centre, there was much activity at the feeding station with a pair of bullfinches and a willow tit being the centre of attraction. As we made our way down to the conifer plantation in which the owls usually roosted, we stopped. In a small silver birch tree sat a little owl; the bird was gazing at us through its half closed eyes. They are the most diurnal of our owls and are frequently seen actively hunting in broad daylight. This bird may not have been hunting, but it was observing us intently enough. We moved on, not wishing to disturb the bird further. The conifer plantation was close by and we commenced our search for the owls. You might remember I have mentioned going there previously, and the birders used to draw a circle in the fallen needles round the tree in which an owl had been seen. This they have had to stop doing. Apparently, some idiots with air rifles had picked up on this and come out to shoot at the owls and two birds had been injured and subsequently died. It is a great pity the owls could not have shot back; the mentality of people, at times, is amazing. With many pairs of eyes, it did not take us long to locate our first long-eared owl, which quickly became four. We were very contented birders now, and walking back through the plantation things got even better. We picked up on a roosting tawny owl. That gave us three different species of owl in less than an hour. Could Tittesworth and the Moors beat this? Yes, it could; well equal it at the very least. Tittesworth was very quiet, but it did provide us with a small flock of four lesser white-fronted geese; these were not to be sneezed at. Axe Edge Moor gave us a flock of nine red grouse, a raven and a passing merlin. We then journeyed on to Swallow Moss, and there we saw four black grouse, all males, and just as we were about to leave, a short-eared owl glided in; the perfect ending to a perfect day. Four owls in one day was most unusual, especially when all were so close to home.

One of the newcomers raised the question, 'Is it always as good as this?' I had to tell him no, that day had been rather exceptional, especially for a local trip. Birds do occasionally drop in your lap, and today 69 had. Not a bad start to a new year.

Our next trip took us further afield, Southport and Leighton Moss, which would bring January to a close. The highlights at Southport were a good selection of waders, pink-footed geese, hundreds of them, and a flock of twenty-three barnacle geese and, the bird of the morning, a magnificent barn owl which was out hunting over the marsh. Owls in January had been very good to us.

Now onto Leighton Moss, and it did not disappoint. A large number of whooper swans were in and a small group of Bewick's swans were also to be seen, just seven of them. It is not often you see our two really wild swans together. Needless to say, there were also mute swans in attendance so we had our three British swans. A goshawk flew through at zero feet, putting most of the ducks up into the air in blind panic, quite a sight as these were well into four figures. The swans just gazed at the hawk and carried on feeding; they were obviously too large for the gos' to be interested in them.

Things quickly quietened down and the ducks returned to feed. On the marshland, a large flock of curlew were feeding away until a male hen harrier decided to interfere with things. This bird flashed across the marsh and was last seen in hot pursuit of a curlew, I did not think the curlew would see that day out.

One of my colleagues brought my attention to a duck which was diving nearby, and I was glad he had. The bird was a drake scaup, and it put on quite a display for us. A quality bird to get so early in the year.

As the day drew to a close, a short-eared owl put on a show for us as it drifted slowly, but very elegantly over a neighbouring meadow. After several missed opportunities the bird finally came up with a small bird held struggling in its claws. The owl had got its supper.

Time to make our way homewards, and another very successful day it had been. Seventy-one species on the day, and our two field meetings so far that year had provided us with over 100 different species. Things could not carry on at that rate, but enjoy it whilst you may!

February saw us make two trips to Wales, one Central Wales via Ludlow and the other the north Welsh coast. Our newcomers were eager to see red kite, which more than suited all of us.

Our initial destination, Ludlow, was an attempt to see the hawfinches which were being reported regularly, and to record these so early in the year would continue the good start to the year. Whitcliffe Common had long been the recommended location, and as you could park alongside the River Teme, you also have the chance of dipper and kingfisher. To get those three birds would be a very satisfactory start.

The day was relatively mild and very clear, and twenty-two of us turned out for the day and we hit the jackpot almost straight away. A dipper gave us a flypast, perched on a rock, and dropped into the river on a few occasions. The bird caught something on one of his dives and flew off with it in its bill. We turned to concentrate on the wooded slopes of Whitcliffe. A mixed flock of titmice and siskins were busily feeding on the silver birches, but our attention was drawn further up the slope to where the beech trees grew. Beech mast is a favoured food of the hawfinches and, after a few minutes, we were rewarded: four birds came down and proceeded to sort through the fallen mast. Their powerful bills were making short work of any seed they found, but our pleasure did not last long. A dog came racing down, barking as it did so, and that was our hawfinches for the day, they did not return. Back to the river. A pair of goosanders came sailing down with the current and commenced to dive, unsuccessfully, unfortunately, but we were happy enough. Then the piercing 'zeeeee, zeeeee' of a kingfisher was heard, which came flashing past, a blur of blue and crimson, to vanish round the bend in the river. I doubt if we saw the bird for above five seconds, but at least we all saw it as well as having heard the bird. No complaints with Ludlow, a most successful start.

On leaving Ludlow, the weather decided to intervene and it did so with a vengeance. A strong wind picked up, accompanied by heavy sleet and rain. We decided not to call in at any of the reservoirs in the valley; instead, we made our way directly to Devil's Bridge, where we could at least get shelter from the trees. As events turned out, it was not a bad decision.

The weather calmed down considerably, although remaining damp. A party of crossbills greeted us on our arrival, now that was not bad, and among the other birds seen were a wintering male blackcap, nuthatch, willow tit, raven, buzzard and treecreeper, but no red kite. As conditions had improved, I suggested we made a stopover at Cwmystwyth where I had seen red kite on many an occasion previously. This we did.

Our luck was in. After about fifteen minutes or so, three red kites came slowly drifting past, almost effortlessly, with hardly a flap of their wings. They are an elegant bird anytime, but these three just seemed intent on impressing us, and they certainly did. That brought another good day's birding to a perfect end and, as if to tell us so, down came the sleet once again. Not the pleasantest of journeys home, but we were content enough. Our next trip to Wales was towards the end of the month. There we were visiting north Wales, and we commenced our trip by looking for the Lady Amhersts pheasants, in the hope they were still to be found. To the delight of the newcomers, they were: five of them, three males and two females. As mentioned previously, the male is an incredibly plumed bird, a perfect way to start the day. Not that it was all over there, as a peregrine falcon flew through, a superb male, and redwing were feeding in the church grounds. Now for the coast.

The tide was just about on the turn, with a goodly variety of waterfowl, the pick of which were common scoters, several hundred of these, and tucked away amongst them were two velvet scoters; these were worth the trip alone. Other duck included goldeneye, red-breasted merganser, pintail and shelduck. The pick of the sea birds were fulmars, guillemots and gannets, with an Iceland gull and kittiwakes being the prime gulls. Waders were well spread and here purple sandpiper, turnstone, sanderling, grey plover and curlew stood out. In total, we saw seventy-one species, '92 was beginning to look a very good year.

March saw us off on a local trip, our regular haunts of Blithfield, Belvide and Chasewater. There we chalked up sixty-one species, the best of which were curlew, great northern diver, Iceland gull, pintail, red-crested pochard, tawny owl and muscovey duck. When you consider this was all less than an hour from home, it was not a bad return.

Later in the month saw us off to Wales again. As on our last visit, we commenced at Ludlow, as other members of the group wanted the opportunity of seeing the hawfinches. They were not disappointed, good views were obtained, as were those of the dipper.

Since our last visit, daylight hours had increased, so we were able to include Aberystwyth on this visit. Via the Elan Valley, we had several sightings of red kites and at Devil's Bridge we saw two choughs and a fleeting glimpse of crossbills.

The tide at Aber' was coming in fast, the waders were collecting along the shore. The usual species were to be seen for that time of the year and the pick being sanderlings, purple sandpipers, turnstones and curlews. Out at sea, a large raft of common scoters was visible, nothing unusual among those that time, a small flock of eiders. the odd red-breasted merganser and several shags were feeding on the in-coming tide. A peregrine falcon came through at speed upsetting the waders, but it did not seem to be in hunting mode, it just hurtled through and that was that. Peace quickly returned. Out at sea a good passage of gannets was taking place and a general movement of gulls was obvious, the number of great black-backed gulls was impressive.

Once again, it had turned out a most pleasant day, and although the range of species was not great, the number of birds seen was. Fifty-two on the day of different species, the total of actual birds I would not even try to guess.

April commenced with a visit to the Dee Estuary, the Point of Air specifically. Waders and sea birds were well represented, as were ducks. We were again lucky to see a velvet scoter, only one this time amongst a large flock of common scoters. A movement of eider ducks was occurring, quite a large flock of those, and gannets, razorbills and guillemots were doing likewise; no doubt, heading for the cliffs of Cumbria. Several Manx shearwaters were out at sea busily feeding.

On shore, the odd willow warbler could be heard singing away, and the call of the chiffchaff was also to be heard as should be expected now April was in. A peregrine was hunting inland, this fortunately did not upset the waders, it was too far away. All in all, we knocked up fifty-nine species, so we were more than happy with our visit. The end of the month saw us return to Spurn Point, full of high expectancy, only to be disappointed. Spurn was the quietest I had ever known. There was a strong off-shore wind, which had not been forecast, and this had driven the sea out far; birds were distant and few, and if it had not been for bar-tailed godwits and brent geese, it would hardly have been worth the effort. But you cannot win them all, and so far the year had been very good.

In May came the Bird Race once again, which we decided to compete in once more; the opportunity of getting one hundred in a day loomed. It was not to be, work as hard as we did, and for twenty-four hours, we only managed eighty-eight which was down on last year. When the full results came through most participants were down on the previous year, so we did not feel so bad.

The end of May, the actual last day, we were again off to Bempton for our annual visit to 'Bird City'; although, this time round, it would be a shorter visit than usual: at nearby South Landing a few interesting warblers had been reported.

Bempton produced its usual gems, the puffins putting on a very good show and out at sea the gannets were very active, with quite a few of last year's birds among them. Sandwich terns were also passing through in good numbers and there appeared to be more shags than usual, we were certainly not complaining. Now for South Landing and the warblers.

At South Landing a lot of activity was going on, bird watchers were everywhere, and a quick question explained why. An icterine warbler had been reported that morning, a bit special this bird and a 'Lifer' for all of us if we were fortunate enough to see it. With a bird of this calibre, you do not have to search out the bird, you just look for the largest group of birders.

After about twenty minutes, this proved to be the case. Round a bend in the path, we came across about fifty birders all gazing excitedly and intently into a small oak tree. Above their heads was a small flock of birds, principally linnets, but amongst them was a much smaller and neater looking bird, our quarry.

Icterine warblers are only slightly larger than the more familiar willow warblers, and are what we term a scarce migrant and are only seen during spring or autumn passage, if you are lucky. Although never having seen the bird, I was more than familiar with certain of its principal features, as it was a bird I had always hoped to see, and here it was. Due to its upright stance and peaked crown, it looked larger than it really was. The light that day was very good and the pale wing panels and yellow ring round the eye also stood out. As it flitted about, the grey legs were also obvious, no problem there, we had our 'Lifer'; this had not been expected. South Landings few unusual warblers had hit the jackpot here, that was for sure. We moved on, serenaded by blackcaps as we did so. Reaching the Landing a party of eider ducks sailed by, all drakes, seven of them, always a superb sight, and close in a drake red-breasted merganser was drifting, looking almost asleep.

We turned to go back up the valley, on the opposite side to that which we came down, and chiffchaffs and willow warblers were very evident, both visually and in song. As we approached the top of the path, I stopped: an unusual call was coming out of a nearby thicket which I instantly did not recognise. This bird had a very wide vocabulary, then it hit me, we were listening to a marsh warbler, another cracker. We searched the thicket very closely, and the bird eventually flicked out onto the top of the bush, gave us a short glare, and flew back down into it. That was that, a burst of song was all heard after that, but we were happy. An icterine and marsh warbler were two magical birds; we would certainly go home happy, that was for sure.

June saw us after a few of our speciality birds, stone curlew, golden oriole and woodlark, should we manage these we would be very happy birders. Fordham, Weeting Heath and Mayday Farm were our destinations, and an early start was called for: 6.00 a.m. saw us on our way. Twelve of us making the trip, and for some the three birds mentioned would be 'Lifers'. For all of us, good 'Year Ticks'. Fordham was for the golden orioles, and we arrived to see several other birders in attendance, always a good sign. We got out of our cars to be greeted by a passing goshawk, that was some start to the day, and this bird turned to put on quite a display for us. If we saw nothing else that day, this would be some memory.

We proceeded to where the majority of birders were collected. The orioles had been seen recently, a male was very active, or so it was claimed. We settled in to wait, and wait we did. It was almost forty-five minutes before a bird flew out, but it was a male, and although I doubt if we saw the bird for ten seconds it was very close and did call twice. The call of the oriole I find to be very evocative, almost straight out of the jungle. I may have mentioned it before, it always reminds me of the sounds heard in the background to Tarzan films. Thank you Fordham, Weeting Heath next. After the wait at Fordham, here it was ridiculously easy. We did not have to go into the reserve. On the opposite side of the road, three stone curlews could be seen strutting their stuff, fully in the open. We stopped and watched them for a few minutes before they vanished over a rise in the ground. These birds had provided us with two benefits. Firstly, we did not need to go into the reserve, which saved us the entrance fees; and secondly, it gave us more time to seek out the larks at Mayday Farm. We were more than happy.

Mayday Farm was only a few minutes' drive away, and although none of us had visited the area previously, we had good directions of where to go, and the necessary map reference. I sometimes wonder what we would do without Ordnance Survey Maps.

We had it all to ourselves, so we spread out and concentrated on the job in hand. Fortunately, most of us had previous experience with woodlarks so we knew what to look for and just as importantly, what to listen out for. On a nearby gorse patch, a family party of stonechats could be seen, two adults and three young which appeared to be busily feeding on ants which were on the gorse. A spotted flycatcher was hawking flies and a family party of grey partridge, seven of them, were feeding in a mown field. Then we had what we came for.

A woodlark came swooping down to land on a solitary tree. After a minute or so it took off, rising into the air, singing away merrily, before returning to the same perch. Woodlarks do not sing in the same manner as skylarks. They do not rise up high in the sky, they tend to sweep out in a curve and then return to their favourite perching spot. We had been fortunate in finding this bird's favourite perch.

We enjoyed the bird for several minutes before it eventually flew off, not to return. We had been very lucky, the three birds we came for, we saw, and we had several additional good species. The Brecks had been a good choice.

Later in the month, Dorothy and I had a week's holiday in Pembrokeshire again, where we renewed acquaintances with a few of our favourite birds; among those being chough, fulmar, gannet, guillemot, Manx shearwater, raven, ruddy shelduck, wheatear and whinchat. We saw sixty species in the week, had some glorious sunshine, and food and wine; could one ask for more?

The following few weeks passed by rather quietly, which suited me in a way. I was busily organising a week's birding for my friends in Norfolk late in August and come the 22nd August, eighteen of us made our way to Norfolk. We stayed at an hotel close to Titchwell Nature Reserve, I had stayed there previously so Dorothy and I knew we would be well looked after, and this proved to be the case.

As is to be expected in Norfolk, the birding was first class and we covered most of the principal locations. During the week, we saw one hundred and eighteen species; a good total for anyone. The highlight for me, personally, was seeing a dotterel, a bird I had never seen in the UK previously. This bird was seen at Cley Marshes, and was a 'Lifer' for everyone. Other quality birds were Arctic skua, avocet, bearded tit, black tern, curlew sandpiper, gargany, honey buzzard, little stint, marsh harrier, Montagu's harrier, peregrine falcon, red-necked phalarope, snow goose, spoonbill and wood sandpiper. Enough there to keep anyone happy, I would have thought. Even the weather was kind, only one damp day in the week.

How could we follow Norfolk? Crosby and Preston did their best. In September, Lancashire called. A passage of great skuas had been reported off Crosby, these were not to be missed. Sixteen of us ventured forth on a most miserable day, light rain was falling and visibility was very poor. Our hopes were not high.

Things at Crosby were slightly better, a breeze was blowing on shore and this improved the light considerably. A group of birders told us that a few great skuas had been seen and that a grey phalarope had been reported at Preston, and they were able to give us full directions. We were more than happy with that news.

The skuas were quickly located, just the odd one or two passed by, heading southwards, but we were happy with that. One of my colleagues shouted out, 'What is this skua Brian, it is not large enough to be a great?' I swung round to look at where he was pointing, and I was glad I did. He had found us an adult pomarine skua, this was not a bird to be sniffed at.

Not as bulky as the great, but still a powerful looking bird. In adult plumage it has one very distinguishing feature: the central tail feathers are extended and have a twist at the end forming quite a blob, clearly seen on this specimen. That bird was a bit special to say the least.

Waders were well accounted for, curlews particularly so, always a marvellous sight – my favourite bird – I can never see too many. Sanderlings were dancing along the edge of the tide, as is their wont, and a wader amongst them caught my attention – a sandpiper – but which one? I was beginning to think it was time to get the field guides out when it hit me: it was a pectoral sandpiper, a rare visitor from across the Pond, a true Yankee. The bird was a juvenile and it was time for the field guides;

I was the only one who had seen this bird previously, a 'Lifer' for everyone else. It cannot get better than that. Crosby was catching up with Norfolk, and we had only been there a few hours!

As we were about to leave for Preston, a gaggle of pink-footed geese flew in – well into three figures – a gannet drifted past and four Sandwich terns flew through. Not a bad send off as far as we were concerned.

We quickly located the area where the grey phalarope was seen, several other birders were in attendance, so the bird was soon found. That day the birding had been easy, and more was to follow. A flock of about fifty golden plovers flew in, many still sporting their beautiful summer plumage, a cracking bird by any standards. Three little gulls were also busily feeding over a small pond, and a few Arctic terns joined in.

I have not mentioned all the birds seen that day, but we totted up sixty-eight with several real top quality birds amongst them; a brilliant day's birding to put it mildly. These are the days you always remember.

The end of the month saw us return to Spurn Point, where we also hoped to include a visit to Sam's Point where a short eared owl was being regularly seen. Spurn lived up to its reputation once again, with the usual range of species to be seen, the best of which were red-throated diver, ring ouzel and the pick of the bunch: a yellow-browed warbler. Not bad by any standards, and we still had time for Sam's Point.

This was a new venue for all of us. The Point sticks out into the Humber with a small car parking area. The owl obviously was a showman. It was just gliding slowly and elegantly over a nearby damp field, they are the ultimate flying machine in many respects; every movement is slow and articulate. I can spend hours just watching them go about their business, nothing seems ever hurried.

Whilst enjoying this bird's prowess a small bird dropped into the edge of the field, a pipit, no doubt just a meadow pipit, but something about the stance of the bird caught my attention. It stood rather upright, with a heavy bill – legs looked long and so did the tail – and as the bird hopped out onto open ground, I was surprised by the length of the hindclaw. What had we here, then it dawned upon me: we were looking at a Richard's pipit, a rare bird in western Europe. What a bird with which to end the day, my only second observation ever; needless to say, for everyone else, a 'Lifer' – a mega one in reality.

Another superb field meeting drew to its conclusion, we were having some year, rarities were just dropping in to see us; you cannot ask for more than that.

Eyebrook and Rutland Water were next on the agenda, and there the best birds of the day were Egyptian goose, kingfisher, ruddy duck, snow goose and twite. Nothing new, but a bit of quality nether-the-less.

November commenced with a visit down to Slimbridge, where we had a chance to see many duck close to hand. The collection provides ample opportunity to really study birds normally only seen in the distance, and there is always the chance of more unusual species dropping in.

The Bewicks's swans had started their arrival, although in small numbers, wild mandarin duck were to be seen; the white-fronted geese had also started to come in and wigeon were plentiful on the wetland meadows along the River Severn. An interesting day was had.

We finished the year off locally, visiting Lea Marston and Kingsbury Water Park, and this turned out to be a good choice. The birds of the day were barnacle geese, ferruginous duck, great northern diver, grey-lag geese, red-crested pochard and ruddy duck. A good way to end the year.

A good year it had been, totalling 221; now what would 1993 bring us?

Our first meeting was a visit to Rutland Water, and we started off with sixty-four species, not a bad start to the year, and amongst those were a few choice birds which it was very good to get out of the way so early in the year. Those being Egyptian goose, jack snipe, pintail, ruddy duck, snow goose and twite. We were more than happy with those.

The end of the month saw us visiting new territory: Wraysbury, Virginia Water and Uxbridge, and two distinct species were on our list, ring-necked parakeets, and smew. Those birds would be 'Lifers' to several of my group, and for those of us who had seen them previously, they were again good birds to get on our Year Lists so early in the year. As far as numbers were concerned, it was not a great day, only forty-six different species were seen on the day, but the important thing was we got the two birds we were after. The parakeets were in a flock of over twenty and the noise they made was ear piercing, I would not have liked them close to my home that was for sure. The smew took some finding at Virginia Water, but we managed eventually, and this was really worth the effort. I had not appreciated there was a group of seven of them, I had expected only one. In all my years of birding, I have never seen so many together; I doubt if I have seen that many in total. The parakeets had been something, this was just extraordinary in comparison. They were a mixture of two drakes, two ducks and four first year birds; no doubt, two families. We were over the moon, our trip south had been worth every mile of it. Most of us now were well over the hundred mark for the year.

Mid-February saw us off to the Elan Valley, after chough and red kite. We failed on the chough but red kite were plentiful and as compensation for missing out on chough, we had a rough-legged buzzard; we were more than happy with that. We also had peregrine falcon, raven, buzzard, kestrel and a sparrowhawk, a good day for birds-of-prey.

The end of the month we travelled north, visiting Southport and Martin Mere, and the day commenced in a brilliant fashion. We arrived at Marshside, Southport, to be told an American wigeon had been seen on the marsh; what a bird to see, a 'Lifer' for us all – presuming we saw it that was.

Further up the coast road, a large group of birders could be seen so we made our way towards them. They were all looking out over the marsh in one direction, so we joined them to be told the bird was out there; and fortunately, it was a drake which made recognition a little easier. Teal are very common duck during the winter months when large numbers migrate to the UK; American wigeon, on the other hand, are a rare bird – few cross the Atlantic to our shores.

Our bird was associating with a flock of about twenty wigeon on open water, and this made finding him quite easy. By comparison, the American wigeon is a duller looking bird, not quite as flashy as our wigeon so we quickly located him. Had it have been a duck, we would not have found things so easy; they are very similarly plumed. What a start to the day, our almost first bird we saw was a 'Lifer'; it cannot get better than that. As a birding friend of mine, Ivor, regularly comments, 'There is only one way it can go now, and that is downhill.'

He was not quite right. We saw bar-tailed godwits, black-tailed godwits, curlews, golden plovers, grey plovers, a hen harrier (a bit special this fellow as it was a male), pink-footed geese, pintails, sanderlings, a singing skylark, turnstones and a large herd of whooper swans. By any standards that was a good day's birding. In total, we saw seventy-one species, not downhill, sorry Ivor!

I had just completed plans for another group visit to Switzerland, exactly twenty of us this time, and we were again staying at the same hotel in Wengen. For ten, plus Dorothy and myself, it was a repeat journey, we were to go on the 23rd June for ten days; something to look forward to. For our next meeting, North Wales called, time to go hunting Lady Amhersts pheasants once again which would be a new bird for a few of the group. We struck lucky, we saw the birds very easily, both a female and two males, so everyone was happy. A peregrine was also swooping round the church tower, we wondered if it was nesting on the building. A good start, now for the coast.

The sea was very calm and fully in, not good for waders, but it brought the water birds in close. The pick of these was three black-necked grebes, many fulmars and the largest number of common gulls I can record, they were really common, I can only presume we had caught them on passage north. Waterfowl were plentiful, common scoter and shelduck especially so, and a small raft of red-breasted mergansers also put in an appearance. As the tide turned, pintails flew in and waders commenced to appear, not in large numbers, but a decent range of species.

On shore, several passerines and the like were visible or audible; among these were the odd chiffchaff calling, a pleasant sound announcing summer was not far away. A small flock of siskins was busily feeding on some gorse and two skylarks were singing their little hearts out way up over the dunes. All in all a most pleasant scene, our trip to Wales had been well worth it.

The end of March saw us visiting Tittesworth Reservoir and the Staffordshire Moorlands. We were off grouse hunting again, but before doing so, we called in at the reservoir and this proved to be the right decision.

Waterfowl were still plentiful, many of the winter visiting teals and wigeons were still to be seen, and these were now is full summer plumage, a most delightful sight. The odd ringed plover and dunlin were still in attendance and out on the water was a large flock of sixty or so barnacle geese.

Whilst enjoying these we had the surprise of our lives, an osprey came swooping down, plunging into the water, to emerge with a catch. A large fish, presumably a trout, was struggling away in the birds claws as the osprey sought to turn the fish face onwards. This it eventually did, and the last we saw was the osprey flying off with its breakfast. That was my earliest record of an osprey which made it more than a little special. How about that for the start of a day's birding? Tremendous!

Off now for the moors, Swallow Moss being our destination, grouse being our targets. Driving across we enjoyed a small party of curlews which flew in front of us for a few seconds. It was a tidy flock of eleven birds and they were calling well; they have a voice of their own, pure magic. Fieldfares and redwing were still to be seen, although their numbers were small, the bulk of them will by now be well on their way back home to Scandinavia. We arrived at Swallow Moss to be greeted by a 'yaffling' green woodpecker; why he should be laughing at us, I did not know! A flock of linnets were actively feeding on some nearby gorse, and we had quite a surprise as two redshanks flew over our heads, calling loudly. These last two birds were totally unexpected in that part of the Moors at that time of the year.

Whilst we were enjoying a male stonechat, which had popped out on the top on a nearby stone wall, we heard the call of one of our target birds. 'Go-back, go-back,' rang out loudly, and turning in the direction from where the call came were three magnificent male red grouse. They stayed on view for several seconds before they took to flight and quickly vanished from sight.

We now commenced to walk down the track towards Fernyford Farm, where a small flock of black grouse was still to be seen. Their numbers were slowly reducing; no doubt, due to close inbreeding. New stock was needed was the considered opinion. Our luck continued. Five black cocks, the male of the species, were roosting up in the trees at the farm, and we had the pleasure of these birds for several minutes before they flew onto the open moorland to feed. We did not see them again, but we were not complaining.

We did have cause to complain about one thing. The sky had been turning very black and down came the rain. Our day was over, but it had been successful, and that is what matters. We had seen our target birds plus a few choice additions. On the day, we actually totted up fifty-nine species, and all within a little over an hour from home; now that cannot be bad.

May saw us have our usual trips to Bempton Cliffs, you cannot miss out on seeing puffins at least once in a year, and an evening on Cannock Chase knocked up nightjars and woodcocks.

Prior to Switzerland, a visit to Anglesey was called for, and we really clicked for a very pleasant day weather-wise. A good selection of birds had been seen, including a few puffins, little terns and a little stint, when we bumped into a friend of mine. After our greetings, he raised the question 'Had we seen the scarlet rosefinch?' the answer to that was obviously no; we did not know anything about the bird. Map out and he showed us where he had seen the bird, and we were off. The opportunity of a 'Lifer' called.

The bird was at Trwyn y Penrhyn, north of Beaumaris, an area I fortunately knew from a past holiday in the area, and once again it was a question of looking for the birders, not the bird.

Thirty or so birders were quickly located and the bird put on quite a display for us; you almost thought it was enjoying itself with all the attention it was receiving. They are an eastern European species, and to see one in June is most unusual, not, I hasten to say, you see many, they are a bit special to say the least.

We were lucky with our bird that day, it was a male and the red on the cheeks and upper breast stood out well in the light, hence the name rosefinch. They also have a very heavy bill for the size of bird, it being only about six inches. It sang frequently, no doubt trying to attract a female; he was going to have no luck there, and we were able to spend a good half an hour enjoying the bird. This had been a totally unexpected bird, and he certainly sent us on our way very happy and contented. The perfect end to a perfect day.

The 23rd June arrived, and twenty of us left Birmingham Airport for our flight to Switzerland, which was its usual comfortable flight. We arrived in bright conditions and travelled on to Wengen, enjoying several black kites from the train as we did so. Not a bad welcoming that. The manager met us at the hotel, made himself known to the newcomers. We had a light tea, and an hour's walk round Wengen; once again enjoying the resident black redstarts, then unpacked and prepared for dinner.

As with previous visits, I organised a day spent locally so everyone could get familiar with the surroundings and have a leisurely day's birding. For the newcomers, some of the birds seen had just been pictures in books prior to that day. Black woodpeckers seemed intent on showing themselves, a pair of nutcrackers were obviously breeding nearby, the resident golden eagle put on a superb flying display and black kites were seen frequently. Even a few chamois put in an appearance. As one of my colleagues said, 'If we see nothing else, this has been worth the money.' He need not have worried, there was obviously more to come.

Once again, we were fortunate with the weather; although, one evening, we had a thunderstorm which was quite spectacular to say the least. The valley seemed to shake with the noise of the thunder, you would certainly not have wanted to be out in it.

We visited the areas we were familiar with and during the holiday we knocked up one hundred and one species, the pick of which were: Alpine accentor, Alpine chough, Alpine swift, black-eared wheatear, black woodpecker, black kite, booted eagle, collared flycatcher, crested titmouse, grey-headed woodpecker, rock thrush, three-toed woodpecker, serin and snowfinch. Dorothy and I had five new species, the rest of the group had many more. Switzerland had done it again.

After Switzerland, the next few field meetings seemed rather quiet; although September saw a good passage of waders pass through the county which was of great interest. Come October, Dorothy and I decided to have a week's holiday and we visited Northumberland. The gods obviously loved us, we had a wonder week of weather, and Northumberland was so quiet it was almost unbelievable. It gave the impression of being a county you drove through and did not stop, a magnificent place as far as we were concerned. We stayed in a very comfortable hotel in Alnmouth which was right on the front.

On our first day, we had a stroll along the beach and were pleased to see a few terns still passing through, mainly sandwich terns and the odd little tern. These birds were probably stragglers from further north, Scandinavia or even Iceland on their winter migration southwards.

Sanderlings were rushing about along the tide line and out at sea a large raft of eider ducks was seen, more than enough to convince us we had chosen well.

After dinner that evening, we met up with another birder who was leaving the following day, but he passed on some very interesting information. Druridge Bay was a must. The brent geese had commenced to arrive, barnacle geese were also in attendance and a good selection of waders was to be seen. The one thing he did mention was to allow at least two days to cover the area well. Our plans were laid, and after breakfast we were on our way. The whole expanse of Druridge Bay is classed as a nature reserve and as far as beaches go, this takes some beating; in summer it must be perfect. We parked up in Druridge and walked towards the beach. Once we had crossed the dunes, sanderlings were again everywhere; curlews were following the retreating tide and a large flotilla of common scoter was drifting out on the tide. Dorothy brought my attention to a large pale looking gull and I was mightily glad she had; a full adult glaucous gull was putting on a superb display for us. They are a very large, almost great black-backed gull size bird, very white with no black at all in their plumage. They breed in the Arctic regions and a few drift down to the UK during the winter, you do not see many so this bird was greatly appreciated – well done, Dorothy. Quite a large number of gulls were out over the sea, all the regular species and further out a number of gannets were fishing away. Shags were also very active, these had no doubt come from The Scars near to Cresswell and the call of oystercatchers filled the air; these birds are rarely, if ever, silent.

We moved on along the beach, enjoying the birds and also the warm autumn sunshine; England is a wonderful place on days like that. Dunlins and golden plovers were in goodly numbers with many of each still flaunting their summer plumages, and in the case of the golden plovers, they looked simply magnificent; mind you, we soon saw a bit of competition. A small flock of grey plovers landed on the shore, seven of them, all in their bright summer plumages, what a sight. Just have a look at them in your field guides, I frequently say they should be called silver plovers; the grey looks more like silver. To see the two species so close together was just superb.

Out at sea more surprises awaited us. Teal were on the move as they flew in from across the North Sea, a pair of red-throated divers, in their summer regalia were also to be seen and a flock of guillemots swam past. Our birder from yesterday had not exaggerated, that was for sure. Time to turn back, our packed lunch to be eaten.

We decided to walk back through the dunes, the sand looked quite firm, and so it was. A small party of wheatears, about a dozen were actively feeding in the dunes; it looked as though they had located an ants nest, and were feeding with gusto. Another case of migrants passing through.

We spotted a damp area in the dunes with a small amount of vegetation growing from it. Here several snipe were to be seen, their long, strong looking bills, probing in the mud. The way they were feeding obviously meant food was readily available. Approaching Druridge, we met up with a small group of local birders who pointed out a firecrest to us that was foraging away in a clump of gorse. We were very pleased, we could easily have missed this bird as it was not showing itself a great deal. Then they gave us some wonderful news.

Down at Cresswell, on a small lake, which they showed me on my map, a pied-billed grebe had been seen for three days now, including that morning, and it was showing well. We had not time to go there at that moment, but tomorrow's birding was already arranged. Pied-billed grebes are a very rare north American vagrant which occasionally crop up in the UK; it was a bird I had never considered I would ever see, but now I had the opportunity

Breakfast was rapidly consumed, we were in 'Twitch' mode. We were able to park up close to the pool near Blakemoor Farm, and quickly approached. We could hear little grebe trilling away – well I presumed it was little grebe – I had no idea what a pied-billed grebe sounded like. We were right, seven little grebes were swimming and diving on the pool, so we settled in to wait. After what seemed an eternity, it was over half an hour, when seriously birding patience is demanded, a dumpy looking bird slowly swam out from a tangle of willow; this was no little grebe, we had our quarry.

They are a larger bird than the little grebe, which they resemble slightly, but this bird, being an adult, fortunately still had the distinctive bill markings which give the bird its name. The bill is short and thick, unlike the more slender and dagger-like bills of our native grebes, which is bluish-white in colour with a black-central band; here, again, we were fortunate in the bird being still in almost summer plumage. In winter, the bill is horn coloured. We enjoyed its company for several minutes, saw it dive several times, once emerging with what looked like a newt, before it vanished from sight and did not return. We were more than happy, we had experienced superb views and saw it make a catch; what more could you ask for? A wonderful and completely unexpected 'Lifer' for both of us, needless to say.

The pool also had two pairs of gadwalls swimming away, grey herons, standing almost sentry-like, their patience is amazing, and a few house martins were hawking flies over the surface of the pool; they would not be there for much longer. As we were about to move off, Dorothy was up to her usual tricks, 'That's a funny looking snipe,' she said. She was right, she had spotted a jack snipe which had walked out of a reed bed and was standing in the water, just visible. Another cracker, and we only had this bird for about thirty seconds before it vanished back into the reeds. Well done, Dorothy.

We spent the rest of the day on the beach, where a large number of knots were assembled. When these took to flight it was most spectacular as there must have been a couple of thousand birds; how they failed to collide, I do not know. Some spectacle, another most enjoyable day.

We decided to have a day away from birding and visit Warkworth Castle and Amble which overlooks Coquet Island; always the chance of the odd bird here in any case.

A very pleasant couple of hours was spent viewing the castle and enjoying the large number of jackdaws congregated therein. Their calls echoed round the remains of the castle, a superb sound, a wonderful bird; ever since I had my pet jackdaw, I have been in love with this bird.

Come the afternoon, this was spent in Amble, where we had a very pleasant lunch and made our way to the front which overlooked Pan Point and Wellhaugh Point. The tide was out and we walked down through the dunes towards Hauxley Haven, and there we were in for a very interesting surprise.

There were many rock pools and in one of the larger pools, two terns were diving; they looked very pale and closer observation proved them to be roseate terns. I had completely forgotten these birds bred on the nearby Coquet Island, and they were a bird we had only seen on the very odd occasion so that was a moment to enjoy. We were very fortunate, I would have thought the majority would have by now been well off on their migration to warmer climes. They are possibly our rarest breeding tern, not a bird to be sniffed at. Our non-birding day had hit the jackpot!

Turnstones were very active searching out food from among the cracks in the rock; they were not living up to their name, no turning of stones there. Ringed plovers were also very evident, curlews and oystercatchers were also to be seen. It had, after all, ended up a birding day!

Friends of ours, who regularly visit Northumberland, insisted we must visit two of the finest sites: Lindisfarne (Holy Island), and the Farne Islands. Lindisfarne is subject to tide times, and the following day was ideal so our plans were made.

On the drive up, we stopped several times to look over Budle Bay, where thanks to the retreating tide large areas were becoming exposed and waders were taking advantage of this. Oystercatchers, curlews, bar-tailed godwits were feeding away in the muddy channels and large flocks of dunlins and knots were moving onto the exposed areas. We were enjoying probably over three thousand birds; the sight and sound of which were wonderful. On to Lindisfarne.

We splashed our way across the causeway to the island, which is called Holy Island for obvious reasons. Saint Aidan arrived there in AD 635 and founded his monastery on the island. It was from here that the Christian message spread throughout the land and many believe the world, as it was known then. Driving across we saw several large flocks of common scoters and eiders and we arrived on The Snook to be greeted by a small flock of brent geese which promptly flew off and were not to be seen again. The island had large numbers of breeding birds, especially gulls and terns, but most of those had departed by then. In the various small bays, a good selection of waders were to be seen, and eiders were again in evidence. Off the Castlehead Rocks shags were busily fishing away and the odd gannet was also to be seen, diving headlong into the sea. A large party of kittiwakes flew past, these were heading out to sea, flying in a northerly direction; where these were going was anybody's guess.

We found an inn for a spot of lunch and went to have a look at the Priory and castle; Lindisfarne had much to offer the historian. We had time for one last look for birds and near Steel End, we hit the jackpot. On a grassy meadow, a group of barnacle geese were feeding away and among them were two geese which looked like pink-footed geese. Dorothy had a better angle than I, and she commented about the bill colour and the fact the legs were not pink. Time for concentration. She was absolutely right, we had two bean geese, two superb birds to finish the day off. On the day, we had seen sixty-two species, several of which were definitely quality birds. I had a feeling we would be back sometime in the future. Conditions were still good, so the Farnes would be next on the agenda. In the breeding season, the Farnes were home to a large range of breeding species – especially terns – most of these would by now have departed, but something of interest would surely be found.

We sailed from Seahouses for a cruise round the islands, we were not landing, all our viewing would be from the sea. Many seals were to be seen; the boat seemed to attract them, they came to see us. Along the rocky coast many shags were sitting out, looking as though they were just enjoying the sun, and eider ducks were bobbing about on the sea. All in all, a very tranquil scene.

On the many rocky outcrops, turnstones and ringed plovers were feeding away. Among the many gulls, goodly numbers of common gulls were to be seen; not a common bird in our neck of the woods – to see them in their hundreds was quite a spectacle. Great crested grebes were also passing through in small numbers; to see these birds on the sea was quite a change to how we usually experience them.

Coming in over the sea were small parties of migrant thrushes, fieldfares and redwings to be precise. These birds were in transit from Scandinavia to spend the winter in the UK, their numbers would greatly increase over the next few weeks. Teals and wigeons were also in attendance, like the thrushes, they too are winter migrants, and the odd red-throated diver could be seen, diving for fish; they are not called divers without reason.

Making our way back to Seahouses, we had a very pleasant experience. A migrating stonechat landed on the boat and hitched himself a lift over the final mile or so of his journey. This bird was no fool. Our final day arrived and we decided to visit the pied-billed grebe once more. The chances were we would never have the opportunity of seeing one again, and who knows what else we might see.

The grebe did not disappoint, although we did not see it catch anything this time. A late reed warbler was calling from the reeds, he should have been well on his way southwards by then. He promptly went silent as a sparrowhawk flew through. The party of little grebes were actively feeding, although they too quickly vanished when the hawk flew across. The odd swallow was also to be seen, it would not be long before they departed our shores. Whilst on the subject of shores, we took ourselves down to the sea shore to have our last look over Druridge Bay, where the tide was returning rather rapidly; it was a high tide too, and the waders quickly departed inland, leaving only ducks and gulls out at sea.

Common scoters and eiders were again the most visible ducks, with just a few wigeons also on the sea; although a small party of seven pochards flew over. These were not stopping, they just vanished from sight. Nothing special was to be seen among the gulls, but a small flock of swans in flight drew our attention. They came closer and we realised we could not hear their wing beats; these birds were obviously not mute swans, you can hear their wing beat. Concentration time was again upon us. These were whooper swans, a real quality bird to finish off with, so after a pleasant walk we returned to our hotel to pack and have our final night. A fine meal, a delightful bottle of wine and a couple of malt whiskies – those were for me – and that was that.

Northumberland would most certainly be visited again. Earlier in the year, when the birds were breeding, it would make a most interesting venue. We saw ninety-one birds during the week, among which were a few choice species, with the pied-billed grebe to remain long in our memories.

The remainder of the year saw me back with the group, visiting familiar areas such as Rutland Water, the Staffordshire Moorlands and the North Welsh coast. Among the birds seen were yellow-legged gull, ruddy duck, ruff, black grouse, hen harrier, little owl, scaup, red grouse, Cetti's warbler, little stint, rock pipit, barn owl, long-tailed duck, water pipit, great northern diver, red-necked grebe and Slavonian grebe. A decent selection to end a year.

The year had provided us with two hundred and nineteen species; we now waited to see what '94 would do.

We commenced the year with a visit to the Moors and, although we had one disappointment as no black grouse were seen, we started the year off with fifty-one species. Included, among which, were: green woodpecker, hen harrier, little owl, long-eared owl, red grouse, red-necked grebe, siskin, snipe and sparrowhawk. Enough quality there to start the year off.

Later in January, we fitted in a visit to Rutland Water; a few choice duck were being reported, and the reports were true. On that day, we saw the following waterfowl: Canada goose, gadwall, goldeneye, goosander, greylag goose, long-tailed duck, mallard, mute swan, pintail, pochard, ruddy duck, shelduck, shoveler, smew, teal, tufted duck and wigeon. Not a bad collection there. If we added the following species, dunlin, golden plover, goldcrest, kingfisher, little owl, Mediterranean gull and water rail, we had a very successful day. Sixty-six species seen. The year had started very well, I had now seen over one hundred species, who knew what the future may hold?

By 1994, and I had been in love with birds for almost sixty years, which I have written about previously. I thought from then on it was time to concentrate more on the exceptional birds I hoped to see and their locations. I visited my regular locations with my groups, and when anything special occurred, I certainly celebrated it. I would not say I was in 'Twitch' mode, but I was sure the odd 'Twitch' would occur.

To start with, an unusual species cropped up locally late February. The bird arrived at Chasewater, which created a bit of excitement, although it was not going to appear on anyone's lists of British birds. A ringed teal was seen for a couple of days, obviously it had escaped from a collection somewhere. They are natives of South America, where they live in the wet forest areas, their chances of flying over the Atlantic and reaching the UK are remote to say the least. These exotics are always of interest, and it makes a change from seeing them in collections.

Late March, we were down in the Lea Valley. There we were after ring-necked parakeets, and we were not disappointed. We saw several of these noisy, colourful birds, which according to one or two of the locals, they were not appreciated. Many people are surprised to think that parrots live in the wild in the UK, but they do, and they are slowly spreading northwards. I have mentioned previously how they came to be living amongst us, and they have certainly settled in well. For some of my group members it was their first experience of the bird, hence our visit.April saw us visit Blacktoft Sands, avocets were on the agenda, once again a first for some of the group. The avocets numbers were increasing annually there, and we had some wonderful views. An osprey was also in attendance; we had not known about this bird so it was a real bonus. The marsh harriers also put on quite a display, there again their numbers were increasing. Blacktoft was slowly becoming a major site for both avocets and marsh harriers.

The pick of the birds, as far as I was concerned, were the spotted redshanks, not because of their rarity, it was due to their beauty. These birds, five of them, were all in their summer plumage, and the best way to describe this is 'star spangled'. They looked absolutely magnificent, well worth the trip alone. Summer migrants were also putting on a show, sand martins and swallows particularly so, and a few yellow wagtails were evident, beautiful birds looking almost like long-tailed canaries. Was summer now there – no, I had yet to hear a cuckoo!

April also saw our organising two holidays. Come May, we would be back in Northumberland for a week, and come July we were off to new territory; Austria called, and there we were staying for a fortnight.

Summer arrived on the 24th April when I heard my first cuckoo of the year, and I actually heard it from my own garden; now that could not be bad. Late April and early May saw us chasing up nightingales, nightjars and golden orioles, all I was pleased to report successfully. We were now ready for Northumberland.

Even in May it was very quiet, ideal from the holiday-makers point of view and the hotel proved to be as good as the previous visit. Being the breeding season we were hopeful of seeing other species, and the prospects on the Farne Islands were something to really look forward to.

A colony of little terns bred near to Alnmouth, those were visited on day one. About fifty pairs were breeding and the noise they created was quite incredible. They are very agile and feisty, and any larger bird which approached, such as a black-headed gull, was swiftly driven off by several of the terns.

The weather on the following day was superb, calm and warm, just the day to visit the Farnes. Our timing was good, we arrived at Seahouses just as a boat was about to sail and that gave us landings on two of the islands, which was perfect for what we wanted.

Our first stop was Inner Farne and there we were greeted by aggressive terns. The Arctic terns, especially, attacked your head and their sharp, pointed bills were like needles being stuck in your scalp. I know, one drew blood on me. Beautiful birds they may well be, friendly they are not. We had been told to look at the Sandwich tern colony very closely as a small number of roseate terns were usually found breeding amongst them, and after a while two were located. In the bright sunlight of the day, one could really appreciate why they were called roseate terns: they had a decided pink tinge to their plumage, a superb looking bird. Common terns also bred on Inner Farne so we had four different terns at one location, a bit special that to say the least.

Shag numbers were very good, and I had never been so close to these birds. They sat tight on their nests just feet away from us. They were obviously used to visitors and saw no danger. A smaller number of cormorants also nested on the island, but these were in more inaccessible locations. They were not so trusting it seemed! Family parties of eider ducks were on the sea; one had nine ducklings – she had done very well. One unusual feature about the Farnes is the lack of trees, a few shrubby bushes and that is about it. All the breeding birds are ground nesting and more easily seen, and the bulk of the birds to be seen was what we loosely term 'seabirds'. Of 'land birds', rock pipits were probably the commonest, and I doubt we saw six of these. There was the odd pied wagtail, feral pigeons, they got everywhere, and near the St. Cuthbert's Chapel, swallow and starling could be seen. Oh, and before I forget, a carrion crow flew over. Back to the seabirds. Their numbers were well up into the thousands and, apart from the birds mentioned previously, there were four species of gulls, several pairs of fulmars, guillemots, razorbills and everyone's favourite bird, puffins. The latter were very accommodating and sat at the entrances to their burrows, slowly turning their heads as they watched people walk by. They gave the impression of studying people just as much we studied them. As I might have said before, they are some bird. A few waders were also present, oystercatchers as would be expected and we also saw a couple of sitting ringed plovers breeding among the shingle. Inner Farne would remain in our memories for ever, and on two counts. Firstly, the number of birds seen and the closeness we got to them; secondly, not quite so pleasant, the smell. With this number of birds, the guano had to be deposited somewhere! On returning to our boat, we were told we could not land on Staple Island, due to a problem which had occurred there. Instead, we were taken for a trip to see the Longstone Lighthouse of Grace Darling fame. This was viewed from a distance.

The skipper of the boat gave a short history of the Grace Darling incident, and two American visitors on the boat were thrilled to bits with this information: they had never heard the story before. A very courageous lady was Grace Darling, a real Victorian heroine, whose story will now be taken back to the States. Our trip out to Longstone Island was accompanied by many grey seals, which were very curious and came close to the boat. Many a photograph was taken of these fascinating creatures. Adequate compensation for not landing on Staple Island.

The Farnes had lived up to their reputation. They are most certainly one of the top, if not the top bird watching location in Northumberland. There may only be 20 to 23 breeding species, it was the numbers of individual birds which made the whole experience so wonderful. A place not to be missed.

The weather forecast for the next few days looked very good, we were in luck once again, so we planned out our next few visits. We would go across to Holy Island, tides were again favourable, and to Kielder Forest Park. Druridge Bay and cross over into foreign parts and visit St. Abbs Head in Scotland.

Our return visit to Druridge Bay was not quite as exciting as the previous year, no pied-billed grebe to be seen, but this was compensated for by the range of species we saw. Among those, out at sea, gannets, fulmars, eiders, common scoters and kittiwakes were seen, whilst along the shore were oystercatchers, redshanks, curlews, the odd bar-tailed godwit, common terns were breeding among the dunes, and a few dunlin showing off their summer plumage. Swallows and swifts were moving through in large numbers and skylarks were joining in with their delightful song. Nothing mega, just a very pleasant and relaxing day. The next day would see us at Kielder.

This is not called a Forest Park without reason. It is the largest man-made forest in Britain I understand, with probably the largest reservoir too. It was woodland species we were after, and we had them in abundance. Ignoring the common species we saw or heard blackcap, chiffchaff, five species of titmice, several crossbills – always something a bit special – lesser redpoll, nuthatch, siskin, spotted flycatcher, treecreeper, tree pipit, willow warbler and wood warbler. Enough there to keep anyone happy and, as we were about to leave, a goshawk gave us a flypast. In total, we had forty-six birds on the day; the bulk of which were woodland species, and this was combined with some very pleasant walks. A most enjoyable day.

Our final day arrived and for this we decided to go north of the border. It is always exciting to visit 'foreign' parts; Scotland, here we come, with no passports required! We commenced our journey in the first rain of the week, but we were assured it would quickly pass and a decent day would follow. It was hoped the BBC weather forecasters had it correct. They had. As we drove through Berwick-upon-Tweed the sun came out and the cloud quickly dispersed. St. Abbs Head is a delightful spot, even if not into birds the cliff walks are wonderful, and several walkers were seen. We spoke to one couple who were walking down to Yorkshire; they were spending their holiday walking down the coast from up further north, a distance of over 250 miles. Good luck to them. St. Abbs Head is jointly managed by the National Trust for Scotland and the Scottish Wildlife Trust; it covers over 80 hectares and has sheer cliffs of 100 metres and, according to reports, is home to over 60,000 birds. It also has a large man-made freshwater lake (remembering where I was I had better call this a loch!), and to be accurate, it is called Mire Loch on my O.S. map. Nearby there were also trees and shrubs in a sheltered valley, and inland it was grazed grassland, an ideal mixture of habitats.

The cliffs supported around 350 pairs of fulmars, 300 pairs of shags, an impressive 16,000 pairs of kittiwakes, 13,000 pairs of guillemots, 1,000 pairs of razorbills and a few pairs of puffins. Also, plus a mixture of gulls, odd pairs of ravens and rock pipits, with a pair or two of wheatears on the tops. No, I had not counted them, a notice I read gave me the numbers! The noise from the kittiwakes would most certainly have kept one awake at night, and there was no need to wonder about their name. Those birds kept on telling you as they called away 'kevi-wake, kevi-wake'. From what one is led to believe, they are the noisiest of birds when at their nesting sites, but silent out at sea.

One thing we found of great interest was the fact the kittiwakes were regularly visiting the loch to bathe. Sea birds usually rarely visit freshwater; you see them bathing in the sea, so why these kittiwakes behaved so there, I had no idea. When I saw the birds at Bempton Cliffs where there was no freshwater, they were bathing in the sea, and unlike many gulls they are rarely seen inland during the winter. They are the most marine of the gulls.

What was also interesting was the fact that teal were to be seen on the loch. We tend to think of teal as winter visitors, there a few pairs were breeding alongside mallards and tufted ducks. The odd curlew could also be heard and skylarks were singing away above the grassy areas. On such a pleasant day as that day turned out to be, St. Abbs Head was a most delightful spot.

On our return journey we stopped at Budle Bay, where the tide was fortunately only just returning. Curlews were well represented, the odd common sandpiper was seen and several Sandwich terns were feeding in the channels. Common snipes were also to be seen – admittedly, only briefly as they skulked among the vegetation – several warblers could be heard from the hedgerow. One blackcap, in particular, serenaded us from a dense thicket of gorse. He was not to be seen, but he most certainly was heard.

We had experienced a wonderful week, and before leaving I discussed with the hotel owner the prospects of bringing a party of birders to stay for a week. He was more than happy with this and he gave me a very attractive price providing I was able to fill the hotel; I did not see this as a problem.

During the week, we broke the hundred mark; we actually saw 107 different species – Northumberland had much to offer.

The next few weeks passed pleasantly enough. We had trips to Wales, the Brecks, Bempton Cliffs and locally where the expected species were to be seen, and enjoyed. The pick of the birds seen during this period were quail, seen at Willington, stone curlew and red-backed shrike at Weeting Heath, choughs in Wales and woodlarks at Mayday Farm.

Come 13th July, Austria called. We flew from Birmingham, landed in Germany and travelled by coach to our destination in Austria. We were staying at a hotel near to Feldwies which was situated on the shores of the Chiemsee, a beautiful crystal clear lake. A most comfortable hotel occupied by many Germans, so little or no English was to be heard, apart from some of the staff. It was there we first experienced the Germanic behaviour regarding reservation of deck chairs. They used to go out early and place their towels on a deck chair, probably an hour or more prior to their occupation of the chair. A few choice arguments used to arise when others removed the towels and occupied the chairs. Although we could not speak German ourselves, it was obvious some rich language was being used. Fortunately, neither Dorothy or I were sun worshippers, so we could just watch and smile to ourselves.

The hotel had small paddle boats which took two people, and these could be hired very cheaply. We spent many a happy hour paddling our way round the shores. Our German friends were not interested in those so there was no competition; they were obviously just sun seekers. The lakes were home to several pairs of red-crested pochards which by now had families of ducklings accompanying them. A pair of mute swans had cygnets but what was noticeable was the fact they did not come for titbits, even though on one occasion we took some bread from the hotel, they were not the slightest bit interested. Back home, they would have been chasing you for it! Great crested grebes seemed at a premium which did surprise us as plenty of small fish could be seen in the clear water, but mallards were just as common as back home.

We had not included a hire car in our arrangements so visits away from the hotel were to be made in public transport so we did not travel too far afield. In consequence, most of our birding was made from walks along the lake and, in these circumstances, we did quite well.

We made a visit to Salzburg, early in the holiday, an interesting city if you are into architecture. We visited two of the parks which were very well laid out, slightly artificial, but we met up again with black redstarts, short-toed treecreepers and black woodpeckers, reminding us of

Switzerland, but as mentioned above, most of our birding was to be done nearer to our base.

We managed one trip to the Kaisergebirge, which had a peak over 2000 metres, and there we were rewarded with several choice species. Amongst which were black kite, crag martin, crested tit, raven, ring ouzel, rock bunting, rock thrush, short-toed eagle and snow finch, enough there to satisfy the keenest of birders.

During our stay we saw eighty-two species, and as well as those mentioned above, other specialities were: black-eared wheatear, citril finch, golden eagle, goshawk, middle-spotted woodpecker, nightingale, nutcracker, Orphean warbler, red-backed shrike, Sardinian warbler, serin, subalpine warbler, white wagtail and woodchat shrike. If those had been seen in the UK it would have been a major 'Twitch'.

Whether we would go back to Austria was debatable. A beautiful country, but from a bird watching point of view, not as rewarding as we found Switzerland. There the birding seemed to be confined and no great distances were required. To do Austria justice, a car seemed to be necessary. Not that we were complaining, we had a most pleasant holiday with many a happy memory. But one warning, should you be thinking of a holiday in Austria, it is an expensive country

The remainder of '94 saw us visiting our regular locations, with one exception which I will come to later, and the pick of species seen were as follows: little stint, osprey, and ruddy shelduck at Rutland Water, curlew sandpiper, garganey, pectoral sandpiper and Temmincks stint at Blithfield – all in August. September saw two trips to Spurn Point, the pick of sightings being as follows – great skua, icterine warbler, marsh harrier, pied flycatcher, red-throated diver and scarlet rosefinch on the first visit, the second produced-Arctic skua, black-winged stilt, great skua, hoopoe, little bunting, Manx shearwater, red-breasted flycatcher and a woodchat shrike, the latter being a UK 'Lifer' for us all. Spurn had done it again.

October was a quiet month until we visited Flamborough Head and South Landing. There we saw brambling, Pallas's warbler, ring ouzel, Slavonian grebe, whooper swan and yellow-browed warbler.

In November, we visited Titchwell and it was up to its usual standard. Seventy-five birds were seen on the day, the best of which were

– bearded tit, Brent goose, eider, hawfinch, hen harrier, marsh harrier, pintail, red-throated diver and pick of the bunch, snow bunting.

December saw us off on two 'Twitches', the first down to Letchlade were we were after a lesser scaup, a rare American vagrant, and I was the only one to have seen the species previously. I was delighted to report we saw it and saw it well, and it was a drake. All were delighted. We also had brambling, green sandpiper, kingfisher and twite, more than enough to keep all happy.

The second December 'Twitch' was a bit more mega. A very rare species had been seen in a car park near to Blackpool, a desert wheatear, this bird, should we be lucky, would be a 'Lifer; for us all. I had seen them when in Egypt all those many years ago; I never dreamed I would have the opportunity of seeing one in the UK. Chances such as those have to be taken.

The weather was vile, but twelve of us ventured forth. In weather such as that, you knew who were the keen birders, or was that just the crazy? Although it was such a poor day from the weather point of view, we quickly spotted a largish group of birders and made our way across. There, rummaging away near a lorry trailer, was our quarry. A rare bird in such a location was unbelievable. It was a lorry parking area, and there, running under H.G.V.s and the like, was this amazing bird. It seemed totally oblivious to the many people close by. The bird kept on running in and out of the pipes; I wondered if it was chasing after ants, not many other insects were active in December. We never found the answer to that one, but we at least enjoyed the moment.

Where to go next was quickly decided. Talking to one of the local birders, he was able to tell us of a Kentish plover being seen on the beach at Blackpool; the seaside called! The chance of two extremely rare birds in one day.

I had checked on my map for the last reported location of the plover and we managed to park our cars close by. There was no crowd of birders to help us there, the beach was very quiet with just the odd dog-walker and jogger, they were of no use to us.

After some time, we located a group of small waders which were dodging the out-going tide and among these were several ringed plover species, which the Kentish plover is. I had explained what we were looking for; the bird, fortunately, being a winter adult, and three distinct differences were being looked for. There was only one Kentish to look for, ringed plovers were several. The ringed plover has a distinctive black face mask, reddish legs and a complete black breast band, in juveniles this is broken. The Kentish, on the other hand, has a smaller face mask, a completely broken breast band, looking more like two black patches and dark grey to black legs. There are other minor differences, but we would concentrate on just the three.

After what seemed a long time, and probably was, one of my colleagues drew my attention to a bird. He had hit the jackpot: he had found his first ever Kentish plover; it cannot get much better than that. We enjoyed the bird for several minutes, it was a very active feeder and at times came in close to us, but unfortunately a large dog came racing along the shore and that was that. With a 'whoosh' the birds were off and the last we saw of them was as they headed further up the beach towards Fleetwood.

As it was still light, we drove up to Fleetwood in the hope of seeing the bird again; we did not, but we had some other choice birds. Whooper swans were flying in to nearby Martin Mere, large numbers of knots and dunlins were evident, a small flock of seven snow buntings were also seen among the dunes, that was twice recently we had seen this species. Pink-footed geese were still feeding along the shores of the Wyre, pintail were in the Wyre and, to finish things off for us, a peregrine falcon gave us a fly past. Lancashire had done us proud today, with two real mega sightings, the desert wheatear and the Kentish plover.

Some of you may be wondering how a bird with a very English name can be such a rarity. Many years ago they used to breed in southern England and they were given the name of Kentish plover to signify this. We literally discovered the bird as a separate species form the ringed plover, and the name has stuck. Throughout the world, where ever the bird breeds, it is the Kentish plover, or to save any confusion – Charadrius alexandrinus, its scientific name. We lost the bird many years ago as a breeding species and now only see the occasional bird, that day's was only my second ever in the UK. Although I did see them breeding in La Camargue.

Nineteen ninety-four has drawn to its conclusion, 221 species seen, four of which were 'Lifers'; happy enough there. What would a new year bring? Our first two trips in '95 took us onto the Moors and into Wales, and we commenced the year in style. The Moors produced black grouse, firecrest, golden plover, hen harrier, little owl, long-eared owl and willow tit; the pick from among fifty-one species seen. Wales, which included calling in at Ludlow produced blackcap, brambling, buzzard, chough, goshawk, hawfinch, peregrine, raven, red kite and rough-legged buzzard, there the best of forty-one birds seen. A good amount of quality to start a new year. Long might it continue.

February commenced with a trip up to Southport, Martin Mere and Seaforth, the latter location for a Ross's gull, a bit special that one, should we be lucky. The anticipated good birds such as Bewick's swan, curlew, dunlin, knot, Mediterranean gull, merlin, peregrine, pink-footed goose, red-breasted merganser, ruff, scaup and whooper swan, were seen at the first two locations, then for the bird of the day, a 'Lifer' called once again.

Seaforth was new to many of us, and it lies just north of Liverpool. Once again, luck was with us. A small party of birders were studying a group of gulls on a small tidal pool, when we approached them. There, swimming away among a party of black-headed gulls was our target bird for the day – the Ross's gull. It was what we termed a 1st winter bird, and the markings were not dissimilar to that of juvenile kittiwake, showing distinctive black 'V' markings on the upper wing surfaces and a black tip to the tail. It is a smaller bird, however, and in flight is tern-like, one for the book this one. They are a north American species – Canada – and are a very rare bird in the UK. Today was most certainly jackpot day for all of us.

March saw us visiting Wraysbury, Staines and Virginia Water. There, we were after four special birds in particular: mandarin, ring-necked parakeet, smew and whooper swan, which we saw. That was a bit of a 'Twitch' and several of my colleagues chalked up a 'Lifer' or two. We had fifty-one birds on the day, so our good run was definitely continuing, '95 was shaping up good.

It was decided another visit to Switzerland was required. Some of my newer course members wished to visit the country, so arrangements were made for a visit in late June for ten days. I had no complaints with leading bird study groups to that country.

333

Blacktoft called again in April and there we saw fifty-six species, the pick of which were avocet, bearded tit, marsh harrier, pink-footed goose and wood sandpiper. Later in the month saw us back in Norfolk, visiting Hunstanton and Titchwell. The usual birds at this time of the year were to be seen; sixty-seven of them, among which were avocets, a large passage of sand martins, a good selection of waders and waterfowl, and an unexpected woodlark. The lark being a new species for some of my colleagues. Early May, Dorothy and I had a week's holiday in the Lakes, clicked for some decent weather with some good food, wine and birds, what else are holidays for? The pick of the birds were bearded tit, bittern, eider, little tern, marsh harrier, ring-billed gull, Sandwich tern and spoonbill. These were seen at Leighton Moss on our journey up to the Lakes, whilst in the Lakes the best were buzzard, cuckoo, dipper, osprey, pied flycatcher, raven, red-breasted merganser, redstart, ring ouzel, tawny owl and wood warbler. Not a bad selection, and in total for the week, we saw fifty-eight species.

Late May we chased up golden oriole at Fordham and stone curlew at Weeting Heath, both being 'Lifers' for some of the party, a bit of a 'Twitch'. We had to work for the golden oriole at Fordham, but did, eventually, have three sightings of a bird much to everyone's enjoyment. The stone curlews were more accommodating, we saw several and one bird in particular put on quite a show for us, a real poser, and we were not complaining. Fifty-six birds on the day, plus a roe deer.

Early June saw us back at Bempton Cliffs, you cannot miss out on a visit to 'Seabird City', and three of our members had never seen puffins previously. They had now.

Come the 25th June and eighteen of us were off to Switzerland, seven being new to the country. Once again the weather was kind to us and the usual locations were visited; why change proven things? The bird watching was a bit quiet when compared with previous visits but we still saw eighty-six species, seven of which were not on the UK List, so all were happy. The chamois put on some most spectacular displays for us, their agility is unbelievable and the marmot numbers seem to have increased every time we saw them. The way they sit up and watch you is almost comical. A great holiday was had once again.

On our return we visited Anglesey in July where roseate terns and black guillemots were on the agenda, and they did not fail us, plus the other forty-seven species we saw. The terns and guillemots were again 'Lifers' for some of my colleagues, and the choughs also put on quite a display for us; two were particularly accommodating and came down for titbits. You cannot get much closer than that.

August was a quiet month spent locally, but come September, we went further afield with Spurn Point being our focus of attention. Among the sixty-four birds seen on that day, the pick were barred warbler, a 'Lifer' for many of my colleagues, merlin, Ross's goose and spotted redshank. Later in the month we had a local 'Twitch', Brandon Marsh in Warwickshire was our destination. A wryneck had been reported, a bit special that one. Years ago they bred in the UK in decent numbers, but now-a-days they are a rare bird with, I understand, just a few pairs breeding in Scotland. For some of my colleagues, a 'Lifer' loomed, and for myself, I had not had the pleasure of seeing one in the UK for a year or two.

On a damp morning, fifteen of us moved off full of expectancy. Brandon Marsh is a Warwickshire Wildlife Trust Reserve, their headquarters in fact, and is a well-appointed reserve with a very good café/restaurant, which in the current conditions would be appreciated. We quickly found out the best spot to see the bird and duly made our way. We did not have to work hard, a group of birders, twenty or so, were all gazing at a fence along the river. Sitting of the top of a post was our quarry; rarity hunting could not be easier than that.

The wryneck was a poser and spent several minutes just climbing up and down the post, providing wonderful views. They are allied to woodpeckers, and their name comes from the fact they can twist their heads round almost like an owl, they are some bird. We had fifty-one species on the day, apart from the wryneck the pick of the bunch were: common gull, dunlin, garganey, greenshank, pochard, ringed plover, ruddy duck, sparrowhawk and yellow wagtail. A good selection there.

The group decided that in the remaining three months of the year they would like to see quality, not quantity. It had been a very successful year so far, most of them had seen, or were approaching the two hundred mark, and were now in 'Twitch' mode. This put more pressure on me; unfortunately, I now had to try to find these birds. My telephone was going to be rather busy I thought.

How did we fare? October saw us chasing after red-necked grebe at Eyebrook Reservoir and snow goose at Belvide. November, we were after a long-billed dowitcher, a rare north American vagrant wader, a 'Lifer' for all of us – this was seen at Beverley – and later in the month, we went up to Tittesworth Reservoir for an American wigeon, a 'Lifer' for most, and called in at Park Hall for the long-eared owls as several of my colleagues had never seen these bird. December saw us once again chasing Ross's goose for those who had not seen the bird previously, this was at Sheerness and then we called at Slimbrdge for the Bewick's swans and white-fronted geese. We finished the year off chasing black-necked grebes off the north Wales coast. We obviously saw many other species, but the birds mentioned were the prime species.

Not all hit the two hundred mark, but the majority did, I finished up on two hundred and sixteen. What had '96 in store for us?

It was again decided we would spend the year chasing quality, my colleagues were still in 'Twitch' mode and that magic figure of '200' called. We would obviously visit all the regular locations as that was where the largest percentage of our birds would be recorded, but they all expressed an eagerness to chase after the special birds. So be it!

Our first field meeting of the year was to the Staffs Moors, where we hoped to knock off a few choice species early on, this we did. Among the fifty-four species seen, the pick were black grouse, hen harrier, lesser redpoll, little owl, long-eared owl, mealy redpoll (a 'Lifer' here for many), red grouse and short-eared owl; a good enough start to the year for any birder.

Later in the month saw us off to Lancashire, Southport and Martin Mere were calling. They were up to standard and the prime birds seen there were as follows: barnacle goose, Bewick's swan, knot, merlin, peregrine, pink-footed goose, pintail, ringed plover, ruff, scaup, snow bunting, snow goose, stonechat, white-fronted goose and whooper swan. All quality birds to see so early in the year. February and we were off to Wraysbury and the Lee Valley. There the pick of the fifty-two species seen were: bittern (a 'Lifer' for some of my colleagues), kingfisher, ring-necked parakeet, smew and water rail. We all hit the hundred mark for the year on this visit. As I told them, two hundred is not going to be so easy!

I finalised a group holiday to Northumberland, where I managed to fill the hotel, and as I mentioned previously, we had very good terms. Eighteen of us would be going, and this would commence on 9th June for a week. Something to look forward to. Late February, we made a quick visit to Kingsbury Water Park. There we saw a smew again, this was just for those who had not made our last field meeting.

March and mid-Wales called. As was usual with this visit, we called in at Ludlow first were we saw a dipper and several hawfinches before moving off into the Elan Valley. Ravens and red kites were accommodating and very good views were obtained and Devil's Bridge was again most productive with crossbills, lesser spotted woodpecker just a single bird and a good flock of siskins. Driving home a goshawk gave us a superb flypast. We went home happy.

Mid-March and Titchwell was our destination. Here we hoped to see the last of the Winter visitors, and an early summer migrant or two. The day was bright and clear and seventeen of us made the journey. And we had a very good day. Seventy-seven birds were seen on the day, the best of which were: Arctic redpoll, avocet, black-winged stilt, brent goose, common scoter, corncrake, eider, lesser redpoll, marsh harrier, red-breasted merganser, sanderling, turnstone, twite and velvet scoter. All of our 'Year Lists' increased on that trip.

April saw us off locally, we were really searching for summer migrants on that one, and we found them. Chiffchaff were very vocal and well spread, as were house martins, we had little ringed plovers at Blithfield Reservoir, where sand martins were also very evident, several hundred of these, swallows were seen in several locations, two wheatears were seen on The Chase and to finish off a yellow wagtail was seen at Belvide. On that day, the 14th April to be precise, we all passed the one hundred and fifty mark, surely that cannot continue?

Several of my group had never seen bearded tits before and I had been told by a friend of mine that they were showing well at Blacktoft Sands, so the end of April saw us off on a 'Twitch' of sorts. The bearded tits did not disappoint, we had several very good views and they were very vocal. To add to their calls, the bittern was booming frequently, and that was a new sound to many; unfortunately, we did not see him. Several summer migrants were seen, common sandpiper, cuckoo (summer must really be here!), garganey, grasshopper warbler, reed warbler, sedge warbler, spotted flycatcher, whinchat and willow warbler among them, all new birds for the year. We saw seventy-four birds on the day. Blacktoft Sands was becoming a very interesting reserve which would see me regularly, that was for sure.

May was mainly local visits, including an evening on Cannock Chase for the nightjars and woodcocks, both seen and heard and we had the added attraction of seeing a long-eared owl. We were not aware of their breeding on the Chase, but it looked as though they might.

With our week's bird watching holiday looming, the first Sunday in June saw us off on a bit of a race round. We hoped to visit, Little Paxton, a new venue, Fordham and Weeting Heath where golden oriole, stone curlew and turtle dove were our objectives.

We had an early start, we were off at 6.00 a.m., and arrived at Little Paxton before 8.00 a.m. We had hardly got out of the cars before we were greeted by a serenading nightingale, some vocalist this bird; we just stood, awestruck, what a greeting. If we saw nor heard anything else, the day was already a success.

After about half an hour, we heard the sound we were really after: a soft purring was coming from some overhead cables, and there sat our turtle dove. For many of my colleagues this was a 'Lifer', and I doubt if they will ever get a better view. Blackcaps and garden warblers were also very vocal, superb songsters those two and a hobby was flashing across the lake; no doubt, hunting sand martins which were plentiful. I was very impressed with Little Paxton, I would most certainly return, but we could not stay any longer as Fordham called.

A few birders were evident at Fordham, but no one had been successful, as the orioles had been inactive and silent, so we decided we would give it just an hour. It was getting very close to our deadline when one called from a nearby line of trees and seconds later flashed across the river to vanish on the other side. That was it, we hung about a little longer, no calls no bird, but we had at least seen and heard one. Would the stone curlews be more accommodating?

Weeting Heath was full of sound. Chiffchaffs and garden warblers were calling and singing loudly respectively, at least two cuckoos were calling, and swifts were screaming away in the sky above. A spotted flycatcher was taking nesting materials into a nest box and the beautiful song of the willow warblers filled the air. A lovely English scene.

We made our way to one of the hides and settled down to look for the stone curlews. It turned out to be a long wait, but patience was finally rewarded, and not by one stone curlew, by three. One of the birds was very close to the hide and provided us with wonderful views. You did not need binoculars for that one. The large head and eyes of the bird were the first things you noticed when that close, they are a partially nocturnal bird which accounts for the eye size. It also has longish legs and thick knees, which were very noticeable. I thought Lars Jonsson, in his book, *'Birds of Europe'* had summed the bird well, to quote: 'An oddity among European birds. Somewhat curlew-like, but its big head and sparrowhawk-like eye and often completely motionless posture produce reptilian associations': I cannot improve upon that. A perfect end to our day; well, not quite, we spotted a pied flycatcher on our return journey to our cars. Sixty-nine birds on the day, the numbers kept rolling on.

Northumberland now awaited us.

The journey up was not very pleasant, continuous rain as far as Newcastle, but afterwards things improved considerably. I had mentioned to my colleagues that I intended to stop for an hour at Warkworth for a walk along the shores of the River Coquet, and upon or arrival I found five of my colleagues were already there. Eiders were swimming in the river, principally drakes, the ducks were no doubt sitting eggs; the odd ringed plover was racing along the shore and reed buntings were calling away. The tide was retreating and terns were feeding actively. I had mentioned to my friends to look at these most carefully as we had the chance of the odd roseate tern which nest on the nearby Coquet Island. This raised concentration levels somewhat and it was not long before a roseate was spotted, and during the next half an hour or so, we saw double figures; a superb start to our holiday.

A pair of whinchats were obviously nest building close by, so we moved away not wishing to disturb them, they had flown a long distance to nest there. A male grey wagtail was busily chasing flies along the waters edge, and he had a nest close by judging by the amount of insects he flew off with. Sedge warblers were also very vocal, with chiffchaffs and willow warblers also competing. We moved on to Alnmouth more than contented.

Being the only members of the group to have visited the area previously it was up to us to sort out the locations, so Dorothy and I put our heads together and came up with the following programme; not necessarily in this order: St Abbs Head, Alnmouth itself, the Farnes, Lindisfarne, Keilder and Wallington Hall Estate, the latter not just for the birds, we had the opportunity of seeing red squirrels there. Sunday dawned bright and clear, so after the drive up the previous day, we chose Alnmouth itself as our first exploration. We spent the morning north of the River Aln, and in the afternoon, we drove round south of the river to visit Alnmouth Dunes and the shore along the Buston Links.

Alnmouth faces directly into the North Sea and out at sea a good selection of sea birds were to be seen. Razorbills and guillemots were very active, not in large numbers, kittiwakes were also feeding out on the sea, along with gulls. A few Sandwich terns could be seen and the little terns, which bred nearby, were their usual noisy and active selves – a great little bird. A few shags were to be seen and the odd eider duck was evident. Skylarks were singing behind us and swallows were hawking flies over the wet sands. A very pleasant scene. Now for the Dunes.

The tide by now was well out and a few waders were to be seen. Oystercatchers were feeding and calling away, as is their wont, the odd curlew was seen and a few pairs of ringed plovers were in situ; all obviously breeding birds. Two late sanderlings were chasing the tide as it retreated, I would have expected these to be much further north and on some shingle a turnstone was ferreting away; always a delightful bird to see when in its full summer plumage as this fellow was. A peregrine falcon came hurtling through putting up skylarks, meadow pipits and a stonechat from out of the dunes, we had not seen those birds prior to the falcon's arrival. A few gannets were also seen, these seemed to arrive just as the tide appeared to be turning; it made us wonder if fish became more active as the tide turned. Our first day had been very pleasant and relaxing after a long drive the previous day. We decided the following day would be spent at St. Abbs Head.

St. Abbs Head was rather busy, a group of birders had arrived by coach, but they quickly dispersed leaving us to our own devices. As I reported when Dorothy and I last visited this location, the high cliffs there are home to a good selection of sea birds. Razorbills and guillemots were very confiding and very good views of those birds were obtained. We were lucky with a very friendly puffin which just sat out on a jutting rock; no further than twenty feet away from us, a few photographs were taken of this fellow. The kittiwakes were their usual noisy selves, they may have a distinctive, call but you would not want to live close to a colony; you would rarely sleep. Rock pipits were flying up and down the cliffs and a group of doves certainly looked like pure rock doves, they looked identical which made us think they were not feral. A pair of whinchats were obviously breeding and several stonechats were calling away. As is usually the case, jackdaws breed on cliff faces and a few of those almost made us think we had choughs, but no, just very agile jackdaws. Fulmars were also busy flying along the cliff face, a superb flying machine they are too.

The kittiwakes were bathing on the loch and teal were again present, that was no doubt a regular breeding location for them. For several of my companions, it was their first opportunity to see teal in full breeding plumage; in that condition, they almost looked exotic. Some bird. Another good day's birding.

After spending two days on the coast, we thought a change was required, so the next day saw us at Keilder Forest and Reservoir. The day was glorious, hardly a breath of wind and the sun was most warm; certainly, no woollies were required on that day.

We commenced looking over the reservoir, the anticipated birds were to be seen little grebes, great crested grebes, mallards, coots, moorhens, mute swans and Canada geese; nothing overly exciting there. The odd lapwing was along the shore and a common snipe gave us a flypast, that bucked things up a little. One of my colleagues then drew our attention to two duck way out on the water, two wigeon, both drakes. That was a bit special as wigeon are winter visitors to our shores and to see two in June was not expected. Could they also be breeding so far north, along with the odd teal?

Time now for the woodlands. These were full of bird song, almost like a delayed 'dawn chorus'. Blackcaps were particularly vocal, but many other species were doing their best to compete; willow warblers and garden warblers especially so.

Moving into the coniferous plantation area coal tits were heard calling and the bird we really wanted joined in, the metallic 'kip, kip' of the crossbill rang out. A magnificent crimson looking bird flew into an adjoining pine tree and commenced to chip away at a cone. Bits were flying everywhere as the bird attacked the cone. In the bright sunlight he looked superb. They are quite a bird, and that one certainly made our day. We all had wonderful views of the fellow one or two of my colleagues commented it was the best view they had ever had. It cannot get better than that!

The crossbill may have been the bird of the day, but in total, we saw sixty-three species; very good numbers for the habitat we were in. Keilder had done its job.

Lindisfarne now called, the tide was perfect for us to drive across. On the Lough the usual birds were to be seen, grebes, mallards, coots and moorhens, along with many black-headed gulls which nested close by. Out at sea gannets, fulmars, gulls -various, terns, auks, one or two family parties of eider ducks, one with quite large ducklings, and occasional shelducks. We were very fortunate that day to also see Manx and sooty shearwaters pass through, the latter most unexpected. We located a male wheatear collecting food, it obviously had a nest near, and the song of skylarks was heard. Ringed plover were no doubt breeding judging by their activity and we were delighted to see a solitary purple sandpiper dressed in full summer plumage – some bird.

Curlews and oystercatchers were spread along the shore line and the odd redshank was to be seen. Stonechat numbers were good, a most attractive bird, especially the male. One family of birds we did not experience were birds of prey.

This did surprise me as kestrels had been seen regularly and the odd peregrine had also put in an appearance, but not that day.

Lindisfarne had not disappointed. A few questions had been raised about the name of Holy Island, so a brief reason may be of interest. The holy relics of St. Cuthbert were originally buried in the Priory and it was to pay homage to his memory that many pilgrims visited the island – hence the name Holy Island. Holy Island is part of the Lindisfarne National Nature Reserve which not only covers the island it also includes

Budle Bay, Fenham Flats and Ross Back Sands, an area of 8,650 acres of wonderful bird watching potential throughout the year. You could spend several days just there.

As a change Wallington Hall Estate now called. For some of us a break from birding was required, so the Hall itself was visited; the remainder went walk-about to see what we could find.

Among the birds seen or heard were the following: little grebes, goosanders, curlews, common sandpipers, a solitary green sandpiper, the inevitable black-headed gulls, great spotted woodpeckers and an audible green woodpecker, nuthatches, a treecreeper, several species of warblers including the wood warblers, spotted flycatchers and a pied flycatcher. Buzzards were consorting overhead and a pair of raven put on quite an aerial display for us. As we drove out, we stopped near to Paine's Bridge where we added dipper and grey wagtail to our list. They gave us forty-eight species for the day. We were more than happy with that. Our final day arrived and the Farnes, was our chosen destination. Only twelve of us made the journey, some wished to visit Alnwick Castle and do a bit of gift shopping. For those of us visiting the Farnes I had been able to confirm that we could visit both Inner Farne and Staple Island. You will remember when Dorothy and I were last here we could not land on Staple Island, so that was new territory for us both. I had warned my companions to make sure they had sturdy hats as they were more than likely to be attacked by the terns, the Arctic terns particularly so, and attack us they certainly did. We quickly moved on to the Sandwich tern colony, they were far more accommodating, although being larger and could do more damage. There we concentrated our attention on searching for the roseate terns.

We were initially surprised to see a large number of car tyres among the colony and a warden happened to be passing, so we raised the question. Apparently, in Canada, they had discovered the fact that terns would nest quite happily inside a tyre, which not only gave them protection from the weather, the tyre also protected them from predation. It was being tried out on the Farnes and appeared to be successful. A pair of roseate terns had taken residence in one of the tyres, and although we could not see the bird once it entered the tyre, we at least knew exactly where to look to see the bird arrive and depart. No complaints from us.

It may not have looked pretty, scattered tyres, but if it worked, and it appeared to be; it was a thought for other tern colonies, as well as an unusual recycling use for old tyres! The shags were very confident again and my group were thrilled to bits to be able to get so close to a bird normally seen out at sea. The eiders were also confiding, the odd female sitting eggs and they were not going to move off, they just sat there studying us, we returning the compliment. The puffins were up to their usual tricks, strutting about and stopping to stare up at us lesser mortals. At times they were only feet away, providing splendid views, and causing many an expression of wonder. They are just an incredible bird. I often joke they look like miniature waiters in their black and white plumage, and they strut about like them too!

Time to sail on to Staple Island. Guillemots and puffins bred there in goodly numbers as do fulmars and kittiwakes along the cliffs. Razorbills were also to be seen although they did seem to be more difficult to find, so much time had to be spent searching along the cliff ledges. One thing which did impress me was the number of 'bridled' guillemots we saw. These are not a different species, it is just the fact that some of the guillemots have white ring round the eye and a white line behind the eye, which makes them quite distinctive.

Our holiday was drawing to a close, one last look round picked up rock pipits and rock doves, and we were on our way.

The weather had been kind, the hotel very comfortable, and the birding was superb. During the week we saw one hundred and nine different species, so who knows, we might return.

Late June saw us in 'Twitch' mode. A rare bird, a river warbler, had been reported from Doxey Marsh, which is near to Stafford. Less than an hour away for us. This could not be passed by, so an evening trip was quickly organised, and twelve of us made the journey. We were all after a 'Lifer' and when one is so close to home you must have a go for it.

We arrived to a scene of chaos, almost; cars were parked in all over the place and suitable parking for three cars certainly took some finding, but we managed. Judging by the number of cars catching up with this bird was not going to be difficult, it was going to be just the question of locating the birders. After a ten-minute walk down into the marsh, the birders were soon seen, and they must have been in almost triple figures;

the bird was a mega sighting after all is said.

We quickly made our way to the group and found one or two familiar faces among the crowd. They quickly put us onto the bird, which was what we typical call an L.B.J. 'a little brown job'. Fortunately, it did have one or two special characteristics, which I had read up about prior to our trip. The first thing was the call, the best way to describe this is as a monotonous insect like sound, not a call you would normally associate with a bird, and it kept this up for very long spells which was helpful. It had pale undersides and a very streaky breast, and when the tail was seen it was quite rounded with rather large pale under tail coverts. This was a bird to thoroughly enjoy, and we did. A most unexpected bird, a 'Twitch' to remember. July saw us back up to The Lakes and Leighton Moss for the day. In The Lakes, Haweswater was our destination; several of my colleagues had never seen golden eagle in England, so it was time to put that right.

It was an early start, we departed at 6.00 a.m. and had a very good drive up. Eleven of us made the journey in three cars, and the weather was good. Walking down to the valley to the spot where the eagles could be viewed we chalked up wood warbler, redstart, pied flycatcher, ring ousel and peregrine falcon. Near the viewing area, we had wheatear and a common sandpiper; not a bad start.

The golden eagle was sitting on a crag near to the nest and the wardens had it in their scopes, so we had very good views. There was also movement on the nest where a large youngster was moving about. It was expected to fly over the next few days, that would have been some sight. The adult bird flew off its crag and we were able to watch the bird circling in the sky before it flew out of the valley. Those of us who had never seen the eagle previously saw it at its best that day. Now down to Leighton Moss.

It was very quiet there, but we spent some time looking at the collection birds. It was a good opportunity of getting close to birds that would never happen in the wild, so it was a very useful exercise.The following few months were very repetitive and with the exception of a Carolina wood duck, seen at Chasewater, nothing special was seen until September. Here we made two visits to Spurn Point. Our first was right at the start of the month, the 1st September, and the best birds we saw that day were Arctic skua, black-tailed godwit, curlew sandpiper, little stint and Sandwich tern. The second visit was on the 23rd September and there we fared better. We saw sixty-five species on the day, the pick of those being bar-tailed godwit, black-tailed again, booted warbler, brent goose, firecrest, goldcrest, icterine warbler, Lapland bunting, little stint, merlin, pied flycatcher, red-backed shrike, ring ouzel, siskin, spotted flycatcher and wryneck – some real quality there. For many of my group, the two warblers and the wryneck were 'Lifers'. Needless to say, we all chalked up a few 'Year Ticks', me included.

Early October saw us on a local 'Twitch'. A Sabines gull had appeared at Blithfield Reservoir. A 'Lifer' for everyone except me, we had to chase this one up. A large number of birders were at Blithfield on that day. Fortunately, being a key-holder, I was able to gain access to the reservoir so we were able to avoid the crush. Twelve of us, packed into three cars, made the journey round the perimeter of the reservoir, heading in the direction of the Angling Club from where the bird had last been reported.

We had hardly entered the reservoir before we had our first 'cracker' of the day. A superb male snow bunting was popping on and off the wire fence, we certainly stopped to admire this fellow; a 'Lifer' for some. Driving on, a Carolina wood duck was picked up on the water, a drake. That was the second time we had seen this species locally, which does not occur very often. We stopped near to the Angling Club H.Q. and set up our scopes, the serious work of the day was now commencing. Sabines gulls are a vagrant from northern America and Greenland, and are a rare bird in the UK. This bird, we understood, was a juvenile. They are a small gull with longish wings for their size and have a slightly forked tail, not unlike a tern in many respects, and the best guide for us was to look for a small gull with very dark markings on the upper wing surfaces. It did not take us long to find our quarry. It was consorting with a group of black-headed gulls and it stood out really well for us. Being a near-Arctic species they are quite accommodating, man is not something they are too familiar with, and at times this bird came in really close to us so we all had splendid views. As 'Lifers' go, my colleagues had a beauty!

On that day, Blithfield was exceptionally rewarding. As well as the birds already mentioned, the pick of other birds seen were – buzzard, common gull, curlew sandpiper, dunlin, greenshank, little stint, ruddy duck, ruddy shelduck and ruff. Not a bad selection less than ten miles from home. Fifty-eight on the day.

Later in the month, Dorothy and I had a four-day break in Dorset and a very pleasant and rewarding time it turned out to be. We found a very good country hotel near to Weymouth from where we were able to have superb walks and also visit the local birding hot spots such as Radipole Lake and Portland Bill, so it was a very relaxing holiday which produced some interesting birds. The Cetti's warblers at Radipole were very vocal, and for once were visible. Kingfishers were also active, providing us with several good views.

On our day at Portland Bill, we really hit the jackpot. We arrived to find much excitement going on, birders were everywhere. After asking the obvious question, we were duly informed that a northern waterthrush and a subalpine warbler were on the Bill, both 'Lifers'. Our holiday suddenly became a 'Twitch'.

It was not difficult to see where the two birds were, all you had to do was look for groups of birders, and two were quickly located. We made our way to the nearest.

Running round on a grassy area was the northern waterthrush, a bird I had never dreamed of seeing in my life. Up till that day it had only been a picture in a book, a real mega 'Lifer' this one. They are a north American species and their recordings in the UK are just about in double figures. Very similar to a warbler in behaviour, with a distinctive eyebrow and spotted chest and belly, the spots almost run into stripes they are so close. Now for the subalpine warbler.

These are a southern European species, which I had seen when abroad, be great to get it onto my UK List.

As we approached the other group of birders, one of them shouted to us and pointed. A small bird was flying low over the ground to stop and perch up on a small bush; we had it, the subalpine was in clear view. As with many of the rarer species seen at this time of the year, the majority are juvenile birds, which explains why they are here and completely lost. This bird was probably just months old and in many respects looked like a small whitethroat, and if your view was just brief, could easily have been mistaken. Not that day, we had the bird sitting out and almost in display mode. Two cracking birds, and just a few yards apart; well, about two hundred to be more accurate! I walked across to the birder who had pointed the bird out to us, and he turned out to be a from Birmingham, quite a coincidence. When chasing rarities, it certainly helps when many other birders are likewise involved. We had not worked for these two birds that was for sure.

Those few days had turned out very well for us. We may have had only fifty-eight birds over the four days, but two 'Lifers' were not anticipated.

The end of the month saw the group in 'Twitch' mode once again. An Isabelline shrike had been reported from Holme Next the Sea in Norfolk, so an early start was again demanded, and twelve of us made the journey. One consolation about Norfolk is the fact that even if you fail to see your target birds there are always plenty of interesting birds to see. Another 'Lifer' had issued out a challenge, which was taken up!

They are a bird from north west Europe and central Asia, and had no rights to be in the UK. We were hundreds of miles from their normal migratory routes, and as with the case of the warbler earlier, this was also a juvenile. In this plumage state they look very similar to a juvenile red-backed shrike, but are slightly longer tailed. Once again it may be the case of looking for the birders rather than the bird, such was the quality of it.

Parking up at Holme we met a birder who was returning from seeing the bird, so he pointed us in the right direction. A group of birders quickly hove into view, and we made our way to join them. We did not need anyone to point the bird out to us on this occasion. Shrikes rarely hide away, and this bird was no exception. It was standing on a fence post giving the impression it was just as interested in us, as we were in it.

A juvenile it most certainly was, of what sex I had no idea, but it could easily have been mistaken for a first winter red-backed shrike, had we not been so close to the bird and having such a clear view. Look in your field guide and you will see what I am saying. Fortunately, it was a more grey-buff colour and not so scaly on the back as the red-backed shrike. Small differences, but importantly so.

Our 'Lifer' was in the bag.

Now for Titchwell, a little further down the coast. Nothing quite as exciting there, but we still had some very interesting birds. The pick of those being barnacle goose, bar-tailed godwit, gannet, grey plover, jacksnipe, little egret, red-throated diver, sanderling, Slavonian grebe and snow goose. We had seventy-three on the day, well worth the effort.

We had not finished 'Twitching', the chance of more 'Lifers' for many of us called. An American golden plover had been reported from Rutland Water, so fourteen of us made our way in early November. We called in at Eyebrook Reservoir first as a ring-necked duck and a scaup had been reported from there and for many of the group these were also 'Lifers', it looked like a very productive day lay ahead.

Both the Eyebrook birds were drakes so that made things a little easier. The scaup was quickly located, which was a wonderful start, now the hard work loomed. They could quickly be passed over as tufted ducks, especially at this time of the year when they were moving into an eclipsed state, moulting out of their summer plumage.

Our luck was in once again. A small party of duck sailed past and amongst them was our duck. It still had much of its summer plumage left so the grey flanks were still showing well which stood out from the white of the tufted ducks. We had the bird for a few minutes before it drifted from sight. We moved on to Rutland in happy state.

The Information Centre provided us with the information we required for the location of the American golden plover, it could actually be seen from the Centre itself. There was only one problem, the bird was a member of a large flock of about two hundred golden plovers, so it was going to take some sorting out

The bird was a juvenile, which could make things a little easier. The American version is slightly larger than ours, slimmer and with a shorter bill. The wings extend marginally beyond the tail and the legs are longer and darker than our golden plover. It is generally darker than our species and has a distinctive pale eyebrow contrasting with a dark line running through the eye. Small detail, but it was at least something to work on. During the next half an hour or so we had several bits of excitement, but nothing conclusive. Then a birder further along the viewing station shouted, 'I believe I have it.' We swung round to see where he was pointing and a dozen or so scopes were concentrated on the area. He was right, the bird was now in full view and twenty or so birders were very happy. The birder who had found this bird certainly deserved a slap on the back. Thanks to him, many of my colleagues had now seen three 'Lifers' that day which cannot be bad.

We could now commence more relaxed birding, the pressure was off! Among the birds seen were: fieldfare, gadwall, goosander, green sandpiper, jacksnipe, pintail, pochard, redshank, redwing, ruddy duck, ruff and short-eared owl. In total, at both locations, we had sixty-seven species with some quality amongst them. A most successful day.

Over the past few months, I had come to a major decision and it was nothing to do with birds. I was now in my sixty-third year and I began to think more and more about retirement. I had been fortunate in making provision over the years and decided the time was now right to retire. The end of the year would see me relaxing at last and spending more time doing the things I enjoyed the most. Dorothy would, unfortunately, have to wait a year or two prior to her retirement, but it would give me the opportunity of doing more in the house which would mean Dorothy and I had more time at the weekends to spend doing the things we liked together. You do only have one life, so make the best of it.

Back to birding. The year to date had been so successful we had all broken the 200 species mark for the year, so it was suggested that for our last two or so meetings; could I possibly sort out a rarity or two, my colleagues were obviously in 'Twitch' mode! Let us hope I could rise to the challenge.

Late November I could. A Bonaparte's gull, a rare north American vagrant had been reported from north Wales, near to Rhyl, and had been seen over a period of three days, the bird looked settled in. Sixteen of us made the journey, all, apart from me, after a 'Lifer', and I had only seen two previously so I was just as happy to chase the bird. The bird was an adult in winter plumage, quite similar to a black-headed gull at a similar age. Fortunately, it had two distinctive differences, it lacked the black primaries and red bill of the black-headed; instead, it had a black trailing edge to the rear of the wing and a black bill. It also behaves differently when feeding picking its food from the surface of the water, and in flight it is more delicate, almost tern-like. Hopefully, we had enough to go on.

We arrived at its last reported location and settled down to study the large number of gulls which were on the scene. We were lucky, although being November, it was a relatively mild day with no wind and the tide was coming in, which at least brought the birds in closer. They do say patience is a virtue, and that day it was needed. We had arrived at 10.30 a.m., and by noon the tide was fully in. We were the only people on that area of beach and I was beginning to wonder if my information was correct, when along the tide line came our bird, and it put on quite a show for us. You would have thought the bird was trying to reward us for waiting so long, at times it was that close binoculars were hardly required. We watched the bird for fully half an hour before it drifted off. What a 'Twitch' and what a bird.

The Bonaparte's was not all we saw that day, we had fifty-three birds on the day; the pick of the remaining being black-tailed godwits, curlews, dunlins (thousands of those), grey plovers, knots, a Manx shearwater, a merlin, a peregrine falcon and shags. A day to remember.

We concluded the year with a trip down to Sheerness and Slimbridge to finish the year off with a few choice geese and swans, and we were not disappointed. On the day, we saw fifty-nine species the pick of which were – barnacle goose, Bewick's swan, brent goose, mandarine, peregrine falcon, pintail, ruddy duck, smew, and whooper swan. Enough there to end the year.

As I had mentioned earlier, all my group members cleared the two hundred mark for the year; I myself had 235, my highest number seen in a single year in the UK.

What would '97 bring in? Initially, not my immediate retirement. I was asked to stay on for a few months in an advisory role, which I could hardly refuse so my retirement was on the back burner slightly.

The year commenced with a local day out within the boundaries of Staffordshire, and an exceptional day it turned out to be. We travelled just over sixty miles and the pick of the fifty-three birds seen were barn owl, gadwall, glaucous gull, goldcrest, little owl, ruddy duck, scaup, shag (a most unusual species so far in land), shorelark, smew and woodlark. What a start to a new year.

Later in the month, we were up to Southport and Martin Mere where more choice species were added to our 'Year's List'. The best of the bunch being barnacle goose, Bewick's swan, brambling, curlew, dunlin, golden plover, knot, merlin, peregrine falcon, pink-footed goose, pintail, red-throated pipit (the bird of the day – a 'Lifer' for most), ruff, white-fronted goose and whooper swan. We had sixty-nine on the day, and most of us had reached the hundred mark before the end of January. No complaints with that start to a fresh year.

Lee Valley and Wraysbury called early February, ring-necked parakeets being again on the agenda, a bit of a 'Twitch' this one. We had fifty-three birds on the day which plus the parakeets, the pick were common gull, goshawk, lesser redpoll, smew and water rail. We were more than happy with those.

The end of February saw us on the Staffordshire Moors, with two birds in particular in mind; long-eared owls and red grouse. Calling in at Park Hall initially, we quickly located the long-eared owls, seven in fact. A bumper owl morning especially as we saw a roosting tawny as we exited. The Moors did not let us down, the red grouse were very active and during a couple of hours we saw those well into double figures. A small number of golden plovers had also returned to their nesting grounds and they looked very smart indeed. The range of species was not great, forty-five in total, but we saw the two we were particularly interested in which is what matters the most.

March and Wales called, the Elan Valley, time for some red kite hunting, and they did not let us down. Their numbers are slowly building up and as we neared Devil's Bridge, we saw seven in the air together; a truly wonderful sight.

Devil's Bridge was not to be out done. The crossbills were very accommodating and the majority were males. Crossbills breed very early and it was a safe guess that the females were already sitting eggs. Studying the crossbills closely we had a great surprise, and an adrenalin rush quickly followed. A superb male parrot crossbill was with the group, and what a bird. For many of my colleagues, the day had taken a new turn; it was 'Lifer' time, and this one was totally unexpected.

We still had time and the light that day was good, so we decided to nip down to Aberystwyth, and this turned out to be a good decision. In transit we picked up buzzard, goshawk, raven and more kites, and at Aber' we saw ringed plovers, turnstones and purple sandpipers. It had turned out a very good day, only forty-eight different species seen, but some quality included.

Towards the end of the month, it was decided a bit of hawfinch hunting was called for. There are certain birds you always wish to have on your 'Year List' and hawfinch are such a bird. We would combine this with a visit to the Clent Hills, new bird watching territory for most of my friends.

Our first stop was Ludlow, and there we were not disappointed. The hawfinch put on quite a display for us; we actually saw four together at one point, which was a bit special. The river provided us with several views of dipper and a pair of goosander were also in attendance, seeing them so late in the year made us wonder if they were settling in to breed. Grey wagtails were also busy, these no doubt would be breeding. Raven were heard calling but not seen. Now for the Clent Hills.

We had a pleasant surprise on our drive across to Clent. We had a red kite, the first I have ever seen in Worcestershire; were they beginning to spread out of Wales and into England?

We had to work hard for our birds at Clent, but it proved worth it. A few of the more difficult birds to get were seen. A goshawk put on a superb flying display for us and seemed as interested in us as we were of him. A pair of buzzards were active, they looked as though they were both food hunting; no doubt, they had a nest with chicks nearby. We stumbled on a long-tailed tit nest building in a gorse bush, we rapidly retreated not wanting to disturb the bird. Titmice were plentiful, as well as the long-tailed we saw blue, coal, great, marsh and willow tits. There are not many days you see all the resident titmice at one location. We also had two woodpeckers, great-spotted and green, plus nuthatch and a crossbill. A very good collection in fact, and as we drove homewards we had the bird of the day, a rough-legged buzzard. That brought a very good day to a happy conclusion. As I have mentioned before, you need not travel long distances to see interesting birds; we are very fortunate in this country of ours. April and Norfolk called. The avocets had commenced their arrival, so along with the bearded tits and marsh harriers we knew what we were after. Hunstanton and Titchwell were our destinations.

We were lucky with the tide, it was fully in when we arrived at Hunstanton and a large flock of scoters were close in, several hundred of them, which had to be studied in detail and we were mighty glad we did.

We spent over half an hour going through these birds and we hit the jackpot: included amongst them were both surf and velvet scoters. Believe me, it is not often you can see all three species together, and for my colleagues, they all had at least one 'Lifer'; unfortunately, not me, I had to settle for 'Year List' birds – not that I was complaining. The fulmars were back on the cliffs sorting out their nesting locations and along the cliff top we had both wheatear and whinchat. Skylarks were also serenading us from above. One last look over the sea produced another cracker for us, a drake long-tailed duck was picked up. We were very pleased we had called in at Hunstanton. Now for Titchwell.

We had not left the car park before we saw our first marsh harrier and heard the avocets calling, we were obviously in for a good day. We quickly saw the avocets and the bearded tits were most co-operative, they came to see us. We had eleven species of waders, plus the best of the remaining, brent goose, common gull, grey partridge, red-breasted merganser, water pipit, water rail, sand martin, shorelark, swallow and a white wagtail. In total we had sixty-nine species on the day.

The end of April saw us locally. Willington, where a decent selection of waders had been reported, and then we would go grouse hunting on the Moors. Willington provided us with seven waders including our first common sandpiper and little ringed plovers of the year. Sedge warblers and reed warblers were also seen and we added house martin to our 'Year Lists'. We were more than happy with that.

The Moors were rather gloomy and our hopes were not high, but fortune favoured us. Driving across Axe Edge Moor we saw several red grouse, many of these were very vocal, and the ring ouzel site really did hit the jackpot. We had a pair of ring ouzels very close in and we saw these birds mate on a few occasions, they obviously were going to breed there, something for the future possibly. We also had wheatear, stonechat and curlew, a very interesting half an hour this turned out to be. Swallow Moss now called, would we be lucky with the black grouse? For one or two of my colleagues this would be a 'Lifer'.

Swallow Moss is at a lower altitude than Axe Edge and the weather was far more agreeable. Red grouse greeted us on arrival and a cuckoo was calling in the distance, not a bad greeting that. We started to walk down towards the farm where the black grouse tended to roost up in a small group of Scot's pines, when one of my friends shouted and pointed, 'What's that?' He had never seen black grouse previously, but he had now found six of them. This quickly brought a smile to his face. You can never beat finding your own 'Lifer', even if initially you do not know what it is, you have commenced a 'learning curve' and you will never forget it. The grouse all flew into their roosting trees and provided us with superb views. They were all males, 'black cocks', the females were quite probably now sitting eggs, and we wished them luck.

Our day was now concluded, and once again we had done very well, reiterating earlier comment regarding the fact you do not have to travel vast distances to see wonderful and exciting birds. They may be nearer than you think, you just have to go and look. Sometimes, they may even come and look at you!

During April, I reached the one hundred and fifty mark, and many of my colleagues were not far behind. The signs were again looking good.

The new month saw me in as one of the great unemployed, my retirement had finally arrived and I had much to look forward to. I became involved with the Staffordshire Wildlife Trust as a volunteer warden at their local nature reserve – Croxall Lakes. I fully intended to keep myself as active as possible.

May saw us on a group holiday once again, these were proving very popular, with the Lake District being our venue. Eighteen of us made the journey. We all met up at Leighton Moss on the way up and there we started well with bittern, common sandpiper, common tern, cuckoo, curlew, greenshank, redshank and ringed plover being the pick. In The Lakes one bird obviously drew us the most, the golden eagle. This was the only English breeding pair, the rest of the UK population are all in Scotland, hence their being a little bit special.

Good weather was required for the walk to the eagle site in Riggindale Valley, and come Tuesday this arrived. On the walk down the pick of the birds seen were garden warbler, great spotted woodpecker, nuthatch, peregrine falcon, raven, redstart, ring ouzel, stonechat, wheatear and wood warbler; plus, obviously, the golden eagle. The eagle was very active and it produced several flypasts for us, and when in flight, and so close at times, you could really appreciate the size of the bird – it cannot be much fun being a rabbit!

On our way home we had a quick look over Haweswater where we saw eider, garganey, red-breasted merganser and a final flypast from the eagle. That was a good wave goodbye! But that was not going to be our final piece of enchantment. Dorothy suddenly pointed, we were in the lead car. On the stone wall, alongside the road, were two red squirrels which just sat there looking at us. We even managed to get out of our cars to enjoy them as they sat there for a good four or so minutes, a few cameras were whirring away that was for sure. All good things come to an end, the squirrels jumped off the wall, dashed across the road, and vanished into nearby woodland. To some of us, who had never seen red squirrels previously, that beat the golden eagles' goodbye!

That day was going to take some beating, and so it proved, although St Bees Head tried. It may not have the number of birds to be seen at Bempton, but it had still the largest numbers of nesting sea birds on the west coast of England. The principal species were kittiwakes, guillemots and razorbills, with a small number of puffins and black guillemots. It is the only breeding site in England for the latter, which was our main reason for visiting; most of the group had never seen the bird before.

It proved not very easy, there are probably only ten pairs or so, but our patience was finally rewarded: one popped out of a crack in the cliff and sat out in full view. The bird may only be black and white, but in that day's sunlight it looked magnificent, and one again the cameras whirred. A solitary bird it may have been, but you only need one for a 'Lifer'. There were a few happy smiles on the journey back to the hotel.

Leighton Moss, the Riggindale Valley and St Bees Head produced the top birds but we saw a good range, walked in some superb country, had many a good meal and wine, so once again we all enjoyed ourselves. As a group, we get on very well together. The total number of species seen during the week was eight-seven.

The remainder of May saw us nightingale and golden oriole hunting, successfully, I am pleased to say, and in early June our annual trip up to Bempton called.

The end of the month brought us into 'Twitch' mode once again. A very rare bird, a great reed warbler had been reported from near to Nottingham, we had to have a go for that, a 'Lifer' for us all.

A lovely June day saw fifteen of us off on our quest. Netherfield Lagoons was our destination, an area none of us had visited previously, but I had taken the usual procedure of obtaining the map reference. I had seen the bird previously when in the Mediterranean region, but to get one on my UK List had never been contemplated. I was as excited with the prospect as all my group, and the one thing which would help us find the bird was its voice, this being exceedingly loud and would carry long distance. We welcomed all the help we could get!

Netherfield Lagoons looked a most unlikely spot, right next door to a large retail park, but birds are not interested in beauty; their requirements are rather basic, food and cover, and the Lagoons had this.

We found parking area and made our way in. I doubt if we had walked many yards before a burst of call rang out, our great red warbler was here alright, and it intended us to know. We followed the sound to the edge of a type of slurry lagoon, and the call was coming from a dense patch of nettles and bramble, nothing reed-like about this location, not that we thought too much about that. We only wanted to see the bird, and this was not easy. It called almost continuously, but steadfastly remained well hidden. Several minutes passed us by when we had the bit of luck always needed in these situations. A blackbird flew into the tangle, very noisily and violently almost, and up flew our bird.

Great reed warblers are not big in the glamour stakes, but we were not interested in that. A little brown job it may well be, but it was a mega 'L.B.J.' to us. They are larger than our own reed warbler, almost thrush size, with a more prominent supercilium, a pronounced forehead and a heavier bill.

One thing which surprised us, and it was not the bird, it was the fact that we were the only birders there enjoying the warbler. For a rarity of this quality, we would have expected a large number of birders present. The bird had only been there for a few days, we could but presume, other birders had been there earlier than us and were now off elsewhere.

We were about to move on as a very large group of birders came into sight, they waved at us, we waved back and pointed, they moved on at a faster gait. They were a party from Liverpool who had come down by coach in the hope of seeing the bird, their hopes were fulfilled. We left them to it and moved on.

Our next destination was Clumber Park, locally to here honey buzzard were regularly seen and reported, from the Wellbeck Abbey Estate. We called in at Clumber, initially, to see if we could find the hawfinches and mandarin ducks; we failed miserably, but at least the coffee etc was very welcomed. Now for the view point over Wellbeck.

This did not take much finding, twenty or so birders were already in attendance and they were able to report that a honey buzzard had been seen on several occasions during the day. Hopefully, it was just a question of waiting. This view point is a well-known raptor viewing location and whilst waiting for the main bird we saw several buzzards, a goshawk, a sparrowhawk and a pair of kestrels, a very good tally, then what we were after arrived on the scene. Arrived is a slight exaggeration, it flew through at speed and was barely in sight for thirty seconds, but that is a long time compared with nothing at all. Fortunately, it flew very close to us so limited in time it may have been, but the view of the bird was crisp and clear.

Unlike the majority of raptors which are red blood or fish eaters, the honey buzzard is an insect eater, hence the name. It does not eat honey, but feeds on the larvae of bees and wasps and will destroy their nests to get at the larvae. Due to this it does not have the large and powerful bill or head of the majority of predators, and for the size of the bird, the head is just about cuckoo size. Other predators have clear nostrils, no feathering which would get covered in blood; the honey buzzard, on the other hand, has feathers covering the nostrils which protect the bird from insect stings.

The bird did not return, but we were happy enough. A great reed warbler and a honey buzzard were enough to satisfy anyone. The majority of my friends went home with two 'Lifers', I was more than content with one plus a 'Year Tick'.

Later in July we visited the south coast, the Dawlish Warren area where we were again after one specific bird, the cirl bunting. They are our rarest breeding bunting with a very small population, and principally located in Devon. A bird which, once again, the majority of my colleagues had never seen – 'Twitch-time' called.

The actual location of where they breed is kept as secret as possible, so please excuse me if I do not divulge this. We arrived at Dawlish just as the tide was turning and we were surprised by the number of birders in attendance. I recognised a couple of them as members of the West Midlands Bird Club, and they quickly explained the reasons for the crowd. A semi-palmated plover, a rare wader from over the Pond was on the beach, and it did not take long to find the bird, there were over a hundred birders looking for it. A cry went up, birders pointed, and there was the little beauty. Prior to our arrival we had heard nothing about this bird, so this was some greeting.

Many of my colleagues had never heard of the bird, and it was not to be found in their field guides and my knowledge of the bird was very scant, we had an unexpected 'Lifer'. They breed in the near-Arctic and at initial glance they are similar to our ringed plover, but luckily for us there was a birder present who was able to point out the minor differences to us; all I can say is that it was a good job he was there. You cannot beat experience, and this birder had seen the bird in the States. It turned out he was the birder who actually identified the bird in the first place; we were glad he was still around.

The tide retreated further out and so did the birds as they followed it, so we made our way further along the shore, where yet another treat awaited us. A small party of Manx shearwaters were feeding and a group of birders called us across and pointed out one of the birds which showed a few minor differences with the rest of the birds, here again it was jackpot time. The bird was a variant of the Manx shearwater, it was a Yelkouan shearwater, another bird which was but a name to me, my colleagues had never heard the name previously. It is a bird from the Mediterranean area and few ever reach as far west as the UK. What a morning, two 'Lifers' in almost as many minutes and we had yet to see the bird we really came for. Devon was on the map as far as birding was concerned.

Now for the cirl bunting, this was at least illustrated in our field guides. I had the map reference once again and we made the journey from the Warren, parking up near to some old and empty buildings, a most unlikely spot for a rare bird. This bird was not so co-operative as the previous two had been and it took us almost an hour before it put in an appearance, but it was the male and well worth the wait. The bird landed on some overhead wires and preened itself, providing us with very good views indeed. It only stayed for a couple of minutes before flying off, and that was the last we saw of it. No one was complaining, we had seen fifty-one birds on the day, three of which were absolute crackers!

August saw us off to Norfolk, visiting Estuary Farm and Titchwell. Estuary Farm was a new area for us and the reason for the visit was the fact a crane had been seen there regularly, once again a 'Lifer' called. Cranes do breed in Norfolk, just a very small colony hung on, so the chances of us seeing the bird were good, and so it proved. We only saw one bird, but one is more than enough as far as 'Lifers' are concerned. We moved on to Titchwell happy in mind.

Titchwell was its usual. Avocets, bearded tits and marsh harriers put on a grand show and various waders also did their best. The pick of these being bar and black-tailed godwits, green sandpiper, grey plover, ruff, sanderling and wood sandpiper; in total, we had seventy-nine species. Another very satisfactory trip.

Late August saw us off to Blacktoft Sands where the usual selection of waders were seen, but the best bird of the day was a Savi's warbler, 'Lifer' time for many of my friends. They are beginning to think this bird watching is easy! September ospreys called. Rutland Water was on the agenda. We had a very productive day, the best of the bunch being black tern, Egyptian goose, green sandpiper, greenshank, osprey, red-crested pochard, red-necked grebe, ruddy duck, ruff and wood sandpiper. A bit of quality there.

The end of the month saw us in 'Twitch' mode. A black-winged pratincole had been reported at Standish, so we decided to chase after that and then call in at Martin Mere to finish the day off.

The pratincole was reported from a small park and this was quickly located. The bird was associating with a flock of lapwings which visited the park regularly throughout the day, so it was just a question of waiting. We were joined by a group of local birders who had just been to Martin Mere and they informed us that a grey phalarope was there. It looked as though we were in for a good day.

After about half an hour the lapwings put in an appearance, landing on a nearby football pitch and the pratincole was quickly located, a 'Lifer' was easily obtained by us all. Smart looking birds pratincoles, almost swallow-like with their forked tails. The bird had a very distinctive throat marking and very dark upper surfaces to wings, hence the name. We enjoyed the bird for several minutes before they all flew off, a grey phalarope now called, some of my colleagues were after 'Lifer' number two.

Martin Mere was very busy, news of the grey phalarope had brought the keen birders in. We quickly found out where the bird was to be seen and made our way there. We had to wait several minutes to gain entry to the hide as quite a queue was patiently awaiting entry, but we eventually did so.

The bird was quickly pointed out to us and it still had plenty of its summer colour. Although called the grey phalarope they have a large amount of red in their plumage, but as there is also a red-necked phalarope, it is called the grey to avoid confusion. In winter the bird is almost a pure grey.

Phalaropes differ from most birds in the fact the females are more brightly marked than the males, who do the majority of the incubating, hence the colour differences. Judging by the amount of red still in the plumage I think it was safe to call this bird a female. Our bird was out on the water, swimming, and picking up small invertebrates from the surface, occasionally spinning round as it did so. A very active way to feed, spectacular really. Due to the queue we could not stay too long, so we departed to let others in.

Although we had sixty-six birds on the day, with some decent quality amongst them, I think it is safe to say the day will be remembered for two birds only: the pratincole and phalarope, they do not come much better than those.

Early in October saw Dorothy and I off for a week's holiday in Kent, a new part of the country for us. We had always wanted to visit Dungeness where many good birds are seen and we also had the opportunity of visiting Charles Darwin's home, Down House. I know he was a Shropshire man by birth but it was Down House where he wrote the 'On the Origin of Species' in which his theories on evolution completely changed the way we understand our place in the world. Genius is a name frequently used now, here was a man worthy of the accolade. Chartwell, home to another very important person, Winston Churchill no less, lies within the county. Should the weather be poor we would also have Scotney Castle, Sissinghurst Castle and Gardens plus you cannot go down to Kent without visiting the White Cliffs of Dover, no matter how bad the weather. A full week lay ahead.

We stayed at a hotel in Maidstone, which proved to be very comfortable. The weather on the first day was not very clever, so we chose Chartwell as we presumed most of the day would be spent indoors, and this proved to be the case. If you are interested in Winston Churchill, this is a place that must not be missed. It was a fascinating visit and his art collection was most impressive. I had always known he was an accomplished artist, but this was the first time I had ever seen his actual work, the man's talent obviously lay in several directions. The weather improved dramatically, Dungeness called, and we responded. I had not realised the area Dungeness covered, we made our way initially to the RSPB reserve area, and this proved to be the choice of choices. As we booked ourselves in, a birder said, 'I presume you've come to see the plover?'

'What plover?' I enquired.

'The spur-winged plover' came the answer.

No, we had not, but we had now.

This was a bird I had only ever seen in Egypt and never a bird I had thought of seeing in the U.K. Our holiday looked as though it may commence with a 'Lifer'.

Spur-winged plovers are similar in some respects to our lapwings, being a black and white looking bird, but there the resemblance ends. They are a slightly smaller bird, with black head, throat and breast, the back is brown and it lacks the long wispy crest of the lapwing. You may find the odd publication referring to the bird as the spur-winged lapwing they are a very rare vagrant to the UK, and many of the reports have been classed as escapees. Our bird, so we were told, has no visible ring on the legs and is likely to be the genuine article. We were not going to get involved in that argument, we just wanted to see the bird and enjoy it.

We made our way to the view point, which was not difficult to find, there were about fifty or so birders congregated in a group watching the bird. It brought back memories for me of watching and photographing this bird in Egypt some forty plus years ago, both the memories and photographs I still have. Now Dorothy can share the bird with me. Over an hour was spent watching this bird, it will probably be the only time I will ever see it again. Some bird.

A good selection of birds were seen, but nothing else of great importance, so we decided to go across to have a look at the nuclear power station, not a pretty sight, but of interest. We were not allowed in obviously, but it was a very interesting structure, certainly nothing like the coal fired power station local to where we live.

At least it was good to know that nuclear power could be used for peaceful purposes.

Whilst studying the structure Dorothy picked up a small, dark looking bird, flitting along the wire fencing. She was up to her tricks again, she had found us a magnificent male black redstart, which for a few minutes put on quite a display for us. I can only presume there must have been an ants nest on the ground just inside the fence, the bird kept dropping onto the same spot and flying up onto the fence with very small insects in its bill. Whatever they were, the bird was enjoying them, and it ate them to its fill before leaving us.

Dungeness had provided us with two great birds, the plover especially so.

The following day was forecast to be showery so we decided Down House would fit in nicely. This was a most interesting visit and was an idyllic location for the man and his works. To walk in his garden, where many of the theories first originated, was though we were meeting the man. To be in the room where he wrote his work that changed the world's attitude to evolution, was mind stretching. Here was a man whose ideas were totally against the current religious beliefs, and he gained many an enemy in the process.

The weather interfered with the rest of the holiday and in consequence birding was put on the back burner. We did, however, manage to visit the White Cliffs of Dover; you cannot miss out on these when in the area. A most impressive 'lump of chalk', and we could just make out the coast of France, well at least we thought we could! The expected sea birds were to be seen including gannets passing down the Channel and the odd kittiwake and fulmar were still present.

Scotney Castle and Sissinghurst Castle and Gardens were included in our agenda, so a very pleasant holiday was concluded. Not quite as we had hoped, but no complaints, the spur-winged plover had assured us of that.

Later in October we visited North Wales and Gibralter Point, not that anything special or unusual was seen on either of those visits, but you cannot win them all.

Early November saw us back in Norfolk, Titchwell and Cley being on the agenda; many birds at least are guaranteed at those two locations.

At Titchwell we hit the jackpot. A black-winged stilt had been reported for several days, and for many of my colleagues this would be a 'Lifer'. Adrenalin rush time!

Brent geese were already in good numbers, always a bird worth seeing, and several avocets were still to be seen, they had not yet moved off. Waders were well represented, as was to be expected, but where was the wader we were really after?

A party of birders, returning from the beach, were able to inform us the stilt was on the shore and was showing very well. To say we moved on quickly is putting it mildly! A long legged, black and white bird, takes little finding, and we quickly picked it up. Long legged birds do have a certain elegance, and the black-winged stilt emphasises this, a truly special bird. Many years ago they used to breed in the UK, now, unfortunately, they are a rare vagrant, hence our interest. We spent many minutes enjoying this spectacle, before moving back onto the reserve proper.

We were losing light very quickly that day, so we made a hurried visit down to Cley and there we saw a very large flock of golden plovers, many of which still showed their summer plumage. You do not have to wonder where the name came from when you see them is that condition. On the dunes we saw five shorelarks, two of which were smartly attired males, a very attractive bird in that state. Sanderlings were dashing along the tide line, as is their wont, and migrating fieldfares and redwings were still coming in over the sea. A very interesting picture. Thanks to the black-winged stilt my group were certainly getting their rare and unusual species. What can the last few weeks of the year provide?

The end of the month saw us on the Moors. One or two of my colleagues had yet to see the red grouse and long-eared owls, so having decided to put that right, we succeeded and had a bonus for some. The wintering hen harrier was back and he provided us with a special flypast. As one of my friends commented 'It cannot get much better than that'. I concurred!

December included Rutland Water and North Wales where little special was seen. A rock pipit in North Wales was about the pick of the month, being a new bird for two of my members.

The year was now over. I had seen two hundred and thirty-three species, another very good year with a few very special birds, and all my course members broke the two hundred mark. No complaints there. What would '98 bring us? Read on!

At our first indoor meeting of the year, my course members again suggested we had several meetings where we chased special birds, and three new members who had only just joined the group were very enthusiastic about this. The course now had twenty-seven members, and they all appeared to be in 'Twitch Mode'. I was only joking there.

To get some of the more special local birds on the list, our first two field meetings were local, Park Hall, Blithfield Reservoir, Kingsbury Water Park and Drakelow Power Station. These locations were chosen for two reasons: the shortage of daylight in January and an easy introduction to our field meetings for our new members. The pick of the birds seen being barnacle goose, barn owl, common gull, gadwall, goldeneye, ruddy duck, smew, teal and wigeon. Enough there to satisfy the newcomers especially.

February saw us venture a bit further afield, Martin Mere and Southport summoned us. The weather was exceptionally bright for the time of the year and twenty-two of us made the trip. On the day we chalked up sixty-six species; the prime birds being Bewick's swan, curlew, green-winged teal, peregrine falcon, pink-footed goose, pintail, red-breasted merganser, ruddy shelduck, ruff and whooper swan. The weather and the birds were very good that day.

Later in the month, Wales called and we had our usual winter visit to the Elan Valley and Aberystwyth. The expected birds were seen and the odd 'Lifer' was chalked up for our new members. The pick of the birds seen were buzzard, oystercatcher, peregrine falcon (we appeared to be doing rather well with this species), purple sandpiper, raven, red kite, ringed plover, rock pipit, shag, stonechat and turnstone. We were all more than happy with those, and for all of us we had passed the one hundred mark for the year. Early March and the Moors called. Our new members had never seen grouse, so we had to put that right. We called in at Park Hall initially to seek out the long-eared owls, and there we did very well. We actually saw seven different birds roosting in the trees, a wonderful introduction to those who had never experienced the birds previously. A tawny also called, but we were unable to locate the bird.

The red grouse on Axe Edge Moor were very vocal and visible and Swallow Moss did not disappoint. We had three black grouse, all black cocks (the male), roosting in the trees and a superb male stonechat was displaying on the top of a gorse bush, we could not find the female who was the obvious cause of his work. The black grouse numbers seem to be reducing rapidly, I was becoming very concerned as to their future there.

April saw us chasing a couple of special birds, 'Twitch Mode' again, and the Lea Valley and Wraysbury were our destinations with bittern and ring-necked parakeets being our target birds. The bittern was seen in flight on several occasions and judging by the amount of booming he made, he was certainly holding territory. A water rail also put in a brief appearance, but at least we all saw it. The ring-necked parakeets were as noisy and active as ever. I love seeing the birds but I would not welcome them as residents in my garden, that was for sure. It is easy to see why the residents on this estate do not love the birds, and they probably feel the same over some of the birders who arrive there. Unfortunately, there are a few birders who do not respect people's privacy.

The 10th May was Bird Race Day, and we decided to enter a team, with Staffordshire again being our chosen county. Midnight saw us start off in reasonably warm conditions. I knew of a barn owl location nearby so we started off with that, we did not see the bird, but we heard it calling, or to be more accurate, 'screeching'. Birds were not plentiful on that occasion and we only had eighty-four on the day; normally, we get near to the one hundred mark. Not to worry, we made a few pounds for our chosen charities, which it was really all about. May 12th came round, an important day for me, I am now officially retired. I have reached my 65th Birthday. As part of the celebrations, we had a day at Slimbridge, where we had a very pleasant lunch and enjoyed the collection. Whilst we were there, Dorothy collected a birthday gift for me, which she had previously ordered, a signed copy by Peter Scott's daughter, Philippa, of a limited edition print of his painting 'Ground Mist – Pinkfeet'. I am in good company regarding this picture, H.R.H. the Duke of Edinburgh has the original of this painting, my copy, proudly hangs in my lounge, and always will. Thank you, Dorothy, a wonderful gift.

Peter Scott was some artist and a great man, and it is still the proudest moment in my life the fact that I interviewed him many years ago for Radio Birmingham. Memories such as those will remain for ever.

Later in the month saw us off visiting Little Paxton, Fordham and Weeting Heath. We were off after a few specialised birds, and they did not fail us. We knocked up crossbill, cuckoo, nightingale, red-legged partridge, spotted flycatcher, stone curlew, turtle dove, woodlark and yellow wagtail, the pick of the sixty-eight species seen on the day. Most of us also passed the one hundred and fifty mark for the year. Another good year looked likely.

June saw us once again at Bempton Cliffs, this was now an annual pilgrimage, the nearest thing you will ever get to a 'bird city'.

July came in with a visit to Anglesey, black guillemot hunting again, and they did not let us down. A 'Lifer' for many of my friends, but better was yet to come. As we approached South Stack, a group of birders caught our attention. We made our way in their direction and as we did we had a most pleasant surprise: a hooded crow flew directly overhead, and landed on some telephone wires nearby. This was a total surprise, none of us had heard about this bird being present on the island. Hooded crows are native in Scotland, but south of the border they are a very unusual species, and especially that far south. This bird was a 'Lifer' for most of my party, and I had only ever seen the bird in Scotland and on the Continent previously. Anglesey was proving to be a good destination. On the day we saw sixty-nine species and, plus the two previously mentioned, we also saw chough, Isabelline shrike (another 'Lifer' for many of my colleagues), raven, roseate tern, Sandwich tern, turnstone, whinchat and a pair of black swans. Where the latter had escaped from was any one's guess, but they were certainly free fliers, as they proved on several occasions. A most productive day.

August, and we were back to Titchwell. The black-winged stilt, seen late last year was still being reported, and many of my group had not seen the bird, so a definite 'Twitch' was required to put that right. We notched up exactly seventy birds on the day, which I am pleased to report, included the stilt, so all were happy. Other quality birds seen included, avocets, both bar-tailed and black-tailed godwits, eiders, marsh harriers, ruddy ducks, ruffs, sanderlings and spotted redshanks. More than enough to keep the most serious of birders happy.

Early September saw us back at Rutland Water and Eyebrook Reservoir, one or two interesting reports had been coming from those two locations of late, so we put this all to the test.

We were not to be disappointed. The pick at Rutland were black-tailed godwits, curlews, curlew sandpiper (just a single bird), Egyptian geese, green sandpiper, a single bird one again, a little stint, a marsh harrier, two ospreys, a red-crested pochard, several ruffs, some of which were still showing remnants of their summer plumage and a snow goose. Eyebrook had the bird of the day, a blue-winged teal ('Lifer' time for some of my friends), also a drake scaup, a female smew and a small herd of whooper swans. A very interesting selection out of the sixty-nine birds seen on the day.

Mid-September, we were back at Spurn Point. Our hopes that day were for a good passage of birds migrating southwards, shearwaters and skuas in particular, birds we do not see locally very often, if at all. Various terns and gulls were passing through, waders were plentiful and smaller passerines such as pied flycatcher, redstart, wheatear and whinchat were also in transit. Out at sea gannets were feeding and three red-throated divers were on the water, accompanied by a large flock of common scoters. Fulmars were busily gliding past and the odd guillemot was seen.

Arctic skuas were plentiful, harassing the gulls, plus the odd shearwater was way out at sea. As the tide turned, these birds drifted in closer and we were able to identify great shearwaters; only two of them, Manx shearwaters, the most numerous, plus the occasional sooty shearwater. We had seen what we came for; in total, sixty-four species on the day. Spurn Point is one of those locations where you rarely fail to see something of interest, pity it is so far away.

The end of the month was group holiday time, and Norfolk was our destination, with eighteen of us venturing forth. We stayed near to

Titchwell in an hotel I had previously visited, where I knew we would be looked after. The usual locations were visited and for seven of the party it was their first time away with us.

During the week we broke the one hundred mark, just: we saw one hundred and one species. I will not list them all, but the choice birds seen were: avocets, a black-throated diver, the black-winged stilt which was still in attendance, brent geese, Cetti's warblers, a firecrest, great skuas, hawfinches, a hobby, a honey buzzard, little egrets, marsh harriers, a Mediterranean race shearwater, the yelkouan shearwater, three ospreys, pink-footed geese, spoonbills and a spotted crake. Not a bad list at all, a few 'Lifers' there for most of us.

Norfolk is the same as Spurn, a bad day is not possible, and just to prove the point we were back at Spurn later in October. We started off with a surprising bird for Spurn, a bearded tit was seen, the first seen there for several years, so we were reliably informed. Early brambling had arrived from across the water, fulmars and gannets were out at sea, with waders well accounted for. Making our way down to an area locally known as Big Hedge (someone there has a sense of humour, it is just a few scattered remains of a hedge), we had the bird of the day. A great grey shrike had dropped in only that morning, so we were very lucky indeed. Quite a bird, shrikes, they are not termed 'butcher birds' without reason. Their diet is small birds such as blue tits and insects, which when caught they will impale on a thorn and return to eat when hungry. This can be very useful when breeding and having young to feed, a larder helps considerably. Other passerines seen were fieldfare, Lapland bunting, shorelark, redwing and yellowhammer. The pick of the fifty-four birds seen on that day. We had by now all past the two hundred mark for the year, we could safely say we were all more than happy with that.

November saw us in 'Twitch Mode'. A night heron had been reported from North Wales, a new bird for all my group, so the decision was made. I obtained the map reference, as the bird was in a very isolated location, and seventeen of us made the trip. This was a case of driving in convoy with five cars making the journey.

We made our way straight to the area from which the bird had last been reported, which we quickly found thanks the large number of parked up cars. The birders were there in number. The bird was walking about in a local field acting more like a cattle egret, as it was in the company of sheep. We were not bothered about this, we just wanted to see the bird well, and we did. What to do now?

The North Welsh coast was only a few miles away so it was easy to make our minds up. Although we saw nothing to compare with the heron, we had one or two good birds, black guillemot, common scoter, curlew, guillemot, jacksnipe, rock pipit, shag and turnstone being the pick. Total seen fifty-two.

With the year now rapidly drawing to its conclusion, we decided to chase after specific birds and two such birds had been reported from Wakefield 'Anglers Country Park', a new location for all of us. The end of November saw us on our way, fourteen of us, and it was a wet and miserable day. There are four main areas of water in the park, and we had our instructions of which two lakes to visit, which was useful as with the heavy rain we did not wish to stay out in it longer than necessary. Telescopes that day would have been useless, it was difficult enough to keep the binoculars dry.

Due to the weather no other birders were in sight, so it was up to us. They do say you have to be mad to bird watch, and on days such as that, I would find it hard to disagree. Fourteen hardy souls moved on. Fortunately, the birds were very cooperative, and both were males which assisted us appreciably. The first we were after was a long-tailed duck, and it lived up to its name. It still had a long tail which was easily visible, so identification, even in such conditions was no problem. Out first target bird was in the bag, and we were not too wet. Now for number two, a ring-billed duck. This fellow proved a bit more difficult and we got rather damp, but success did not evade us. We found him and he proved to be a bit of a poser, so good views were enjoyed by all. Other birds were seen, the best two being water rail and ruddy duck, but the ultimate winner was the weather. Fourteen, by now very damp birders, returned to their cars, to make their journeys home. Damp we may have been, but we were successful, for most of my colleagues they had also chalked up at least one 'Lifer' each. We were thankful for the cars all having heaters, we dried out slowly.

For our final field meeting of the year, we decided to visit Park Hall and the Moors. We intended to have an owl hunting day, as well as mopping up the grouse. For those who had not seen them previously during the year, Park Hall was most successful. The long-eared owls had obviously heard of our coming, and they sat out in full view. The tawny owl was calling once again, and this time we found him, and as we returned to our cars a little owl was spotted in the quarry. Most successful. Now for the Moors: Axe Edge Moor quickly supplied us with red grouse, so we moved on swiftly to Swallow Moss. A stonechat greeted us on our arrival, no complaints there, and we made our way down towards the farm. We then had to work very hard before we located any black grouse, and it was just a solitary bird, admittedly it was a male, but you know my concern for this species. I really did hope for a few more. From a birding point of view, one is enough to get it on your 'Year List'. As if to compensate for black grouse numbers, one of my colleagues shouted, 'What's that?' Swinging round, two short-eared owls were gliding, low and sedately, over the ground. What a finish to our day. We were able to enjoy those two magnificent birds for several minutes before they vanished from sight. The Moors had done their job that day.

That brought '98 to its conclusion, and another very successful year. It had been not so great in numbers as previous years, but well up for the quality of the birds seen. I had seen two hundred and seventeen species, I was happy with that. We now awaited '99, the final year of the decade.

As well as now being retired, I was also in my sixtieth year of being in love with birds. From my early days of feeding the ducks in the local park and seeing the kingfisher on my father's fishing rods, it has been a life of pure enjoyment and learning. We only have one life, I have no complaints regarding mine, well not so far anyway!

After my initial indoor meeting, the bird study group wished to continue with seeking out the more unusual birds, they did not intend me to have any rest!

We again had a few new faces, so to introduce them to the field meetings we went local, and the Moors called us. Would it be as good as the closing meeting last year? Park Hall was our first calling in point and there the pick of the birds seen were brambling, fieldfare, lesser redpoll, little owl, long-eared owl, redwing, treecreeper and willow tit. The Moors threw in red grouse, short-eared owl, sparrowhawk and yellowhammer. Not a bad start to a new year, we had forty-six species on the day. The newcomers were more than happy with that.

Later in the month saw us travelling further afield, Southport and Martin Mere called. We did rather well, as usually is the case at those two locations. In total we saw sixty-three species, the best being barn owl, curlew, goshawk, knot, mandarin duck, merlin, peregrine falcon, ruff, sparrowhawk and whooper swan. One of my new members commented that he did not know so many different birds could be seen in the UK. I told him to wait until he had completed his first year at it.

Early February saw us have just a couple of hours on a Sunday morning. A great northern diver had been reported at Chasewater, a quality bird to get so early in the year. For the newcomers to birding this was indeed a special bird, as they commented, just a picture in a book, so we hoped to put that right.

No problem. The bird was as good as gold, and showed up well. It was a juvenile, unfortunately, so it did not look as splendid as a full adult, but it was still one hell of a great bird. All of us were happy to chalk this one up so early. As one of my colleagues said, 'Gaffer, you have something to keep it up to now.' He was right, we could only but try!

February and Wales called, time for red kite and the like. We had an early start to make the most of the daylight and called in at Ludlow initially. There we quickly notched up hawfinch, dipper, peregrine falcon and raven. On now to the Elan Valley.

The red kite did not disappoint us, several put on spectacular aerial displays, worth the trip alone. A covey of seven grey partridge was also worthy of note, they are not our commonest game bird, that is for sure.

Approaching Aberystwyth a goshawk gave us a good flypast, which was greatly appreciated by us all. At Aber' we had a chough out at sea, not a place we usually associate with this bird and oystercatchers were very noisy, as is their wont. The peak bird at Aber' is the purple sandpiper, this took us some time to locate, but to everyone's joy, we found it – well to be more accurate, found four. As the tide started to retreat a turnstone appeared on a gravel spit which was quickly joined by a small flock of ringed plovers. Returning to our cars a rock pipit popped up on the sea wall as if waving us good-bye. Another most interesting day, sixty birds seen and we had now all passed the hundred mark for the year. Things looked good for the year ahead.

It had been suggested that I arrange another birding holiday, so this I had done. Nineteen of us would be going away for a week to the Lakes once again, commencing 25th April. It would appear more people wished to have a chance of seeing the golden eagle, and who can blame them.

This holiday will also be a way of celebrating Dorothy's retirement. She was sixty on 12th February, but she was asked to stay on for a few weeks to train up her replacement, so she actually finished in early April. That could not come soon enough.

The end of February saw Dorothy and I having a short break in Norfolk, just two full days, but it was most enjoyable. We had seventy-three birds over the period, including the black-winged stilt; Dorothy had not seen this bird previously. Two early avocets were also seen, and brent geese, pink-footed geese and white-fronted geese were also still to be seen. No marsh harriers had returned as yet, but a superb male hen harrier was at Cley, now they are a bit special. During the weekend I added fifteen birds to my 'Year List', so I was more than happy; plus, the odd drop of wine went down well. As Dorothy put it, 'A very pleasant late Birthday Present.' I could not argue with that. Here's to many more in the future!

Late in March saw the group at Blacktoft Sands, chasing a few interesting 'Year Ticks', and they did not disappoint; for our newcomers, those birds turned into 'Lifers'. The top birds that day were avocet, bearded tit, bittern, curlew, golden plover, marsh harrier, ringed plover, stock dove and a wood sand piper. We totalled fifty-two on the day.

As we were going to The Lakes we did not organise an April field meeting, our week away would more than cover that. On the way to The Lakes, we called in at Leighton Moss for the bearded tits and bittern; we saw the first and heard the second, that was a good start to the week.

In The Lakes the golden eagle put on an aerial display for us and we could just make out the female which was on the nest. The nest, which had been used several times was becoming very large. Part of the mating process is the male bringing in fresh nesting materials which the female adds to the structure, so the nest grows larger as each year passes. At least this makes it easy to see for us birders, although I would not like to climb up to it. The nest is obviously guarded throughout the breeding season, egg collectors would love to have a clutch of English golden eagle eggs.

We saw eighty-seven species during the week and as well as those previously mentioned, the pick of the remainder were, common sandpiper, curlew, dipper, lesser spotted woodpecker, marsh harrier, marsh tit, merlin, peregrine falcon, pied flycatcher, raven, red-breasted merganser, ring ouzel, ruddy duck, siskin, tawny owl and wood warbler. A few 'Lifers' and 'Year Ticks' for many of my colleagues among those.

May saw us on our, by now, regular trip down to Little Paxton, Fordham and Weeting Heath. As usual we were after cuckoo, hobby, nightingale, spotted flycatcher, stone curlew, turtle dove and woodlark. I am pleased to report, we saw the lot, plus another fifty-six species.

Bempton Cliffs called in June. My new members had been waiting for this trip with intense anticipation, I do not believe they thought such a place existed in the UK, they were due to find one did.

The day was bright and clear, a perfect June day in fact, and the birds performed as usual, the puffins especially so. Everybody loves puffins, they are a bird everyone recognises, but in reality, few have seen them. For three of my colleagues, that was put right that day, and one of the puffins was so close you could almost touch the bird, although as I know to my pain, do not: their bill is one hell of a weapon!

As the day drew to its conclusion and we were walking back to our cars, one of my colleagues stopped, and pointed, 'Hear that Brian?' The sea birds may have provided the glamour and colour of the day, but from a pure birding point of view, he had hit the jackpot. From a nearby bramble tangle a grasshopper warbler could be heard, and I was very pleased he had picked it up. Their call was now just on the fringe of my hearing capabilities; I think they call it age, and due to this I miss out on them frequently. I was able to approach close to the tangle and hear this bird well. This to me was very special, it could be my only encounter with the bird that year, many a year I did not get it on my 'Year List', I now had. The 'gropper' as we call it, may not have the magic of the puffin, but for me it was the bird of that day. We may have only seen thirty-six species, but we had seen many thousands of birds as well as hearing them and smelling them. There must be a fortune in guano on those cliffs!

July saw us visit Titchwell, where although over seventy species were seen, the best bird there was a small party of snow geese, which pleased several of my group.

August saw us in 'Twitch' mode. A corncrake had been reported from Willington Gravel Pits, just over the border in Derbyshire, that bird could not be ignored. Corncrakes are now a rare bird with just a few pairs hanging on in Scotland and Eire; they are a summer migrant with just the very occasional bird being reported on passage through the Midlands. I had not seen one for many a year, so we had to chase this bird up.

The news about the bird had spread and we only just managed to park our cars up before joining in the rush. A 'Twitch' can be quite amusing. Many birders are only interested in seeing the bird, a couple of minutes doing so and they are off chasing their next quarry. We joke about them, saying it is on a par with train number collecting, tick it off and await the next one.

I suppose over fifty birders were collected on the edge of a field of rough grazing, sheep were in the field, and the latest news was that the bird had flown beyond a rise in the ground and all were awaiting its re-appearance. It was a case of the waiting game. We had no other plans so if it meant we waited, then so be it.

After what seemed eternity, a call broke out, a rasping, 'crex, cres' was heard. I swung round to my colleagues, 'That's it,' I shouted. The bird was most definitely there, waiting was no longer a problem; when you know the bird is about, waiting is just part of the game.

Sixteen of us had made the meeting that day, and I was the only one who had ever seen or heard the bird previously, fifteen now had an audible 'Lifer'; could we get it visually?

The bird was in no mood to co-operate and we must have waited well over an hour before our patience was fully rewarded. Over the top of a ridge walked our bird. It had not a care in the world, it just pecked away at the earth and slowly walked across our vision, before vanishing once again.

For many of the birders, that was that, in true 'Twitch' mode, off they shot. We hung about for a little longer, heard the bird call again, but it did not show, not that we were complaining. Willington had a few other choice birds to search out. We saw an adult curlew sandpiper which was still in almost full summer plumage, a delightful sight that, a small party of golden plovers gave us a fly past, and a greenshank could be heard but not seen. As we were about to leave a family party of five grey wagtails popped in, the male, female and three juveniles; some send-off that.

That trip again proved you did not have to travel miles to see interesting birds, we were less than half an hour from home. I frequently tell people to get to know their own patch.

September saw us make two trips to Spurn Point, where we again did very well: several 'Year Ticks' and 'Lifers' were obtained. The pick of those being Arctic skua, bar-tailed godwit, great skua, grey plover, Manx shearwater, pectoral sandpiper, pomarine skua, red-backed shrike and whimbrel. Spurn rarely lets you down.

The end of the month saw us visiting Titchwell. This was done as a bit of a mopping up exercise, a chance to see some of the regular waders missed so far that year by course members. But as always is the case with Norfolk, the unexpected is frequently encountered. A grey phalarope was found, 'Lifer' time for one or two of the members. A red-necked grebe was on the sea, another quality bird, and two wood sandpipers were along the shore. Those three species alone had made the visit worthwhile, apart from the other sixty-four species seen.

Early October we visited Rutland Water and Eyebrook Reservoir. There we saw many birds but nothing outstanding, just a pleasant day's birding. Later in October we had a local visit to Blithfield Reservoir, where we saw ruddy shelduck, twite, whooper swan and a yellow-legged gull.

The latter are becoming seen more often. It is a race of herring gull which frequents the Mediterranean region and it is a bird which many feel should have full status as a nominate species, so birders are looking out for it more seriously. The principal difference between it and the herring gull is leg colour. The herring gull has pink legs, the yellow-legged, obviously, has yellow. We were more than happy to have had such a clear view of this bird, a 'Lifer' for many, even if in 'lower case' at present.

November, we visited the Point of Ayr, on the Dee Estuary. The tide was right for us so we decided on a few hours' sea watching as a change from our normal ventures. The day was relatively mild with little or no wind coming in from over the sea, we had chosen well as far as the weather was concerned.

There was plenty of activity out at sea, black-headed gulls, common gulls, herring gulls and lesser black-backed gulls were well represented, with the odd great black-backed causing consternation at times to their smaller colleagues. Fulmars were gliding past and several ducks were out at sea, particularly pintails, shelducks and common scoters, a few hundred of the latter.

After much scoping one of my colleagues picked up a diver, closer scrutiny proved this to be a black-throated diver. A small party of pink-footed geese were also on the sea, which was slightly unexpected and three great crested grebes swam by.

Being so used to seeing those grebes on our local lakes and reservoirs we tend to forget that they can also be seen out at sea. Whilst musing over the grebes I picked up a smaller grebe swimming by, much closer in. I quickly re-focused my scope and found myself looking at a winter plumaged Slavonian grebe, that bird certainly made our day.

The tide had now started to turn; unfortunately, so had the weather. The wind had suddenly risen and with it came the rain, and rain it did. Nothing for it but to call it a day, but it had been quite a day up to that point. For our final meeting of the year, we decided to visit Martin Mere. Being a Wildfowl Trust Reserve it had a very good café and many hides, ideal should the weather choose to be inclement. We chose well, it was a cold and damp December day, and only ten of us made the effort. After an early coffee, we set forth.

Quite a few whooper swans had arrived from the Arctic north, and listening to those it did not need much imagination to realise where their name came from, whoop they certain can! A small flock of six bean geese were in among the swans and several barnacle geese were moving through the other birds, most of those were probably collection barnacle geese

You have to be careful at Wildfowl Trust Reserves as many of the birds you see can quite easily be collection birds. It is a question of can they fly or can you see two full sets of primary feathers? If not, you cannot count it.

We were studying a hen harrier which was quartering a damp meadow behind one of the lakes, when I spotted a small white heron moving between the grazing cattle. I initially thought little egret, but as the bird turned I picked up the shape and colour of the bill, it was a stout looking bill, yellowish in colour; we had a cattle egret. A superb bird to get, and it certainly brightened up the conditions. Incidentally, had it been a little egret, the bill would have been longer and black in colour. We had heard nothing about this bird so we were absolutely delighted to see it. 'Lifer' time again for many of my party.

Several waders were to be seen including ruffs, of which there were over fifty, the largest number I have ever seen together, curlews, golden plovers, redshanks and three spotted redshanks. A flock of pink-footed geese flew in from off the nearby estuary, the tide was no doubt coming in and these birds were returning to Martin Mere to roost up.

The light was fading rapidly due to the time of year and the weather conditions prevailing, so our last field meeting of not only the year, but the century, drew to its close. The cattle egret was our final quality bird of the year, not a bad note to go out on.

It had been another good year for birds, I saw two hundred and twenty-three, and the majority of my class members cleared the two hundred mark. The newcomers just could not believe what they had seen, pictures in books had now become reality, and the golden eagle they will treasure for ever, and I would jolly well hope so!

What did a new century have in store? could we include our wishes as New Year Resolutions?

A NEW CENTURY STARTS

Dorothy and I only made one resolution, a joint one as it turned out, and that was to enjoy our time together, and with that in mind we booked ourselves two holidays for the year: a week in The Lakes during May, and a week in Anglesey during June. My group also wanted a week's birding so I arranged this for Norfolk, in September, so that gave us three holidays to look forward to. Retirement sounded quite good!

The year commenced with a visit to Rutland Water, where we chalked up sixty birds on the day, not a bad start to a new year, especially as it was only the 9th January. Among the birds seen were barnacle geese, dunlin, gadwall, goldeneye, goosander, great northern diver (the bird of the day), green sandpiper, redshank, ruddy duck, shelduck, shoveler, smew (another first class bird) and snipe. Some quality with which to commence a new year.

Later in the month, Southport and Martin Mere called. There pick of the birds seen were black-tailed godwit, the cattle egret again, this bird seemed well settled in, curlew, golden plover, hen harrier, knot, merlin, peregrine falcon, pink-footed goose, pintail, ruff, stonechat, teal, whooper swan and wigeon. We totalled seventy-two species on the day, and the majority of us reached the one hundred mark on that occasion. The prospects of another good year ahead seemed likely, especially with three holidays to look forward to.

Early February saw us on our annual pilgrimage to Wales. Ludlow, the Elan Valley and Aberystwyth called and by now you probably know exactly what we were after. They did not disappoint. Buzzard, chough, dipper, hawfinch, purple sandpiper, raven, red kite, ringed plover, rock pipit. shag, and turnstone all put in an appearance. Some wag commented, 'This birding is easy.' I quickly informed him as the year progresses things will get more difficult. You can only see a 'Year Tick' once, after that it is pure repetition.

February saw us back in Norfolk, Titchwell being our destination. It was a little early for the return of the avocets, although a bird had been reported, but not for a couple of days or so. We saw several bar-tailed godwits, the black-winged stilt was still in attendance, so were the brent geese, tucked away amongst which were two brant geese, the North American race. A 'Lifer' for us all. Common scoters and eiders were on the sea, with fulmars passing by. Golden plovers and grey plovers were on the reserve, a good opportunity to see the differences between these two species. A Mediterranean gull was among the black-headed gulls, with sanderling dashing along the tide line. The way these delightful small waders chase the tide looks almost as though they are having a game. Two returning marsh harriers were also seen. We had a very good selection of species, sixty-one of them.

As we still had time and the light was holding, we decided to spend a few minutes inland at a spot locally known as the barn. Here grain and other farm produce is stored which attract a variety of the smaller birds. Buntings and larks are regularly seen there; a spot not to be missed if you have the time.

We arrived to find a group of about twenty or so birders all in very excited mode. Two of them came rushing across to us as we got out of our cars. One of them shouted, 'Brian, you are just the bloke we need, come and tell us what we have got here?' I did not like the sound of that, there were twenty odd birders as I have already said, probably many were local, and they needed a 'foreigner' to tell them what they were looking at. I arrived to look at the bird, and I had not got the foggiest idea of what I was looking at. It was a bunting of some species, but not one I had ever seen previously. Including my own group, I now had over thirty pairs of eyes staring at me, all waiting for an answer. I started to put my brain into gear as they say. When confronted by this type of situation I always go through the birds I know, eliminate those, then you may only have a few to concentrate upon. But I do not usually have to do this with an audience, I cursed the fact that two birders here knew me, and had voiced their thoughts so loudly. The bird was obviously a male and it had very pronounced facial markings, and slowly a thought occurred to me. I had recently been looking at pictures of rare buntings and finches in a book I carried in my car, this could be a meadow bunting, a bird from Asia; in that case, it was some rarity. I asked one of my friends to pop back to my car and bring the book 'A Field Guide to the Rare Birds of Britain and Europe' for me. I told the group what I thought, some quickly looked in their field guides, but they were not going to find it there, it was not on the British List.

The book came, I looked, breathed a silent sigh of relief, a meadow bunting it certainly was. The excitement was intense, several were going to report it to the Rarities Committee, and took my name and address to include in their reports. They were surprised to hear I had no intention of reporting the bird myself, but as I told them, there was no way this bird would be accepted. It was a non-migratory species so there was no chance of it having flown all the way across Europe to arrive in the UK, it must just be an escapee.

As I told my friends, put the bird on your 'Life Lists', but put a question mark by it and await to see if it ever appears on the British List. (I do not think it ever has.) But that does not take away the fact we all saw it, and it was certainly a free flyer.

I was very pleased to have got out of that one, and I had a very quiet word with my old friend who had put me on the spot. The threats, should he do it ever again, were gruesome.

The Lapland buntings, reed buntings, yellowhammers, shorelarks and twite we saw afterwards all paled into insignificance after the meadow bunting. We certainly had a day to remember, that was for sure, me especially!

With our Norfolk holiday coming up on 23rd March, we did not have a field meeting that month. Eighteen of us made the trip, Dorothy included. We tried a new hotel this time, The Pheasant, at Kelling, and we chose well a very comfortable hotel: good food, a good selection of Scotch whisky and wines (what more could one ask for?), and a handy man who was a very good birder and a Brummie to boot. He certainly helped us find some good birds, and accompanied us on occasion.

During the week we visited Hunstanton, Holme-next-the-Sea, Thornham, Titchwell, Holkham Hall (where some had a break from birding), Holkham Meals, Wells-next-the-Sea, Cley-next-the-Sea, Salthouse Heath and The Quags at Kelling. The prime bird watching areas on the north west coast of Norfolk.

The weather at times was very chilly, but at least we had little rain, and several of the places visited either had, or were very near to, good catering establishments.

The birding was first class, we saw one hundred and five species during the week, the pick of which were as follows. Avocet, bean goose, bearded tit, brent goose, Cetti's warbler, crane, Egyptian goose, golden pheasant, goshawk, kingfisher, marsh harrier, merlin, our first sand martins of the year, snow goose, spotted redshank and turtle dove. Apart from me, everyone went home with both 'Lifers' and 'Year Ticks'; I only had 'Year Ticks', but I was not complaining. A great week was had by all. After all the excitement of Norfolk, April saw us visiting locally, and our initial meeting was a bit of a 'Twitch'. Belvide Reservoir had a marsh warbler reported, a very unusual species in the county, and Blithfield Reservoir had a Ross's goose. Two quality birds such as those, on our doorstep, could not be missed. I am pleased to say they were not, very good views of both were obtained. 'Lifer' time again for some. Visit two was to Cannock Chase. There we saw little owl, raven (it was believed they were actually breeding on the Chase for the first time in many years), redstart, tawny owl, tree pipit, willow tit and woodlark. The pick of the fifty-eight species seen, and all less than ten miles from home.

The 7th May duly saw Dorothy and I off for our week in The Lakes. We could not have picked a better week, the weather was ideal, and apart from calling in at Leighton Moss on the way up, we did more walking than birding. Having said that we knocked up ninety-eight species, quite a number without really trying.

Leighton Moss obviously gave us a good help towards that total; included there were: barnacle goose, bean goose, bearded tit, little gull, little tern, marsh harrier, Mediterranean gull, pink-footed goose, red-breasted merganser, ruddy duck and wigeon. The Lakes themselves chipped in with buzzard, crossbill, curlew, goldcrest, the golden eagle obviously (you do not visit The Lakes without seeking out this bird), honey buzzard, peregrine falcon, pied flycatcher, raven, ring ouzel, siskin, wheatear and wood warbler, to mention but a few. A good selection with little effort. Later in the month saw us on our usual May hunt for cuckoo, hobby, nightingale, spotted flycatcher, stone curlew and woodlark, all seen. Little Paxton, Lakenheath and Weeting Heath again produced the goods. Sixty-four birds seen on the day. Bempton Cliffs drew us back in June and we combined this with a short visit to nearby Flamborough Head. Bempton Cliffs provided us with their customary spectacle, but Flamborough provided us with the bird of the day.

A Forster's tern, a rare American vagrant had been reported, not that we were lucky, we did not see it, but whilst there searching for the bird a colleague of mine kept on commenting about a yellow bird he was looking at. I took it he was looking at a yellowhammer, and we had more important things to do, tern hunting. Eventually, to more or less shut him up, I looked at the bird and I was mighty glad I had, this was no yellowhammer: he had found us a golden oriole. I think it is safe to say he will never be ignored again.

The 13th June saw Dorothy and I off for our holiday in Anglesey, where we stayed near to Beaumaris. Once again the gods favoured us with wonderful weather. Although I had previously visited Anglesey on birding trips, this we the first opportunity I had of really exploring the 'island', which was what we did.

As usual, birding was a big part of it, and we saw seventy-five species during the week. The pick of these were black guillemot, chough, nutcracker (this was only the second time I had seen this species in the UK), stonechat and a woodchat shrike. The nutcracker and the shrike were real top quality birds, worth the holiday alone.

We visited the Newborough Forest area and there we were amazed by the variety of orchids to be seen, a truly amazing area, also rich in bird song. The cliff top walks near to Llaneilian were also impressive as long as you kept away from the caravan sites. Black guillemots were seen from the cliffs and orchids were again in evidence. The choughs put on their usual displays at South Stack and the peregrine falcon was nesting on the cliff side, but no hooded crows that time. You cannot win them all. A very pleasant holiday drew to its conclusion.

In July, we visited Blacktoft Sands and called in at the Wellbeck Estate on our return, an osprey had been reported at the latter which some of my colleagues needed for their 'Life Lists'.

Blacktoft was as good as usual. The avocet numbers and marsh harrier numbers were increasing annually, a wide selection of waders were now in, the spotted redshanks looking particularly smart, several still in their summer plumage. The bird of the day was a spoonbill; well, three of them to be more accurate – two adults and a juvenile. According to a local birder they had flown in from Holland, they were welcome visitors that was for sure.

The osprey did not disappoint, it put on a very good display and actually caught a fish which it flew off with. We also had goshawk, buzzard and a sparrowhawk whilst we were osprey hunting, a very good raptor watching spot obviously.

Whilst waiting I became conscious of a bird calling, I swung round to my friends, 'Listen, a quail is calling.' From out of the nearby field a quail was in full voice, 'pit pil-it' rang out repeatedly for a few minutes. A male quail was letting rip. Unfortunately, we did not see the bird, but several of my colleagues now had an audible 'Lifer'; not a bad end to a day out, that was for sure.

That day saw many of my colleagues pass the two hundred mark for the year; thanks to my holidays, I had completed that number some time ago.

Early August was a local trip, Blithfield Reservoir and Belvide Reservoir, we were just mopping up the odd bird we required for some of our 'Year Lists'. Arctic tern, black-necked grebe, green sandpiper, hobby, mandarin duck and wood sandpiper. We were not to be disappointed, we saw them all, so a few of us went home really happy, others contented.

Later in the month Rutland Water drew our attention, a green-winged teal had been reported, a 'Lifer' for some of my colleagues, and a 'Year Tick' for many. It was also an opportunity to see red kite nearer home, they had been introduced near to Rutland, so we had a very good chance.

Rutland did not fail us. Curlew sandpiper, a small group of four, Egyptian geese, kingfisher, osprey, red kite, ruff all showed well, and the green-winged teal, a drake, put on a very good show. All in all, a most satisfactory day, with over fifty species seen.

September saw our return to Spurn Point, where I had been reliably informed, a good passage of sea birds was taking place. That meant we had a chance of skuas and shearwaters, and so it turned out.

Arctic skuas were quickly picked out, as they harassed the local black-headed gulls, and as the morning progressed we saw the following out at sea. Cory's shearwaters, great skuas, just the occasional bird, and sooty shearwaters. Additional to these we also had common scoter, red-backed shrike and snow bunting. As we had time we made our way down to the point where the bird ringing is carried out and there is a large area of gorse, much favoured by the smaller birds.

We arrived to a scene of excitement. A dozen or so birders pointed to a specific gorse bush, and shouted, 'There he is.' What 'He' was we had no idea, but a quick look told us. A barred warbler was sitting out on the top of the bush, almost saying, 'What a pretty boy I am.'

Pretty is probably an over-statement. They look like a small greyish cuckoo, but what they may lack in glamour they more than make up in rarity. What a bird to end the day on, at least a 'Year Tick' for everyone and a 'Lifer' for most. Spurn had certainly done it again. The birds I have mentioned were just the cream of the sixty-eight seen.

Dorothy and I thought a few days away would be very pleasant, so we booked ourselves in at The Pheasant once again, and the end of the month saw us back in Norfolk.

We had four nights so we could not cover Norfolk as well as in the past, but the birder at The Pheasant was able to point us in the right direction, which was a great help.

We saw ninety-seven birds in those four days, but it was a period of concentration and effort, not for the faint hearted. The pick of the birds seen were avocet, bean goose, bearded tit, brent goose, curlew, curlew sandpiper, eider, gannet, grey plover, honey buzzard, jacksnipe, Lapland bunting, peregrine falcon, red-necked grebe, red-throated diver, snow goose and spotted crake.

Early October, Spurn Point called us once again. Those who had been unable to make our last visit wanted to have a go, I was more than happy to say yes. Spurn, like Norfolk, always has something to offer.

We had sixty-six species on the day, the mixture much as expected with one very special inclusion. It was 'Lifer' time, for all of us. A large number of birders were gazing, very intently at 'Big Hedge', an area I have mentioned previously. As we approached a birder pointed, we looked in the direction to find ourselves looking at a Radde's warbler, I could not believe what we were looking at. We had heard nothing about this bird from any birders we had seen earlier, so it was with complete surprise. Radde's warblers are natives of Siberia, so to arrive in the UK they have travelled all the way across Europe, quite a journey and quite a rarity. For those of us who had made the journey to Spurn, it was jackpot time. Our last two visits to Spurn had produced two wonderful birds: the barred warbler and now the Radde's warbler. You could not ask for more.

The reminder of the year did not produce too much excitement, apart from a scaup and snow goose at Kingsbury Water Park, a black redstart at Sharpness, with Bewick's swans and white-fronted geese at Slimbridge.

It had turned out to be a very good year, and I had recorded my highest number in a year, two hundred and thirty-nine. I was beginning to think the magic two hundred and fifty may arrive yet.

We commenced 2001 with a local trip, which covered Kingsbury Water Park, Lea Marston, the Ladywalk Reserve and Cannock Chase, and this proved to be a good start to the year. We saw sixty-two birds on the day and at no time were we above twenty miles from home. We picked up several quality birds the pick being, brambling, buzzard, common gull, crossbill, green sandpiper, lesser redpoll, mandarin duck, marsh tit, ruddy duck, siskin, water rail and woodcock. A very good start to the year, long may it continue.

Before moving on birding. I had been giving a lot of thought recently to my future involvement with the University run courses. A big change had occurred regarding these. Originally, they had been extra-mural courses, but recently they had become continuing study courses with much more an educational flavour to them. Written work etc., was now expected from students, and bird watchers were not interested in that side of things. All they wanted to do was to learn about birds and, more importantly, learn how to identify birds. Also, I needed to consider my own capabilities. I was not a qualified teacher and my birding expertise, such as it was, was self-taught and based on my own experiences. I did not believe I was capable of judging written work, and to be perfectly honest, as I had approximately thirty students a time, I did not feel I had the time available to judge their work fairly. I finally came to the conclusion it was time to retire as a part-time lecturer, and this I would do come August when my summer course was completed. This course had already been advertised and a small number of students were already enrolled, so I did not wish to disappoint them.

We also visited the Moors and Park Hall during January, where we saw three species of owl, grey partridge, red grouse, siskin and snipe among forty-eight species seen.

Later in the month, we visited Martin Mere; the usual species were seen, fifty on the day, and that gave most of us our one hundred species for the year, not a bad start.

Several of my course members asked me whether I would still be organising bird watching holidays. I had not really thought about that, but as enough were interested, I decided to continue doing so. I suggested we had a week in Norfolk come late September, when bird passage should be good, and this was agreed.

February saw us visiting Rutland Water, there smew were again the top target bird, which I am pleased to say we saw – especially as Rutland was the quietest I had ever seen it.

To improve matters, Ludlow, the Elan Valley and Aberystwyth were our targets for the end of the month; things there would surely be up to standard. They were, fifty-four species seen on the day. As well as the expected birds such as buzzard, crossbill, dipper, hawfinch, purple sandpiper, raven, red kite, rock pipit stonechat and turnstone, we had a speciality, a 'Lifer' for most. A Carolina wood-duck was in the harbour at Aberystwyth, a superb drake, and according to a local birder this was the second year the bird had appeared for the winter. Was this a true migrant from across the 'Pond'? We shall never know the answer to that question, we were just thrilled to see the bird. It had really made our trip worthwhile.

I had seen two or three Carolina wood ducks previously, of doubtful pedigree, this bird was the first which could well be the real thing. It went on my 'List' most definitely. March saw us visiting the North Wales coast where sea birds were our targets, they did not disappoint. Common gulls, common scoters, fulmars, gannets, great black-backed gulls, little gulls, the occasional passing Manx shearwaters and various of the commoner gulls, all helped our numbers progress. We had local meetings during April as we chalked up returning migrant, fooling ourselves Summer was nigh. They do say one swallow does not make a summer, as we saw several, we hoped.

May and Dorothy and I were off to The Lakes again, it was not quite our second home, but we did love the area. The weather was not up to the expected standard and we spent much time on the 'Stately Home' trail, and for the first time in many a year, we did not see the golden eagle. We had eighty-one birds during the week, so we were not complaining.

Later in that month, we were off chasing cuckoo, hobby, nightingale, pied flycatcher, turtle dove and woodlark, which all performed well for us. Bempton called in June; we could not miss our visit to 'Bird City'. It was much as usual. We had seventy-two birds on the day, the only real consideration was the puffin situation. Very few views of this fellow were obtained, and most of those that were, were on the sea, few birds on the cliffs. Puffins are a species that will be badly affected by climate change, much talked about. Their food is very dependent on water temperatures. a couple of degrees is all it needs to drive it off. There is a real fear now that with the oceans warming up the puffins prey will slowly move ever northwards, with the puffin following on. We could lose the bird as an English breeding species, perish the thought.

Later, during June, Dorothy and I had a few days holiday in Norfolk, where I was able to finalise our arrangements for the group holiday in September. Once again, I was able to obtain good terms, so all will be happy. During the four days, we saw ninety-eight species with one or two surprises among them. On the sea at Titchwell, we saw common scoter and a small party of eider; these we did not expect during summer. Two whooper swans were also on the reserve these should have long since departed north. Gannets were also seen way out fishing and the little tern colony was as noisy and active as ever. The pick of the week was a red-necked phalarope seen on The Quags. This bird had really brought the locals in. By now this bird should have been well north where they breed, as with the whoopers, what it was doing there we could but guess at. Not, I hasten to add, that anyone was complaining.

It had been a very pleasant few days, and The Pheasant Hotel really did look after us, the prospects looked very good come September.

I was now approaching my final two months working for Keele University, so we decided to visit Titchwell, Blacktoft Sands and Spurn Point, in the hope we could chalk up as many species as possible. We were hoping to 'Go out with a bang!'

Titchwell started us off with seventy-six species, among which were avocet, bar-tailed godwit, curlew, honey buzzard, marsh harrier, ruddy duck, ruff, Sandwich tern, spoonbill – five of them, turtle dove and an escapee – a swan goose. Now for Blacktoft. Among the sixty-six birds seen at Blacktoft, the pick were avocet, bearded tit, curlew sandpiper, green sandpiper, greenshank, marsh harrier, red-necked grebe, spoonbill – only one this time, sparrowhawk, spotted redshank, Temminck's stint and wood sandpiper.

Now for our final event – Spurn Point. Here we saw seventy-two species, the best of the bunch were as follows. Avocet, curlew, curlew sandpiper, gannet, golden plover, grey plover, pomarine skua, red-throated diver, ringed plover, sanderling, Sandwich tern, scarlet rosefinch (needless, to say the bird of the day, a 'Lifer' for some of my colleagues), wheatear, whimbrel, whinchat and yellow wagtail. Not a bad list to bow out on.

Our Norfolk week arrived, and this time the weather was a bit mixed, but as most of the reserves we visited had hides, it did not concern us too much. During the week we saw one hundred and twenty-seven species, an exceptionally good total, among which were one or two cracking species. Bar-headed geese, buff-breasted sandpiper, great skua, Greenland wheatear, Lapland bunting, Montagu's harrier, red-throated diver, scaup, short-eared owl, Slavonian grebe and yellow-browed warbler are worthy of mention. A good mixture of 'Year Ticks' and 'Lifers' for all of us. My friends hoped that, even though the bird study classes were now over, further birding holidays could be arranged. I was sure they could.

The remainder of the year saw Dorothy and I having a few trips out, visiting several of the locations I usually took the course members to. Nothing really exceptional was seen, but we had some very pleasant excursions out, and there was now no longer any pressure to find birds, we just enjoyed what we saw.

My retirement from teaching did not last long. Forest Enterprise had opened a new visitor centre at nearby Rosliston, just over the borders in Derbyshire, and it was suggested I ran a bird study course there for the retired and un-employed. This was to be a weekly course run on a

Monday morning. I decided to do this and Dorothy was also involved with the National Trust so she was able to work for them as a volunteer guide at Sudbury Hall, also on a Monday morning.

Species seen during the year were again good, two hundred and twenty-eight, which included some quality species.

Two thousand and two saw us both occupied once again. Prior to commencing these, we managed to fit in a three-day break north of the border, visiting Caerlaverock on the north Solway coast. Here a very large winter flock of barnacle geese could be seen. Although barnacle geese are seen throughout the year, they are what we term feral. Here the bird are the genuine wild stock who visit the area every winter from their breeding grounds in the far north. It is estimated that the Solway flock of over 12,500 birds is the entire breeding population from Svalbard, and when you add these to the large numbers of pink-footed geese and greylag geese, you are approaching 20,000 birds. Well worth the journey.

To see geese in these numbers is a memorable event, and it was something we enjoyed on several occasions over the few days of our stay. Whooper swans were also to be seen in goodly numbers, and fifty or so Bewick's swans and mute swans were also in attendance. A good selection of ducks were to be seen and over our stay we saw goshawk, hen harrier, peregrine and merlin, but the top bird was probably a great grey shrike we saw at the nearby village of Glencaple. It was a lovely break, a good hotel, with a superb selection of a certain Scottish 'brew'. What more could you ask for?

The Rosliston Bird Study Group, as we called ourselves commenced later in the month, and it had twenty-six members, a few of my University students also joined, so it was not all new faces. We initially commenced with just indoor meetings as the bulk of the members were newcomers to the hobby, just taking it up as they were retired and wished for something to do.

During the following two months or so Dorothy and I enjoyed a few trips out to places I regularly visited with previous groups. Park Hall, the Moors, Martin Mere and Southport, Wales, Rutland Water and Titchwell.

You will, by now, be aware of the species we hoped to see on those occasions, and we were not let down. Additional to the expected we also saw green-winged teal, Ross's goose and smew at Martin Mere, an

Australian shelduck (obviously an escapee) and Mediterranean gull at Rutland Water. Titchwell still had the black-winged stilt, plus crane. By now I was well over the hundred species mark.

Nightingales called late April, and many of my new course members were interested in the chance of hearing this master songster, so we had a field meeting to Little Paxton. For many it was their first serious attempt at birding, so it was going to be a good indicator as to their interest levels.

I need not have concerned myself, they all thoroughly enjoyed themselves. The nightingales put on a special show, one in particular sat out on the top of a small bush and serenaded us for several minutes, much to everyone's enjoyment. We also had three hobbies pass through and common terns had arrived, these too put on an aerial display as only terns can. As we had time, we decided to drive on to Weeting Heath, the chance of stone curlews could not be passed over. Weeting Heath did not let us down, we had very good views of stone curlews, chiffchaffs called, willow warblers sang and even woodlarks showed. We could not have asked for more, well we could. When can we go out next they asked? It looked as though Monday field meetings would not be all local, as I had first thought when I agreed to run this course. Dorothy had been asked to do voluntary work at the hospital in Burton-on-Trent so she finished at Sudbury Hall and agreed to do her session on a Monday, which freed me up for longer field meetings. This gave me the opportunity to take my group up to Bempton Cliffs for an experience many of them had never had previously. We clicked for a good day from a weather point of view, and the birds behaved themselves well, even the puffins obliged, a special sighting for many. As one or two said, they had never expected to see a puffin in their lives, they did that day.

For those new to the game, a place such as Bempton is unbelievable. For those of us who regularly visit, most of what we see is expected, and to be fair, if not seen we would be tremendously disappointed and wonder what had gone wrong. For many of my companions that day, the birds seen had only ever been pictures in books prior to that visit. They were real now.

July saw us visiting Backtoft Sands, another opportunity to see many interesting species which would be new birds to many of the course members. They were not disappointed. Avocets, bearded tits, black-tailed godwits, a cuckoo gave us a flypast, did not call, green sandpiper, greenshank, and the bird of the day, a marsh sandpiper, a 'Lifer' for us all. This bird was totally unexpected, but it did not end there. A birder told us of a rose-coloured starling that was being seen in the grounds of an inn in Swinefleet, no need to say where we shot off to.

The bird was not difficult to find, car parking was the problem! This we managed, and then we just joined a large group of birders who pointed out the last direction the bird had flown. It was with a small flock of starlings which kept on returning to a tree in the inn grounds. I think the inn keeper was rather pleased with the number of people wanting to see the bird. A few pints were being consumed that was for sure.

A shout went up, 'Here they come,' and so they did. About twenty of them, they all landed in the tree, and there, for all to see, was the rose-coloured starling. I have only ever seen one previously, and that was a juvenile, this bird was a full adult, and really did look the part. It is just two colours, pink and black, with a slight crest; at a distance, you could almost think it was pied. A wonderful bird to finish off the day. When added to the marsh sandpiper seen earlier, it was some day.

As far as the Rosliston Birders were concerned our next few meetings were a collection of indoor and local field meetings, I was having trouble with my walking. A visit to hospital was called for and I was told a knee replacement was required, and due to a cancellation I was able to have that done far quicker than anticipated. September saw me in hospital and temporarily out of circulation. For the remainder of the year my birding was done from the car or near to the car; Dorothy had become my chauffeur.

The year closed, in the circumstances my 'Years List' was not too bad, two hundred and seven species were seen and included amongst those were a few choice specimens.

Come 2003, and I was almost back to normal, the surgeon had done a wonderful job as far as I was concerned, and serious birding was back. Our first field meeting late January was local; a trip over the border into Derbyshire where we visited Carsington Water. We had a very good start to the year. Fifty-eight species seen, the pick of which were barnacle goose, buzzard, gadwall, mandarin, red-crested pochard, scaup and a sparrowhawk. The bird of the day, however, was kept on the back burner for our return journey home.

Locally to where we lived, at Handsacre, a great grey shrike had been seen over a couple of days, and we called in hoping to see this bird; a 'Lifer' for many.

Judging by the number of cars parked up, we had no need to worry. Several birders whom I knew well where there, and the bird was quickly pointed out to us. As I have mentioned previously, shrikes do not hide away, and this was no exception. It sat out on the top of small bushes and gave us many a fly past. On one occasion, it chased after a blue tit which just managed to evade the shrike. The blue tit lived to fight another day, the shrike went hungry. That is the way of the wild world.

A better ending to a day was hard to imagine, we all went home happy in frame of mind, and I was also happy with how I had managed the day. Compliments to the surgeon once again. As I mentioned earlier, a good start to a new year.

Another local meeting followed at the end of the month. The Staffordshire Moorlands and area was visited. We saw the long-eared owls, five of them on that occasion, but the bird of the day, and that was a very local one, was seen at the Branston Golf Club, just six miles from home, and that was a small group of waxwings.

Many of the newcomers had never dreamed of seeing such an exotic bird in the U.K., and local to their homes made it even more unbelievable. The waxwings were flying in and out of a garden bordering the golf course, and the lady of the house was thrilled to bits with it all. She was quite happy to invite us into her back garden where we were able to see the birds more closely, and she was most interested to learn all she could about the birds. They were feeding on her many cotoneaster bushes, which had a good berry crop, although these were vanishing at quite a rate of knots!

As with our previous trip, we had kept the best bird till last; long may it continue, I was told!

The following day I was back with Dorothy, she was most interested in seeing the waxwings. Unfortunately, the lady of the house was not at home, so we had to chase after the birds a little more. We had good views, however, so we were more than satisfied.

February saw us local once again, a bit of a chase round really. We visited Ladywalk N.R, Kingsbury Water Park, Chasewater, Cannock Chase and ended up at Whitemoor Haye. We had fifty-eight species on the day and amongst them were some very good quality birds. At Ladywalk we had a bittern – we do not see many of those so close to home – and the Chase provided us with buzzard, raven and a mealy redpoll; the latter being a 'Lifer' to many of my colleagues. We had all passed the one hundred mark for the year by this stage.

An advertisement in the local paper caught our attention. A local tour operator was arranging a cruise to Norway for later in the year. They had hired the cruise liner from an Italian company and were only advertising the accommodation locally. It sounded ideal and as the cost was not too excessive, we decided to take a chance and booked up. It was a ten-day cruise; sailing on the 25th July, something to look forward to and an excuse to splash out on some smart clothing. Well, for Dorothy anyway, I only needed evening attire.

Back to birding. We had a good mixture of local meetings, including nightingale hunting; Bempton, needless to say, and Wales for the red kites. These had now become 'hardy annuals' as they do say. We also called in at Rutland Water where black-necked grebe, red-necked grebe and Slavonian grebe were all in attendance. To see our three rarest grebes on the same day and at the same location was not to be missed, and they were not. When you add the great crested grebe and little grebe to those three, we saw all our breeding grebes on one occasion. I doubt if that will ever occur again.

Early May, Dorothy and I had a short holiday in Pembrokeshire, staying at a small licensed private hotel; the owner of which was a keen birder. He was able to point us in the direction of breeding choughs, and also the best places to see the sea birds from. The best thing of all, however, was to be seen in the grounds of his hotel.

After dinner, as dusk came in, he regularly put out the left-overs from the evening meal onto the lawn in his garden. Those who were interested, sat in the lounge with a tot of their favourite brew, and waited. The first creatures to arrive were two foxes which were so tame they came up to the windows and looked in at us. After a short while, a badger lumbered in; the foxes did not like him and they moved off, leaving the badger to finish off the pickings. It was half an hour of sheer delight, and to top it all he had a bat colony in his roof; as darkness drew in, they came out to complete the scene. We had a few magical evenings, that was for sure.

We intended to return, but unfortunately, he was selling up later that year; he and his wife were off to Spain to live. I have frequently wondered if the new owners continued to feed the animals.

Our annual visits to Little Paxton and Bempton cliffs followed, with the customary results, much to everyone's pleasure, and an evening early June saw us nightjar and woodcock hunting on The Chase, also successfully.

Prior to our cruise a trip to Blacktoft was arranged. A small party of five spoonbills had been reported and for many of my colleagues this would be a new species, a 'Twitch' was called for.

Once again Blacktoft proved successful, the spoonbills were seen, to every one's delight and waders had commenced their arrival. The avocets were very accommodating and we saw black-tailed godwits and spotted redshanks still in their summer plumage. Those two species alone were worth the visit, they are most colourful in their summer regalia.

Whilst at Blacktoft I spoke to a local birder who told me he had just been across to Denaby Ings, a reserve near to Mexborough, where he had seen two great white egrets. Fortunately, I had the required OS map in the car, the reserve was a new name to me, and we quickly located the spot on the map. No need to say we were well and truly into 'Twitch' mode; a new species for all, except me that is, but if seen they would only be the second I had seen in the UK. The spoonbills had been a bit of a 'Twitch', the egrets were mega by comparison. Off we shot, four cars driving in convoy, but traffic was light and we arrived at Denaby Ings safely. It's only a small reserve and we arrived to find we had it all to ourselves, the news of the egrets obviously had not yet broken. The only problem was that we now had to do all the searching, but looking for two white birds, the size of a heron, should not prove difficult! The largest area of water is known as Main Ing, and part of this was reed lined. The Ing was over looked by a hide, so we made ourselves comfortable. After a few minutes, out of the reeds stalked a great white egret, closely followed by its partner. They are not called great white without reason.

As mentioned above, they are the size of our grey heron, and both of the birds had black bills, which showed them to be adults. Another distinguishing feature is the pronounced kink in their necks, it really stood out on those two. Great whites are rare vagrants from central and southern Europe, although reports do seem to be slightly more frequent, so who knows. Will they become a more regular sighting, as the little egret has become? Climate Warming – is this part of it? Another very successful field meeting, now Dorothy and I had Norway to look forward to. We sailed from Dover, and I must say The White Cliffs certainly look something special from the sea. We had seen them previously from the air and walked along the tops, but from the sea they are really something.

The cruise proved to be a great success, not especially from a birding point of view. Just the fact that Norway is a beautiful country, the Norwegians seemed to all speak English and were very friendly, and the food and accommodation on the liner were excellent.

We had several marvellous experiences with the birds. We were in a park in Bergen, it was lunchtime, and we were enjoying a drink and cake we had bought. The weather was fine and many Norwegians were also enjoying their lunches, most of the park benches were occupied. We had hardly sat down before a fieldfare joined us. We had never been so close to the bird before, and it just sat there looking at us. We threw it a piece of cake, and we then realised what it was after. Looking around the park, we saw this was going on at several locations; the Norwegians are obviously as daft as we are when it comes to feeding the birds. We had fed robins and chaffinches like this back home, we never thought of feeding fieldfares.

Sailing through the Lofoten Islands we had a white-tailed sea eagle accompanying the liner for almost half an hour, it hardly seemed to flap its wings. An incredible sight, the bird is large, our largest bird of prey in northern Europe, a 'flying bedstead' in fact. That was our first sighting of such a memorable bird, and it will not be forgotten that is for sure.

As we sailed further north, North Cape being our next destination, we had another special experience. We were sitting out on deck when an announcement was made, 'Whales on the port side.' A mass exodus was made to the left hand side of the liner, and there were two whales sailing majestically past us. As they dived, up came the spouts of water, the height of which was amazing. This they repeated for several minutes before disappearing from view. Unfortunately, they were going in the opposite direction to us. An amazing sight, another one we shall not forget. I do not know which whale they were, all I can say is they were large.

We arrived at Honningsvag, where we had to moor up and go by tender to land. A coach was waiting for those of us who were visiting North Cape. On the way, we stopped at a display of Lapland culture. Here in traditional clothing, plus a few reindeer, which visitors could feed and stroke; a chance to study traditional Lapland life was displayed. I must confess, Dorothy and I were more interested in looking at the local bird population and there we had Lapland buntings and hooded crows in an abundance. Although Lapland buntings are seen in the UK during winter, to see them on their breeding grounds in full summer plumage, was not a chance to be missed. We also saw a large owl way out in the distance, it could have been an eagle owl, but we will never know. One thing was for sure, it was too dark to be a snowy owl.

We had been lucky on the coach, we had the front seat alongside the driver, so we had uninterrupted vision. Reindeer were everywhere, almost like looking at a field of sheep back home, and I was surprised at how slender their legs were. Living in the tough conditions they do, I had expected a much heavier looking animal. At North Cape itself, we visited the museum and spent some time studying the birds on the cliffs which towered just over one thousand feet. The usual cliff nesting species were seen with one very special addition for us: Brunnich's guillemots, an exceptionally rare bird in the UK – the first we had ever seen. North Cape was worth the visit if only just for that bird.

Whilst having a light snack, where we sat outside, another delightful bird visited us at the table. You will remember the fieldfares that came begging for food, here it was snow buntings. We see snow buntings in the UK, but they are a winter visitor to our shores, so to see them in full summer plumage was another great delight.

We also had an amusing incident with reindeer; a group of Japanese tourists were also enjoying a meal, and watching them was a small group of reindeer, five of them. The Japanese finished their meals and moved on. The reindeer quickly trotted across to their table and promptly devoured whatever was left. This just did not seem right, but if you live in such a hard environment, anything else you can get is a supplement to your diet.

That was not our last encounter with reindeer that day. On returning back to the liner we came across a reindeer which just stood, stock still, in the roadway in front of us, leaving no way round it. Our driver, who incidentally was a lady, stopped, and we just sat there looking at the reindeer, which returned its glare on us. I mentioned earlier that we had the seat at the front of the coach, so I asked the driver whether I should go out and gently shoo the animal off. I was told no, reindeer are a highly protected animal and they always have the right of way, and to drive them off is an offence. Eventually, the reindeer got fed up with it all, and slowly moved off and we were able to continue on our way. So should you ever be driving in Norway and come across a reindeer, it is boss, not you! Sailing back southwards we experienced the mid-night sun and glimpsed the Northern Lights, both extremely memorable events. It was the only time we ever had sat out at 2.00 a.m. in almost bright sunlight, enjoying a drink. We also had the pleasure of great and long-tailed skuas escorting the liner. Life cannot get much better than that!

We also cruised in some of Norway's famous fjords and although most of the birding was done from onboard, we saw some most interesting species, many rarely seen back home. To see flocks of long-tailed ducks and scaups was incredible, those two ducks are only seen on occasion in the UK. One flock of long-tailed totalled forty-seven, prior to that I doubt if I had seen more than a dozen in my life. White-billed divers were also regular sightings, a bird never seen previously, and king eiders and Stella's eiders were also regularly seen.

On the birds-of-prey front we had golden eagles, four of them in total, a possible gyrfalcon, but the bird was at distance and flew through rapidly, goshawks, buzzards and a rough-legged buzzard. On one occasion we managed a walk along the shores of the fjord and we enjoyed seeing a nutcracker, this brought back memories of Switzerland. Lapland buntings were also frequent sightings and we saw a pair of shore larks, the male still sporting his tufts, sticking up on his head, looking almost like a pair of stunted horns. Shore larks were a new species to us so we studied them for several minutes before they became bored with things, and flew off.

Further whale sightings we obtained and, on one occasion, it was announced that it was a grey whale, so that resolved all discussion. They are some creature that is for sure, their size as they rise up in the water had to be seen to be believed. What an amazing sight and to think people hunt them, it is so sad. Size does not make you safe where man is concerned.

We had a feeling this will not be or only visit to Norway, nor our last cruise. We could not think of a more comfortable way of seeing the world.

On my return home, a few subtle hints were dropped out about my organising another week's bird watching holiday. So this I did and come November we would visit Norfolk to see what it had to offer as winter draws in. The Pheasant again being our destination.

August saw us locally. We had two interesting species to see, an osprey and a spotted crake, the latter being a 'Lifer' for most of my colleagues so we went in pursuit of that bird first. It had been reported from Belvide Reservoir and was in the reed bed near to the first hide. We arrived to find the hide empty, which was not a good sign, although it meant we could all get in, eleven of us. Reed warblers were still vocal and a water rail was grunting away and occasionally showing itself well, when the bird we were after put in an appearance. It walked out of the reeds to stand in a channel which separated the reeds. It stood motionless for several seconds, providing us with an exceptional view, before it commenced to probe in the shallow water for food. It looked as though it was feeding on emerging insects, but before we could study this, the water rail shouted, and the crake vanished into the reed bed. We waited for several minutes, but it did not reappear. Time now for Blithfield Reservoir and the osprey. Before we did so, however, two black-tailed godwits dropped in and commenced to feed in front of the hide. As goodbyes go, we had no complaints with that.

The osprey had been reported from Tad Bay, so we made our way down to the hide in Stansley Wood. We arrived just as two birders, whom I knew, were leaving. The osprey was to be seen and was perched in a tree on the opposite side of the bay. This tree was well known to me and was a regular roosting spot for passing ospreys. Telescopes were quickly mounted, and there, for all to see, sat our osprey.

Ospreys on passage are now an annual feature at Blithfield Reservoir, both on spring and autumn passage. Occasionally, one lingers on and we hope it may stay to breed, but no such luck; but who knows, one year they may. They are now regularly breeding outside Scotland.

We spent time studying this bird, which was an adult, probably a non-breeding bird making an early return migration. The bird repaid our attention by flying down and catching a fish, which it carried back to its perch and slowly devoured. A wonderful sight as long as you were not the trout it had caught!

Once again, we had hit the jackpot by birding locally. We actually had fifty-seven birds on the day, including, additional to those already mentioned, barnacle goose, buzzard, dunlin, little egret, little ringed plover, red-breasted merganser, ringed plover, ruddy duck and ruff, were the pick of the bunch.

September provided us with two trips to Spurn Point, one with Dorothy and the other with my group. The expected birds were to be seen plus Arctic skua, black guillemot, this most unexpected, great northern diver, great skua, little gull, little tern long-eared owl, purple sandpiper, red-throated diver and Sandwich tern. Enough there to satisfy the most serious of birders.

In October, Rutland Water and Eyebrook Reservoir were our destinations, and they did not disappoint. On the day, we totted up seventy-four species, among which were three superb birds. At Rutland we had a drake ferruginous duck, probably one of the rarest ducks seen in the UK, it was only my fifth record, and a yellow-legged gull, well two of them to be more accurate. At Eyebrook, we had the yellow-legged gull's closest 'mate', a Caspian gull. You are unlikely to find those in any field guides of the period as they are both races of the herring gull, but they are becoming more and more likely to become full species in their own rights in the not too distant future. Thanks to DNA tests etc.

It all comes to him who waits, and for eighteen of us, it finally did Norfolk here we come. Many of the usual places were visited, Titchwell and Cley Marshes are 'must visit' locations, no matter what the time of year. We just failed to register the one hundred for the week, we died in the hole on ninety-seven, but no one was complaining. We had some new faces among us and they were delighted with how things had gone. I have a feeling more will be required!

The pick of the birds seen were avocet, bean goose, black redstart, brent goose, Egyptian goose, eider, goshawk, hen harrier, marsh harrier, pink-footed goose, red-throated diver, rock pipit, ruff and turnstone. Apart from 'yours truly', all had 'Lifers'; I at least, had a few 'Year Ticks'. The important thing was all enjoyed the experience.

The year concluded with visits to Slimbridge and northern Wales. At Slimbridge, we enjoyed close up views of the wildfowl collection as well as seeing the Bewick's swans which winter there and the white-fronted geese. A merlin also put on a spectacular aerial display as it chased a meadow pipit, at zero feet, before finally catching it. The speed of the merlin was simply amazing, and the way it chased its prey was most impressive. It is not much fun being low down in the pecking order. Our trip to Wales include Rhos on Sea, the Little Orme, and on the return journey calling in at Worlds End, near Wrexham. Conditions on that day were not good. It commenced with heavy rain which persisted all the time we were at the coast, visibility was very poor in consequence. Shortly after lunch, the rain lightened so we decided to make our way to Worlds End, hoping that inland conditions would improve – they did.

Blue sky actually appeared, with briefly, a wintery sun. We were there after black grouse and the chance of hen harrier, and after a short time we saw what we came for. Initially, a female hen harrier was seen quartering, low, over the moor. She disturbed a small flock of red grouse, not that she seemed the slightest interested in them. Things quietened down, a raven croaked, and two red grouse flew over the rim of a hill. One of my colleagues pointed, 'What are these coming in?' he asked. Bingo time. Seven black grouse, all black cocks, came hurtling in to crash land in the gorse, and vanish from sight. Grouse are not the most elegant of fliers, they just hurtle in, on whirring wings, crashing into cover. They will never win prizes for grace, that is for sure, not that we were complaining. We had seen what we came for, which brightened up a damp day that was for sure. Another year drew to a close, even allowing for my slow start, I saw two hundred and thirty-one species in the UK. Now we would see what 2004 has to say. We commenced the year with familiar field meetings, the Staffordshire Moorlands and the Elan Valley, where the expected species were readily available. Come the 1st February, Southport and Martin Mere were on the agenda, and there the one hundred mark was passed with ease.

A few days later, Dorothy and I had a short break in Norfolk, where we knocked up eighty-seven species. Included among these were a couple of avocets, several barn owls, the black-winged stilt still (this bird had been there so consistently the locals had named him; he is now known to all as, I believe, 'Sammy'), a marsh harrier, spotted redshanks and a short-eared owl were also on show. Some high quality birds to see so early in a year. After the success of last year's cruise, we booked another for later that year. A fifteen days cruise by the Fred Olsen line which would take in Scotland, the Faroes, Holland, Iceland, Spitsburgen and Norway, enough there to keep us happy we thought, sailing on the 20th June. During the next two months we visited mainly local areas in Staffordshire and Derbyshire, but here we saw several quality species, amongst which were brambling, dipper, firecrest, hawfinch, little owl, long-eared owl, mandarin duck, peregrine, pink-footed goose and ruddy duck. Enough there to keep the keenest of birders happy.

Come May and it was time to venture further afield once again. Nightingales called, or should that be sang? The lure of stone curlews, golden orioles and woodlarks drew us. To see those special birds, we had to travel; the occasional nightingale and woodlark had appeared locally, but if you wish to be certain of seeing them, then travel you must. They are never guaranteed needless to say, but our luck was in, the four species were all seen, and well. The newcomers to our group were delighted with the results of those visits.

Prior to our cruise a 'Twitch' called. A scarlet rosefinch was being reported from Tophill Low Nature Reserve, a new location for us and a new bird for several of my colleagues. The reserve lies alongside the River Hull in Yorkshire, map reference obtained, and we were on our way. I had previously made contact with the warden as an entrance fee was payable and I needed to make sure we could all gain access. Not much fun to drive a hundred miles or so and not be allowed in.

The rosefinch was quickly located, a group of over thirty birders saw to that. On a 'Twitch' you do not need to look for the bird, just look for the birders. The bird, which was a male in almost full summer plumage, put on a superb show for us. They are a vagrant from Eastern Europe and Asia, and when seen, which is not very frequently, they are usually juvenile birds seen in autumn. A summer vagrant was a bit special to say the least; a bird to be savoured, and we did. Not a lot else was seen on that occasion – it was definitely a one bird 'Twitch', not that anyone complained.

Our cruise arrived and on the 20th June, 2004, we set sail. What wonders lay ahead?

Our first stop was Scotland. There we had the choice of several excursions. We chose a coach trip which included visiting Loch Ness; you cannot visit Scotland and miss out on this opportunity. We all dream of seeing 'Nessie', some people seriously so.

The day was bright and clear and the views were wonderful. I always knew the Loch was large, but the length of it took me by complete surprise. We made several stops at selected viewpoints, at one of them we had wonderful views of a golden eagle which sailed majestically by. We were able to bring this to the attention of several of our companions, much to their great pleasure. An osprey also put in a brief appearance, we were on our own when this occurred, so no one else was able to share the event. It was a very pleasant few hours, in glorious countryside, and no – we did not see 'Nessie'. We sailed on to the Faroes. We decided to look after ourselves there and see what birdlife we could find. Some of our companions went whale watching; some small craft were plying for their trade. It did surprise us a little, the locals were making a living taking tourist's whale watching whilst at the same time, or so we understood, continuing whale hunting.

The birdlife did not let us down. A good array of auks, gulls, eider ducks, common scoters, skuas, terns, plus a few hooded crows. A few waders were also seen, bar-tailed godwits with fledged young, a sight we had never seen previously, turnstones and the inevitable oystercatchers. We were more than satisfied.

Iceland was on the horizon, our main reason for taking this particular cruise. We had two days to explore Iceland, so we took one tour which included Lake Myvatn and the Reykjanes Peninsula and the second day we intended to visit Reykjavik, which included a visit to Lake Tjomin, two full days in which we hoped to see some of Iceland's spectacular birds and equally spectacular scenery.

The trip to Lake Myvatn was most enjoyable. The English translation for the name is Lake of Flies, or so we were informed, and on a warm day the mosquitoes are unbearable, so we were told. You can well imagine our delight when that day dawned cloudy and with a distinct chill, not a day for flies to enjoy! Most of our companions on that excursion had gone to see the meteor craters which were famous in the area, we left them to it, birds were our objective, and we were not let down. Round the perimeter of the lake were several small ponds and it was almost a case of each one having a pair of red-necked phalaropes in attendance. These birds were not frightened of people and we had wonderful views of them, some I doubt were above ten feet away from us. Phalaropes are unusual birds, the female is the more brightly coloured and the male does most of the incubating and looking after the young. Here it certainly is not a man's world, the women have never had it so good!

Two pairs of great northern divers were out on the lake, and one pair sailed in very close to us. They are a superb bird and this was the first time we had seen them in their full summer plumage, some bird. Whenever we had seen the species previously, it had been either in winter or in juvenile plumage. Lake Myvatn had not let us down. Now for the Reykjanes Peninsula.

The Peninsula hosts one of Iceland's largest colony of seabirds, a mixture of thousands of terns, gulls, skuas and auks, and the skuas were the birds which interested us the most. Gulls, terns and auks we are familiar with back home, Bempton Cliffs provides most of those, but skuas in the UK are mainly Scottish. We were not to be disappointed. Arctic skuas were there in an abundance and great skuas were not far behind. We had mentioned to one or two of our colleagues not to go close to the skua colonies, some ignored our advice and returned with head wounds inflicted by the aggressive birds, skuas are not frightened of people; I doubt they are frightened of anything, especially the great skua. They are not called great for nothing, they are the size of a great black-backed gull and far more vicious. The Arctic skuas are also equally aggressive, birds to be viewed from afar. Among the auks nesting on the cliff ledges, were several Brunnich's guillemots, a very rare bird back home and a species we had only previously seen in Norway, here they were quite numerous. On our return journey, we were driving along the side of a fast flowing river of ice melt, it was almost pure white in colour, but more interestingly, on it was a small flock of Barrow's goldeneyes, all drakes. These were a bird completely new to us and we managed to get the coach driver to pull over and stop for a few minutes. We were very pleased she did so, it was the only occasion we saw any of them.

Our second day was spent in Reykjavik, where after a coffee and a look round, we made our way to Lake Tjomin. Here we again saw great northern divers, red-necked phalaropes and a pair of grey phalaropes with several large gulls out on the lake. Among these were Iceland gulls (Where else would you expect to see them?), and glaucous gulls, all again in summer plumage. As with the divers, the few we see at home are usually winter birds or juveniles, and these are only seen rarely. Along the shore were snow buntings and Lapland buntings, and from the scattered bushes redwings could be both heard and seen, all of these being winter visitors to the UK. The snow buntings and Lapland buntings looked particularly smart in their full summer plumage, not that this was new to us, we had seen these previously in Norway, but we were not complaining. Iceland had certainly lived up to its reputation.

We sailed round the northern coast of the country as we made our way to Spitsbergen and we saw many whales. Two great grey whales in particular drifted by totally oblivious to our cruise ship just a few feet away, not that they need have worried, they looked almost as large as we were.

On one occasion a group of killer whales was following the liner, these put on a very spectacular display. They followed us for some considerable time, just cruising along in the wake of the liner, they gave the impression of just enjoying it all; although, on the other hand, they may have been hoping someone fell overboard!

The sea looked a large and open expanse, but the more you looked at it the more you realised just how much lived in it, and above it. Your major marine birds such as shearwaters, auks, kittiwakes and gannets can be seen well away from land and the distances they must travel in search of food is vast indeed. I am never bored when looking over vast expanses of open sea, there is always something to attract your attention, spectacularly so on occasion, as with whale spotting.

As we approached Spitsbergen we were well into the Arctic Circle, and to talk of the 'land of the mid-night sun is no myth', or to be more accurate, in our case it was 'sea of...' I had mentioned when on our cruise to Norway of sitting out on deck well into the night, in bright sunlight, here it literally did not set. How wildlife and the few people living on Spitsbergen adapt to life I do not know.

Sailing down Kongsfjord we were thrilled with the number of little auks which flew past the liner. Spitsbergen has a very high population of these delightful small birds, and they gave us the impression they had all come out to greet our arrival. With their fast blurring wings, they looked almost like a large dark bee. An amazing sight. And they were not all. Spitsbergen also has a good selection of Arctic breeding gulls, glaucous and Iceland, but the specialities, specially for us, was the hope of seeing adult Ross's gulls, which breed on Spitsbergen in small numbers, and the ivory gull, another speciality of the area. We were fortunate with the Ross's gull, we saw a few of those, and they were pretty special, in their summer plumage they are very distinctive. The ivory gull however did not oblige. Unfortunately, we only had a few hours to spend on land, but the landscape was incredible and we were surprised by the temperature; it was relatively mild, this was no doubt due to the fact the sun did not set. Where we landed, if my memory serves me right, was Ny Alesund.

Here an International Research Village is located, and amongst the buildings snow buntings and Lapland buntings were breeding, almost like starlings and house sparrows back home, and they were relatively tame. In the tundra areas Arctic terns had large colonies, why else are the known as Arctic terns, and ringed plovers were breeding among the dry shingle. All very peaceful, and all very tolerant of man. We cruised back round the north of the island, whales again evident, and on one of the small islands we saw what looked like sleeping walruses, we could not get good enough views to be sure, but they were certainly large. But joy of joys, a small flock of twenty or so, very white looking gulls came drifting past; we had our ivory gulls, looking more like large snowflakes than birds. What a bird, if for nothing else, Spitsbergen was worth it.

I remembered reading somewhere that over 60% of Spitsbergen is glaciated, and when sailing round the island it is easy to understand this, it is hard to imagine such ice and snow. The liner stopped at one or two of the more spectacular glaciers, one of which was known as the blue glacier, and in the clear light of the Arctic; it was easy to understand where the name came from. One of the glaciers treated us to a spectacular ice fall. A large area of the glacier just broke off and tumbled into the sea, it made a sound like thunder; how many tons of ice fell into the sea was hard to imagine. We were just pleased to see it and not be underneath it. I am pretty sure of one thing, both Iceland and Spitsbergen will see us again, after all, we did not see a polar bear, Norway was next. We arrived in Norway in very poor weather. Our first stop was at a location where we could not berth, we had to moor up and travel by tender as the conditions were so poor; this we were unable to do. We spent the day cruising round the northern coast, although this was spectacular, I cannot say I enjoyed it greatly. Dorothy on the other hand was able to sit out on the deck and thoroughly enjoy being tossed around by the waves. It was at times like this I realised why I had joined the RAF and not become a sailor! The number of empty tables at dinner that evening told the story, I did at least manage my meal.

The birds seen in Norway on that occasion were much as we had experienced on our previous cruise, with two major exceptions, a superb hawk-owl and very large numbers of sea eagles. If we take the eagles first. We saw just the odd few on the previous cruise, but on this occasion we saw many. One of the fjords had a large island near to the entrance, on which was a fish processing plant, and here – after the day's processing had been completed – remains of the fish were put out for the sea eagles and other scavengers. To see twenty or thirty eagles in the air together was not unusual, this illustrated the large number of birds living in the country. I have read that half the European sea eagle population live in Norway, and this is estimated at 4,500 birds; I wondered how many came here? The hawk owl on the other hand was a one off, but what a one off! In flight could easily be mistaken for a sparrowhawk, but our bird, fortunately for us, landed on a telegraph pole and sat there for several minutes just surveying us. They are a very diurnal owl, very whitish in colour, particularly on their breast – and although we had never experienced the bird previously – there was no mistaking this fellow.

Next came a brief visit to Holland, Amsterdam in fact, and not much birding was expected from here, but even so we had a few surprises. Bar-headed geese and Egyptian geese were seen in goodly numbers. Back home Egyptian geese are only to be seen in the odd location where escapees have set up small breeding colonies of now wild birds, and bar-headed geese are usually single birds which have escaped from collections. In Holland, they must have been breeding for several years to be seen so frequently; it raises the question: were they from escapees or have they been deliberately released and introduced? Whatever the answer is to that question, they are certainly now looking part of the Dutch scene.

Swifts were very common, especially round the older parts of the city, and the other feature of Amsterdam are its cyclists. I have never seen so many cyclists in all my life, cycles were parked up, one leaning against the other. It made you wonder how you sorted your own cycle out, or as I heard one wag say, 'It probably does not matter, you just take the first available machine; you don't own it, you just borrow it.' Wonder if that could happen on car parks?

We cruised back across the North Sea. Enjoying a few passing shearwaters and skuas before darkness descended. Another most enjoyable holiday was drawing to its conclusion, where to go next was the question upper most in our thoughts. This cruising certainly had its advantages. During the cruise we had seen ninety-three species, many of which you would have been unlikely to see back home. This is the beauty of foreign travel of course; you just have to know what you are looking at or have the necessary field guides to assist you. As least on a cruise there is not the same problem with weight restrictions, and you do not change rooms as you travel. The remainder of 2004 saw us visiting our usual haunts, but even so we saw a few very high quality species. At Tamworth, not usually noted for mega species, we had a hooded merganser: a rare North American species, and a 'Lifer' for all. Rutland produced another cracker, a red-breasted goose. With both of these species, the 'purists' were out, claiming they were escapees. It seems that every time you see a rare waterfowl species, they have to be escapees, other types of birds are more readily accepted. If these unusual waterfowls are all escapees, someone is being very careless, they are expensive birds to buy, and collection birds are not usually just clipped, they are pinioned, and their primaries do not grow again, the bird remains flightless. The merganser and red-breasted goose could certainly fly, and did so frequently. They went on my listings. The red-breasted goose is a rare vagrant from the Siberian tundra, and I think it is fair to say, if they arrive here they are most certainly lost.

I organised another group holiday for Norfolk which took place in September, the 19th to the 26th to be precise, and The Pheasant was again our venue. We are now well known here and they do look after us. The weather that week was a little mixed to say the least, but we thoroughly enjoyed ourselves and visited all the usual locations. I think we are getting to know Norfolk very well. We had a marvellous week totting up one hundred and fourteen species in the week, the pick being: black-winged stilt, crane, Egyptian goose, great skua, lesser yellowlegs (a rare North American vagrant), a 'Lifer' for most, long-tailed skua, Manx shearwater, pectoral sandpiper (another Yankee vagrant), red-necked grebe, red-throated diver, Ross's goose, sooty shearwater and spotted crake. Enough there to keep us all happy.

Mid-October we were back in North Wales, Rhos on Sea, the Little Orme and Worlds End were our destinations. The weather was very calm which did not help us, the birds remained far out at sea, but we did at least pick up a red-throated diver at Rhos and a great northern diver off the Little Orme. Worlds End did not let us down good views of both black and red grouse, plus a flypast by a merlin, were enough for all. My group had been talking about another bird watching holiday, so I organised another week away in Norfolk for late May the next year. The Pheasant Hotel were only too pleased to book us all in, and once again we obtained good terms. Seventeen of us on this occasion, nine of whom who had never been away with us previously. November saw us at Rutland Water and Eyebrook Reservoir, where not a lot happened, a pleasant enough day, but not a lot on the bird front, a curlew sandpiper being the best of that day. We finished the year at Slimbridge, which was up to its usual standard. Barnacle geese, bean geese, Bewick's swans, a lesser spotted woodpecker, mandarin ducks, white-fronted geese and whooper swans brought it down on another good year.

The year saw me reach my highest ever total seen in the UK, I reached two hundred and forty-two species. My dream of two hundred and fifty in a year was beginning to look possible! What had 2005 in store? To start off we booked ourselves another cruise – this time with P&O a cruise round the Mediterranean which included calling in at Egypt, that should bring back some memories, and who knows, I may get to see the pyramids this time? A ten-day cruise in May should be quite pleasant at that time of the year. The year commenced with a series of local visits, which included the Moors, Tittesworth Reservoir, the Chase, Blithfield Reservoir, Belvide Reservoir and Carsington Water. The usual quality birds expected were picked up during those first few weeks, which always helps to start your 'Year List' off well. The pick of those early species were bean goose, black redstart, corn bunting, long-eared owl, merlin, red grouse, short-eared owl, stonechat, water pipit, waxwing and white-fronted goose. Not a bad haul that, and I also reached my hundred mark by the end of January, a very good start to the year.

As the daylight hours increased we ventured further afield. Southport and Martin Mere increased our waterfowl and wader numbers considerably. The usual highlights being curlew, golden plover, a superb male hen harrier, peregrine, pink-footed goose, pintail and whooper swan. In total, seventy-six on the day. Early March saw us visit Aberystwyth and the Elan Valley, calling in at Ludlow in transit, where the dipper, goosander and hawfinches put on their usual display. Driving through the Valley red kite and buzzard were seen, the numbers of red kite are slowly increasing, no doubt due the fact they are being re-introduced from, I believe, Spain. Where ever they have originated, we can never have too many, they are a magnificent flying machine! Chough and raven added to the list at Aber. Another good day.

We had a local meeting late April at Blithfield Reservoir, and there disaster struck, I passed out; paramedics were summoned and I was transported to hospital in Burton. Dorothy was not with us on that occasion so one of my friends raced home to bring her into hospital to see me, what she expected to find I can only guess. She arrived to see me sitting up in bed, wired up to a piece of medical apparatus to be told it looked like I had suffered a stroke; fortunately, not too serious – if there is such a thing as not serious. I must admit I was feeling fairly reasonable, but the hospital decided to keep me in for a few days' observation and further checks. Our cruise was but days away, and this was quickly kicked into touch, no chance we were told. Fortunately, it was covered by insurance, so we did not lose out financially; we just missed out on a cruise we were looking forward to. The other problem was I could not drive until further examinations cleared me.

On my release, I was referred to a heart specialist at Leicester, and there a pacemaker was suggested and this would be fitted in a couple of months or so. The main thing for me was that I was told I could drive again.

To compensate for missing out on the cruise, we did at least have Norfolk to look forward to, not quite as exotic as cruising the Med, but The Pheasant was up to its usual standard and looked after us well. The birds were to their usual high standards and we saw one hundred and twenty-five during the week, including two mega specimens, purple heron and lesser spotted eagle, but more about those later. The other prime species seen were avocet, crane, gargany, hobby, Montagu's harrier, nightingale, pink-footed goose – a very late record for this species – turtle dove, woodchat shrike and wryneck. Enough there without our two mega's, but back to those.

We were driving towards Cley when Dorothy told me to stop. She had seen a very dark looking heron land on the edge of a reed bed. Luckily, there was a wide grassy verge to the road and all of our cars were able to pull up on it, there were five vehicles. A quick look through our binoculars, and Dorothy had hit the jackpot: it was a superb purple heron, a bird none had ever seen in the UK previously. I had seen them abroad on a few occasions, but there is nothing like seeing them back home. We enjoyed the bird for several minutes before it stalked off into the reed bed, to vanish for ever. Seventeen very happy birders moved on to Cley, and there it got even better.

We drove down to the car park on Cley Eye to carry out some sea watching, and there we enjoyed a few gannets and fulmars plus odd terns when one of my party shouted, 'What is that large bird of prey flying low over the water?' The bird was quite a distance, but it was easy to tell it was large, an eagle type, but which? Telescopes were quickly focused on the bird and now a little of the birds detail could be gleaned.

The bird was long winged and as it glided, which it did a lot, the wings were held angled downwards, but this was only obvious from its carpal joint. The head and shoulders looked pale compared with the rest of the bird's darker plumage, and as it banked it showed a pale, almost 'V' shape on the rump area. My friends were looking at me expecting some comment, I was struggling. I then remembered seeing spotted eagle on occasion in Europe, so I suggested we looked at that in our field guides. I was a lucky man, a spotted eagle it certainly was, but which? There are two species: the spotted eagle and lesser spotted eagle, and they were not easy to split, especially at that distance. Here a stroke of luck came our way. Two birders came dashing up, shouted to us about the eagle, and they were able to tell us that the bird had been flying along the coast for a few miles and giving some very good views. It had actually flown over the beach at Cromer and here it was decided it was the lesser spotted eagle, we were happy with that. The paler head and shoulders certainly supported that diagnosis, what a bird. To think we had seen two mega birds within a couple of miles of each other. No wonder Norfolk is looked on as the prime U.K. birding county. Now you know why we keep on going back.

That was another great week, and missing out on the Med did not seem so bad after all. We would no doubt book it for another year. I had only been home a few days before my birding went on to the back burner so to speak. A letter arrived from Leicester, an appointment for my pacemaker was therein. Late June and Dorothy took me across for this to be carried out, and although I was only in hospital for three days, I was not able to drive for eight weeks so my birding was limited somewhat.

After three weeks I was able to get out as a passenger, but carrying a telescope was a no go due to the weight resting upon the area where the pacemaker was implanted.

Due to my pacemaker, this was going to be a year I had to miss out on a visit to Bempton Cliffs, but for my first trip out I was driven to the Blacktoft Sands and North Cave reserves, both in Yorkshire. Walking is limited at Blacktoft as the hides are close to each other and at North Cave you are able to drive right up to the hides, perfect for me in the current circumstances. On the day, we had seventy-one species with the pick of them all being quail. As I have mentioned before, quail are our smallest game bird, they are only here during the summer, and they are rarely seen. Their best identification feature is voice, when the male calls, usually in the evening, you may hear a three note call – quite liquidy – frequently repeated, 'wet my lips' or 'quip ip ip'; I prefer the latter translation! The only problem was the time of the year, late July and the quail only called briefly, but we were fortunate to see a bird. Once again, we travelled home happy birders.

The year passed by quietly in many respects, and although we made two visits to Spurn Point, Old Moor and Rutland Water, we had little of what you may call extra special – apart from on our second trip to Spurn – where it was jackpot time again. A mega bird and a 'Lifer' for all.

Near 'Big Hedge' we saw a group of very excited birders, there were over forty of them, so we quickly made our way across to be greeted by news of a lesser grey shrike. Great grey shrikes are regular winter visitors to the UK, lesser certainly are not, and this was the first time any of us had the chance of seeing the bird; they are not on your list of expectancies!

Unlike great grey, which are usually showmen and sit out in full view, this bird was intent with playing games with us and only fleetingly popped out. Times like this can become very frustrating. Fortunately, it repeated its antics so we all eventually managed to get a good view of the bird, patience is the name of the game, and with a 'Lifer' you do like to see it well. The year closed on two hundred and twenty-four, not bad in the circumstances, and among those birds were a few very choice specimens. A new year awaited, what would 2006 bring in?

Before any birding took place, two holidays were booked. Firstly, another cruise – this time round the Baltic Sea, which included a day in Russia visiting St. Petersburg in late May – but before then I organised another group holiday to Norfolk. This was a winter break for a change, a chance to chase up the winter visitors; all we hoped for was some decent weather to do it in.

Now back to actual birding. Our first two meetings were local where the customary birds were quickly chalked up, and at the end of the month we visited Rutland Water. There is always the chance of the odd quality duck being seen there, and we were not to be disappointed.

We had barnacle goose, Egyptian goose, pintail, red-breasted merganser, scaup and smew. Enough there to interest the most serious birder. A few waders were also present, curlew, dunnock, golden plover, redshank and snipe being the pick of those. In total we saw sixty-nine species on the day, and we had all reached the hundred mark before the end of January. Signs of another good year we hoped.

Prior to our Norfolk week, we visited Martin Mere and Southport, and clicked for a foul day; fortunately, in one respect, it was rain not snow. We managed one or two quality sightings, early avocets and marsh harriers, the anticipated whooper swans, and a mixture of waders; wet we may have got, but we chalked up sixty-two species in the rain. Now for the serious stuff of Norfolk.

I must confess as the holiday got ever nearer the weather took a turn for the worse, and snow was experienced in many parts of the country with the eastern side suffering the most. What were we heading in to?

At least we drove over in dry conditions, although the landscape looked very winterish; but birders are hardy souls, or at the worst, just plain stupid! We had made the decision to drive straight to the hotel in case of bad weather and we all met up in time for a light lunch and refreshments, and we were very pleased we had done so. Another birder was in the hotel who had just come up from visiting The Quags, a collection of small pools near to the hotel, and there he had seen a grey phalarope. Unpacking went straight onto the back burner, and off down The Quags we strode with the prospects of a super bird to start off the week – for some it was 'Lifer' time on Day one. It cannot get much better than that. The phalarope did not disappoint: it performed well, right in the open and in front of us; the bird had not a care in the world as Dorothy commented, 'It was almost like being back in Iceland.' She was not quite right there, it had been warmer in Iceland!

There were also redshank, ruff and ringed plover along with the grey phalarope, on the sea, which was very calm, two red-throated divers were slowly drifting southwards and a decent flock of meadow pipits were on the shoreline. These would need closer observation as the week progressed just to make sure some unusual pipit was not tucked away amongst them. Time that day was against us; it was, after all, February and the days were not light for long.

After dinner that evening, we all agreed we had just experienced a great start to our holiday; here's hoping it was to continue. The malt tasted very good that evening and we decided that tomorrow we would visit Titchwell. We understood early avocets and marsh harriers had been seen, and due to the poor weather, barn owls were actively hunting in broad daylight; good enough reason for that decision.

The morning dawned white over, but at least it was frost not snow, and by the time we had breakfasted, it had mostly gone. In the hotel grounds, we had a good quality bird to start off the day: a little owl popped in to see us, he was welcome anytime.

The journey to Titchwell was uneventful, and we arrived at Titchwell to find it almost deserted, hardly a car in the car park, I had never seen this before. The reserve was up to its usual standard, avocets were indeed back, well three of them were and we saw at least two marsh harriers, both males. As it was a calm day the bearded tits were quite active and we were treated to many a flypast by those little beauties. Whilst enjoying those one of my colleagues brought my attention to a flock of brent geese which were on the water in front of us: two of them he thought were very dark and did not look right. I was very pleased he had picked those out, they were two of the North American race known as brant geese, which occasionally pop up. It is a continual argument between the birders and the purists, as to whether they are escapees or not. We later found out those two were not ringed, so they go on our lists. As to be expected at Titchwell, there were large number of waders present, black-tailed godwits, curlews, dunlins, knots, golden and grey plovers, and along the shoreline sanderlings and the odd turnstone. The waders seen at The Quags were also here in larger numbers, plus many oystercatchers. When you talk of waders at Titchwell you are looking at thousands on occasion, and that day was one such. Just as we were about to leave, a birder arrived – almost out of breath – he was so excited. Up the lane near to the barns I have previously mentioned, where we saw the meadow bunting, you will recollect another mega bird was seen; this time, a cinereous bunting. What a bird from the extreme eastern end of the Mediterranean was doing so far west I do not know, but all thoughts of returning to our hotel quickly vanished; we were on an adrenalin rush. 'Twitch' time really called.

The bird was this time near to the junction at Choseley Farm, and was associating with a small flock of reed buntings. Cinereous buntings are unlikely to be confused with reeds, they are a much paler looking bird, and as the bird was being reported as a male, things were definitely better. A quick look in our field guides so we all knew what we were looking for, and the chase was on. The word chase was a little exaggerated. We quickly spied a group of about twenty birders and pulled in to join them. The bunting was feeding in a nearby field along with the reed buntings, and the bird stood out quite easily. We all had a 'Lifer' and, when added to what we had seen previously, we certainly had experienced a brilliant day. We all hoped it would continue for the remainder of the week. The malt that evening tasted even better than usual.

Day two saw us visiting Cley and Salthouse, and the weather had made a decided change for the worst. Although only a short distance from The Pheasant, the journey was not pleasant: snow had drifted across the road in several places and we were all very pleased to arrive at Cley safely. Gum boots were the order of the day as the snow was quite thick in places. It did not seem to overly concern the birds as the water was not frozen, fortunately, so the waterfowl were happy enough and the damp margins to the lakes were also clear of snow, so the waders had mud to explore. A barn owl was already out hunting and a large flock of brent geese were on the water, no brants this time. Pink-footed and greylag geese were also in good numbers. The waders were much as seen the previous day at Titchwell, although not in quite the same numbers. Out at sea was a very large flock of scoters, so we concentrated our efforts on those; you never know what may be tucked in amongst them. Wigeon were quickly picked out and after a good deal of searching three velvet scoter were found, two drakes and a duck; our hard work had been rewarded. A peregrine falcon flew through at one stage and this certainly flushed the smaller waders. A large flock of golden plovers took to the air, we had not even seen those birds as they were on the far side of an island, so the peregrine did us a favour. A quick warm snack was had at Cley and we made our way down to Salthouse. The car park was almost deserted, which in the conditions was understandable, only real hardy souls come out on days like this. A red-necked grebe was on the water, just drifting slowly further out to sea on the out-going tide, and curlew could be heard on the heath behind us; what they had to call about on a day like that I did not know. A merlin came flashing across, he did not look to be in hunting mode, probably rushing about to keep warm. Some local birders regularly put seed out there which attracted turnstones and small birds. The turnstones had been and eaten their fill by the time of our arrival, but a flock of small, very pale looking birds dropped in. We were glad they had. We had seven snow buntings, five males and two females, memories for Dorothy and I of a recent cruise. Seven is a very good number, the most I have ever seen together in the UK, so this was more than a bit special. They were quite accommodating, so we were able to watch them for many minutes, and cameras whirred away. Miserable weather we may have experienced, but we had no complaints on the bird front. Another very pleasant evening was had at The Pheasant, with the malt getting ever better. That is probably a silly thing to say, malt cannot be improved, it is already perfection; the thing which can change is our appreciation of it! We studied the tide tables that evening and saw things were just about perfect for visiting Snettisham. Norfolk and North West Norfolk in particular: hosts the largest winter collection of waders to be seen in England. Thousands congregate along this stretch of coast along the shores of The Wash, and for many of my colleagues this was going to be a first time adventure.

We needed an incoming tide and that day it was just perfect, high tide was round 11.00 a.m. and it just happened to be one of the highest of the winter we were informed.

The journey up was not difficult, no more snow had fallen, although it was still very cold. As we would be exposed to any wind off the sea we made very sure that we had adequate clothing; watching birds in cold weather is not the most pleasant of occupations. Frozen fingers do not operate binoculars or telescopes easily.

On arrival we found it to be a calm day, just the slightest of breezes, and this was off shore so it was to our backs. Thousands of birds were flying out at sea, hundreds of thousands may be a more accurate statement, and these birds were being driven in ever closer by the tide. How many dunlins and knots could be seen was impossible to judge, the sky at times just looked full of them, and their accompanying calls just filled the air with sound. The hair on the back of your neck just rose – well, it did if you had any soul. They were right about the height of the tide, we also had to quickly retreat its incoming. Eventually, it was fully in. The waders were now congregated on dry land, and they were everywhere; we, by the way, had now moved into a hide from where we could view the birds in comparative comfort. There was a very good selection needless to say, and not just in numbers, the range of species was also high. I will run through them. Dunlin and knot I have already mentioned, additional to these were: oystercatcher, lapwing, golden plover, grey plover, ringed plover, bar-tailed godwit, black-tailed godwit, redshank, curlew, spotted redshank, greenshank, green sandpiper, common sandpiper, a solitary avocet, snipe, sanderling and turnstones. Almost a who's-who of British waders.

As what seemed a relatively short period of time a certain amount of restlessness appeared among the birds, particularly the oystercatchers, and then small groups commenced to fly out. The tide had turned, food was now becoming available, and the birds moved off to seek this. In a comparatively short period of time, the majority of the birds had gone so we returned to the shore to watch the birds follow the tide, instead of previously retreating in front of it. To put it bluntly, this had been one hell of an experience. I had seen it all previously, but as I mentioned earlier, it still raises the hair on the back of my neck. This was real birding, this was what it is all about, and as one or two of my colleagues said, 'This was a day they would never forget.' Mind you, it was not quite all over. As we walked back to our cars, a short-eared owl came out and put on a display for us. The perfect finish to a perfect morning. After a warm snack at a nearby café, we popped down to Hunstanton to do some sea watching. The tide, unfortunately, had raced out and many of the birds were way out at sea. A few gulls remained on the cliffs and the odd fulmar gave us a flypast, so all was not lost. On the beach below, a few waders were to be seen, curlews and oystercatchers mainly and a small flock of gannets were picked up, way out at sea. It may have been a quiet ending to the day, but after the excitement of the morning, it was probably good to relax.

The following day saw us at Holkham, and here we had a pleasant surprise, no one was taking parking money. I can but presume that, due to the bad weather, it was not worth having anyone there to collect the fees from so few vehicles. When we parked up at Holkham Gap, the only cars were ours. It was another very sharp morning, so we quickly made our way into the shelter of the Meals; the trees here were of some benefit. Parties of titmice were very active, and we had five species in many of the groups. Blue, great, coal, marsh and long-tailed tits. Goldcrests were also well accounted for, and we even heard a chiffchaff. That was totally unexpected so early in the year, but we are getting reports of occasional over-wintering chiffchaffs. These are not necessarily birds born in the UK, they are more likely to be birds which have arrived here from Scandinavia and the like.

We were enjoying a pair of bullfinches, always a superb sight, when one of my colleagues said, 'Hi Bri, I have a funny looking goldcrest here.' I swung round to see just what he had got, and he had found the bird of the morning so far. He pointed out a magnificent male firecrest to us, what a bird. He may not have known what he had found, but we were mighty glad he had. Unlike the goldcrest which breeds through the UK, firecrest are a relatively rare species – a few pairs do breed – but the birds we usually see are winter visitors from further north and we do not see many of them. I have years when I do not see any at all, this could well be my only one of the year, so I was delighted to see the bird. Along with the goldcrest, they are our smallest bird.

Making our way out of the Meals and onto the area commonly known as West Sands, we concentrated our efforts on picking up the snow buntings which regularly feed here, or so it was claimed. Many meadow pipits were to be seen and a small party of reed buntings were picked up, but it was several minutes before we found a snow bunting; well, to be more accurate, four of them – three females and one male.

Whilst enjoying these, they were disturbed by a passing sparrowhawk; they vanished, so did the hawk, and that was that for the morning. We then drove down to Wells, Wells Next the Sea to give it it's full name, and here we drove down to the car park near the coastguard and lifeboat stations; the local café being our number one target. It was open and some warm food was quickly obtained and almost as quickly digested. Feeling somewhat invigorated, we made our way down to the coastguard station which overlooked the now large area of mud flats, which were exposed now the tide was out, and well out. A narrow channel ran through the mud and several seals were swimming in this, looking almost lazy as they did so.

On the bird front, curlews, oystercatchers, redshanks and godwits were feeding in the mud and overhead skeins of brent geese were flying in and out of nearby Cley. A quick look at the nearby conifer plantation was called for, and this turned out to be a good call: crossbills could be heard, now to try to find them.

When we did finally locate them, it was not the call that drew our attention, it was the bits of cone falling out of the trees. There must have been at least thirty birds in that flock, and so many birds chiselling away at fir cones does cause quite an amount of sawdust – fortunately!

They are very agile birds and to see them hanging onto a cone with one foot and the other keeping them in position on the twig; it was quite amazing. Where the cones were large, the crossbill just hung on the cone. The more you watch birds the more you learn about them.

Crossbills were not the only inhabitants of the plantation, a small party of siskins were also feeding away. They were probably not after the cone seeds, their preference was probably for small insects which lived in the cone. Whatever the reason, the crossbills and the siskins had certainly brought some colour to the scene, and also concluded our trip out most pleasantly.

We decided that a day in The Broads would not go amiss, the problem is the area is quite large so you had to be rather selective of which area to visit. We chose Hickling Broad; it was here where there was always the chance of bittern and, more importantly, a small colony of cranes are to be found nearby – that is rather special. They are probably the only breeding group in the UK, one of our rarest breeding birds. Visiting this area also had the advantage of nearby Horsey Mere should time be available.

Arriving at Hickling Broad, which is a Norfolk Wildlife Trust reserve, we had an unpleasant shock: it was closed up, as work was being carried out on some of the hides. Fortunately for us, at that moment, the warden arrived on the scene; when he realised where we were from, he let us in without charge. He pointed out the hides which were being renovated and told us we could not visit those areas, but showed where we could go. At least half the reserve was open to us, and one of the hides we could go in overlooked one of the larger pools. More importantly, he was able to show us the field which the cranes favoured.

On some feeders near the visitor centre, two blackcaps were feeding, both females and a male marsh harrier was flying across in the distance; not a bad greeting. We made our way down to the hide and were delighted to see a flock of thirty-four whooper swans on the pool and amongst those were two family parties: one pair with three cygnets; the other with two. The young still had large areas of colour in their plumage, so there was no problem in deciding they were cygnets. Decent numbers of teals and wigeons were also to be seen, plus the odd goldeneye and goosander.

In the distance, a large flock of golden plovers was in the air; they kept on vanishing as they landed, only to take to the air a short while later. We realised why they were so active, the marsh harrier repeatedly flew in their direction and the golden plovers were not amused! Wading in the water were curlews and black-tailed godwits, along with both Canada and grey-lag geese, plus a pair of great crested grebes.

Two grey heron were stalking the pool edges, these briefly disturbed a water rail which flew out of the reeds to vanish as quickly as it appeared. We nodded a thank you to the heron. A Cetti's warbler could just about be heard, quite a voice this little fellow possesses, they are slowly moving northwards from their home in southern England. Could this once again be a sign of 'Climate Change?'

As we could not cover all the reserve, we decided to move on and try to find the cranes, then we might have enough time to visit Horsey Mere. We walked down the track which ran round the edge of the reserve, enjoying a large flock of fieldfare and redwing as we did so. Dorothy was in the lead, when she suddenly stopped, pointed and put her fingers to her lips. She moved back a few paces and as we caught her up she whispered, 'Cranes.' Peering through a gap in the hedge, thirteen cranes were visible, more than I have ever seen in my life in total. They were feeding on a damp meadow; what they were finding to eat I do not know, although I have a suspicion it was probably worms. They were slowly progressing across the field in an almost stately manner, looking very elegant on their long thin legs. Most of us may have seen cranes previously, but never like this. Two of my colleagues turned to me and said, 'Brian, if we had seen nothing else this week, this alone would have been worth it.' I could not help but agree.

Remembering the quote my old friend Ivor regularly comes up with,

'After this, there is only one way it can go and that is down hill.' Horsey Mill proved him correct. A lovely spot with a marvellous mill, but bird life was almost non-existent. Had it not been for a moorhen, two coots, a pair of mallards and a hovering kestrel, it would have been so. Not that we were complaining, thirteen cranes had made sure of that, and to think some say thirteen is an unlucky number!

Our final day arrived, and we decided we would re-visit Titchwell.

From a weather point of view, this was our best day: cold, but clear, and we drove off in convoy towards Titchwell. In transit, as we approached the entrance to Holkham Hall, we spotted a group of birders staring – very intently – down the drive to Holkham Gap. We pulled in and parked up. Once again, no parking attendants were in view so we parked up for free.

Joining the birders there we saw their attention was focused on a large flock of grey geese, pink-foots being our initial thought, but one of the birders drew our attention to a group of about twenty birds just away from the main flock, and we were pleased he had. These were white-fronted geese, a great addition to our week's list. We stayed on for several minutes enjoying the geese, before moving on to Titchwell.

Titchwell was far busier than when we were last there, and after a quick coffee, we made our way into the reserve. The birds were much the same as seen earlier in the week, although with the calmer conditions the bearded tits were very active, providing us with some marvellous views. Even a bittern joined in and stalked across a channel right in front of the hide. If we saw nothing else, we would have been happy with that.

The bird of the day, however, was to be seen on the marshland to the left of the main pathway as we walked down to the beach. Three geese were walking away from us, these we initially thought to be white-fronted when they turned to face us, and we were mightily glad they had. These were three lesser white-fronted geese, a bird rarely seen. In the space of just a few miles, we had seen both white-fronted and lesser white-fronted geese, that could only happen in Norfolk!

After a warm snack for lunch, we decided to go back and have a few minutes down at The Quags prior to doing our packing. The grey phalarope had by now moved off but the pipit flock was still very active and we did wish to study those more closely. There was well in excess of fifty birds, and meadow pipits are not the most stationary of birds, they continually run or flit about. Our patience was finally rewarded, two birds ran from the flock – they looked very erect, almost like small thrushes – we had two rock pipits. Not a bad way to finish the week. Now for the packing.

A very enjoyable evening was had, the odd drink flowed, and we all agreed we must do it again. During the week, we had seen one hundred and eighteen species and included amongst those was a few very choice birds. Norfolk had done it yet again. We also learned something else on this holiday. People talk of the south east as being the warmest place in the UK, our week in Norfolk completely debunked that notion!

March, April and early May saw us making our usual visits, chalking up the few special birds we try to see every year, and they did not let us down, apart from one particular favourite. A day trip was made up to The Lakes to see the golden eagles, and this failed completely; no eagles were seen and, from reports I heard, a solitary bird had been seen for just a few days before it vanished from the scene. It now looked as though England had lost its only pair of breeding golden eagles, after so many years of enjoying those dramatic birds; The Lakes would never be the same.

May 26th finally arrived, Dorothy and I were off cruising once again. The Baltic called. On that cruise, we visited Denmark, Norway, Sweden, Finland, Russia, Estonia, Germany and Belgium; six of those were new countries to us both.

On that cruise, birds did not score greatly. Many of the expected species such as bramblings, fieldfares, redwings, nutcrackers, and waxwings were seen when on shore, and long-tailed ducks, scaups and scoters – various divers and a good mixture of gulls and terns, were seen daily from the liner. Ospreys were seen on several occasions, especially as we sailed along the Swedish coast. On one occasion, two wheatears actually landed on the liner; it was as though they were cadging a lift. These two charming little birds raised a few smiles from passengers.

It had been most enjoyable visiting some of Europe's top cities, such as Oslo, Copenhagen, Stockholm, Helsinki and Tallinn, all unique in their own way, and now St. Petersburg loomed ahead. One thing which had surprised us both was the ease of access we had experienced to all the countries so far visited, even Estonia, an Eastern Bloc state, welcomed us. No doubt the cruise companies have much experience on this and they do a great deal of preparation. Before we went on our first cruise, I was very concerned about entry due to my pacemaker, as passage through the electrical apparatus used at ports was to be avoided. I was assured this was no problem. I had my European Pacemaker Patient Identification Card and all I had to do was show this and, if required, I would have a quick hand search – few bothered.

Things were about to change. Russia was our next destination and they very much had their own thoughts on things. Arrival at St Petersburg lacked in glamour that was for sure. They did not have a separate arrival area for shipping, cargo or cruise was all the same to them. We were escorted through customs, which looked like the set of a James Bond film. I had become separated from Dorothy who had gone through before me. When my turn came, I was roughly pushed forward to the electrical checkpoint; I protested and waved my Pacemaker Card at them which was completely ignored – no English was obviously being spoken – and the struggle became a little rough. Dorothy watching all of this looked worried to death. I had obviously caused a blockage, and no one was getting through. Watching all of this was a female police officer who was sitting high on the top of a ladder/chair, who shouted something and clambered down, pushing her way through the line of people and stomped up to us. She jabbed me and shouted something and pointed at the checkpoint; I waved my card, almost in front of her nose.

She grabbed this and her manner to me changed almost instantly, and the customs officer who had challenged me felt her full wrath. I was waved through, and we all eventually arrived in Russia. The only question was, would I get out?

A coach awaited us to take the party to the centre of the city. A female guide – who spoke very good English, as she had apparently been to a university in England – was explaining the various points of interest; although near to the docks, there were few of those. She stopped the coach at one point, near a most dismal looking building imaginable, to tell us this had been the headquarters of the Russian secret police. If only a small percentage of what we have heard about their exploits is true, no wonder the area looked dismal.

Once in the city proper, it changed completely. Some of the buildings are just incredible, the cathedral itself stood out, architecture of the highest standards. If what we were told is correct, at the height of Communism, the cathedral was used as a grain and potato store; it must have taken some work and much money to bring it back to its current splendour. We were unable to go in as a large queue had formed and our guide told us it would take over two hours to clear, and it was still growing. This suited us, after looking at some of the interesting buildings and statues round the cathedral, we visited the famous Heritage Museum.

This has to be seen to be believed, just a few statistics. It covers 233,345 square metres (do not ask me who measured those), and it has over three million works of art and world culture artefacts, plus many other exhibits. You could spend a week going round the Heritage, and even then not seeing it all. In the three hours available to us, we did as much as we could. It had a very good gift shop, where we spent some time sorting out a gift for our daughter; we settled on a set of Russian Dolls, which were modelled on owls. Buying those was an experience. The shop listed prices in four currencies, dollars, sterling, Euros and, finally, roubles. We had been told on the liner, that when buying anything in Russia, try to buy items which had complete Euros as the price and preferably in units of five. Russia seeked foreign currency, and if you bought anything for say three Euros, they gave you the change in roubles – which you had difficulty in then spending – and if you brought this back onboard, it was useless.

They may have made it difficult to get in, but once in they certainly were after your money. An incredible city, but somehow I do not think we will return. A great experience world travel, it certainly broadens the mind, but Russia is not for us. Incidentally, I 'got out' and lived to tell the tale.

On our return journey we briefly called in at North Germany where a very pleasant stroll was enjoyed, accompanied by many black redstarts and a nutcracker put on quite a show for us. A colony of common terns were nesting among the dunes, and these were just a noisy and aggressive as they would have been back home. There is obviously little or no difference between the 'Germanic' common tern and ours.

Two more countries left to visit, Belgium and Holland. Firstly, Holland and a re-visit to Amsterdam. We enjoyed a boat trip on this occasion which enabled us to do two things: one, avoid being run over by cyclists and a second to see the city from a different angle. We also visited a diamond museum, which proved very interesting. The Egyptian geese and bar-headed geese noted on our previous visit, were just as plentiful and widespread. Finally, Belgium and the city of Brussels. This was a coach trip of two hours away from where we docked, but it was well worth it. The parts of the city we visited were most interesting with some amazing architecture and splendid cafes. Whilst there we made sure of buying some Belgium chocolates, and the shop we chose was a chocolatiers delight. A few Euros were handed over, but the price was less than they would have been back home, and there they let you taste one or two before purchase. We rather liked the idea. Home we arrived, another marvellous experience, even our Russian friends could not dampen that!

Back to UK birding once again. Before the month was out, we made our usual trip up to Bempton Cliffs to enjoy 'Seabird City', which we most certainly did. My concern over puffin numbers increased, they are becoming harder and harder to find. Several were on the sea, but birds on the cliffs were difficult to locate. Speaking to a volunteer, she expressed the thought that numbers had decreased by 50% in the last decade, that is a frightening number.

Early July saw us visit Anglesey for a day's birding; needless to say, an early start was required for that trip – 6.00 a.m. saw five cars leaving Lichfield, carrying eighteen very keen birders. Dorothy thought us mad, she sat this one out.

The trip was most successful. Black guillemots, again, obliged as did choughs, gannets, little terns, Manx shearwaters well out at sea, peregrine, two puffins, roseate terns and Sandwich terns; in total, seventy-eight pieces. A long journey it may have been, but we journeyed home happily enough.

The remainder of the year was relatively quiet and the only trip of any real significance was to North Wales and Worlds End. Here we chalked up seventy-two species on the day, the pick of which were black grouse, chough, common scoter, hen harrier, little egret, red-throated diver, rock pipit, Slavonian grebe and stonechat. The year closed on two hundred and sixteen species, down on recent years, but I heard no complaints 2007 now loomed; let us see what that would bring.

One thing the new year would see us do was another cruise. This time, we were visiting the Mediterranean and the Black Sea; a fourteen-day cruise, which included a day in Egypt, that could bring back memories. This would take place late September, some time ahead, so let us concentrate on the months before.

We commenced the year with the usual local visits, with the pick of the birds being Bewick's swan, buzzard, crossbill, curlew, Dartford warbler (this being a bit special as it was seen on Cannock Chase), glaucous gull, great norther diver, hen harrier, Iceland gull, long-eared owl, mandarin, red grouse, ruddy duck and willow tit.

I will look at two of those records in more detail. The Dartford warbler has been spreading northwards in recent years, and last year was reported from The Chase – although I was not fortunate enough to see it – so come February I was delighted to see the bird. Not one, a pair, so they were obviously breeding on The Chase; let us hope successfully so. Now the ruddy duck.

The ruddy duck population in the West Midlands was, until recently, very good. The birds are all due to escapees from collections and they found conditions in the UK, England specifically so, to their liking and they bred very successfully. Unfortunately, on the Continent, they started to inter-breed with the white-headed duck – a rare species – and due to their close relationship, the young from this were fertile. Consequently, the concern was raised over the future of the white-headed duck and it was decided to eradicate the ruddy duck. As the largest population of the ruddy was in the UK, the major cull was to be carried out here. To say this raised a storm of protest amongst birders is putting it mildly. It certainly put my blood pressure up.

The white-headed duck on the Continent was rare because of two major factors, not inter-breeding with the ruddy. Its habitat had been reduced considerably, and in Spain especially, it had been almost shot out of existence. On the ruddy duck's part, it is not a great migrant, so the numbers crossing the Channel were minimal, thus my argument was do not shoot the birds here: if any cross the water, shoot them there. Another alternative, which did not go down well, was in a protest letter I sent to the RSPB, where I suggested shooting the shooters – the white-headed duck would then have a good chance of increasing in numbers.

Ten years or so ago, I regularly saw ruddy duck in good numbers, at Blithfield Reservoir for instance, flocks of fifty or sixty were not unusual; now if I see two or three, I am very lucky. Another thing which concerns me is how good are the shooters; can they recognise the ruddy fully so they do not shoot another species in error? I doubt it. Now I have got that off my chest, back to birding.

Early summer saw us off nightingale, turtle dove, stone curlew, woodlark and ring-necked parakeet hunting, and all successfully so. Bempton Cliffs produced the usual birds, with puffins again looking low in numbers. The other species did not seem to be suffering any decline, but much concern is being expressed regarding puffin numbers. It is a big worry when one of our favourite birds shows such a reduction in numbers.

Our evening on Cannock Chase was most productive. Nightjar numbers seemed up, several calling birds, two or three woodcock were seen roding their territories, two young long-eared owls were seen – a marvellous breeding record for The Chase – and the peak of it all was to see a male Dartford warbler with food.

Confirmation that the bird was breeding on The Chase is a wonderful addition to the Staffordshire list of breeding species. As possible compensation for the decline in puffins, the number of red kites I see now are really on the increase. The re-introduction of this bird is working wonders and red kite are now being seen in places where they have not been seen for many, many a year. I no longer have to go to the wilds of Wales to see this bird, you can see them now as you drive down the M40 in Oxfordshire; at times, they keep you company as you cruise along. It takes the monotony out of motorway driving!

In the time remaining before our cruise, we visited Spurn Point on two occasions, Norfolk likewise, and the Welsh coast, where we had a few choice species. Amongst them were bearded tit, bittern, black-necked grebe, curlew sandpiper, great grey shrike, grey phalarope, honey buzzard, jacksnipe, osprey, peregrine, pied flycatcher, red-necked grebe, red-throated diver, ring-necked duck, rough-legged buzzard, scaup, short-eared owl, Slavonian grebe, twite, water pipit, white-fronted goose and whooper swan. Some quality sitting among those.

Then came the cruise. Our first call was Portugal, and here we chose a scenic coach tour which took in a mountainous region of the country where birds-of-prey were likely. We left Lisbon for Rio Tejo where some of the peaks reached over three thousand feet and, although birds were not easy to find, we had a few distinctive species. Black-shouldered kites were seen from the coach, and we stopped at a café where, whilst drinking a coffee, we saw a little bustard; two cracking birds to start our cruise off.

As we were driven round we saw black kites, alpine swifts, choughs, alpine accentors, short-toed eagle, great spotted cuckoo, spotless startling, short-toed larks and Thekla larks – not a bad selection – seen without leaving the coach.

Approaching our berth, we drove across a long bridge over the estuary and, whilst stuck in a bit of a traffic jam, were able to enjoy greater flamingos seen below. We did not grumble about that traffic jam, it could have lasted longer.

It was interesting to see the acres of cork oak that were growing; what the birdlife would have been like amongst these we could but imagine. We were informed that Portugal produces about 50% of the world's cork, and looking at some of these plantations, that was not hard to believe. We left Portugal for Spain, rounding the Rock in the dark, although we were due to land on the return leg of our voyage. We only had a day in Spain so we decided to see Barcelona on our own, no organised trip this time, and no expectation of birding. Two locations we particularly wished to visit were Barcelona Cathedral and Barcelona Aquarium. The Cathedral was everything it is claimed to be: a magnificent building in every sense of the word, built I believe in the 14th century. We only managed to view the exterior of the building, as with St, Petersburg, a large queue was waiting to enter. The Aquarium was rather expensive in our opinion, but as it had one of the finest collections of corals to be seen, hang the expense.

It was probably going to be our only chance of seeing it, and it was a bit special. After lunch, for which we returned to the liner, we went a walk along the front. Here we found a few small park-like strips of land, with many trees and flower beds, probably a place for butterflies and some interesting birds. Butterflies, for some reason, were not seen in number; could the flowers have been scentless? We did have a few birds, though. Familiar species from home were seen and heard, but for us two birds in particular were of interest, bee-eaters and hoopoes, these two would brighten up any scene. They were not the only birds to catch our attention. The end of one park was a small wooded area of date palm type trees, and from these a most raucous sound was to be heard. In the trees was a colony of ring-necked parakeets, their old nests could be clearly seen, this was obviously where they bred. In the spring, one can but imagine the noise to be heard here; it was bad enough now. They may be a very colourful bird, but they certainly are not musical. We had not expected any birds, but we had picked up three very colourful and interesting birds; we were more than happy with Barcelona.

Now France, and Monaco in particular, called. We were not particularly interested in this stop, we are not car racing fans and Monaco just seemed to be a very expensive built up area. We need not have worried.

We could not berth at Monaco due to weather conditions; instead, we were to berth some twenty miles from Monaco and for those who wished to visit they would be taken in by coach. This suited us fine, we would spend the day locally and see just what we could find. We understood fine walks were available along the coast, and although it was a quiet location, a few choice cafes were available.

Our journey to the shore by tender was most pleasant; a beautiful, calm sea and Audouin's gulls were flying overhead. Not many, they are a rare bird even in the Med. This part of France seemed fine to us.

We had a pleasant coffee at a café before walking off along the shore line. It was an area of sand dunes and many small areas of water left behind as the tide retreated. A few waders were evident, little ringed plovers were already on passage, we had two possible Kentish plovers, but we just could not get the view we wanted.

A pair of collared praticoles were also seen these could quite easily have bred here. The pick for us was to see several black-winged stilts, a bird rarely seen in the UK – you probably remember 'Sammy' of Norfolk fame.

After a very pleasant walk or, to be more accurate, a meander – we returned to the tenders and had lunch on the liner. In the afternoon, we came back ashore and walked in the opposite direction. Here the sand dunes were replaced by low cliffs and, as the tide was now returning, we were able to walk along the tops of those. In the fields, many larks could be seen – they were not very vocal at that time of the year – they were just running on the almost bare ground, seeking food. After a lot of hard, work we decided we had both crested larks and the odd Thekla larks there and whilst we were enjoying those Dorothy drew my attention to two, much larger looking larks. She had hit the jackpot this time: she had found two calandra larks. These birds were quite flighty, which was a good thing. We were able to see their very dark underside to the wings, a key identification feature at this time of the year when they have moulted out of their summer plumage. I was very pleased I had experienced these three birds previously; otherwise, splitting them would not have been easy.

A little while later and Dorothy was up to her tricks once again 'What on earth have we here!' she exclaimed. I looked, and I had not the foggiest idea. I needed to take notes of this bird. It was a small bird, 10 cm or so in length, a pale greyish-brown with a white rump, creamy white underparts and a very black and pointed tail, not rounded or squared off as is the usual case. It had an unusual bill, pale grey-blue, a thick base and an arched culmen (the upper bill). I was glad I had a couple of my field guides on board, I had work to do.

Time to return, and whilst Dorothy was showering, I got my field guides out. I concentrated my efforts on sparrows and finches, and I picked the right group. The bird was an Indian silverbill, native to India west to the Persian Gulf; what on earth was it doing so far west? I also read it was occasionally reported from Israel, and was possibly an introduced species. This was a bird I had never expected to see in my life. Up till then, it had been just a name, now thanks to Dorothy, it was a reality. One hell of a substitute for missing out on Monaco! We now sailed on to Corsica. There, we were only having a short stay and as it was a big night on board, and the ladies liked to look their best, Dorothy stayed on board to have her hair dressed. I took the tender to shore and walked out of the village to see what I could find. Hooded crows were quite common and I was able to identify Corsican nuthatch, citril finch, spotless starling once again, Italian sparrow, Marmora's warbler, the odd bee-eater with, out at sea, Cory's and Mediterranean shearwaters, and Audouin's gulls again. A more than reasonable collection for such a short stay.

Our next stop was Italy, and there we chose to have a full day's tour of Rome; you can hardly visit Italy without doing so. The major sights were seen and enjoyed, but I wished the Italians did not drive on the horn, the noise was ceaseless. We were warned whilst walking in Italy to be careful of motor-scooter muggers. Apparently, they would drive down the roadway and race onto the pavement areas, where the passenger on the scooter would snatch any cameras or bags that were being carried by unsuspecting pedestrians. Care was taken that day, we carried nothing.

Greece was our next destination. Prior to arriving there, the opportunity to book further cruises in 2008 was available. P&O were offering passengers good discounts if they booked whilst on the cruise, so we took the opportunity of booking two cruises. Two thousand and eight was going to be an important year for us, I would reach my 75th birthday in May and, come October, we would be celebrating our Golden Wedding Anniversary. May would now see us visiting Greenland, Iceland, Spitsbergen and Norway, October the West indies. They do say travel broadens the mind!

Greece was another destination where birding did not top the priority list. The ancient history of the country was our main interest, and with only one day in the country, we chose a Greek mythological tour. Perhaps you may like to join us and learn a little about ancient Greece? Our tour commenced at the Temple of Olympian Zeus, here we were told of the legend of Deucalion and Pyrrha – Greece's version of the flood myth. Then on to the Theatre of Dionysus and then on to the top Acropolis to visit the Temple of Athene Nike (birding returns here, Athene was the goddess of wisdom and war, and the owl was her bird. So it was only right that an owl should be named after her, and the little owl is – its' scientific name being Athene noctua). The Erechtheion temple followed and then the marvellous Parthenon. Greek mythology comes to life as you explore this area. Down from the Acropolis, we next visited the Ancient Agora, where it is believed democracy was born. Socrates extolled his intellectual thoughts here it is claimed. Then across to the Temple of Hephaestus where we heard about the exploits of his mother,

Hera, and his wife, Aphrodite. We finished by hearing the story of Thesseus and the Minotaur.

This had been an exhaustive day, both mentally and physically, but well worth the effort. The guide spoke perfect English and was only too pleased to answer any questions. What we needed now, apart from a good shower and evening meal, was to get back to birding. After the exploits of that day, birding seemed more relaxing; hopefully, Turkey and the Bosporus would provide just that.

We docked at Istanbul, having cruised up the Sea of Marmara, our journey up there had been escorted by a school of dolphins. They seemed to have followed the liner for several miles, enjoying themselves in the wake of the liner. Needless to say, we also enjoyed watching them. Another interesting feature of our journey was the number of cormorants we saw, and those were all the southern race; a far more attractive looking bird than the ones we see back home. Our cormorant is known as Phalacrocorax carbo; the southern race, Phalacrocorax carbo sinensis. A few of the latter are now being seen in the UK, but it is still an unusual bird back home.

We decided not to take any tours in Turkey, we would spend the day in Istanbul, and when here there is one thing you must do and that is visit the Blue Mosque.

Prior to doing so we went to the Topkapi Palace, now a museum, and had almost interesting time there. As well as a museum, it has some pleasant gardens to relax in, and a very special exhibit is the Topkapi Diamond; some stone this. We also visited the Snake Column, an interesting monument brought from Delph, and the Egyptian Obelisk brought from Luxor. You notice I said brought, they certainly were not bought; the old Turkish Empire took what it liked. Didn't we all!

The Blue Mosque was all it was claimed to be, the blue tiling on the building was quite incredible, and so was the architecture. Although known as the Blue Mosque, its name is the Sultan Ahmed Mosque and he had it built in the early 1600s I believe. It is in a typical Islamic style of architecture, and it over powers everything local to it. Those sultans certainly had power and money.

After a few hours of culture, we decided enough was enough. After Rome, Athens and now Istanbul, a relaxing afternoon was required – or at least what was left of it – so we returned to our liner.

We showered early and sat out on the balcony of our cabin, enjoying an aperitif prior to going down to dinner, when two darkish birds flew past the liner. We could not believe our eyes, two pygmy cormorants had just given us a flypast. Those were totally unexpected birds, which had not been considered as possibilities. They were a bird never reported in the UK and according to what I had read about them, they were not a marine bird like the cormorant; instead, they were more an inland species seen on small lakes and ponds. My field guide even went as far as stating never in the Mediterranean unlike the larger species. These may not have been in the Med, but they were close to it. They flew on up the Bosporus, we were pleased we had returned to the liner a little earlier than anticipated, the aperitif now went down very well. So well, we had two!

We sailed early the next morning on our way towards the Black Sea, and after breakfast we returned to our cabin and set up the telescope on our balcony and studied the eastern shores of the Bosporus. Most of this was agricultural land with many of the fields divided by ditches, and we were very interested to see many members of the egret family in the ditches and fields. Little egrets were the commonest, with an occasional squacco heron – the latter probably on migration to tropical Africa, where it winters – but the bird for us was the great white egret. Those large white looking herons favoured the damp ditches, where frogs and other amphibians lived.

Due to their size, they were easily recognised and several were close enough to see their pronounced curve in the neck. A very good diagnostic feature. It was now October, and several flocks of martins and swallows were flying down the Bosporus, migrants from eastern Europe and Asia, and several of these landed on the liner to rest. Little did they realise, the liner was taking them back up north! We were very pleased they had dropped in because amongst them were the odd red-rumped swallow, a bird I have only seen once in the UK. It was a treat to see them so close.

On entering the Black Sea, we met up with quite a movement southwards of terns. Many were the common tern, familiar back home, but tucked in amongst them were small groups of little terns and the occasional, lumbering, gull-like, gull-billed tern; a very rare bird back home. To see those so close to hand was marvellous, and it was interesting to see just how many juvenile birds were within the flocks.

It was here we received some disappointing news, we would not be visiting Egypt; the reason was a bit vague, but it would appear there was some political unrest. Instead, we would visit Madeira. Having visited Madeira previously, we did not mind; it would now be wild canaries instead of pyramids!

Back to the Black Sea. Flocks of migrating waders were very evident, but as we moved further from the shores these became so distant that positive identification was not possible. This was very disappointing, but we had at least managed to identify a few of the more familiar waders: redshanks, a few curlews, plovers, mainly little ringed, our old friend the lapwing and, the pick of the bunch, a small group of seven collared pratincoles almost landed on the liner. A lovely bird to see so close.

The further we entered the Black Sea the fewer the birds became, apart from gulls and terns, but we were happy enough. One flock of black terns in particular was most impressive. There were over a hundred birds in this flock which was more black terns than I had ever seen in my life, and once again many juveniles were included. That is the way to bird watch, just sitting down and letting the birds come to you; that cannot be bad!

We arrived in the Crimea in the dark, after a journey of several hundred miles, so we had to wait till daylight to see what we had. We were having a pre-breakfast coffee on our balcony, surveying the scene in front of us, when Dorothy commented about some funny looking swans she could just about see. I swung round to look in the direction she was pointing, funny swans they certainly were not; she had picked up a group of nine white pelicans, a quick rush for the telescope followed.

The white pelican is as large as a swan, when including the preposterous bill, so it was no wonder Dorothy first thought they were swans as she did not have her binoculars to hand. Some arrival in the Crimea, it only lacked the red carpet. We had been undecided what to do in the Crimea. Many of the passengers were going to visit Yalta, where the Yalta Conference was held in February 1945. There, Churchill, Roosevelt and Starlin decided what to do with Germany once the war concluded. We all know the outcome of that, Germany was carved up and the Cold War followed.

We had considered going, but we observed that surrounding the small port where we would disembark was a large area of what could best be called wasteland. In this, a few dilapidated buildings stood, but the remainder was a collection of bushes, trees and open areas that just looked ideal as a staging post for small migrants about to cross the Black Sea – their last food for many miles. No Yalta for us.

Thanks to having no pressure, we enjoyed a leisurely breakfast and left the liner well after the maddening throng had departed. I am pleased to report, that once we entered this 'wasteland', it was far more attractive than when viewed from a distance and it certainly had birds. This late in the year, the birds were not singing, they were just calling away and doing their best to frustrate us by hiding away in the undergrowth. In those foreign parts, we had little or no idea of what we were listening to; we had to see them. The first bird we saw clearly enough to identify was a great grey shrike. A bird known to us, that was a help. It was busily feeding away on large insects, which looked like crickets, and there appeared to be many of them. Eventually, a small warbler species popped out and sat on top of a bush glaring straight at us; thank you. I knew this one, having seen them in Egypt, it was a melodious warbler. Two down, and both identified, nothing like a bit of confidence building! That was quickly shattered, we saw two other birds and had no idea of what we were looking at. To improve matters, a flock of black terns flew overhead and on to the Black Sea, we could at least recognise them!

A warbler dropped onto the ground where we saw it eating ants, and this bird at least gave us a very good view. It was a very erect and active warbler, looking larger than our willow warbler and had, what can best be called, a peaked forehead – almost like it was wearing a cap. It was a washed out yellow on the underside and had a pale wing panel. Dorothy was busily looking at the warblers in her field guide when it hit me, 'Look at the icterine warbler Dot,' I said. I had it right. I was very pleased I had spent time myself the previous evening, looking at the likely warblers.

The birds of the Crimea were not making it helpful, that day we really had to work for our birds. Who knows Yalta may have been more relaxing!

Two hoopoes put in an appearance, these brightened the morning up considerably; you can never see too many of those, that is for sure.

Lunch was approaching and as we turned to go back on board another shrike put in an appearance, and this was no great grey. We found ourselves staring at a male masked shrike, a bird we had not really considered as being likely. We went on board for lunch in a very happy frame of mind. It had been hard work, but well worth it. We returned after lunch to view another part of the area, this part had more bushes and less tangled undergrowth; we may have it slightly easier here.

The first birds we saw was a passing small flock of serins, twenty or so of those, which, unfortunately, did not hang around; they were obviously in transit. A small warbler caught our attention, a really washed out looking bird. I first thought could be a chiffchaff, but the bird was too pale on the undersides. Another field guide job, but this bird sat out posing for us, so we were able to identify it without too much trouble – a juvenile Bonelli's warbler.

A pair of very striking looking warblers were next in line. These both had the most pronounced submoustachial you are every likely to see, a pair of Rupppell's warblers. There is no mistaking this bird that is for sure. I like my field guides description of the bird, it commences 'Male unmistakable', and I for one will not argue with that.

The afternoon had started really well. Several Sardinian warblers were seen, which was to be expected, they were a resident not a warbler on passage. Olivaceous warblers, another resident in this part of the world, which also did not hide their light under a bushel.

To finish the afternoon off, a very secretive small bird kept on annoying us; all we had were flashes of a dark headed bird, not unlike a Sardinian warbler, but behaving totally differently. Eventually our patience was rewarded: it sat out on the top of a bush for several seconds. We had the view we wanted, it was a male Orphean warbler, a cracking bird to end the day. Well not quite, just as we almost reached our liner a woodchat shrike flew through, a male and that bird did end the day.

Instead of our visiting wasteland, it had turned out to be a wonderland, and how many birds we failed to identify we do not know. We were more than happy with those we had. The Crimea goes high on our list of bird watching locations.

The following day, we were only cruising a short distance from the Crimea, our next stop being Odessa: 'The Pearl of the Black Sea' as it is frequently called. As our birding the previous day had been so interesting, we decided to explore the city. We went on a walking tour in the morning, which was very informative and we saw many of the principal buildings etc. After lunch, we had a quiet meander and visited two of the city's parks; here, we hoped for a few birds, but we were not very successful. You cannot win them all.

As we were not visiting Egypt, we were now due for a long cruise down the Black Sea and out along the Mediterranean before our next stop, Gibraltar. The birds over the Black Sea were much as seen two days before, although one group of pelicans which flew past us made me think they could have been Dalmatian pelicans; they looked decidedly greyer than the white and the black prairies were not so obvious. They were too distant to obtain a clear view, and you do not claim them if you are not sure. A 'Nearly' bird as we term them.

Back in the Med, and time to just relax and look out at sea. Gulls and terns were again active, and shearwaters were still to be seen. The larger ones were probably Cory's shearwater and the darker looking types were likely to be Yelkouan shearwaters. The latter, now a species in their own right, they were until recently, considered to be a race of the Manx shearwater.

Approaching The Rock, several pods of dolphins were to be seen. They escorted the liner for some distance before racing off; they had more power than we had, that was for sure.

Gibraltar was not new to us, having spent a holiday there previously, so we decided to go up the Rock and see the monkeys. The Barbary macaques are the only wild monkey living in Europe, so when visiting Gibraltar, they are a must see attraction. I have mentioned previously that they are a not a tame animal and should be treated with respect; they have teeth and know how to use them.

After a coffee, we took the cable car up the Rock and were quickly greeted by a troop of monkeys. There must have been over twenty of them, but as soon as they realised we had nothing for them, they raced off to seek out others who might. They are rarely still and must cover miles as they race about – to see them leaping down the Rock face is quite amazing – they are so sure of foot. Bird life on the Rock was quiet. The large colony of yellow-legged gulls which nest there each year – had, by then, all departed. There was only a limited passage of birds-of-prey passing through that day, these were very high and we guessed they were honey buzzards. I doubt if above twenty birds came through, the wind was in the wrong direction.

We took the easy way down the Rock, and did not walk it; after our day in Gibraltar, we set sail for Madeira.

The liner moored at Funchel, the capital of Madeira. Here we had an early breakfast as we had booked for a morning Levada walk in the Serra D'Agua Valley. This was a guided walk of approximately four hours, and was most enjoyable. We saw a few wild canaries on this walk, and another bird, the endemic chaffinch on Madeira was also seen. This is a race of the chaffinch we have back home, and is commonly known as the blue chaffinch, due to its blue tinged back. Both of those sightings brought back memories of our holiday on Maderia.

On the afternoon, we spent some time in Funchel and here we visited the Jardim Publico da Ajuda; a delightful small park which we understood had only been opened a few years ago. Here, we had a few late monarch butterflies. When we were last here, we saw this exotic butterfly in its hundreds, not so many that day – but even one would have been very special, they are some insect.

That completed our last landfall until we arrived back in the UK. We had seen some wonderful sights, some incredible birds and visited several countries, which prior to the cruise, were just names on a map.

We had been home just two short weeks, when our lives took a devastating turn. Dorothy became unwell and was quickly referred to hospital, her appointment came through very rapidly. After her initial appointment, where several tests and an X-ray was taken, we were called back and told the news: Dorothy had cancer and in a very advanced state. To say our world fell apart is putting it mildly. Several months undergoing various treatments were to no avail, and come May, she was admitted to hospital. From here she later went to a nursing home and finally on 28th July, she passed away. If there is any consolation, she passed away peacefully. A year which promised so much, ended so tragically. Dorothy fought tooth and nail to survive, and one of the final things she said to me was, 'Concentrate on the good memories, the great times spent together, and whatever you do with your life is live it to the full. That is the best compliment you can make to me.' Those few words have remained with me, and will always do so. Birding over the past few months had gone onto the back burner, although Dorothy insisted, I continued with my Monday Bird Study Group. This I did, but I changed things so we only had a morning meeting and most of those were indoor sessions or field meetings taken at Rosliston Forestry Centre. That way, I was never more than fifteen minutes or so from home should the need have arisen.

As Dorothy's condition worsened we rarely had the opportunity to go out together, although just prior to her going into hospital, we did manage such a day. It was early May, a beautiful day too, and Dorothy felt a little brighter so we had a trip across to Blithfield Reservoir. Part of the perimeter of the reservoir is accessible by car, so we were able to drive in and park up. Many hirundines were to be seen flying low over the water along with swifts, and the common terns had commenced their arrival. Dorothy then pointed out a large bird to me, an osprey was flying across the reservoir, straight in our direction, and it commenced to dive for fish. After several abortive attempts, it finally caught a fish and flew off with its catch.

Dorothy's final bird watch had turned out to be memorable, and it stayed with her up to her final hours; she mentioned it to me two days before she died. It not only stayed with her, it still has with me, and it will always do so. A new life now lies ahead and the birds will become the integral part of it, apart from the memories that is. Thank you, Dorothy, for all you gave me.

To be continued...

Previously Published by Author

The Birdwatchers Day List co-edited with Chaz Mason - Curlew
Countryside Publications
English Churchyard Flora – Curlew Country Publication
The Wild Flowers of a Gravel Pit – Birmingham University
A Journal of a Year in the Life of a Blue Badge Birder – Derby Books
Publishing CO. Ltd.